WORKBOOK FOR WRITERS

Lynn Quitman Troyka
Douglas Hesse

Prentice Hall
Upper Saddle River   London   Singapore
Toronto   Tokyo   Sydney   Hong Kong   Mexico City

© 2009 by Pearson Education, Inc.
Upper Saddle River, NJ 07458

All rights reserved. No part of this book may be reproduced, in any form or by any means, without permission in writing from the publisher.

Printed in the United States of America

10 9 8 7 6 5 4 3 2 1

ISBN 13: 978-0-205-62070-8
ISBN 10: 0-205-62070-1

CONTENTS

PART 3: WRITING RESEARCH

PART 4: WRITING ACROSS THE CURRICULUM AND BEYOND

PART 5: WRITING WHEN ENGLISH IS A SECOND LANGUAGE

PREFACE

The *Workbook for Writers*, First Edition, continues the tradition, established by prior Troyka Workbooks, of serving dual purposes: functioning as a supplement and a self-contained textbook. As a supplement to the *Workbook for Writers*, First Edition, it contains exercises and writing activities at the end of each module. As a self-contained textbook, it presents concise explanations of key concepts followed by numerous opportunities for practice. To those ends, this *Workbook* offers:

- Complete coverage of all basic topics—grammar, punctuation, mechanics, the writing process, and critical thinking.

- Many integrated sections for multilingual writers, with special emphasis on count and non-count nouns, articles, verbals, prepositions, word order, and modal auxiliary verbs.

- Focus on integrating quotations and writing paraphrases and summaries—topics not usually included in workbooks on writing.

- Charts and checklists throughout to summarize and highlight key information.

- Sequenced exercises that lead students to independent work so that students progress from simple tasks such as identifying sentence elements; advance to guided writing, such as sentence combining; and, finally, graduate to original sentences, paragraphs, and essays.

- Exercise content in connected discourse to replicate more closely the activities of revising and editing real writing. The topics from across the curriculum engage interest.

PART 1: | *The Writing Process and Writing Effectively*

MODULE 1: THINKING LIKE A WRITER

1a What is the current scene for writers?

In this age of information, more people write than ever before. With the aid of computers, ordinary people now write what used to be considered work for professionals, such as brochures, newsletters, articles, and essays.

In addition, people share their writing, both formal and informal with more people than in the past. Students used to give their essays, considered formal writing, to their teachers who were usually the only ones to read their students' work. Now through the use of computers, students may share their work with all the other students in their class getting more comments and ideas to help them improve their papers while gaining a better understanding of the criteria for good formal writing. Traditionally, a letter considered informal writing, was written by one person and sent to another. Now you may forward the same email to four or five friends who in turn may email a few more of their friends with the information you provided. As more people write for school, work, and pleasure, they have a greater understanding of the importance of having good writing skills.

1b What are the major purposes for writing?

Students often think their purpose for writing is to complete a class assignment. However, purpose means more than that: It refers to what the writing seeks to achieve. Although writing to express yourself and to create a literary work are important, this workbook concentrates on the two purposes most frequently found in academic writing: to provide information for your reader and to persuade your reader.

Expressive writing is usually the private recording of your thoughts and feelings. A personal journal is an example of expressive writing.

Informative writing (also known as expository writing) seeks to give information and, when necessary, to explain it. Informative writing focuses on the subject being discussed. Informative writing includes reports of observations, ideas, scientific data, facts, and statistics. It can be found in textbooks, encyclopedias, technical and business reports, nonfiction books, newspapers, and magazines.

CHECKLIST FOR INFORMATIVE WRITING

1. Is its information clear?

2. Does it present facts, ideas, and observations that can be verified?

3. Does its information seem complete and accurate?

4. Is the writer's tone reasonable and free of distortions?

Persuasive writing (also known as **argumentative writing**) seeks to convince the reader about a matter of opinion. Persuasive writing focuses on the reader whom the writer wants to influence. Examples of persuasive writing include editorials, letters to the editor, reviews, sermons, business or research proposals, opinion essays in magazines, and books that argue a point of view.

CHECKLIST FOR PERSUASIVE WRITING

1. Does it present a point of view about which opinions vary?

2. Does it support its point of view with specifics?

3. Does it base its point of view on sound reasoning and logic?

4. Are the parts of its argument clear?

5. Does it intend to evoke a reaction for the reader?

1c What does "audience" mean for writing?

Good writing is often judged by its ability to reach its intended audience. The more information you have about your audience's background, beliefs, and concerns, the better you can think about how to reach that audience.

CHECKLIST OF READER AUDIENCE CHARACTERISTICS

WHAT SETTING ARE THEY READING IN?

Academic setting?

Workplace setting?

Public setting?

WHO ARE THEY?
Age, gender

CHECKLIST OF READER AUDIENCE CHARACTERISTICS *(continued)*

Ethnic backgrounds, political philosophies, religious beliefs

Roles (student, parent, voter, wage earner, property owner, veteran, and others)

Interests, hobbies

WHAT DO THEY KNOW?

Levels of education

Amount of general or specialized knowledge about the topic

Probable preconceptions and prejudices brought to the topic

GUIDELINES FOR PARTICIPATING IN PEER-RESPONSE GROUPS

AS A RESPONDER

1. Think of yourself in the role of a coach, not a judge.

2. Consider all writing by our peers as "works in progress."

3. After hearing or reading a peer's writing, briefly summarize it to check that you and your peer are clear about what the peer said or meant to say.

4. Start with what you think is well done. No one likes to hear only negative comments.

5. Be honest in your suggestions for improvements.

6. Base your responses on an understanding of the writing process, and remember that you're reading drafts, not finished products. All writing can be revised.

7. Give concrete and specific responses. General comments such as "This is good" or "This is weak" aren't much help. Say specifically what is good or weak.

8. Follow your instructor's system for putting your comments in writing so that your fellow writer can recall what you said. If one member of your group is supposed to take notes, speak clearly so that the person can be accurate. If you're the note taker, be accurate, and ask the speaker to repeat what he or she said if it went by too quickly.

AS A WRITER

1. Adopt an attitude that encourages your peers to respond freely. Listen and try to resist any urge to interrupt during a comment or to jump in to react.

2. Remain open-minded. Your peers' comments can help you see your writing in a fresh way, which, in turn, can help you produce a better-revised draft.

3. Ask for clarification if a comment isn't clear. If a comment is too general, ask for specifics.

4. As much as you encourage your peers to be honest, remember that the writing is yours. You "own" it, and you decide which comments to use or not use.

1d What is "tone" in writing?

As an adult writing to an adult audience, you are expected to sound sensible and even-tempered. This stance is reflected in your **tone**—*what you say* and *how you say it*. Tone can be broadly described as **informal** or **formal**. Tone is informal in journals and freewriting. As you move from writing for the private you to writing for an audience, you are expected to move toward a more formal tone. This does not mean that you should use overblown language or put on airs that make you sound artificial. Most audiences expect a tone midway between informal and highly formal. Your tone should take into account the topic, purpose, and audience of your piece.

HOW TO USE TONE IN WRITING

1. Reserve a highly informal tone for conversational writing.

2. Use a formal or medium level of formality in your academic writing and when you write for supervisiors, professionals, and other people you know from a distance.

3. Avoid an overly formal, ceremonial tone.

4. Avoid sarcasm and other forms of nastiness.

5. Choose language appropriate for your topic and your readers.

6. Choose words that work with your message, not against it.

7. Whatever tone you choose to use, be consistent in each piece.

1e What does "sources for writing" mean?

You are your first source for writing. For many college writing assignments, you can draw on your own prior knowledge. For others, you will be expected to use outside sources, sources outside of what you already know.

GUIDELINES FOR USING SOURCES IN WRITING

1. Evaluate sources critically. Not all are accurate, true, or honest.

2. Represent your sources accurately. Be sure to QUOTE, PARAPHRASE, and SUMMARIZE well so that you avoid distorting the material.

3. Never PLAGIARIZE.

4. Know the difference between writing a SUMMARY and writing a SYNTHESIS.

5. Credit your sources with clear and complete DOCUMENTATION. Be sure to ask your instructor which DOCUMENTATION STYLE you should use.

1f What resources can help me with writing?

Your personal bookshelf needs to contain three essential volumes: a dictionary, a thesaurus, and a handbook for writers. Most college bookstores offer a good variety of hardback "college dictionaries." Before choosing one, browse through it and read some definitions you want to learn or to understand more clearly. A portable, paperback dictionary in your backpack can also be very handy. For a more comprehensive resource, unabridged dictionaries list every word in English. The reference section of every library has one (usually on display) that everyone can consult.

Another valuable resource for writers is a thesaurus, which is a collection of synonyms. The easiest to use are arranged alphabetically. Check for this feature, as it is not an automatic arrangement for a thesaurus. *Roget's 21st Century Thesaurus* is an excellent volume arranged alphabetically.

A handbook—such as the one you're using as you read this—is another important reference that gives you detailed information about [sometimes forgotten] rules of grammar, punctuation, and other writing conventions. It also offers extensive advice about how to write successfully, whether for college, business, or the public. You need all this information to write successfully in other courses and in your career after college.

A college library, sometimes called a learning resources center, is fully stocked with all manners of reference books, circulating books, resources for online access, and more. Before you need the library, spend some time getting to know what's available. Then you can dive right in when the time comes.

1g How do computers shape the writing process?

Most writing, whether for school or work is now done on computers using word processing programs and printers. Students who do not own a computer or a printer may be able to use computers and printers in their school library, writing center, or computer lab, or they may be able to use a computer and printer at their public library. If you need to use the school's computers and printers, get a schedule of open lab hours. Do this early in the semester before your first assignment is due.

1g.1 Creating documents

Word processing programs, such as Microsoft WordPages and WordPerfect, include aids for writers. They offer some advantages, but they also have severe limitations. In no case are such tools substitutes for your own careful editing and proofreading. Software, after all, can't "think" and make distinctions between *form* and *from* in spelling; between the way you use or misuse *deep* and *profound*; or between an unjustified and a justified use of a passive construction. Here's a list of some of these helpful applications:

- Spell-check programs
- Thesaurus programs
- Grammar or style-check programs

1g.2 Finding resources

In addition to helping you produce and revise writing, computers help you find sources. Most library catalogs and databases are now searchable with computers. Many colleges and universities also allow you to access these resources off campus. Check with the library to learn how to access these resources.

1g.3 Managing your work

Computers allow you to save different drafts of your papers as they evolve or to organize your work into various folders. Many people take notes from sources directly into computer files. Often, you can save .PDF versions of articles from library databases to a folder on your computer.

1g.4 Communicating with others

You're probably familiar with e-mail and instant messaging as ways to communicate with your friends and others. These and similar technologies can sometimes also help you with formal writing projects. Discussing a topic online with classmates can help generate ideas for writing. Computers can also allow you to share drafts of your work with others without physically meeting them. Some instructors post student papers on class Web pages so that other students can read and respond to the writing. Finally, computers also offer many advantages for working on colaborative projects.

1h What forms of writing do computers enable?

Computers enable new kinds of writing. Instead of traditional diaries, writers can keep Web logs (blogs), which are online journals that anyone can read through the Internet. In addition, writers can copy and paste photographs or illustrations into documents, and they can use different fonts and graphic elements such as ruler lines or textboxes. Interestingly, certain documents today can exist only in digital form on computers because they contain audio or video files, or they connect to other documents and Web sites. In fact, a website that allows anyone to edit content is called a wiki. Another way of writing is through digital portfolios which have links between and within texts. More and more people use software such as PowerPoint to create presentations. Finally podcasts, online broadcasts, may be used by writers who want people to hear what they've written.

Adapting to Your Audience and Purpose

Look at this picture of an earthquake. Describe the scene as part of your response to each of the four different audiences described below. Use your own paper.

1. You have just seen a news report of a serious earthquake in South America. Some people are still trapped in the wreckage, while thousands are in need of shelter, food, and medical help. You work for a charity which offers rapid response volunteers in situations like this. Prepare a statement to be read out on local TV and radio which explains the services your organization offers and why people should donate money for an immediate relief mission to the area.

2. You recently moved to San Francisco to attend college. Your grandmother has seen a TV show about the 1904 earthquake and is worried about you. She doesn't know how you can live in a place where disaster might strike at any time. Write back explaining your attitude to this risk. Reassure her that you are taking what precautions you can and that, in the event of any tremors, you would know what to do.

3. While on a Study Abroad program recently, you were caught up in an earthquake which totaled the school building yet, miraculously, cost no lives. Write a short piece for the college newspaper back home detailing this experience.

4. A minor earthquake has destroyed your apartment building and an adjacent strip mall, yet all the surrounding buildings are unscathed. You discover that cheap materials were used in the construction of both the apartment building and the mall. Write a letter to the builders in which you hold them responsible for this disaster. Make a clear link between their negligence and the collapse of the buildings.

MODULE 2: PLANNING, SHAPING, DRAFTING AND REVISING

2a What is the writing process?

Experienced writers know that **writing is a process**, a series of activities that starts the moment they begin thinking about a subject and ends when they complete a final draft. Experienced writers also know that good writing is rewriting. Their drafts are filled with additions, cuts, rearrangements, and rewordings.

For the sake of explanation, the different parts of the writing process are discussed separately in this module. In real life, you will find that the steps loop back and forth as each piece of writing develops.

STEPS IN THE WRITING PROCESS

Planning means discovering and compiling ideas for your writing.

Shaping means organizing your material.

Drafting means writing your material in sentences and paragraphs.

Revising means evaluating your draft and then rewriting it by adding, deleting, rewording, and rearranging.

Editing means checking for correct grammar, spelling, punctuation, and mechanics.

Proofreading means reading your final copy to eliminate typing or handwriting errors.

2b What terms describe different kinds of writing?

Terms that describe different types of writing are often used interchangeably. For example, the words *essay*, *theme*, and *composition* usually—but not always—refer to writing of about 500 to 1,000 words. Similarly, the word *paper* can mean anything from a few paragraphs to a complex research project. Another option is the general term *piece of writing* to refer to all types of writing.

2c What is a "writing situation"?

The writing situation is the place to start with thinking about your writing. Its four elements are **topic**, **purpose**, **audience**, and **special requirements**.

TOPIC:	What topic will you be writing about?
PURPOSE:	What is your purpose for writing?
AUDIENCE:	Who is your audience?
SPECIAL REQUIREMENTS:	How much time do you have to complete the assignment? What is the length requirement?

2d How can I think through a writing topic?

Some assignments leave no room for making choices. You may be given very specific instructions, such as "Explain how plants produce oxygen." Your job with such assignments is to do exactly what is asked and not go off the topic.

Some instructors will ask you to write on whatever topic you wish. In such situations, you need to select a topic that is suitable for informative or persuasive writing in college, one that reflects your ability to think through ideas. You need to demonstrate that you can use specific, concrete details to support what you want to say. Be careful not to choose a topic that is too narrow, or you will not have enough to say.

When you choose or are assigned a topic that is very broad, you have to **narrow the subject**. To do this, you must think of different areas within the subject until you come to one that seems workable for an essay.

Any broad subject may contain hundreds of possible essay topics. Do not try to think of them all, but also do not jump on the first topic that occurs to you. Consider the purpose of the assignment, the audience, the word limit, the time available to you, and your own interests and knowledge. A suitably narrowed topic will enable you to move back and forth between general statements and specific details.

Techniques for gathering ideas, sometimes called **invention techniques**, can help you while you are narrowing your topic. For example, they help you to discover how much you know about a topic before you decide whether or not to write on it. Experienced writers use many techniques for gathering ideas; we will discuss the most common ones in this module.

2e What can I do if no ideas occur to me?

If you've ever felt you'll never think of anything to write about, don't despair. Instead, use structured techniques, sometimes called **prewriting strategies** or **invention techniques**, for discovering and compiling ideas. For a list of the techniques, see the box below. Experiment to find out which techniques suit your style of thinking. Also, even if one technique produces good ideas, try another to see what additional possibilities might turn up.

WAYS TO DISCOVER AND COMPILE IDEAS FOR WRITING

- Keep an idea book and a journal.
- Freewrite.
- Brainstorm.
- Ask the "journalist's questions".
- Map.
- Talk it over.
- Use a good Internet search engine.
- Incubate.

2f How do I use an idea log and a journal?

Many writers carry an **idea log**—a small notebook—with them at all times so that they can jot down ideas that spring to mind.

A **journal**, like an idea log, is a record of your ideas, but it is built from daily writing sessions. In your journal you can write about your opinions, beliefs, family, friends, or anything else you wish. The content and tone can be as personal and informal as you wish. Nevertheless, a journal is not a diary for merely listing things done during the day. It is a book for you to fill with what you want to think about.

Keeping a journal can help you in three ways. First, writing every day makes it easier for you to write. Second, a journal encourages close observation and thinking. Third, a journal is an excellent source of ideas when you need to write in response to an assignment.

2g What is freewriting?

Freewriting is writing down whatever comes into your mind without stopping to worry about whether the idea is good or the spelling is correct. You do nothing to interrupt the flow. Do not go back to review. Do not cross out. Some days your freewriting might seem mindless, but other days it can reveal interesting ideas. Freewriting works best if you set a goal, such as writing for ten minutes or until one page is filled. Sometimes you may decide to do focused freewriting—writing on a set topic—in preparation for an essay.

2h What is brainstorming?

In **brainstorming**, you make a list of all the ideas you can think of associated with a topic. The ideas can be listed as words, phrases, or complete sentences. List making, like freewriting, produces its best results when you let your mind work freely, producing many ideas before analyzing them.

Brainstorming is done in two steps. First make your list. Then go back and try to find patterns in the list and ways to group the ideas into categories. Set aside any items that do not fit into groups. The groups with the most items are likely to reflect the ideas that you can write about most successfully.

2i What are the "journalist's questions"?

Another commonly used method for generating ideas is the **journalist's questions**: *who? what? where? why? when?* and *how?* Asking such questions forces you to approach a topic from several different points of view.

2j What is mapping?

Mapping is much like brainstorming, but it is more visual. When you map, begin by writing your subject in a circle in the middle of a sheet of unlined paper. Next draw a line out from the center and name a major division of your subject. Circle it, and from that circle move out to further subdivisions. Keep associating to further ideas and to details related to them. When you finish with one major division of your subject, go back to the center and start again with another major division. As you go along, add anything that occurs to you for any section of the map. Continue the process until you run out of ideas.

2k How can "talking it over" help?

Talking it over is based on the notion that two heads are better than one. When you talk it over with someone interested in listening and making suggestions, you often think of new ideas. Ways of approaching a point of discussion include debating, questioning, analyzing, synthesizing, and evaluating. If your instructor sets up peer-response groups in your class, you might ask the other members to serve as sounding boards—a term meaning someone you trust to tell you if your ideas are complete and reasonable. Otherwise, talk with a good friend or another adult.

2l How can an Internet search help?

Internet search engines are good sources for finding ideas, understanding your subject, and for locating information you can use in your writing.

Perhaps one of the best search engines for moving from general to specific categories is <http://www.yahoo.com>. Other search engines include <http://www.google.com>, <http://www.hotbot.com> (which is currently part of lycos.com), <http://altavista.com>, but there are many more. Click on the "search" function and type in the word you want to explore. If it's more than one word, use Boolean codes so that the search engine will "understand" what you are looking for.

2m How can incubation help me?

When you allow your ideas to **incubate**, you give them time to grow and develop. Incubation works especially well when you need to solve a problem in your writing (for example, if material is too thin and needs expansion, if material covers too much and needs pruning, or if connections among your ideas are not clear for your reader). Time is a key element for successful incubation. You need time to think, to allow your mind to wander, and then to come back and focus on the writing.

One helpful strategy is to turn attention to something entirely different from your writing problem. After a while, guide your mind back to the problem you want to solve. Another strategy is to allow your mind to relax and wander, without concentrating on anything special. Later, return to the problem you are trying to solve. At this point you might see solutions that did not occur to you before.

2n How can shaping help me?

To shape the ideas that you have gathered, you need to group them and sequence them.

An essay has three basic parts: an introduction, a body, and a conclusion. The body consists of a number of paragraphs. The introduction and conclusion are usually one paragraph each. Review various types of paragraphs in your handbook.

2o How can looking for levels of "generality" help me?

Effective writing includes both general statements and specific details. In both informative and persuasive writing, general statements must be developed with facts, reasons, examples, and illustrations.

To group ideas, review the material you accumulated while gathering ideas. Look for general ideas. Next, group under them related, but less general ideas. If you find that your notes contain only general ideas, or only very specific details, return to gathering techniques to supply what you need.

2p How can a subject tree help me?

A **subject tree** shows you visually whether you have sufficient content to start a first draft of your writing. A subject tree also visually demonstrates whether you have a good balance of general ideas and specific details. If what you have are mostly general ideas—or, the other way around, mostly specific details—go back to techniques for discovering and compiling ideas so that you can come up with the sorts of material that are missing.

2q What is a thesis statement?

A **thesis statement** is the main idea of an essay. Because it prepares your reader for what you will discuss, the thesis statement must accurately reflect the content of the essay. Following is a list of the basic requirements for a thesis statement.

BASIC REQUIREMENTS FOR A THESIS STATEMENT
1. It states the essay's subject—the topic that you discuss.
2. It conveys the essay's purpose—either informative or persuasive.
3. It indicates your focus—the assertion that presents your point of view.
4. It uses specific language, not vague words.
5. It may briefly state the major subdivisions of the essay's topic.

Many instructors also require that the thesis statement appear as a single sentence at the end of the introductory paragraph.

In most writing situations you cannot be certain that a thesis statement accurately reflects what you say in the essay until you have written one or more drafts. To start shaping your essay, however, you can use a preliminary thesis statement. Even if it is too broad, it can guide you as you write. When the essay is completed, be sure to revise so that your final thesis statement accurately reflects the content of your essay.

Here are some thesis statements written for 500- to 700-word essays. The first two are for essays with an informative purpose, and the last two are for essays with a persuasive purpose.

TOPIC	rain
No	Rain is important. [too broad]
YES	Rain is part of the earth's water cycle.
TOPIC	radio
No	Everyone listens to the radio. [too broad]
YES	The variety of radio programming ensures there is a program for every taste.
TOPIC	drunk driving
No	Drunk driving is dangerous. [too broad]
YES	Unless drunk drivers are taken off our roads, they will continue to kill and injure thousands of people each year.
TOPIC	adoption
No	Sometimes, adopted children have problems. [too broad]
YES	Adopted children should be able to find out about their birthparents for psychological, medical, and moral reasons.

2r What is outlining?

Many writers find outlining to be a useful planning strategy. An **outline** helps pull together the results of gathering and ordering ideas and preparing a thesis statement. It also provides a visual guide and checklist. Some instructors require outlines because they want you to practice the discipline of thinking through the arrangement and organization of your writing.

An **informal outline** does not have to follow all the formal conventions of outlining. It simply *lists* the main ideas of an essay—the major subdivisions of the thesis statement—and the subordinate ideas and details.

A **formal outline** follows strict conventions concerning content and format. The material must be displayed so that relationships among ideas are clear and so that the content is orderly. A formal outline can be a **topic outline** or a **sentence outline**: each item in a topic outline is a word or phrase, whereas each item in a sentence outline is a complete sentence.

Here are the conventions to follow in a formal outline.

1. **Numbers, letters, and indentations**: All parts of a formal outline are systematically indented and numbered or lettered. Capitalized Roman numerals (I, II, III) signal major divisions of the topic. Indented capital letters (A, B) signal the next, more specific level of informa-

tion. Further indented Arabic numbers (1, 2, 3) show the third, even more specific level of information, and so on.

2. **Grouping in pairs:** At all points on an outline there is no I without a II, no A without a B, and so on. If a heading has only one subdivision, you need either to eliminate that subdivision or expand the material so that you have at least two subdivisions.

3. **Levels of generality:** All items in a subdivision are at the same level of generality. A main idea cannot be paired with a supporting detail.

4. **Overlap:** Headings do not overlap. What is covered in A, for example, must be quite different from what is covered in B.

5. **Parallelism:** All entries are grammatically parallel. For example, all items might start with -*ing* forms of verbs or all might be adjectives and nouns (see 18f).

6. **Capitalization and punctuation:** Capitalize only the first word of each heading. In a sentence outline, end each sentence with a period. Do not put periods at the end of items in a topic outline.

7. **Introductory and concluding paragraphs:** The introductory and concluding paragraphs are not part of an outline. Place the thesis statement above the outline.

Here is a formal topic outline of an essay on living alone.

THESIS STATEMENT
Chances are high that adult men and women will have to know how to live alone, briefly or longer, at some time in their lives.

I. Living alone because of circumstances

    A. Grown children moving to other cities

        1. Going away to school

        2. Taking jobs

    B. Married people not being married forever

        1. One out of two marriages ending in divorce

        2. Eight out of ten married women becoming widowed, usually late in life

II. Taking care of practical matters

    A. Opening a checking account

        1. Comparing bank services

        2. Comparing advantages of different kinds of checking accounts

    B. Making major purchases

        1. Replacing a refrigerator

        2. Buying a car

III. Establishing new friendships

    A. Students getting used to going to classes without old friends

        1. Being able to concentrate better

        2. Being able to meet new friends

IV. Dealing with feelings of loneliness

   A. Understanding the feeling

   B. Avoiding depression

     1. Not overeating

     2. Not overspending

     3. Not getting into unwanted situations

       a. Taking the wrong job

       b. Going into the wrong relationship

   C. Keeping busy

2s What can help me write a first draft?

If you have trouble getting started when the time arrives for drafting, you are not alone. Even professional writers sometimes have trouble getting started. Here are some time-proven methods experienced writers use to get started when they are blocked.

1. Write a discovery draft. Put aside all your notes from planning and shaping, and write a discovery draft. This means using FOCUSED FREEWRITING to get ideas on paper or onto your computer screen so that you can make connections that spring to mind as you write. Your discovery draft can serve as a first draft or as one more part of your notes when you write a more structured first draft.

2. Work from your notes. Sort your notes from planning and shaping into groups of subtopics. When you start writing, you can systematically concentrate on each subtopic without having to search repeatedly through your piles of notes. Arrange the subtopics in what seems to be a sensible sequence, knowing you can always go back later and re-sequence the subtopics. Now write a first draft by working through your notes on each subtopic. Draft either the entire essay or chunks of a few paragraphs at one time.

3. Use a combination of approaches. When you know the shape of your material, write according to that structure. When you feel "stuck" and don't know what to say next, switch to writing as you would for a discovery draft.

First drafts are not meant to be perfect; they are meant to give you something to revise. The direction of drafting is forward: keep pressing ahead. Do not stop to check spelling or grammar. If you are not sure a word or sentence is correct, circle it or put an X in the margin so that you can return to that spot later.

No single method of drafting an essay works for everyone. Following are a pair of methods you might try—or you might prefer to use another method that you have developed for yourself.

1. Put aside all your notes from planning and shaping. Write a "discovery draft." As you write, be open to discovering ideas and making connections that spring to mind during the physical act of writing. When you finish a discovery draft, you can decide to use it either as a first draft or as part of your notes when you make a structured first draft.

2. Keep your notes from planning and shaping in front of you and use them as you write. Write a structured first draft, working through all your material. If you are working on a long essay, you may want to draft in chunks, a few paragraphs at each sitting.

2t How can I overcome writer's block?

Writer's block is the desire to get started, but not doing so. Often, writer's block occurs because the writer harbors a fear of being wrong. To overcome that fear or any other cause of your block, think about it honestly so that you can shed light and gain understanding of whatever is holding you back. Also, a variety of techniques have become popular to overcome it.

WAYS TO OVERCOME WRITER'S BLOCK

1. Check that a myth about writing such as "writers are born, not made"; "writers have to be 'in the mood' to write"; "writers have to be really good at grammar and spelling"; "writers don't have to revise"; or "writing can be done at the last minute" isn't stopping you.

2. Avoid staring at a blank page.

3. Visualize yourself writing.

4. Picture an image or a scene, imagine a sound that relates to your topic.

5. Write about your topic in a letter or e-mail to a friend.

6. Try writing your material as if you were someone else.

7. Start writing in the middle of your essay.

8. Use FREEWRITING or FOCUSED FREEWRITING.

9. Change your method of writing.

10. Temporarily switch to writing about a topic that you care about passionately.

2u How do I revise?

To revise your essay, you must first evaluate it. Then you make improvements and in turn evaluate them in the context of the surrounding material. This process continues until you are satisfied that the essay is in final draft.

STEPS FOR REVISING

1. Shift mentally from suspending judgment (during idea gathering and drafting) to making judgments.

2. Read your draft critically to evaluate it. Be guided by the questions on the Revision Checklist below.

3. Decide whether to write an entirely new draft or to revise the one you have.

4. Be systematic. You need to pay attention to many different elements of a draft, from overall organization to choice of words. Most writers work better when they concentrate on specific elements during separate rounds of revision.

MAJOR ACTIVITIES DURING REVISION

Add. Insert needed words, sentences, and paragraphs. If your additions require new content, return to idea-gathering techniques.

Cut. Get rid of whatever goes off the topic or repeats what has already been said.

Replace. As needed, substitute new words, sentences, and paragraphs for what you have cut.

Move materials around. Change the sequence of paragraphs if the material is not presented in logical order. Move sentences within paragraphs, or to other paragraphs, if arrangements seem illogical.

When you revise, you need to pay special attention to your essay's title and thesis statement. Both of these features can help you stay on track, and they tell your reader what to expect.

The title of an essay plays an important organizing role. A good title can set you on your course and tell your readers what to expect. A title always stands alone. The opening of an essay should never refer to the essay's title as if it were part of a preceding sentence. For example, after the title "Knowing How to Live Alone," a writer should not begin the essay with the words, "This is very important." The title sets the stage, but it is not the first sentence of the essay.

The thesis statement expresses the central idea that controls and limits what the essay will cover. A thesis statement contains the topic, narrowed appropriately; the focus, which presents what you are saying about the topic; and the purpose. If your thesis statement does not match what you say in your essay, you need to revise either the thesis statement or the essay—sometimes both.

A revision checklist can help you focus your attention as you evaluate your writing. Use a checklist provided by your instructor or compile your own based on the Revision Checklist below.

Revision checklist

The answer to each question on this checklist should be yes. If it is not, you need to revise.

THE GLOBAL VIEW: WHOLE ESSAY AND PARAGRAPHS

1. Is your essay topic suitable and sufficiently narrow?
2. Does your thesis statement communicate your topic, focus, and purpose?
3. Does your essay show that you are aware of your audience?
4. Is your essay arranged effectively?
5. Have you checked for material that strays off the topic?
6. Does your introduction prepare your reader for the rest of the essay?
7. Do your body paragraphs express main ideas in topic sentences as needed? Are your main ideas clearly related to your thesis statement?
8. Do your body paragraphs provide specific, concrete support for each main idea?
9. Do you use transitions and other techniques to connect ideas within and between paragraphs?
10. Does your conclusion give your essay a sense of completion?

THE LOCAL VIEW: SENTENCES AND WORDS

1. Are your sentences concise?
2. Do your sentences show clear relationships among ideas?
3. Do you use parallelism, variety, and emphasis correctly and to increase the impact of your writing?
4. Have you eliminated sentence fragments? Have you eliminated comma splices and fused sentences?
5. Have you eliminated confusing shifts?
6. Have you eliminated disjointed sentences?
7. Have you eliminated misplaced and dangling modifiers?
8. Have you used exact words?
9. Is your usage correct and your language appropriate?
10. Have you avoided sexist language?

2v How do I edit?

When you edit, you check the correctness of your writing. You pay attention to grammar, spelling, and punctuation, and to correct use of capitals, numbers, italics, and abbreviations. You are ready to edit once you have a final draft that contains suitable content, organization, development, and sentence structure. Once you have edited your work, you are ready to transcribe it into a final copy.

As you edit, be systematic. Use a checklist supplied by your instructor or one you compile from the following Editing Checklist.

Editing checklist

Your goal is to answer yes to each question below. If you answer no, you need to edit. The numbers in the parenthesis tell you which chapters in this handbook to go to for more information.

1. Is your grammar correct?
2. Is your spelling, including hyphenation, correct?
3. Have you used commas correctly?
4. Have you used all other punctuation correctly?
5. Have you used capital letters, italics, abbreviations, and numbers correctly?

2w How do I proofread?

When you **proofread**, you check a final version carefully before handing it in. You need to make sure your work is an accurate and clean transcription of your final draft. Proofreading involves a careful, line-by-line reading of an essay. You should proofread with a ruler so that you can focus on one line at a time. Remember that no matter how hard you have worked on other parts of the writing process, if your final copy is inaccurate or messy, you will not be taken seriously.

2x What is collaborative writing?

Collaborative writing or peer-group writing refers to students working together to write a paper. The underlying idea is that two (or more) heads are better than one.

Here are guidelines for collaborative writing.

GUIDELINES FOR COLLABORATIVE WRITING

STARTING

1. Learn each other's names and exchange e-mail addresses and/or phone numbers so that you can be in touch outside of class.

2. Participate actively in the group process by helping to set a tone, include people and set limits if someone tries to dominate the group.

3. As a group, assign work to be done between meetings. Distribute the responsibilities as fairly as possible.

4. Make decisions regarding the technology you will use.

5. Set a timeline and deadlines for the project. Agree what to do in the event that someone misses a deadline.

PLANNING THE WRITING

6. After discussing the project, brainstorm as a group or use other techniques for discovering and compiling ideas.

7. Together agree on the ideas that seem best. Incubate, if time permits, and discuss your group choices again.

8. As a group, divide the project into parts, and distribute assignments fairly.

9. As you work on your part of the project, take notes in preparation for giving your group a progress report.

10. As a group, OUTLINE or otherwise sketch an overview of the paper to get a preliminary idea of how best to use material contributed by individuals.

DRAFTING THE WRITING

11. Draft a thesis statement.

12. Draft the rest of the paper. Decide whether each member of the group should write a complete draft or a different part of the whole. Use photocopies to share work.

REVISING THE WRITING

13. Read over the drafts. Are all the important points included?

14. Use the revision checklists, and work either as a group or by assigning portions to subgroups. If different people have drafted different sections, COHERENCE and UNITY should receive special attention in revision, as should your introduction and conclusion.

15. Agree on a final version. Assign someone to prepare the final draft and make needed photocopies.

EDITING AND PROOFREADING THE WRITING

16. As a group, review printouts or photocopies of the final draft. Don't leave the last stages to a subgroup. Draw on everyone's knowledge of grammar, spelling, and punctuation. Use everyone's eyes for proofreading.

17. Use the editing checklist to double-check for errors. If you find more than one or two errors per page, correct and print out the page again.

18. If your instructor asks, be prepared to describe your personal contribution to the project and/or to describe or evaluate the contributions of others.

Using Idea-Gathering Techniques   EXERCISE 2-1

Select four topics from this list, and prepare to write by narrowing each one. Use a different idea-gathering technique for each: freewriting, brainstorming, the journalist's questions, and mapping. Use your own paper, but record your narrowed topic on the line next to each subject you use.

1. talent _____

2. someone I can count on _____

3. traveling alone_____

4. happiness _____

5. graduation _____

6. breakfast _____

7. the beach _____

8. my grandparents_____

9. a personal loss _____

10. choosing a car_____

Grouping and Ordering Ideas   EXERCISE 2-2

Select two of the topics you explored in Exercise 2-2. For each, group ideas in clusters of related material and then order the clusters. Remember that not every item in an idea-generating exercise has to appear in the final essay. Feel free to omit items that do not fit your pattern. If there are gaps, return to idea-gathering techniques to get more material. Your end products will be informal outlines. Use your own paper.

Writing Thesis Statements

A: Most of the following thesis statements are unacceptable because they are too broad or too narrow. Label each thesis *acceptable* or *unacceptable*. Then revise each unacceptable thesis to make it suitable for an essay of about 500 words.

EXAMPLE   Canada is a nice place to visit.
            Its nearness to the United States, its cultural variety, and the lack of a language barrier make Canada an attractive choice for a family vacation.

1.   Planned budget cuts will do terrible damage to the university.

    _____

2.   Many students do not study as much as they should.

    _____

3.   My parents blame today's violence on movies, but I blame it on society.

    _____

4.   I saw several interesting auto races last week.

    _____

5.   I fell in love when I was seventeen.

    _____

6.   In interviews a job applicant should not beat around the bush.

    _____

7.   The local post office provides services that I use regularly.

    _____

8.   Remodeling an older home involves three major steps.

    _____

9.   In May I visited Turkey.

    _____

10.   The Norman Conquest occurred in 1066.

    _____

B: Write thesis statements for the four topics you narrowed in Exercise 2-2 and for six original topics. Be sure that each topic is suitably narrow for an essay of about 500 words and that the thesis statement shows a purpose and a point of view.

EXAMPLE   Topic: *how shopping has been changed by the development of closed malls*

Thesis Statement: *The development of closed malls has led to a revolution in the way Americans shop: we can shop easily at night and in rough weather, we see a greater variety of goods than in any single store, and we are encouraged to think of shopping as fun rather than as a chore.*

1.   Topic _____

    Thesis Statement _____

2. . Topic _____

    Thesis Statement _____

3.   Topic _____

    Thesis Statement _____

4.   Topic _____

    Thesis Statement _____

5.   Topic _____

    Thesis Statement _____

6.   Topic _____

    Thesis Statement _____

7.   Topic _____

    Thesis Statement _____

8.   Topic _____

    Thesis Statement _____

9.   Topic _____

    Thesis Statement _____

10. Topic _____

    Thesis Statement _____

The following topic outline contains twelve errors in form and logic. Revise the outline, using the guidelines in your handbook and in section 2r of this workbook. Draw a single line through each error and write your revision beside it.

Thesis Statement: Leaving a roommate for a single apartment can have definite drawbacks.

I. Unsatisfactory Furnishings
    A. Appliances
        1. Major
            a. Stove
            b. Refrigerator
        2. Minor
            a. Microwave
            b. Blender
            c. Toaster
            d. Mixer
        3. Washer
    B. Furniture
        1. Futon
        2. Living room
            a. Sofa
            b. Chairs
            c. Tables
        3. Kitchen
            a. Table
            b. Chairs
    C. Equipment
        1. For entertainment
            a. VCR
        2. Exercise
II. Not enough money to pay the bills
    A. Rent
    B. Utilities
        1. Gas
        2. Electricity
        3. Phone
    C. Food
        1. Groceries
    D. Entertainment

III. Inadequate companionship
  A. Loneliness is a frequent problem
  B. Occasional fear
  C. Friendly neighbors

Making a Formal Outline

Convert one of the informal outlines you developed in Exercise 2-3 into a formal outline. Write a sentence outline or a topic outline, but be sure not to mix the two types. Begin by placing the thesis statement you developed in Exercise 2-4B at the top of your page. Use the list of conventions in 2r and in your handbook for guidance and as a checklist when you are done.

Revising, Editing, and Proofreading Essays

A: Here is a middle draft of a short essay. It has already been revised, but it has not yet been edited. Edit the essay, using the Editing Checklist. If you like, you may also make additional revisions. When you are done, submit a carefully proofread copy of the completed essay to your instructor.

Forks, knives, and spoons seam so natural to most of us that its hard to imagine eaten dinner with out them. Yet many people, such as the chinese, use chopsticks instead, and other's use their hands to eat.

Knives are the oldest western utensils. The first ones were made of stone 1.5 million years ago. It was originally use to cut up dead animals after a hunt. The same knife were used to: butcher game slice cooked food, and kill enemies. Even later in History, nobles was the only ones who could afford separate knives for different uses. People use all-purpose knives, pointed like todays steak knives. The round-tipped dinner knife is a modern invention. It became popular in 17th cen. France because hosteses want to stop guests from picking they're teeth with the points of there dinner knives.

The spoon is also an anceint tool. Wooden spoons twenty thousand years old have been found in Asia; spoons of stone, wood, ivory, and even gold have been found in Egyptian tombs. Spoons scoop up foods that were to thick to sip from a bowl.

The fork is a newcomer. Forks did not become widely accepted until the eighteenth century; when the French nobility adopted the fork as a status symbol, and eating with ones hands became unfashionable. At about the same time, individual place settings became the rule to. Previous, even rich people had shared plates and glasses at meals, but know the rich demanded individual plates, glasses, forks, spoons, and knives. Today in America, a full set of utensils is considered a necessity. We forget that as recently as the american revolution some people still considered anyone who use a fork to be a fussy showoff.

B: Here is the first draft of an essay. It needs a great deal of work, as most first drafts do. Revise the essay, using the Revision Checklist. Then edit your work, using the Editing Checklist. Finally, submit a carefully proofread copy of the completed essay.

The Suburbs

This morning at registration the clerk who was reviewing my program insulted me when she said, "Why do you live all the way out there?" She said it as if I was a fool to live in the suburbs. It was really crowded, so I didn't tell her what was on my mind. In this essay I will tell you why I like living in the suburbs.

City slickers always have pity on me. "Your so far away from everything" they say. This remark only shows how stupid they are. First, I am not as isolated as they think. To get to school, I drive about 40 minutes on a smooth highway. The highway is uncrowded too. My city friends take an overcrowded bus for forty minutes. Or longer, if there is a traffic jam. When I graduate and begin to work, I probably will not have even the forty-minute drive because local businesses are growing by leaps and bounds. There are factories, shopping malls, and large insurance, law, and advertising firms. All within twenty miles of my home.

I think that if my classmates knew how pleasant suburban life can be, they would join me in a flash. People here are friendlier. First moving onto my block, people I didn't recognize waved to me as I walked my dog. I thought they had me confused with someone else. I later found out that they were just been friendly. I use to live in the city. The only people who notice me when I was walking my dog were the ones who sternly reminded me to "keep the dog off their lawns." Neighbors here keep an eye on one another. Once when I did not move my car for three days a neighbor knocked on my door to see if I was feeling alright. When I lived in the city, no one cared what I did or how I was, as long as I kept the volume down on the stereo.

Maybe I do not live in the most sophisticated area in the world, but I am not deprived. My stores carry the same fashions as stores in the city, my television receives the same programs, and my radio carries the same stations. So everything is equal except the suburbs have some advantages I have described to you in this essay. The city is a nice place to visit, but I wouldn't want to live there.

MODULE 3: WRITING PARAGRAPHS

3a What is a paragraph?

A **paragraph** is a group of sentences that work together to develop a unit of thought. Paragraphing permits you to subdivide material into manageable parts and, at the same time, to arrange those parts into a unified whole that effectively communicates its message.

To signal a new paragraph, you indent the first line five spaces in a typewritten paper and one inch in a handwritten paper.

A paragraph's purpose determines its structure. In college, the most common purposes for writing are *to inform* and *to persuade*. Some paragraphs in informative and in persuasive essays serve special roles: they introduce, conclude, or provide transitions. Most paragraphs, however, are **body paragraphs**, also called **developmental paragraphs** or **topical paragraphs**. They consist of a statement of a main idea and specific, logical support for that main idea.

3b How can I write effective introductory paragraphs?

Introductory paragraphs: In informative and persuasive writing, an introductory paragraph prepares readers for what lies ahead. For this reason, your introduction must relate clearly to the rest of your essay. If it points in one direction and your essay goes off in another, your reader will be confused—and may even stop reading.

In college writing, many instructors want an introductory paragraph to include a statement of the essay's **thesis**—its central idea. Although professional writers do not always use thesis statements in their introductory paragraphs, they can help student writers who need to practice clear essay organization. Here is an example of an introductory paragraph ending with a thesis statement.

1   Basketball is a team game. Individual stars are helpful, but in the end, the team that plays together is the team that wins. No one player can hog the ball; no one player should do all the shooting. Every player, every coach and every fan knows that. But once in a while, a team needs a super effort by an individual. **In a National Basketball Association playoff game between Boston and Syracuse, Boston's Bob Cousy made one of the most spectacular one-man shows ever seen.**

—HOWARD LISS, *True Sports Stories*

An introductory paragraph often includes an **introductory device** to lead into the thesis and to stimulate reader interest. To be effective, an introductory device must relate clearly to the essay's thesis and to the material in the topical paragraphs. Some of the most common introductory devices are listed below.

INTRODUCTORY PARAGRAPHS

STRATEGIES TO USE

1. Providing relevant background information

2. Relating briefly an interesting story or anecdote

3. Giving one or more pertinent—perhaps surprising—statistics

4. Asking one or more provocative questions

5. Using an appropriate quotation

6. Defining a key term

7. Presenting one or more brief examples

8. Drawing an analogy

STRATEGIES TO AVOID

1. Don't write statements about your purpose, such as "I am going to discuss the causes of falling oil prices."

2. Don't apologize, as in "I am not sure this is right, but this is my opinion."

3. Don't use overworked expressions, such as "Haste makes waste," as I recently discovered, or "Love is grand."

3c What are body paragraphs?

Body paragraphs appear between an introductory and a concluding paragraph and consist of a main idea and support for that idea. To be effective, a body paragraph needs unity, development, and coherence. Here's an overview of those three elements:

Three characteristics of effective body paragraphs: UDC

U = **U**nity: Have you made a clear connection between the main idea of the paragraph and the sentences that support the main idea?

D = **D**evelopment: Have you included detailed and sufficient support for the main idea of the paragraph?

C = **C**oherence: Have you progressed from one to the next in the paragraph smoothly and logically?

3d How can I create unity in paragraphs?

A paragraph has **unity** when the connection between the main idea and its supporting sentences is clear. Unity is ruined when any sentence in a paragraph doesn't relate to the main idea or to the other sentences in the paragraph. A paragraph is unified when all its sentences relate to the main idea. Unity is lost if a paragraph contains sentences unrelated to the main idea.

3e How can topic sentences create paragraph unity?

The sentence that contains the main idea of a paragraph is called the **topic sentence**. The topic sentence focuses and controls what can be written in the paragraph. Some paragraphs use two sentences to present a main idea. In such cases, the first is the topic sentence and the second is the **limiting** or **clarifying sentence** which narrows the focus of the paragraph.

Topic sentence at the beginning of a paragraph: Most informative and persuasive paragraphs have the topic sentence placed first so that a reader knows immediately what to expect. Placing the topic sentence first also helps to ensure that the entire paragraph will be unified.

2   **Many first-jobbers suffer from the "semester syndrome."** Students can usually count on being "promoted" at least twice a year—into the next semester. "Promotions" came regularly and at fixed intervals in school. At work, it's a different story. Promotions don't necessarily occur with any regularity, and sometimes they don't occur at all. This point may seem like a very obvious one, but the fact that students are used to rapid advancement can make their transitions to work harder. Since as students they become so conditioned to advancement at a fixed rate, many first-jobbers become impatient when they are required to remain in one job or at one task without a promotion for longer than a "semester." They begin to feel they're not moving anywhere, and as a result many leave their first jobs much too soon.

—The staff of *Catalyst, Making the Most of Your First Job*

Topic sentence at the end of a paragraph: Some informative and persuasive paragraphs present the supporting details before the main idea. The topic sentence, therefore, comes at the end of the paragraph. This technique is particularly effective for building suspense, but it should be used sparingly. In the following paragraph, notice how concrete details build up to the main idea.

3   I read Dreiser's *Jennie Gerhardt* and *Sister Carrie* and they revived in me a vivid sense of my mother's suffering: I was overwhelmed. I grew silent, wondering about the life around me. It would have been impossible for me to have told anyone what I derived from these novels, for it was nothing less than a sense of life itself. **All my life had shaped me for the realism, the naturalism of the modern novel, and I could not read enough of them.**

—RICHARD WRIGHT, "The Library Card," *from Black Boy*

Topic sentence implied: Some paragraphs make a unified statement without the use of a topic sentence. Writers must construct such paragraphs carefully, so that a reader can easily see the main idea. Paragraphs with implied topic sentences are rare in academic writing.

3f How can I develop my body paragraphs?

A topic sentence is usually a generalization. A topical paragraph is **developed** by the sentences that support the topic sentence, offering specific, concrete details. Without development, a paragraph fails to make its point or capture a reader's interest.

The key to successful development of topical paragraphs is detail. Details bring generalizations to life by providing concrete, specific illustrations. A paragraph developed with good detail often has RENNS—an acronym that stands for *reasons*, *examples*, *numbers*, *names*, and appeals to the five *senses*. Use RENNS as a memory device to help you check the development of your paragraphs, but do not feel that every paragraph must have a complete menu of RENNS to be well-developed. Here is a paragraph with two of the five types of RENNS.

4   However, the first ride I got took me on the way to New York rather than Washington. It was a big Standard Oil truck, heading for Wellsville. We drove out into the wild, bright country, the late November country, full of the light of Indian summer. The red barns glared in the harvested fields, and the woods were bare, but all the world was full of color and the blue sky swam with fleets of white clouds. The truck devoured the road with high-singing tires, and I rode throned in the lofty, rocking cab, listening to the driver telling me stories about all the people who lived in places we passed, and what went on in the houses we saw.

—THOMAS MERTON, *The Seven Storey Mountain*

This paragraph offers concrete, specific illustrations which describe Merton's first ride on the way to New York. It has *names* such as Standard Oil truck (not the general term *truck*), Wellsville, November country, and red barns (not the general term *buildings*). It appeals to the senses by including many references to light and specific colors, as well as to the rocking motion of the cab and the sound of the tires.

THE RENNS TEST: CHECKING FOR SUPPORTING DETAILS

R = **Reasons** provide support.

E = **Examples** provide support.

N = **Names** provide support.

N = **Numbers** provide support.

S = **Senses**—sight, sound, smell, taste, touch—provide support.

3g How can I write coherent paragraphs?

A paragraph is coherent when its sentences are related to each other, not only in content but also in grammatical structures and choice of words. The techniques of coherence are transitional expressions, pronouns, repetition of key words, and parallel structures. Though they are discussed separately in this section for the sake of clear example, techniques of coherence usually work in unison.

TECHNIQUES FOR ACHIEVING COHERENCE

Using appropriate transitional expressions

Using pronouns when possible

Using deliberate repetition of a key word

Using parallel structures

Using coherence techniques to create connection between paragraphs

Transitional expressions—words and phrases that signal connections among ideas—can help you achieve coherence in your writing. Here are the most commonly used transitional expressions.

TRANSITIONAL EXPRESSIONS

SIGNAL	WORDS
Addition	also, in addition, too, moreover, and, besides, further, furthermore, equally, important, next, then, finally
Example	for example, for instance, thus, as an illustration, namely, specifically
Contrast	but, yet, however, on the other hand, nevertheless, nonetheless, conversely, in contrast, on the contrary, still, at the same time, although
Comparison	similarly, likewise, in like manner, in the same way, in comparison
Concession	of course, to be sure, certainly, naturally, granted
Result	therefore, thus, consequently, so, accordingly, due to this
Summary	as a result, hence, in short, in brief, in summary, in conclusion, finally, on the whole
Time sequence	first, firstly, second, secondly, third, fourth, next, then, finally, afterwards, before, soon, later, during, meanwhile, subsequently, immediately, at length, eventually, in the future, currently
Place	in the front, in the foreground, in the back, in the background, at the side, adjacent, nearby, in the distance, here, there

Notice how transitional expressions (shown in boldface) help to make the following paragraph coherent.

5   The role of stress in the development of schizophrenic symptoms is particularly hard to study since what is stressful for one person may not be stressful for another. **Nonetheless**, two conclusions can be drawn. **First**, the biological predisposition to become mentally disorganized

lowers a schizophrenic's resistance to stress in general, although some people who are so predisposed can tolerate more stress than others. **Second**, the issue of becoming independent from one's family of origin appears to pose special difficulties for individuals predisposed to schizophrenia. This is not surprising in view of the fact that mental, emotional, and social competence are requirements of successful completion of this task. The predisposed individual may be impaired in each of these areas.

—Kayla F. Berneim and Richard R. Lewine, *Schizophrenia*

When you use **pronouns** that clearly refer to nouns and other pronouns, you help your reader move from one sentence to the next. Notice how the pronouns (shown in boldface) help make the following paragraph coherent.

6   The men and women who perform the daring and often dangerous action that is part of almost every television and motion-picture story today are special people. **They** are professional stunt men and women. **They** know precisely what **they** are doing and how to do it. **Most** are extraordinary athletes with the grace and timing of dancers. **They** plan ahead what **they** must do. And **they** have no intention of getting hurt, although sometimes **they** do.

—Gloria D. Miklowitz, *Movie Stunts and the People Who Do Them*

You can achieve coherence by repeating **key words** in a paragraph. Notice how the careful repetition of the words *demand, difficulty, game(s), fun,* and *rules* (shown in boldface) help make this paragraph coherent.

7   We **demand difficulty** even in our **games**. We **demand** it because without **difficulty** there can be no **game**. A **game** is a way of making something hard for the **fun** of it. The **rules** of the **game** are an arbitrary imposition of **difficulty**. When the spoilsport ruins the **fun**, he always does so by refusing to play by the **rules**. It is easier to win at chess if you are free, at your pleasure, to change the wholly arbitrary **rules**, but the **fun** is in winning within the **rules**. No **difficulty**, no **fun**.

—John Cardi, "Is Everybody Happy?"

Parallel structures can help you achieve coherence. Using the same form of phrase or clause several times sets up a rhythm which gives unity to the paragraph. Notice how the parallel structures (shown in boldface) make this paragraph coherent.

3h How can I arrange a paragraph?

Here are some of the most common ways to organize paragraphs.

WAYS TO ARRANGE SENTENCES IN A PARAGRAPH
1. By time
2. By location
3. From general to specific
4. From specific to general
5. From least to most
6. From problem to solution

From general to specific: An arrangement of sentences from the general to the specific is the most common organization for a paragraph. Such paragraphs often begin with a topic sentence and end with specific details.

8   **This** is our hope. **This is** the faith with which I return to the South. **With this faith we will be able to** hew out of the mountain of despair a stone of hope. **With this faith we will be able to** transform the jangling discords of our nation into a beautiful symphony of brotherhood. **With this faith we will be able to work together, to pray together, to struggle together, to go to jail together, to stand up for freedom together,** knowing that we will be free one day.

—MARTIN LUTHER KING, "I Have a Dream"

9   **Gifts from parents to children always carry the most meaningful messages.** The way parents think about presents goes one step beyond the objects themselves—the ties, dolls, sleds, record players, kerchiefs, bicycles and model airplanes that wait by the Christmas tree. The gifts are, in effect, one way of telling boys and girls, "We love you even though you have been a bad boy all month" or, "We love having a daughter" or, "We treat all our children alike" or, "It is all right for girls to have some toys made for boys" or, "This alarm clock will help you get started in the morning all by yourself." Throughout all the centuries since the invention of a Santa Claus figure who represented a special recognition of children's behavior, good and bad, presents have given parents a way of telling children about their love and hopes and expectations for them.

—MARGARET MEAD AND RHODA METRAUX, *A Way of Seeing*

From specific to general: A less common arrangement moves from the specific to the general. The paragraph ends with a topic sentence and begins with the details that support the topic sentence.

10   They live up alongside the hills, in hollow after hollow. They live in eastern Kentucky and eastern Tennessee and in the western part of North Carolina and the western part of Virginia and in just about the whole state of West Virginia. They live close to the land; they farm it and some of them go down into it to extract its coal. Their ancestors, a century or two ago, fought their way westward from the Atlantic seaboard, came up on the mountains, penetrated the valleys, and moved stubbornly up the creeks for room, for privacy, for a view, for a domain of sorts. **They are Appalachian people, mountain people, hill people. They are white yeomen, or miners, or hollow folk, or subsistence farmers**.

—ROBERT COLES, "A Domain (of Sorts)"

From least to most important: A sentence arrangement that moves from the least to the most important is known as a **climactic sequence**. This arrangement holds the reader's interest because the best part comes at the end.

11   Joseph Glidden's invention, barbed wire, soon caught on—though not with everyone. Indians called it "devil's rope." Ranchers often cut it down so their cattle could graze freely. Most farmers, however, liked barbed wire. It kept cattle away from their crops. Cattle could break through most wire fences. With barbed wire, they quickly got the point. Eventually, ranchers started using barbed wire. With it, they separated the best cattle from the others to produce better breeds. Barbed wire helped railroads keep cattle off the tracks. As a result, the railroads expanded into new territory. **Glidden probably didn't realize it at the time, but the few hours he spent twisting wires would help speed the taming of the West.**

—*Small Inventions That Make a Big Difference*, National Geographic Society

According to location: A paragraph that describes the relative position of objects to one another, often from a central point of reference, uses **spatial sequence**. The topic sentence usually gives the reader the location that serves as the orientation for all other places mentioned.

12   The bay in front of the dock was framed by the shores of the mainland, which curved together from both sides to meet in a point. At that vertex another island, rocky and tall, rose from the water. It looked uninhabited; and although a few cabins were scattered along the mainland, between and behind them was unbroken forest. It was my first sight of a natural wilderness. Behind our tent too, and several other tents here and a house in their midst, was the forest. Over everything, as pervasive as sunshine, was the fragrance of balsam firs. It was aromatic and sweet and I closed my eyes and breathed deeply to draw in more of it.

—SALLY CARRIGHAR, *Home to the Wilderness*

According to time: A paragraph arranged according to time uses a **chronological sequence**.

13   About 30 years ago, a prince in India found a rare white tiger cub whose mother had been killed. The prince decided to raise the cub, which he named Mohan. When Mohan grew up, he fathered some cubs that were white. One of his cubs, Mohini, was sent to the National Zoo in Washington, D.C. Mohini was used to breed more white tigers for other zoos in the United States.

—"Who-o-o Knows?" *Ranger Rick*

3i How can rhetorical strategies help me write paragraphs?

If you know a variety of patterns for paragraph development, you have more choices when you are seeking ways to help your paragraphs deliver their meanings most effectively. Although, for the purpose of illustration, the patterns shown here are discussed in isolation, in essay writing paragraph patterns often overlap. Be sure to use the paragraph pattern that communicates your meaning most effectively.

COMMON RHETORICAL STRATEGIES (OR PATTERNS) FOR PARAGRAPHS

- Narrative
- Description
- Process
- Examples
- Definitions
- Analysis
- Classification
- Comparison and Contrast
- Analogy
- Cause-and-Effect Analysis

Narration: Narrative writing tells about what is happening or what happened. Narration is usually written in chronological sequence.

14   During the 1870s, the business world was not yet ready for the typewriter. Inventor C. Latham Sholes and his daughter Lillian faced two major objections as they demonstrated

Sholes's writing machine. "Too expensive and too slow," the businessmen protested. The response discouraged the inventor, but he didn't give up. At his home in Milwaukee, Wisconsin, he designed improvements for his machine. He also invented touch-typing, a system that enables a person to type fast without looking at the keys. Touch-typing was faster than handwriting. It could save both time and money. That caused businessmen's interest to perk up. By 1900, in offices all over the United States, the clickety-clack of typewriters was replacing the scratching of pens.

—*Small Inventions That Make a Big Difference,* National Geographic Society

Description: Descriptive writing appeals to a reader's senses—sight, sound, smell, taste, and touch—creating a sensual impression of a person, place, or object.

15   The forest was quiet except for the shrill cries of faraway toucans. Then many leaves began to rustle nearby. Seconds later crickets and cockroaches were hopping and crawling frantically in my direction. What could be causing these creatures to run for their lives? I wondered. Then I saw them: Tens of thousands of army ants were marching toward their fleeing prey—and me! The swarm of ants looked like a huge moving triangle, with the ants at the head of the swarm forming the widest part. And this part was as long as a school bus.

—DOUG WECHSLER, "I Met the Rambo Ants"

Process: A process describes a sequence of actions by which something is done or made. It is usually developed in chronological order. If it is to be effective, a process must include all steps. The amount of detail included depends on whether you want to teach the reader how to do something or you merely want to offer a general overview of the process.

16   To keep the big teams as nearly even as possible in the level of performance, a system called the draft has been devised. This is the way it works. Names of top college players who are graduating and want to turn pro are listed. Team representatives meet for a few days, usually in New York, to select the players they wish from this list. The team that placed last in the standings that year, gets first choice. The team next lowest in the standings gets the next choice, and so on. Naturally the representative will select the player the team needs the most. If one team gets a player that another team wants, that other team may trade an established team member or members for the draft choice. Naturally, a lot of wheeling and dealing goes on at this time.

—BOB AND MARGUITA MCGONAGLE, *Careers in Sports*

Example: A paragraph developed by example uses one or more illustrations to provide evidence in support of the main idea.

17   Getting right down to the gory details, ever since the earliest days of movie making, stars have been gushing, oozing, trickling, or dripping blood, as the case may be, on screen. Victims in silent movies "bled" chocolate syrup, which looked just like the real McCoy on the kind of black-and-white film used then. If a cowboy in a Western was to get shot, just before the scene was filmed a little chocolate syrup would be poured into the palm of his hand. Then, when the cameras started rolling and the cowboy got "blasted," he merely slapped his hand to his chest and what audiences saw was the bloody aftermath.

—JANE O'CONNOR AND KATHY HALL, *Magic in the Movies*

Definition: A paragraph of definition explains the meaning of a word or concept. Because it is more thorough than the definition offered by a dictionary, such a paragraph is called an **extended definition**.

An extended definition may contain any of several elements, but it rarely includes all of them: (1) a dictionary definition, (2) a negative definition—what the term is not, (3) a comparison and contrast of definitions used by other people, (4) an explanation of how this term differs from terms with which it is often confused, and (5) an explanation of how the term originated. If the subject is a human quality, the definition may include (6) a discussion of how a person develops the quality and how the quality shows up in the individual's personality.

18   Now, consider for a moment just exactly what it is that you are about to be handed. It is a huge, irregular mass of ice cream, faintly domed at the top from the metal scoop, which has first produced it and then insecurely balanced it on the uneven top edge of a hollow inverted cone made out of the most brittle and fragile of materials. Clumps of ice cream hang over the side, very loosely attached to the main body. There is always much more ice cream than the cone could hold, even if the ice cream were tamped down into the cone, which of course it isn't. And the essence of ice cream is that it melts. It doesn't just stay there teetering in this irregular, top-heavy mass; it also melts. And it melts fast. And it doesn't just melt— it melts into a sticky fluid that cannot be wiped off. The only thing one person could hand to another that might possibly be more dangerous is a live hand grenade from which the pin had been pulled five seconds earlier. And of course if anybody offered you that, you could say, "Oh. Uh, well—no thanks."

—L. RUST HILLS, *How to Do Things Right*

Analysis and classification: **Analysis** divides things up, and **classification** puts things together. A paragraph developed by analysis, also known as **division**, divides one subject into its component parts. Paragraphs written in this pattern usually start by identifying the one subject and then explain that subject's distinct parts. For example, a football team can be divided into its offensive and defensive teams, which can be divided further into the various positions on each.

A paragraph developed by classification discusses the ways that separate groups relate to one another. The separate groups must be from the same class; that is, they must have some underlying characteristic in common. For example, different types of sports—football, Rugby, and soccer— can be classified together according to their handling of the ball, their playing fields, the placement of their goals, and the like.

19   **There are three kinds of book owners.** The **first** has all the standard sets and best sellers—unread, untouched. (This deluded individual owns wood-pulp and ink, not books.) The **second** has a great many books—a few of them read through, most of them dipped into, but all of them as clean and shiny as the day they were bought. (This person would probably like to make books his own, but is restrained by a false respect for their physical appearance.) The **third** has a few books or many—every one of them dog-eared and dilapidated, shaken and loosened by continual use, marked and scribbled in from front to back. (This man owns books.)

—MORTIMER J. ADLER, "How to Mark a Book"

Comparison and contrast: **Comparison** deals with similarities, and **contrast** deals with differences between two objects or ideas. Paragraphs using comparison and contrast can be structured in two ways. A **point-by-point structure** allows you to move back and forth between the two items being compared. A **block structure** allows you to discuss one item completely before discussing the other.

POINT-BY-POINT STRUCTURE

Student body: college A, college B
Curriculum: college A, college B
Location: college A, college B

BLOCK STRUCTURE

College A: student body, curriculum, location
College B: student body, curriculum, location

Here is a paragraph structured point-by-point for comparison and contrast.

20   Some people say the business about the jolly fat person is a myth, that all of us chubbies are neurotic, sick, sad people. I disagree. Fat people may not be chortling all day long, but they're a hell of a lot *nicer* than the wizened and shriveled. Thin people turn surly, mean, and hard at a young age because they never learn the value of a hot-fudge sundae for easing tension. Thin people don't like gooey soft things because they themselves are neither gooey nor soft. They are crunchy and dull, like carrots. They go straight to the heart of the matter while fat people let things stay all blurry and hazy and vague, the way things actually are. Thin people want to face the truth. Fat people know there is no truth. One of my thin friends is always staring at complex, unsolvable problems and saying, "The key thing is...." Fat people never say that. They know there isn't any such thing as the key thing about anything.

—SUZANNE BRITT JORDAN, "That Lean and Hungry Look"

Here is a paragraph structured block style for comparison and contrast.

21   Many people think that gorillas are fierce and dangerous beasts. Stories have been told about gorillas attacking people. Movies have been made about gorillas kidnapping women. These stories and movies are exciting, but they are not true. In real life, gorillas are gentle and rather shy. They rarely fight among themselves. They almost never fight with other animals. They like to lead a quiet life—eating, sleeping, and raising their young.

—SUSAN MYERS, *The Truth about Gorillas*

Analogy: Analogy is a type of comparison. By comparing objects or ideas from different classes, an analogy explains the unfamiliar in terms of the familiar. For example, the fight to find a cure for a disease might be compared to a war. Often a paragraph developed with analogy starts with a simile or metaphor.

22   If clothing is a language, it must have a vocabulary and a grammar like other languages. Of course, as with human speech, there is not a single language of dress, but many: some (like Dutch and German) closely related and others (like Basque) almost unique. And within every language of clothes there are many different dialects and accents, some almost unintelligible to members of the mainstream culture. Moreover, as with speech, each individual has his own stock of words and employs personal variations of tone and meaning.

—ALISON LURIE, *The Language of Clothes*

Cause-and-effect analysis: Cause-and-effect analysis involves examining the origin or outcome of something that happened or might happen. Causes are what lead up to an event; effects are what result.

23   When a person is weightless, the slightest exertion causes motion. For example, if you pushed yourself away from a chair, you would continue to move away from it. There would be nothing to stop the motion. You would float in space. Should you let go of your book, it would hang in space. Push it ever so slightly, and the book would move in a straight line. Splash water, and it would form into round drops moving in all directions.

—FRANKLIN M. BRANLEY, *Mysteries of Outer Space*

3j What is a transitional paragraph?

Transitional paragraphs: A transitional paragraph usually consists of one or two sentences that help the reader move from one major point to another in long essays. Here is a transitional paragraph that moves the reader between a series of details and an explanation of their possible source.

24   Now that we've sampled some of the false "facts" that clutter our storehouse of knowledge, perhaps you'd like to consider some of the possible reasons why we seem so susceptible to misinformation.

—WILLIAM GOTTLIEB, *Science Facts You Won't Believe*

3k How can I write effective concluding paragraphs?

Concluding paragraphs: In informative and persuasive writing, a conclusion brings discussion to a logical and graceful end. Too abrupt an ending leaves your reader suddenly cut off, and a conclusion that is merely tacked onto an essay does not give the reader a sense of completion. In contrast, an ending that flows gracefully and sensibly from what has come before it reinforces your ideas and increases the impact of your essay. The most common ways of concluding an essay are listed below.

STRATEGIES FOR CONCLUDING PARAGRAPHS

STRATEGIES TO TRY

1. A strategy adapted from those used for introductory paragraphs but be careful to choose a different strategy for your introduction and conclusion

   • Relating a brief concluding, interesting story or anecdote

   • Giving one or more pertinent—perhaps surprising—concluding statistics

   • Asking one or more provocative questions for further thought

   • Using an appropriate quotation to sum up the thesis statement

   • Redefining a key term for emphasis

2. An ANALOGY that summarizes the thesis statement

3. A SUMMARY of the main points, but only if the piece of writing is longer than three to four pages

4. A statement that urges awareness by the readers

5. A statement that looks ahead to the future

6. A call to readers

STRATEGIES TO AVOID

1. Introducing new ideas or facts that belong in the body of the essay

2. Rewording your introduction

STRATEGIES FOR CONCLUDING PARAGRAPHS *(continued)*

STRATEGIES TO AVOID

3. Announcing what you've discussed, as in "In this paper, I have explained why the price of oil dropped."

4. Making absolute claims, as in "I have proved that oil prices don't always affect gasoline prices."

5. Apologizing, as in "Even though I'm not an expert, I feel my position is correct."

The concluding paragraph below summarizes Cousy's "show."

25   In that game Bob Cousy scored a total of 50 points. He made 25 of them in regulation time, and 25 more in the four overtime periods. And he made 30 out of 32 foul shots. Even more important, he had scored his points at the right time. Four times he scored in the final seconds to keep the game going. Then he helped his team pull away. Basketball may be a team game, but most teams would not be sorry to have an individual performer like Bob Cousy.

—*HOWARD LISS, True Sports Stories*

Here is a list of what to avoid when writing concluding paragraphs.

WHAT TO AVOID IN WRITING CONCLUDING REMARKS

1. Don't go off the track. Avoid introducing an entirely new idea or adding a fact that belongs in the body of the essay.

2. Do not merely reword your introduction. Also do not simply list the main idea in each topic sentence or restate the thesis. While a summary can refer to those points, it must tie them into what was covered in the essay. If the introduction and conclusion are interchangeable, you need to revise.

3. Don't announce what you have done. Avoid statements such as "In this paper I have tried to show the main causes for the drop in oil prices."

4. Don't use absolute claims. Avoid statements such as "This proves that..." or "If we take this action, the problem will be solved." Always qualify your message with expressions such as "This seems to prove..." or "If we take this action, we will begin working toward a solution of the problem."

5. Don't apologize. Avoid casting doubt on your material by making statements such as "I may not have thought of all the arguments, but..."

Identifying Sentences That Do Not Fit the Topic Sentence   EXERCISE 3-1

Identify the topic sentence in each paragraph, and write its number in the first column. Then, identify any irrelevant sentences (ones that do not fit the topic sentences), and write their numbers in the second column.

	TOPIC SENTENCE	IRRELEVANT SENTENCES

EXAMPLE   ¹The flute is a very old instrument. ²It existed as long ago as 3500 B.C. ³My brother plays the flute. ⁴Archaeologists digging in the cities of ancient Sumeria and Egypt have found well-preserved flutes. ⁵When these flutes were tested, they sounded much like modern flutes. ⁶However, they look different. ⁷My brother's flute is silver. ⁸Ancient flutes were played vertically, and they were 1 1/2 feet long but only a 1/2 inch wide.

TOPIC SENTENCE: ___1___   IRRELEVANT SENTENCES: ___3, 7___

1.   ¹Many people associate the clarinet with jazz or the Big Bands of the forties. ²However, the clarinet has been around since ancient times. ³The clarinet can be hard to play. ⁴The first clarinet appeared in Egypt before 2700 B.C. ⁵The double clarinet appeared about eight hundred years later. ⁶The first modern Westerner to compose for the clarinet was a sixteenth century German, Johann Christoph Denner. ⁷He improved the clarinet by making it of wood, using a single rather than a double reed, and increasing its length from one foot to two feet.

2.   ¹The lute is the ancestor of many modern stringed instruments. ²There is even a mural, dating from 2500 B.C., that shows a Babylonian shepherd playing a lute. ³The guitar, the ukulele, and the sitar are descendents of the lute. ⁴The sitar became popular in the West after the Beatles George Harrison studied with Indian musician Ravi Shankar. ⁵The violin, fiddle, and

cello also are descended from the lute. [6]The bows used to play these instruments are an eighth century Islamic addition to the tradition of stringed instruments.

3. [1]The trumpet is another instrument with a long history. [2]The first trumpets were made of bamboo cane or eucalyptus branches. [3]The eucalyptus tree is found in Australia and is the chief food source for koalas. [4]The first metal trumpets, made of silver, were found in the tomb of King Tutankhamen of Egypt, who died about 1350 B.C. [5]The Greek trumpets of the fifth century B.C. were made of carved ivory. [6]Like us, the Romans had both straight and J-shaped trumpets. [7]The Romans are often depicted in paintings as enjoying music.

    _____   _____

4. [1]The first bagpipes were very unusual instruments. [2]They were made from the complete hide of a sheep or goat. [3]The chanter, a pipe with finger holes, was set in a wooden plug placed in the animal's neck. [4]The drones, the pipes that produced the bagpipe's sound, were set in wooden plugs placed in the forelegs. [5]Then as now, a blowpipe was used to fill the bag with air. [6]The player pressed the bag under one arm, forcing air out the drones, and fingered the chanter, making the bagpipe's famous sound. [7]The bagpipe originally came from Asia.

    _____   _____

5. [1]Many people assume the piano is an improved version of some older keyboard instrument, such as the harpsichord. [2]Actually, the harpsichord, the clavichord, and the piano are widely different. [3]In a harpsichord, the strings are plucked. [4]This plucking enables the instrument to sustain a note. [5]In the clavichord, the strings are struck by blades of metal. [6]Once a blade moves off a string, the note stops. [7]The first clavichord dates back to about 1385. [8]In the piano, the strings are struck by small hammers that rebound immediately. [9]The piano did not become popular until the eighteenth century.

    _____   _____

Identifying Transitions

Underline all the transitional words and expressions in these paragraphs. Then list the transitions on the lines provided.

1. The lion is called the King of Beasts, but the tiger really deserves the title. Male lions are six to eight feet long, not counting their tails. They are about three feet high at the shoulder, and they weigh four to five hundred pounds. In contrast, the tiger can grow up to a foot longer, several inches taller, and a hundred pounds heavier.

   _____

2. Most people think the boomerang is found only in Australia; however, this is not so. People use curved hunting sticks in four other parts of the world: Indonesia, eastern Africa, the Indian subcontinent, and the southwestern United States. In the United States, the Hopi, Acoma, and Zuni Indians use such sticks to hunt small animals. Few boomerangs are designed to return to their owners, but the Australian aborigines have perfected a kind that does return. In fact, the word "boomerang" comes from the aborigines' name for such a hunting stick.

   _____

3. Despite its name, *The Encyclopaedia Britannica* is not a British enterprise, nor has it ever been. The Britannica was founded in 1771 by a group of "Gentlemen in Scotland" who ran it until 1815, when a second group of Scotsmen took over. The British finally became involved in 1910, but as partners to Americans. Since the 1920s, the Britannica has been a completely American project. From 1928 to 1943, it was owned by Sears, Roebuck. Since 1943, the Britannica has been owned by the University of Chicago.

   _____

4. Everyone knows the story of Cinderella. She was treated as a servant by her stepmother and stepsisters, helped by a fairy godmother, and finally rescued by a prince who identified her because her small foot fit the glass slipper that his "mystery woman" had left behind at the ball. Were glass slippers fashionable centuries ago, or did someone make a mistake? Someone certainly made a mistake. In 1697, Charles Perrault translated Cinderella from Old French into English. Unfortunately, he mistranslated *vair* as "glass." Actually, *vair* means "white squirrel fur." So, Cinderella's shoes were much more comfortable than we had been told.

   _____

5. Dr. Joseph Guillotin did not invent the guillotine, although it was named after him. The guillotine had been in use throughout Europe since at least the early fourteenth century. In most places, the guillotine was reserved for executing nobility. During the French Revolution, Dr. Guillotin suggested to the French National Assembly that the machine become the country's official form of capital punishment. He wanted it to be used on criminals regardless of their social class. The Assembly agreed. The first victim of the French guillotine was a highwayman in 1792. Within a year, the heads of the nobility began to fall in the infamous Reign of Terror.

   _____

Identifying Devices That Provide Coherence

Read this paragraph carefully, and then answer the questions that follow.

¹Have you ever wondered how the painted lines in the road are made straight? ²No one painting freehand could consistently keep lines straight, so machines are used. ³Before a small road or street is painted, a highway crew marks it at twenty-foot intervals, following an engineer's plan. ⁴Then a gasoline-powered machine, about the size of a large lawnmower, is pushed along by one person. ⁵The operator follows the marks on the road, while air pressure forces out a stream of paint or hot plastic. ⁶Hot plastic lasts from eighteen months to three years; paint lasts from three to six months. ⁷Of course, this machine is too slow for use on highways. ⁸Instead, four-person crews use a large truck equipped with a pointer that can be used to follow the median strip, so there is no need to mark the road before painting. ⁹The truck is faster than the one-person machine for other reasons as well: it has two adjustable sprayguns that paint lines at the required distances apart, and it moves at five miles an hour. ¹⁰Crew members must have great skill. ¹¹In fact, they receive up to a year of training.

1. Which words and phrases serve as transitional devices?

2. What key words are repeated (include all forms of the words)?

3. How does parallelism function in sentences 6 and 9?

4. What key words are later replaced by pronouns? List the nouns and the pronouns that substitute for them.

Organizing Sentences to Create a Coherent Paragraph

Rearrange the sentences in each set to create a coherent paragraph. Write the letters of the sentences in their new order. Then write out the paragraph.

1. a. Second, compare fees for special services, such as stopping checks.

    b. Always compare several banks before you open a checking account.

    c. Finally, make sure the bank's hours are convenient for you.

    d. First, find out the monthly fee each bank charges.

    e. Next, see if you will be earning interest on your account.

2. a. Early humans imitated these "natural bridges" by chopping down tall trees and placing them across water.

    b. It was built of many logs tied together with rope.

    c. The first bridges were simply trees that had, by chance, fallen across streams.

    d. The bridge over the Euphrates River lasted for decades.

    e. The first genuine bridge was laid across the Euphrates River at Babylon about 700 B.C.

3. a. Sir Alexander Fleming discovered the penicillin mold, the first modern antibiotic, by accident in 1928.

    b. For the next 200 years, scientists sought a cure for infection.

    c. The Chinese used this soybean mold to treat skin infections.

    d. The first antibiotic was made from moldy soybeans around 500 B.C.

    e. Soon after, other cultures began using moldy bread and cobwebs to treat infected wounds.

    f. Strangely, they never looked into these folk remedies.

4. a. Two years later, Long's wife became the first woman to deliver a baby under anesthesia.

    b. Before the introduction of ether by Long, doctors had relied on crude methods of anesthesia.

    c. The use of ether in surgery started in 1842.

    d. In 1846 in Boston, the word "anesthesia," meaning "lack of feeling," was coined after the first use of ether in major surgery.

    e. In that year, Dr. Crawford W. Long used ether to anesthetize a young man who was having a cyst removed from his neck.

    f. These early methods included alcoholic intoxication, freezing the area of the operation, and having the patient inhale the fumes from burning narcotic plants.

For each topic sentence below, supply three to five relevant details. Then, using your own paper, write a unified and coherent paragraph using the topic sentence and your supporting details.

1. Topic Sentence: Parenting class should (should not) be required for high school graduation.

    Details:

2. Topic Sentence: Buying on credit can be disastrous.

    Details:

3. Topic Sentence: The _____ have contributed many things
          (members of an ethnic group)
          to American culture.

    Details:

4. Topic Sentence: _____ is an exciting spectator sport.

    Details:

5. Topic Sentence: The laws regarding _____ should be changed.

    Details:

6. Topic Sentence: Choosing a college can be difficult.

    Details:

Organizing Details within Paragraphs   EXERCISE 3-6

Details in a paragraph are often organized in one of four patterns: chronological order (time), spatial order (location), general to specific, or climactic order (least important to most important). For each pattern, select a subject from the ones given, construct a topic sentence, and list three to five supporting details. Then, on your own paper, use the topic sentence and details to write a unified and coherent paragraph of at least four sentences. It may be possible to combine two closely related details in one sentence.

1. CHRONOLOGICAL ORDER: the steps in applying to college; preparing for vacation; painting a room

   Topic Sentence:

   Details:

2. SPATIAL ORDER: the view from the classroom window; the floor plan of the local video rental store; the layout of a basketball court

   Topic Sentence:

   Details:

3. GENERAL TO SPECIFIC: the advantages (disadvantages) of working while attending school full time; the mood on New Year's Eve; the reasons _____ is my favorite meal

   Topic Sentence:

   Details:

4. CLIMACTIC ORDER: why I've chosen my career; how I control anger; how I would raise responsible children

   Topic Sentence:

   Details:

Using Examples in Paragraphs

Write two paragraphs in which examples are used to support your topic sentence. In the first paragraph, use three to five short examples; in the second, use one extended example. First compose a topic sentence. Next, list the supporting example(s) you will use. After that, write your paragraph, using your own paper.

Select your topics from this list: the risks of walking alone at night; my favorite actor/actress; the advantages (disadvantages) of playing on a school team; how peer pressure can be hard to resist; professional athletes are overpaid (underpaid); the difficulty of adjusting to a new neighborhood, school, or job.

1. MULTIPLE EXAMPLES

   Topic Sentence: _____

   Examples: a. _____

   b. _____

   c. _____

   d. _____

   e. _____

2. EXTENDED EXAMPLE

   Topic Sentence: _____

   Example: _____

48

Name _____   Date _____

Using Paragraph Development Strategies   EXERCISE **3-8**

Most paragraphs are developed through a combination of several of the strategies discussed in this chapter. Usually one strategy predominates, however. For each development strategy listed below, select a topic from the list; compose a topic sentence; list three to five details, examples, or other pieces of support; and then, using your own paper, write the paragraph.

1. NARRATIVE
   Topics: a time I surprised my friends; a success story; meeting someone special; recovering from a tragedy

   Topic Sentence: _____

   Events: a. _____

              b. _____

              c. _____

              d. _____

              e. _____

2. DESCRIPTION
   Topics: the locker room between classes; a weekend evening at a local dance club; Malcolm X or Martin Luther King Jr.; an odd person in my neighborhood

   Topic Sentence: _____

   Details: a. _____

              b. _____

              c. _____

              d. _____

              e. _____

3. PROCESS
   Topics: how to study for a test; how to plan a Halloween party; how to select a pet; how to read a map

   Topic Sentence: _____

   Steps: a. _____

              b. _____

              c. _____

              d. _____

              e. _____

4. DEFINITION
   Topics: my ideal job; a perfect day; fear; science fiction

   Topic Sentence: _____

   Qualities: a. _____

                b. _____

                c. _____

                d. _____

                e. _____

5. ANALYSIS AND CLASSIFICATION (pick one)
   Topics for Analysis: types of sports shoes; types of cars; types of fear; types of dreams

   Topic Sentence: _____

   Subgroups: a. _____

              b. _____

              c. _____

              d. _____

              e. _____

   Topics for Classification: movies; desserts; baby sitters; bosses

   Topic Sentence: _____

   Individual
   Components: a. _____

               b. _____

               c. _____

               d. _____

               e. _____

6. COMPARISON AND CONTRAST
   Topics: my brother (sister) and I; being a high school senior and a college freshman; team sports and individual competition; Michael Jackson's stage personality and that of another performer

   Topic: _____

   Points of Comparison
   and Contrast: a. _____

                   b. _____

                   c. _____

                   d. _____

                   e. _____

50

Name _____ Date _____

7. ANALOGY

Topics: a possessive person and a spider in its web; starting a new job (attending a new school) and jumping into a cold pool; a lie and a forest fire; daydreaming and going for a walk

Topic Sentence: _____

Similarities: a. _____

b. _____

c. _____

d. _____

e. _____

8. CAUSE AND EFFECT

Topics: why I chose the college I am now attending; why I dropped an old friend; how a new baby affects a family

Topic Sentence: _____

Causes or
Effects: a. _____

b. _____

c. _____

d. _____

e. _____

Revising Introductions and Conclusions

Each of these introductions and conclusions is inadequate as part of a 500-word essay. Determine what is wrong with each. Then, using your own paper, revise each paragraph. Some may need to be completely rewritten.

1. ### THE EXPLORATION OF THE ANTARCTIC

   Introduction: I think the Antarctic is very interesting, so even though I didn't have time to do a lot of research I'm going to tell you what I know about its exploration.

   Conclusion: In this paper I have tried to show how brave all these explorers were to face the terrible cold and loneliness of Antarctica. By the way, Antarctica is the *South Pole*.

2. ### THE CAUSES OF VOLCANIC ERUPTIONS

   Introduction: There are 850 active volcanoes in the world. More than 75 percent of them are located in the "Ring of Fire," an area that goes from the west coasts of North and South America to the east coast of Asia, all the way down to New Zealand. Twenty percent of these volcanoes are in Indonesia. Many are also in Japan, the Aleutian Islands (off Alaska), and Central America. Other big groups of volcanoes are in the Mediterranean Sea and Iceland. In contrast, there are only six volcanoes in Africa and three in Antarctica.

   Conclusion: So this is why volcanoes erupt.

3. ### SHOULD CAPITAL PUNISHMENT BE RESTORED IN OUR STATE?

   Introduction: Yes, I agree with the question. Every year the rate of serious crime in our state rises. Now is the time to get the murderers and rapists off the streets.

   Conclusion: In this essay, I have proven beyond any doubt that the death penalty will discourage people from committing violent crimes, that it will save the taxpayers a lot of money, and that hardly anybody will be executed by accident.

4. ### LET'S NOT LIMIT PRESIDENTS TO TWO TERMS

   Introduction: The twenty-second amendment to the Constitution, limiting presidents to two elected terms, should be repealed.

   Conclusion: Fourth, the twenty-second amendment was ratified in 1951 as a Republican reaction to the earlier four-term election of Democrat Franklin Roosevelt. Now the strategy has backfired; although the American people may be very happy with a president, they cannot keep him in office long enough to successfully put all his policies to work.

5. ### LEARNING A SECOND LANGUAGE

   Introduction: In this essay I will discuss why it is important for Americans to speak and read more than one language. Knowing a second language helps people to explore another culture, keeps them in touch with their roots, and can make traveling abroad much easier and more interesting. Therefore, all Americans should learn a second language.

   Conclusion: There are, then, three good reasons to learn a second language. First, knowing a language such as French or German enables a person to read some of the world's most important literature, philosophy, and science. Second, learning the language of our ancestors may help us to learn about our families and ourselves and may help us to preserve vanishing ways. Third, travel in Europe, Asia, or South America is easier when the traveler is able to speak to the inhabitants in their own language. Finally, once we have struggled to learn a new language we can understand how newcomers struggle to learn English. This can make us more patient and understanding, leading to better relations with our neighbors and co-workers.

Writing Introductions and Conclusions

EXERCISE 3-10

Write introductory and concluding paragraphs for three of the topics listed here. Refer to the chapter for suggested strategies. Before writing, list your thesis statement and strategies on the lines below. Use a different strategy for each paragraph. Use your own paper.

Topics: selecting a sensible diet for life; violence in the stands at sports events; applying for a student loan; dealing with difficult neighbors; noise pollution; motorcycles; old movies; talking to your doctor; teenage marriage; computers in the classroom; science fiction monsters

ESSAY 1

Thesis Statement: _____

Strategy for Introduction: _____

Strategy for Conclusion: _____

ESSAY 2

Thesis Statement: _____

Strategy for Introduction: _____

Strategy for Conclusion: _____

ESSAY 3

Thesis Statement: _____

Strategy for Introduction: _____

Strategy for Conclusion: _____

MODULE 4: THINKING, READING, AND WRITING CRITICALLY

4a What is critical thinking?

Although thinking comes naturally to you, awareness of *how* you think does not. Thinking about thinking is the key to thinking critically.

The word **critically** here has a neutral meaning. It does not mean taking a negative view or finding fault. Critical thinking is an attitude. If you face life with curiosity, you are a critical thinker. If you do not believe everything you read or hear, you are a critical thinker. If you enjoy contemplating the puzzle of conflicting theories and facts, you are a critical thinker.

4b How do I engage in critical thinking?

Critical thinking is a process that evolves from becoming fully aware of something, to reflecting on it, to reacting to it. The general process of critical thinking used in academic settings is described in the following chart.

STEPS IN THE CRITICAL THINKING PROCESS

1. **Summarize:** Extract and restate the material's main message or central point. Use only what you see on the page. Add nothing.

2. **Analyze:** Examine the material by breaking it into its component parts. By seeing each part of the whole as a distinct unit, you discover how the parts interrelate. Consider the line of reasoning shown by the EVIDENCE offered and logic used. Read "between the lines" to draw INFERENCES—gaining information that's implied but not stated. When reading or listening, notice how the reading or speaking style and the choice of words work together to create a TONE.

3. **Synthesize:** Pull together what you've summarized and analyzed by connecting it to your own experiences, such as reading, talking with others, watching television and films, using the Internet, and so on. In this way, you create a new whole that reflects your newly acquired knowledge and insights combined with your prior knowledge.

STEPS IN THE CRITICAL THINKING PROCESS *(continued)*

4. **Evaluate:** Judge the quality of the material now that you've become informed through the activities of SUMMARY, ANALYSIS, and SYNTHESIS. Resist the very common urge to evaluate before you summarize, analyze, and synthesize.

4c What is the reading process?

Purposes for reading vary. In college, most reading involves reading to learn new information, to appreciate literary works, or to review notes on classes or assignments. These types of reading involve rereading.

Your purpose in reading determines the speed at which you can expect to read. When you are hunting for a particular fact, you can skim the material until you come to what you want. When you read material about a subject you know well, you can move somewhat rapidly through most of it, slowing down when you come to new material. When you are unfamiliar with the subject, your brain needs time to absorb the new material, so you have to read slowly.

The full meaning of a passage develops on three levels: the literal, the inferential, and the evaluative. Most people stop reading at the literal level, but unless you move on to the next two steps you will not fully understand what you read.

STEPS IN THE READING PROCESS

1. **Reading for literal meaning:** Read "on the lines" to see what's stated.

2. **Reading to draw inferences:** Read "between the lines" to see what's not stated but implied.

3. **Reading to evaluate:** Read "beyond the lines" to form your own opinion about the material.

A major evaluative reading skill is **differentiating fact from opinion**. The difference between fact and opinion is sometimes quite obvious, but at other times telling fact from opinion can be tricky. Keep in mind that facts (numbers, statistics, dates, quotations) can be proven. Opinions, in contrast, reflect individual biases. Consider these examples:

OPINIONS	FACTS
California is too crowded.	California has the largest population of any U.S. state—over 29 million people.
Living in Alaska must be lonely.	Alaska has a population density of only .96 persons per square mile.
New Jersey has the best scenery on the East Coast.	New Jersey's official nickname is the Garden State.

4c.1 Reading for literal meaning

Reading for literal meaning is reading for comprehension. Your goal is to discover the main ideas, the supporting details, or, in a work of fiction, the central details of plot and character.

WAYS TO HELP YOUR READING COMPREHENSION

1. **Make associations.** Link new material to what you already know, especially when you're reading about an unfamiliar subject. You may even find it helpful to read an easier book on the subject first in order to build your knowledge base.

2. **Make it easy for you to focus.** If your mind wanders, be fiercely determined to concentrate. Do whatever it takes. Arrange for silence or music, for being alone or in the library with others who are studying. Try to read at your best time of day (some people concentrate better in the morning, others in the evening).

3. **Allot the time you need.** To comprehend new material, you must allow sufficient time to read, reflect, reread, and study. Discipline yourself to balance classes, working, socializing, and family activities. Reading and studying take time. Nothing prevents success in college as much as poor time management.

4. **Master the vocabulary.** If you don't understand the key terms in your reading, you can't fully understand the concepts. As you encounter new words, first try to figure out their meanings from context clues. Also, many textbooks list key terms and their definitions (called a *glossary*) at the end of each chapter or the book. Of course, nothing replaces having a good dictionary at hand.

4c.2 Reading to draw inferences

When you read for **inferences**, you're reading to understand what's suggested or implied but not stated. This is similar to the kind of critical thinking discussed in your handbook. Often, you need to infer the author's PURPOSE.

DRAWING INFERENCES DURING READING

1. Is the **tone** of the material appropriate?

2. Can I detect **prejudice** or **bias** in the material?

3. Is the separation of **fact** and **opinion** clear or muddy?

4. What is the writer's **position**, even if he or she doesn't come out and state it?

4d How do I engage in critical reading?

To read critically is to think about what you are reading while you are reading it. You can use some specific approaches such as reading systematically and reading actively and closely.

To **read systematically** is to use a structured plan for delving into the material. First preview the material. Then read it carefully, seeking full meaning at all levels. Finally, review what you have read.

To **read closely and actively** is to annotate as you read. Annotation means writing notes in a book's margin or in a notebook, underlining or highlighting key passages, or using other codes that alert you to special material. Experiment to find what works best for you.

4e How do I tell the difference between summary and synthesis?

A crucial distinction in critical thinking, critical reading, and writing resides in the differences between summary and synthesis. In the process of critical thinking, summary comes before synthesis.

To **summarize** is to condense the main message or central point of a passage. It is the gist of what the author is saying.

To **synthesize** is to connect what you are reading to what you already know or are currently learning. You cannot synthesize effectively until you have first summarized the material.

4f How do I write a critical response?

A critical response essay has two missions: to summarize what a source says and then to discuss the main idea by giving your thoughts and opinions. A well-written critical response accomplishes these two missions with grace and style.

GUIDELINES FOR WRITING A CRITICAL RESPONSE

1. Write a SUMMARY of the main idea or central point of the material you're responding to.

2. Write a smooth TRANSITION between that summary and what comes next: your response. This transitional statement, which bridges the two parts, need not be a formal THESIS STATEMENT, but it needs to signal clearly the beginning of your response.

3. Respond to the sources based on your prior knowledge and experience.

4. Fulfill all DOCUMENTATION requirements. See your handbook for coverage of four DOCUMENTATION STYLES (MLA, APA, CM, and CSE). Ask your instructor which to use.

4g How do I assess evidence critically?

The most important part of reasoning is **evidence**—facts, statistics, examples, and expert opinion.

4g.1 Evaluating evidence

You can evaluate evidence by noting the following statements to guide your judgment.

GUIDELINES FOR USING EVIDENCE EFFECTIVELY

1. **Evidence should be sufficient.** In general, the more evidence, the better. A survey that draws upon 100 people is more likely to be reliable than a survey involving only ten.

2. **Evidence should be representative.** Do not trust a statement if it is based on only some members of the group being discussed; it must be based on a truly *representative*, or typical, sample of the group.

3. **Evidence should be relevant.** Be sure the evidence you present truly supports your point and is not simply an interesting but irrelevant fact. For example, declining enrollment at a college *might* indicate poor teaching—but it also might indicate a general decline in the student population of the area, a reduction in available financial aid, higher admissions standards, or any number of other factors.

4. **Evidence should be accurate.** Evidence must come from reliable sources.

5. **Evidence should be qualified.** Avoid words such as *all, certainly, always,* or *never.* Conclusions are more reasonable if they are qualified with words such as *some, many, a few, probably, possibly, may, usually,* and *often.*

4g.2 Recognizing primary versus secondary sources of evidence

Primary sources are firsthand evidence. They're based on your own or someone else's original work or direct observation. **Secondary sources** report, describe, comment on, or analyze the experiences of others. As evidence, a secondary source is at least once removed from the primary source.

EVALUATING A SECONDARY SOURCE

1. **Is the source authoritative?** Did an expert or a person you can expect to write credibly on the subject write it?

2. **Is the source reliable?** Does the material appear in a reputable publication—a book published by an established publisher, a respected journal or magazine—or on a reliable Internet site?

3. **Is the source well known?** Is the source cited elsewhere as you read about the subject? (If so, the authority of the source is probably widely accepted.)

EVALUATING A SECONDARY SOURCE *(continued)*

4. **Is the information well supported?** Is the source based on primary evidence? If the source is based on primary evidence, is the evidence authoritative and reliable?

5. **Is the tone balanced?** Is the language relatively objective (and therefore more likely to be reliable), or is it slanted (probably not reliable)?

6. **Is the source current?** Is the material up to date (and therefore more likely to be reliable), or has later authoritative and reliable research made it outdated? (Old isn't necessarily unreliable. In many fields, classic works of research remain authoritative for decades or even centuries.)

4h How do I assess cause and effect critically?

Cause and effect is a type of thinking that seeks the relationship between two or more pieces of evidence. You may seek either to understand the effects of a known cause or to determine the cause or causes of a known effect.

GUIDELINES FOR EVALUATING CAUSE AND EFFECT

1. **Clear relationship.** Causes and effects normally occur in chronological order: *First* a door slams; *then* a pie that is cooling on a shelf falls. However, a cause-and-effect relationship must be linked by more than chronological sequence. The fact that B happened after A does not prove that it was caused by A.

2. **A pattern of repetition.** To establish the relationship of A to B, there must be proof that every time A was present, B occurred.

3. **No oversimplification.** The basic pattern of cause and effect—single cause, single effect—rarely gives the full picture. Most complex social or political problems have *multiple causes*, not a single cause and a single effect.

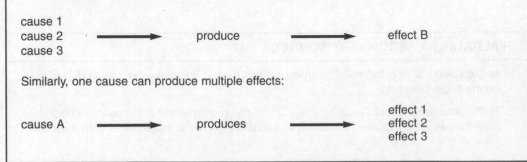

4i How do I assess reasoning processes critically?

Induction and **deduction** are reasoning processes. They are natural thought patterns that people use every day to think through ideas and to make decisions.

Induction is the process of arriving at general principles from particular facts or instances. Suppose you go to the supermarket and when you get home you notice that the eggs are smashed because the packer put a melon on top of them. The next week you come home from the market after the same person has bagged your groceries to find that a package of spaghetti has split open. The week after that the same packer puts a container of yogurt in upside down. It opens and you have to wash your groceries before you can put them away. You decide never to go on that person's line again because you want your groceries packed properly. You have arrived at this conclusion by means of induction.

Once you have become convinced that a certain grocery packer at your supermarket does a sloppy job, you will probably stay off that person's line—even if it is the shortest one. Your reasoning might go like this:

A. That grocery packer smashes groceries.

B. I can choose to get on that person's line or not.

C. If I choose to get on that person's line, my groceries will get smashed.

You reached this decision by means of deduction. Deduction moves from two or more general principles (A and B above) to a conclusion (C) about a specific instance.

COMPARISON OF INDUCTIVE AND DEDUCTIVE REASONING

	INDUCTIVE REASONING	DEDUCTIVE REASONING
Argument begins	with specific evidence	with a general claim
Argument concludes	with a general statement	with a specific statement
Conclusion is	reliable or unreliable	true or false
Purpose is	to discover something new	to apply what's known

INDUCTIVE REASONING

- **Inductive reasoning moves from the specific to the general.** It begins with specific evidence—facts, observations, or experiences—and moves to a general conclusion.

- **Inductive conclusions are considered reliable or unreliable, not true or false.** Because inductive thinking is based on a sampling of facts, an inductive conclusion indicates probability—the degree to which the conclusion is likely to be true—not certainty.

- **An inductive conclusion is held to be reliable or unreliable in relation to the quality and quantity of the evidence on which it's based.**

- **Induction leads to new "truths."** It can support statements about the unknown based on what's known.

DEDUCTIVE REASONING

- **Deductive reasoning moves from the general to the specific.** The three-part structure that makes up a deductive argument, or SYLLOGISM, includes two premises and a conclusion drawn from them.

DEDUCTIVE REASONING *(continued)*

- **A deductive argument is VALID if the conclusion logically follows from the premises.**

- **A deductive conclusion may be judged true or false.** If the argument contains an assumption, the writer must prove the truth of the assumption to establish the truth of the argument.

- **Deductive reasoning applies to what the writer already knows.** Though it doesn't yield new information, it builds stronger arguments than inductive reasoning because it offers the certainty that a conclusion is either true or false.

4j How can I recognize and avoid logical fallacies?

Logical fallacies are flaws in reasoning that lead to illogical statements. They tend to occur most often when ideas are being argued. Most logical fallacies masquerade as reasonable statements, but they are in fact attempts to manipulate readers. Logical fallacies are known by labels that indicate how thinking has gone wrong during the reasoning process. Some examples of logical fallacies are *hasty generalization, false analogy, begging the question, irrelevant argument, false cause, self contradiction, red herring, argument to the person, guilt by association, bandwagon, irrelevant authority, card-stacking, the either-or fallacy, appeal to ignorance,* and *ambiguity.*

Distinguishing Fact from Opinion   EXERCISE 4-1

Identify each passage as fact or opinion. Be prepared to explain your answers.

EXAMPLES   Once people had little choice in what they ate.   *fact*
               They would have preferred our food.   *opinion*

A. 1. The diet of prehistoric people was confined to what they could gather or catch.   _____

2. Control of fire enabled people to cook their food.   _____

3. Cooking undoubtedly improved the taste.   _____

4. Gradually people learned to plant seeds and tame animals.   _____

5. Planting and herding allowed people to settle in one place.   _____

6. Some people must have longed for their former nomadic life.   _____

7. Early civilizations sprang up in areas that could pro- duce bountiful crops.   _____

8. The fact that some could produce more than they needed freed others for nonagricultural chores.   _____

9. Farming cannot have been very difficult if one person could produce so much food.   _____

10. With such abundance I imagine many became wasteful.   _____

11. People gradually learned to preserve food by curing, drying, and pickling.   _____

12. My favorite pickle is the sweet gherkin.   _____

13. Bacon is a form of cured meat still popular today.   _____

14. Dried fruit does not taste as good as fresh fruit.   _____

15. Some dehydration machines on today's market are great.   _____

B. 1. In 1781 Nicolas Appert developed the first canning method.   _____

2. He sealed cooked food in glass bottles.   _____

3. Today's stores are filled with cans of every kind of food.   _____

_____

4. The canning industry should give Appert more credit than it does. _____

5. Refrigeration, one of the oldest methods of food preservation, is increasingly popular. _____

6. Cave dwellers kept food in cool recesses. _____

7. Ancient Romans imported ice to cool food. _____

8. Most of it probably melted before it got to Rome. _____

9. In the United States ice used to be delivered door to door. _____

10. Today electricity has made refrigerators and freezers common. _____

11. In fact, living without a refrigerator would be impossible. _____

12. Refrigeration enables many grocery stores to offer fruits and vegetables grown far away. _____

13. Grocery freezer sections are kept too cold. _____

14. The different methods of food preservation have added variety to the contemporary diet. _____

MODULE 5: WRITING ARGUMENTS

5a What is a written argument?

When **writing an argument** for your college courses, you seek to convince a reader to agree with you concerning a topic open to debate. A written argument states and supports one position about the debatable topic. Support for that position depends on evidence, reasons, and examples chosen for their direct relation to the point being argued.

Written argument differs from everyday, informal arguing. Informal arguing often originates in anger and might involve bursts of temper or unpleasant emotional confrontations. An effective written argument, in contrast, sets forth its position calmly, respectfully, and logically.

5b How do I chose a topic for an argument?

When you choose a topic for written argument, be sure that it is **open to debate**. Be careful not to confuse facts with matters of debate. A fact is the name of a college course or how many credits are required in a college curriculum. An essay becomes an argument when it takes a position concerning the fact or other pieces of information. For example, some people might think that college students should be free to choose whatever courses they want, while other people might think that certain courses should be required of all students.

A written argument could take one of these opposing positions and defend it. If you cannot decide what position to agree with because all sides of an issue have merit, do not get blocked. Instead, concentrate on the merits of one position, and present that position as effectively as you can.

5c How do I develop an claim and a the thesis statement for my argument?

An **assertion** is a statement that reflects a position about a debatable topic that can be supported by evidence, reasons, and examples. The assertion acts as a preliminary form of your thesis statement. Although the wording of the assertion often does not find its way into the essay itself, the assertion serves as a focus for your thinking and your writing.

TOPIC   Wild animals as domestic pets

ASSERTION   People should not be allowed to own wild animals.

ASSERTION   People should be allowed to own wild animals.

Before you decide on an assertion—the position you want to argue—explore the topic. Consider all sides. **Remember that what mainly separates most good writing from bad writing is the writer's ability to move back and forth between general statements and specific details.** Before you start drafting, use the RENNS formula to check whether you can marshal sufficient details to support your generalizations.

To stimulate your thinking about the topic and your assertion about the topic, use the techniques for gathering ideas. Jot down your ideas as they develop. Many writers of arguments make a list of the points that come to mind. Use two columns to visually represent two contrasting points of view. Head the columns with labels that emphasize contrast: for example, *agree* and *disagree* or *for* and *against*.

5d Why might I need to define key terms?

Key terms in an essay are the words central to its topic and message. While the meanings of some key terms might be readily evident in your writing, others may be open to interpretation.

5e What is the structure of a classical argument?

No one structure fits all written argument. However, for college courses, most written arguments include certain elements.

5f How do I support my argument?

To support an argument's claim, you must use reasons, examples, and evidence. One good method for developing reasons for an arguemnt is to ask yourself *why* you believe your claim. Another method is to write a list of pros and cons about your claim.

THE STRUCTURE OF A CLASSICAL ARGUMENT

1. **Introductory paragraph:** Sets the stage for the position argued in the essay. It gains the reader's interest and respect.

2. **Thesis statement:** States the topic and position you want to argue.

3. **Background information:** Gives readers the basic information they need for understanding your thesis and its support. As appropriate, you might include definitions of key terms, historical or social context, prior scholarship, and other related material. You can include this as part of your introductory paragraph, or it can appear in its own paragraph placed immediately after the introduction.

4. **Evidence and reasons:** Supports the position you are arguing on the topic. This is the core of the essay. Each reason or piece of evidence usually consists of a general statement backed up with specific details, including examples and other RENNS. Evidence needs to meet the standards for critical thinking and reasoning to be logical. Depending on the length of the essay, you might devote one or two paragraphs to each reason or type of evidence. For organization, you might choose to present the most familiar reasons and evidence first, saving the most unfamiliar for last. Alternatively, you might proceed from least important to most important point so that your essay builds to a climax, leaving the most powerful impact for the end.

5. **Response to opposing position:** Sometimes referred to as the *rebuttal* or *refutation*. This material mentions and defends against an opposite point of view. Often this refutation, which can be lengthy or brief according to the overall length of the essay, appears in its own paragraph or paragraphs, usually immediately before the concluding paragraph or immediately following the introductory paragraph, as a bridge to the rest of the essay. If you use the latter structure, you can choose to place your thesis statement either at the end of the introductory paragraph or at the end of the rebuttal paragraph. Yet another choice for structure consists of each paragraph's presenting one type of evidence or reason and then immediately stating and responding to the opposing position.

6. **Concluding paragraph:** Ends the essay logically and gracefully—never abruptly. It often summarizes the argument, elaborates its significance, or calls readers to action.

5g What types of appeals can provide support?

An effective argument relies on three types of persuasive appeals: logical appeals, emotional appeals, and ethical appeals.

GUIDELINES FOR PERSUASIVE APPEALS IN WRITTEN ARGUMENT

- **Be logical:** Use sound reasoning.

- **Enlist the emotions of the reader:** Appeal to the values and beliefs of the reader by arousing the reader's "better self."

- **Establish credibility:** Show that you as the writer can be relied on as a knowledgeable person with good sense.

5h What is the Toulmin model for argument?

The Toulmin model for argument has recently gained popularity among teachers and students because it clarifies the major elements in an effective argument.

The terms used in the Toulmin model may seem unfamiliar, but the concepts are ones you have encountered before.

THE TOULMIN MODEL OF ARGUMENT

Toulmin's term	More familiar terms
claim	the main point or central message, usually expressed in the thesis statement
support	data or other evidence, from broad reasons to specific details
warrants	underlying assumptions, usually not stated but clearly implied; readers infer assumptions

---

5i What part does audience play in my argument?

When a topic is emotionally charged, chances are high that any position being argued will elicit either strong agreement or strong disagreement in the reader. For example, topics such as abortion, capital punishment, and gun control arouse very strong emotions in many people.

The degree to which a reader might be friendly or hostile can influence what strategies you use to try to convince that reader. For example, when you anticipate that many readers will not agree with you, consider discussing common ground before presenting your position. Common ground in a debate over capital punishment might be that both sides agree that crime is a growing problem. Once both sides agree about the problem, there might be more tolerance for differences of opinion concerning whether capital punishment is a detterent to crime.

5j How can Rogerian argument help me reach opposing audiences?

Rogerian argument seeks common ground between points of view.

THE STRUCTURE OF A ROGERIAN ARGUMENT

1. **Introduction:** Sets the stage for the position that is argued in the essay. It gains the reader's interest and respect.

2. **Thesis statement:** States the topic and position you want to argue.

3. **Common ground:** Explains the issue, acknowledging that your readers likely don't agree with you. Speculates and respectfully gives attention to the points of agreement you and your readers likely share concerning the underlying problem or issue about your topic. As appropriate, you might include defintions of key terms, historical or social context, prior scholarship, and other related material. This may take one paragraph or several, depending on the complexity of the issue.

4. **Discussion of your position:** Gives evidence and reasons for your stand on the topic, elaborated similarly to the parallel material in classical argument.

5. **Concluding paragraph:** Summarizes why your position is preferable to your opponent's.

5k What is a reasonable tone in an argument?

To achieve a reasonable tone, **choose your words carefully**. Avoid exaggerations and artificial language. No matter how strongly you disagree with opposing arguments, never insult the other side. Name-calling is impolite, shows poor self-control, and demonstrates poor judgment.

5l How do I handle opposing arguments?

Dealing with opposing positions is crucial to writing an effective argument. If you don't acknowledge arguments that your opponents might raise and explain why they are faulty or inferior, you create doubts that you have thoroughly explored the issue.

- Examine the evidence for each opposing argument.
- Use the Toulmin model to analyze the opposing argument.
- Demonstrate that an opposing argument depends on emotion rather than reasoning.
- Redefine key terms.
- Explain the negative consequence of the opposing position.
- Concede an opposing point, but explain that doing so doesn't destroy your own argument.
- Explain that the costs of the other position are not worth the benefits.

PART 2: | *Understanding Grammar and Writing Correct Sentences and Using Punctuation and Mechanics*

MODULE 6: PARTS OF SPEECH

6a Why learn the parts of speech?

Knowing grammar helps you understand how language works. Grammar describes the forms and structures of words. In this way, it offers an explanation of how language operates and how words make meaning to deliver their messages. Grammar also sets down the standards accepted by people who write and speak for educated audiences.

If you know the parts of speech, you have a basic vocabulary for identifying words, their various forms, and the sentence structures they build. The first part of this chapter explains each part of speech to help you identify words and their functions. Being able to do this is important because sometimes the same word can function as more than one part of speech. To identify a word's part of speech, you have to see how the word functions in a sentence.

We drew a **circle** on the ground. [*Circle* is a noun.]

Sometimes planes **circle** the airport before landing. [*Circle* is a verb.]

Running is good exercise. [*Running* is a noun.]

Running shoes can be very expensive. [*Running* is an adjective.]

6b What is a noun?

A **noun** names a person, place, thing, or idea.

Most nouns change form to show number: *week, ox* (singular); *weeks, oxen* (plural). Nouns also change form for the possessive case: *the **mayor's** decision*. Nouns function as subjects, objects, and complements: ***Marie** saw a **fly** in the **soup*** (subject, direct object, object of preposition); ***Marie** is a **vegetarian*** (subject, subject complement).

NOUNS		
TYPE	**FUNCTION**	**EXAMPLE**
Proper	Names specific people, places, or things (first letter is always capitalized)	**John Lennon** **Paris** **Buick**
Common	Names general groups, places, people, things, or activities	**singer** **car** **talking**
Concrete	Names things that can be seen, touched, heard, smelled, tasted	**landscape** **pizza** **thunder**
Abstract	Names things *not* knowable through the five senses	**freedom** **shyness**
Collective	Names groups	**family** **team** **committee**
Noncount or Mass	Names "uncountable" things	**water** **time**
Count	Names countable items	**lake** **minutes**

Articles often appear with nouns. The articles are *a, an*, and *the*, and they signal whether a noun is meant generally or specifically in a particular context.

Give me **a** pen. [General: any pen will do.]

Give me **the** pen on the desk. [Specific: only one pen will do.]

6c What is a pronoun?

A **pronoun** takes the place of a noun.

Peter is an engineer. [noun]
He is an engineer. [pronoun]

The word (or words) a pronoun replaces is called its **antecedent**.

Some pronouns change form to show **number**: *I, she, yourself* (singular); *we, they, themselves* (plural). Many pronouns change form to show **case**: *I, who* (subjective); *me, whom* (objective); *my, mine, whose* (possessive).

PRONOUNS

TYPE	FUNCTION	EXAMPLE
Personal *I, you, they we, her, its, our*, and others	Refers to people or things	I saw **her** take **your** books to **them**
Relative *who, which, that, what, whomever*, and others	Introduces certain noun clauses and adjective clauses	**Whoever** took the book **that** I left must return it.
Interrogative *who, whose, what, which*, and others	Introduces a question	**Who** called?
Demonstrative *this, these, that, those*	Points out the antecedent	Is **this** a mistake?
Reflexive; Intensive *myself, yourself, herself, themselves*, and all *-self* or *-selves* words	Reflects back to the antecedent; intensifies the antecedent	They claim to support **themselves**. I **myself** doubt it.
Reciprocal *each other, one another*	Refers to individual parts of a plural antecedent	We respect **each other.**
Indefinite *all, anyone, each*	Refers to nonspecific persons or things	**Everyone** is welcome here.

6d What is a verb?

A **verb** expresses an action, an occurrence, or a state of being.

I **leap**. [action]

Claws **grab**. [action]

The sky **becomes** cloudy. [occurrence]

He **seems** sad. [state of being]

A **linking verb** connects a subject with one or more words—called a **subject complement**—that rename it or describe it.

Eleanor Roosevelt **was** First Lady. [*Eleanor Roosevelt* = subject, *was* = linking verb, *First Lady* = subject complement]

Eleanor Roosevelt **was** popular. [*Eleanor Roosevelt* = subject, *was* = linking verb, *popular* = subject complement]

VERBS		
TYPE	**FUNCTION**	**EXAMPLE**
Main *ask, begin, choose, dangle, eat, follow, go, hear, investigate,* and thousands more	Delivers verb meaning	I **drove** yesterday.
Linking *be, appear, become, look, seem,* and others	Acts as main verb but delivers meaning by linking a subject to a complement	You **seem** angry.
Auxiliary *can, could, may, might, must, should, would,* and others	Combines with main verb to make a verb phrase that delivers information about tense, mood, and voice	If I **had** driven last week, you **would be** driving now.

The most common linking verb is *be* (8e). Verbs describing the workings of the senses sometimes function as linking verbs: *feel, smell, taste, sound, look,* and so on. Other linking verbs include *appear, seem, become, remain,* and *grow.*

Auxiliary verbs, also known as **helping verbs,** are forms of *be, do, have,* and several other verbs that combine with main verbs to make verb phrases.

This season many new television series **have imitated** last year's hit shows. [*have* = auxiliary, *imitated* = main verb, have *imitated* = verb phrase]

Programs **are becoming** more and more alike. [*are* = auxiliary, *becoming* = main verb, are *becoming* = verb phrase]

Soon we **may** not **be able to tell** the programs apart. [*may be able* = auxiliary verb, to *tell* = main verb, *may be able to tell* = verb phrase]

6e What is a verbal?

Verbals are made from verb parts but they cannot function as verbs, because they do not change form to show time (tense) changes. They function as nouns, adjectives, or adverbs.

VERBALS

TYPE	FUNCTION	EXAMPLE
Infinitive *to* + simple form of verb	1. Noun: names an action, state, or condition	**To eat** now is inconvenient.
	2. Adjective or adverb: describes or modifies	Still, we have far **to go**.
Past participle *-ed* form of regular verb	Adjective: describes or modifies	**Boiled, filtered** water is usually safe to drink.
Present participle *-ing* form of verb	1. Adjective: describes or modifies	**Running** water may not be safe.
	2. Noun; see *gerund*, below	
Gerund *-ing* form of verb	1. Adjective: describes or modifies	**Hiking** gear is expensive.
	2. Noun: names an action, state, or condition	**Hiking** is healthy.

6f What is an adjective?

An **adjective** modifies—that is, describes—a noun or a pronoun. Adjectives also modify word groups—clauses and phrases—that function as nouns.

He received a **low** grade on the first quiz. [Low modifies noun grade.]

His second grade was **higher**. [Higher modifies noun phrase his second grade.]

That he achieved a B average was **important**. [*Important* modifies noun clause that he *achieved a B average*]

Descriptive adjectives such as *low* and *higher* show levels of "intensity," usually by changing form (*low, lower, lowest*).

Determiners are sometimes called **limiting adjectives**. **Articles** are one type of these limiting adjectives. The chart that follows lists types of determiners.

DETERMINERS (LIMITING ADJECTIVES)

Articles
a, an, the

The students made **a** bargain.

Demonstrative
this, these, that, those

Those students rent **that** house.

Indefinite
any, each, other, some, few, and
others

Few films today have complex plots.

Interrogative
what, which, whose

What answer did you give?

Numerical
one, first, two, second, and others

The **fifth** question was tricky.

Possessive
my, your, their, and others

My violin is older than **your** cello.

Relative
what, which, whose, whatever,
whichever, whoever

We don't know **which** road to take.

6g What is an adverb?

An **adverb** modifies—that is, describes—a verb, an adjective, another adverb, or a clause.

In winter the ice on ponds may freeze **suddenly**. [*Suddenly* modifies verb *may freeze.*]

It is **very** tempting to go skating. [*Very* modifies adjective *tempting.*]

People die **quite** needlessly when they fall through the ice. [*Quite* modifies adverb *needlessly*]

Always wait until the ice has thickened enough to hold your weight. [*Always* modifies entire clause.]

Most adverbs are easily recognized because they are formed by adding *-ly* to adjectives (*wisely, quickly, devotedly*). Yet some adjectives also end in *-ly* (*motherly, chilly*). Also, many adverbs do not end in *-ly* (*very, always, not, yesterday, well*).

Conjunctive adverbs are a group of adverbs that function (1) to modify the sentences to which they are attached, and (2) to help create logical connections in meaning between independent clauses.

CONJUNCTIVE ADVERBS (WORDS OF TRANSITION)

FUNCTION	EXAMPLES
Indicate addition	**also, furthermore, moreover**
Indicate contrast	**however, still, nonetheless, nevertheless, conversely**
Indicate comparison	**similarly**
Indicate summary or result	**therefore, thus, consequently**
Indicate time	**next, then, meanwhile, finally**
Indicate emphasis	**indeed, certainly**

Construction has slowed traffic on the interstate; **therefore**, people are looking for other routes to work. People have been complaining for weeks. **Finally**, one more lane has been opened during rush hour.

6h What is a preposition?

A **preposition** signals the beginning of a prepositional phrase. It is followed by a noun or pronoun (called the **object of the preposition**), and it indicates the relationship of that noun or pronoun to another word. The object of the preposition is never the subject of the sentence. Here is a complete list of prepositions.

about	despite	over
above	down	past
across	during	regarding
after	except	round
against	excepting	since
along	for	through
among	from	throughout
around	in	till
as	inside	to
at	into	toward
before	like	under
behind	near	underneath
below	next	unlike
beneath	of	until
beside	off	up
between	on	upon
beyond	onto	with
but	out	within
by	outside	without
concerning		

Prepositional expressions are formed by combinations of single-word prepositions.

according to	due to	instead of
along with	except for	in the midst of
apart from	in addition to	on account of
as for	in back of	on top of
as regards	in case of	out of
as to	in front of	up to
because of	in lieu of	with reference to
by means of	in place of	with regard to
by reason of	in regard to	with respect to
by way of	in spite of	with the exception of

A **prepositional phrase** consists of a preposition (or prepositional expression), its object, and any modifying words. A prepositional phrase always starts with a preposition: *above their heads, in the pool, in front of the store.*

6i What is a conjunction?

A **conjunction** connects words, phrases, or clauses. **Coordinating conjunctions** join two or more grammatically equivalent structures.

COORDINATING CONJUNCTIONS

and	or	for
but	nor	so
		yet

And, but, yet, or, and *nor* can join structures of any kind: two or more nouns, verbs, adjectives, adverbs, phrases, and all types of clauses.

Joe is majoring in Computer Technology **and** Engineering. [nouns]
He finds his course interesting **but** demanding. [adjectives]
In his spare time, he works on his car, **and** he helps care for his grandfather. [independent clauses]

For and *so* can connect only independent clauses.

Joe helps his grandfather, **for** he does not want the man to move to a nursing home.

Correlative conjunctions function in pairs, joining equivalent grammatical constructions.

CORRELATIVE CONJUNCTIONS

both . . . and	neither . . . nor
either . . . or	not only . . . but (also)
whether . . . or	

Both industrialized *and* agricultural nations are developing new strategies to protect the environment.

Subordinating conjunctions begin certain dependent clauses that function as modifiers.

SUBORDINATING CONJUNCTIONS

after	even though	though	where
although	if	unless	wherever
as	once	until	whether
because	since	when	while
before	so that	whenever	

Because of the unpredictability of hurricanes, many lives are lost each year. People sometimes refuse to evacuate *although* they are warned in plenty of time.

6j What is an interjection?

An **interjection** is a word or expression used to convey surprise or other strong emotions. An interjection can stand alone, usually punctuated with an exclamation point, or can be part of a sentence, usually set off with commas. Interjections occur only rarely in academic writing.

Oh no!
Darn! I lost my keys.
Well, how much will it cost to fix my car?

SENTENCE STRUCTURES

6k How is a sentence defined?

The *sentence* can be defined in several ways. On its most basic level, a sentence starts with a capital letter and finishes with a period, question mark, or exclamation point. Sentences can be classified according to purpose. Most sentences are **declarative**; they make a statement:

Pizza is fattening.

Some sentences are **interrogative**; they ask a question:

How fattening is pizza?

Some sentences are **imperative**; they give a command:

Give me a pizza!

Some sentences are **exclamatory**; they exclaim:

What a large pizza!

Grammatically, a sentence contains at least one **independent clause**, that is, a group of words that can stand alone as an independent unit, in contrast to a **dependent clause**, which cannot stand alone. Sometimes a sentence is described as a "complete thought," but the concept of "complete" is too vague to be useful.

To begin your study of the sentence, consider its basic structure. A sentence consists of two parts: a subject and a predicate.

61 What are a subject and a predicate in a sentence?

1 Recognizing subjects

The **simple subject** is the word or group of words that acts, is acted upon, or is described. In the sentence *The saxophonist played*, the simple subject is the one word *saxophonist*. The **complete subject** is the simple subject and all the words related to it.

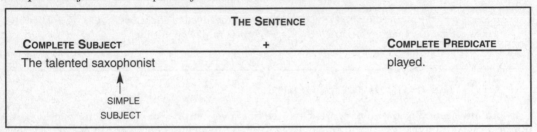

The **pianist** sang. [simple subject]
The new pianist sang. [complete subject]

A subject can be **compound**, that is, can consist of two or more nouns or pronouns and their modifiers.

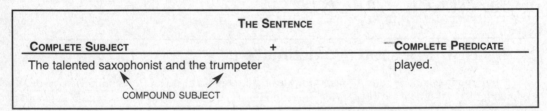

The **audience** and **the club manager** applauded. [compound subject]

2 Recognizing predicates

The **predicate** is the part of the sentence that says what the subject is doing or experiencing, or what is being done to the subject. The predicate usually comes after its subject, and it always contains a verb. The **simple predicate** contains only the verb. The **complete predicate** is the simple predicate and all the words related to it.

THE SENTENCE		
COMPLETE SUBJECT	+	**COMPLETE PREDICATE**
The talented saxophonist		played passionately.

SIMPLE
PREDICATE

The pianist **sang**. [simple predicate]

The pianist **sang** beautifully. [complete predicate]

A predicate can be **compound**, that is, consisting of two or more verbs.

THE SENTENCE		
COMPLETE SUBJECT	**+**	**COMPLETE PREDICATE**
The talented saxophonist		strutted and played. ↖ ↗ COMPOUND PREDICATE

The pianist **sang** and **swayed**. [compound predicate]

6m What are direct and indirect objects?

1 Recognizing direct objects

A **direct object** occurs in the predicate of a sentence. It receives the action of a transitive verb, completing its meaning.

THE SENTENCE		
COMPLETE SUBJECT	**+**	**COMPLETE PREDICATE**
Their agent		negotiated a contract ↑ ↑ VERB DIRECT OBJECT

Their agent called the **music critics**. [direct object]

To find the direct object, make up a *whom?* or *what?* question about the verb. (The agent negotiated what? *A contract.* The agent called whom? *The music critics.*)

A direct object may be compound:

They played **their hit** and **a new song**.

2 Recognizing indirect objects

An **indirect object** occurs in the predicate of a sentence. It answers a *to whom?*, *for whom?*, *to what?*, or *for what?* question about a verb.

THE SENTENCE			
COMPLETE SUBJECT	**+**	**COMPLETE PREDICATE**	
Their agent	got ↑ VERB	the group ↑ INDIRECT OBJECT	a contract. ↑ DIRECT OBJECT

He tried to get **them** an album deal. [indirect object]

6n What are complements, modifiers, and appositives?

1 Recognizing complements

A **complement** occurs in the predicate of a sentence. It renames or describes the subject or object. A **subject complement** is a noun or adjective that follows a linking verb, such as *was* or *seems*, and renames or describes the subject.

THE SENTENCE		
COMPLETE SUBJECT	+	**COMPLETE PREDICATE**
The club manager		was the owner.

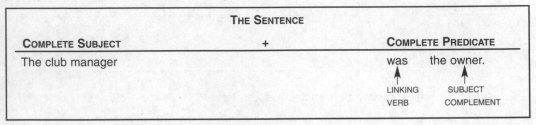

The owner was a **jazz lover**. [noun as subject complement]
The owner was **generous**. [adjective as subject complement]

An **object complement** is a noun or adjective that immediately follows the direct object and either renames or describes it.

THE SENTENCE		
COMPLETE SUBJECT	+	**COMPLETE PREDICATE**
The owner		called himself Artie.
		VERB DIRECT OBJECT
		OBJECT COMPLEMENT

The group considered itself **lucky**. [adjective as object complement]
Artie called them **exceptional**. [adjective as object complement]
He began to consider himself **a patron of the arts**. [noun phrase as object complement]

2 Recognizing modifiers

Modifiers are words or groups of words that describe other words. There are two basic kinds of modifiers: adjectives and adverbs.

Adjectives modify only nouns or words acting as nouns, such as pronouns, noun phrases, or noun clauses. They may appear in the subject or the predicate of a sentence.

THE SENTENCE		
COMPLETE SUBJECT	+	**COMPLETE PREDICATE**
The talented saxophonist		played a mellow tune.
ADJECTIVE		ADJECTIVE

Adverbs modify verbs, adjectives, other adverbs, or independent clauses. They may appear in the subject or the predicate of a sentence.

	THE SENTENCE	
COMPLETE SUBJECT	+	**COMPLETE PREDICATE**
The saxophonist		played very passionately.
		ADVERBS

The audience responded **warmly**. [Adverb *warmly* modifies verb *responded*.]

They swayed **quite** excitedly in their seats. [Adverb *quite* modifies adverb *excitedly*.]

Enthusiastically, they demanded more. [Adverb *enthusiastically* modifies independent clause.]

3 Recognizing appositives

An **appositive** is a word or group of words that renames the word or group of words preceding it. Generally, appositives are nouns used to rename other nouns, although adjectives and verbs are also sometimes renamed by appositives.

	THE SENTENCE	
COMPLETE SUBJECT	+	**COMPLETE PREDICATE**
The group, Diamond in the Rough		looked like a hit.
APPOSITIVE		

Their manager, **Jon Franklin**, was ready to take the next step. [*Jon Franklin* renames the noun *manager*.]

He picked his targets: **the record companies and the television shows**. [*The record companies and the television shows* renames the noun *targets*.]

---

60 What is a phrase?

A **phrase** is a group of words that lacks a subject or a predicate. Phrases function as parts of speech. They cannot stand alone as sentences.

A **noun phrase** functions as a noun in a sentence.

Some political terms have unusual histories.
The seating plan in the French congress during their Revolution gives us our names for political radicals, conservatives, and moderates.

A **verb phrase** functions as a verb in a sentence.

The members **were seated** in a semicircular room. The most radical members **were located** to the left of the chairperson's platform, the more conservative to the right.

A **prepositional phrase** functions as an adjective or adverb. It is formed by a preposition followed by a noun or pronoun.

This arrangement enabled members **with similar views** to talk **during meetings**. [*with similar views* modifies *members*; *during meetings* modifies *to talk*.]

An **absolute phrase**, which consists of a participle preceded by a subject, modifies the entire sentence to which it is attached. An absolute phrase cannot stand alone as a sentence because it lacks a true verb.

The moderates being in the center, physical fights were avoided. [*Being* is the present participle of *to be*; *the moderates* acts as a subject.]

Verbal phrases use forms of verbs that do not express time, so they cannot function as verbs in sentences. Instead, they function as nouns or modifiers. Verbal phrases are formed with infinitives, past participles, or present participles.

Infinitive phrases contain a verb's simple form preceded usually, but not always, by the word *to*. Infinitive phrases function as nouns, adjectives, or adverbs.

Politicians love **to debate every issue**. [infinitive phrase = noun as object of verb *love*]

Physically separating politicians works **to prevent debates from becoming fist fights**. [infinitive phrase = adverb modifying verb *works*]

Gerund phrases use the present participle—a verb's *-ing* form—as nouns.

Understanding the origin of certain terms helps us recognize the repetition of historical patterns. [gerund phrase = noun functioning as sentence subject]

(In the preceding example, notice *recognize the repetition of historical patterns* too. It is an infinitive phrase, but one that does not use *to*.)

Participial phrases function as adjectives. They are formed from a verb's present participle—its *-ing* form—or from its past participle—the *-ed* form of a regular verb.

Imitating the French plan, we now call radicals leftists, conservatives right-wingers, and moderates centrists. [present participle phrase = adjective modifying *we*]

These labels, **copied by many governments**, continue long after the revolution that gave them birth. [past participle phrase = adjective modifying *labels*]

Telling the difference between a gerund phrase and a present participle phrase can be tricky because both contain a verb form that ends in *-ing*. Remember that a gerund phrase functions *only* as a noun, and a participial phrase functions *only* as an adjective.

Seeing liver on the dinner menu, I decided to fast. [participial phrase as adjective describing]

Seeing liver on the dinner menu made me want to fast. [gerund phrase as subject of sentence]

6p What is a clause?

A **clause** is a group of words that contains a subject and a predicate. Clauses are divided into two categories: **independent clauses** (also known as **main clauses**) and **dependent clauses** (including **subordinate clauses** and **relative clauses**).

1 Recognizing independent clauses

An **independent clause** contains a subject and a predicate. It can stand alone as a sentence. However, it cannot begin with a subordinating conjunction or a relative pronoun because those words make a clause dependent.

THE SENTENCE		
COMPLETE SUBJECT	+	**COMPLETE PREDICATE.**
The saxophonist		played.

2 Recognizing dependent clauses

A **dependent clause** contains a subject and a predicate and usually starts with a word that makes the clause unable to stand alone as a sentence. A dependent clause must be joined to an independent clause.

Some dependent clauses start with **subordinating conjunctions** such as *although, because, when, until*. A subordinating conjunction indicates a relationship between the meaning in the dependent clause and the meaning in the independent clause.

THE SENTENCE				
DEPENDENT (ADVERB) CLAUSE SUBJECT		+	**INDEPENDENT CLAUSE**	
When **the applause** stopped			**the saxophonist** played.	
SUBORDINATING CONJUNCTION	COMPLETE SUBJECT	COMPLETE PREDICATE	COMPLETE SUBJECT	COMPLETE PREDICATE

Because clauses that start with subordinating conjunctions function as adverbs they are called **adverb clauses** (or sometimes **subordinate clauses**).

They modify verbs, adjectives, other adverbs, and entire independent clauses. Adverb clauses may appear in different parts of sentences, but they always begin with a subordinating conjunction. They usually answer some question about the independent clause: *how? why? when?* or *under what conditions?*

Many Americans wait to travel to Europe **until they can get low air fares**.
If a family has relatives in another country, an international vacation can be relatively inexpensive.
The number of Americans visiting China has grown rapidly **since full diplomatic relations were established in 1979**.

✤ PUNCTUATION ALERT: When an adverb clause comes before an independent clause, separate the clauses with a comma. ✤

Since full diplomatic relations were established in 1979, the number of Americans visiting China has grown rapidly.

Other dependent clauses act as adjectives. These **adjective clauses** (also called **relative clauses**) start with relative pronouns such as *who, which,* and *that* or relative adverbs such as *when* or *where*. Adjective clauses modify nouns, pronouns, and groups of words functioning as nouns.

THE SENTENCE		
FIRST PART OF INDEPENDENT CLAUSE	**DEPENDENT (ADJECTIVE) CLAUSE**	**SECOND PART OF INDEPENDENT CLAUSE**
The talented saxophonist	who led the band	signed autographs.
COMPLETE SUBJECT	RELATIVE PRONOUN	COMPLETE PREDICATE

The word starting an adjective clause refers to something specific—an antecedent—in the independent clause.
The concert hall, **which held 12,000 people**, was sold out in one day.
The tickets **that I bought** were the last ones in the balcony.
See 10k for a discussion of when to use *who, which,* or *that*.

Noun clauses function as subjects, objects, or complements. Noun clauses begin with many of the same words as adjective clauses: *that, who, which,* (in all their forms), as well as *when, where, whether, why,* or *how.* Noun clauses do not modify. They replace a noun or pronoun with a clause.

It depends on your generosity. [pronoun as subject]
Whether I can buy the camera depends on your generosity. [noun clause as subject]
Whoever wins the contest will appear in publicity photos. [noun clause as subject]

Because they start with similar words, it is easy to confuse noun clauses and adjective clauses. A noun clause *is* a subject, object, or complement; an adjective clause *modifies* a subject, object, or complement. The word at the start of an adjective clause has a specific antecedent elsewhere in the sentence; the word that starts a noun clause does not.

Elliptical clauses are grammatically incomplete in order to be brief and to the point. Usually the omission is limited to *that, which,* or *whom* in adjective clauses, the subject and verb in adverb clauses, or the second half of a comparison.

Lima is one of the places **[that] I want to visit this summer**. [relative pronoun omitted from adjective clause]
After **[I visited] Sao Paolo**, I decided to return to South America. [subject and verb omitted from adverb clause]
An apartment has less storage space **than a house [has]**. [second half of comparison omitted]

6q What are the four sentence types?

Sentences have four basic structures: simple, compound, complex, and compound-complex.

A **simple sentence** is composed of a single independent clause with no dependent clauses. It has one subject and one predicate. However, a simple sentence is not always short. The subject or predicate may be compound, and the sentence may contain modifying words or phrases.

The beagle is one of the world's most popular dogs.
It is a member of the hound family.
The basset and the harrier are also hounds.

A **compound sentence** is composed of two or more independent clauses joined by a coordinating conjunction or a semicolon. There are seven coordinating conjunctions: *and, but, or, nor, for, so,* and *yet.* Compound sentences operate according to principles of coordination. ❖ PUNCTUATION ALERT: Always use a comma before a coordinating conjunction that joins two independent clauses.❖

The beagle is known for its large, velvety ears, **but** its hazel eyes are even more attractive.
The beagle is believed to be one of the oldest breeds of hounds, **and** it is still used to hunt.

A **complex sentence** is composed of one independent clause and one or more dependent clauses. ❖ PUNCTUATION ALERT: Always use a comma after a dependent clause when it occurs before an independent clause. ❖

Because it has an erect, white-tipped tail, the beagle can be seen and followed even in high grass and bushes.
Although the beagle lost some of its popularity at the beginning of this century, it has become recognized as the ideal pet for anyone **who wants a medium-sized hound**.

A **compound-complex** sentence contains two or more independent clauses and one or more dependent clauses.

The beagle gets along well with other dogs **since it is a pack animal, and** it is patient with boisterous children **who might be too rough to allow near less sturdy pets**.
Although the beagle can be a delight, it is not an easy animal to keep **because it loves to wander off hunting and investigating, so** an owner needs to be alert.

Identifying Nouns

Underline all the nouns. Write them on the lines to the right.

1. Many people have now seen, or at least heard about, "e-books."   _____

2. They may replace traditional, manuscript-based books.   _____

3. It is essential, however, to distinguish between a digital book and a book-reading appliance.   _____

4. At its simplest, a digital book is a literal translation of a printed work.   _____

5. It is created by scanning or generating a PDF file.   _____

6. Book-reading appliances are devices resembling small laptops.   _____

7. They enable you to read digital books.   _____

8. Costing a few hundred dollars, the appliances feature high-quality screens but no keyboards.   _____

9. They run for a long time on batteries and can store several books.   _____

10. Some book-reading appliances are designed to work with your own library of downloaded digital books.   _____

11. Without the appliance, you would be unable to read the books, which are encrypted and stored on your computer.   _____

12. Other book-reading appliances use modems to download works directly from library services over phone lines.   _____

13. Some companies are working on software which will enable digital books to be displayed on general-purpose computers.   _____

14. Even so, digital books may never be as popular as their traditional counterparts.   _____

15. Screens do not offer a pleasant environment for reading very long texts.   _____

16. In addition, highlighting or making notes in a digital book is awkward.   _____

17. Certain types of books, however, are very popular in electronic form.   _____

18. They include dictionaries, encyclopedias, directories, product catalogs, and maintenance manuals.   _____

19. Readers of this type of book are generally in search of a small amount of specific information. _____

20. When doing lengthy reading, however, people seem to prefer to print on-screen text. _____

21. They are using paper – a simple but effective viewing technology – as their preferred user interface. _____

Identifying Pronouns

Underline all the pronouns. Write them on the lines to the right. If a sentence contains no pronouns, write *none* on the line.

EXAMPLE Since the 1930s, scientists them have been trying to get chimpanzees to communicate with <u>them</u>.   *them* _____ _____

1. In the 1940s, one couple raised a chimpanzee named Vickie in their home. _____ _____

2. They treated her as if she were a human child. _____ _____

3. They tried to teach Vickie to say English words by shaping her mouth as she made sounds. _____ _____

4. She learned to say only three words: *Mama*, *Papa*, and *cup*. _____ _____

5. Even that was amazing because chimpanzees do not have the right vocal structures to produce human sounds. _____ _____

6. Realizing this, scientists in the 1960s began teaching sign language to their chimpanzees. _____ _____

7. Chimpanzees have their own ways of communicating among themselves. _____ _____

8. One chimpanzee was taught over a hundred words in American Sign Language. _____ _____

9. She also formed her own original sentences. _____ _____

10. She would even hold simple conversations with anyone who knew sign language.

      _____   _____

11. Other chimpanzees were trained to ask for what they wanted by pressing a series of symbols on a computer keyboard.

      _____   _____

12. Chimpanzees are not the only animals whose trainers "talk" with them.

      _____   _____

13. Gorillas, dolphins, and even parrots supposedly can communicate with us.

      _____   _____

14. Not everyone believes this is possible.

      _____   _____

15. Some say members of different species can have only limited communication with one another.

      _____   _____

16. What do you think about animal speech?

      _____   _____

17. Would you want to have conversations with your pets?

      _____   _____

Identifying Verbs

Underline all the verbs, including complete verb phrases. Write them on the lines to the right.

EXAMPLE Everyone <u>desires</u> a happy life. _____desires_____ _____

1. These tips can lead to such a life. _____ _____

2. Always recognize your good qualities. _____ _____

3. Everyone has positive traits, such as sympathy or generosity. _____ _____

4. You should think of these qualities often. _____ _____

5. Sometimes, another person may cause us problems. _____ _____

6. Discuss that problem with a friend or a loved one. _____ _____

7. You might also ask yourself several questions. _____ _____

8. Who is at fault, and why is that person at fault? _____ _____

9. Always take responsibility for your part of the problem. _____ _____

10. A solution to the problem may require a joint effort. _____ _____

11. What else might lead to a happy life? _____ _____

12. Tolerate other people's behaviors. _____ _____

13. Accept their differences. _____ _____

14. Also, do not dwell upon the past mistakes of your own life. _____ _____

15. Mistakes are part of a continuous learning process. _____ _____

16. Without mistakes, you might not learn the right way. _____ _____

17. Look back at all your successes, not your failures. _____ _____

18. Be available to assist others. _____ _____

19. They would do the same for you in most cases. _____ _____

20. Above all, always find time for relaxation, and enjoy everything around you. _____ _____

Identifying Forms of Verbs

Decide if each italicized word or phrase is a verb, an infinitive, a past participle, a present participle, or a gerund. Write your answers on the lines to the right.

EXAMPLE   Perfume *refers* to a fragrant fluid preparation with an appealing scent. _____*verb*_____

1. The word "perfume" *originates* from the Latin "per fumem," which can be translated as "through smoke." _____

2. *Scenting* the body is a custom that dates back to the ancient Egyptians. _____

3. Once the Egyptians had learned how *to extract* the scent from flower petals, they then burned natural oils to scent temples, private homes, and royal palaces. _____

4. There *is* evidence that even Egyptian tombs were scented with fragrant ointments and oils. _____

5. The Egyptian discovery eventually *spread* to all parts of Europe. _____

6. An Arab physician discovered a way to produce a *distilled* fluid that could be used in the perfume-making process. _____

7. This process greatly *reduced* the cost of making the essential oils that went into perfume. _____

8. The first modern perfume to combine *scented* oils that were blended into alcohol was made in 1370. _____

9. Europeans *called* it "Hungary Water," since the perfume was created by order of Queen Elizabeth of Hungary. _____

10. Some records *suggest* that the perfume industry prospered in Renaissance Italy. _____

11. *To improve* the industry, Catherine de Medici's personal perfumer searched for a way to refine perfume in the sixteenth century. _____

12. During the 1500s, many *considered* France to be the perfume center of Europe. _____

13. Louis XIV, who was dubbed the "perfumed king," was responsible for the industry's *increasing* popularity. _____

14. Much later, fragrance makers in Paris, like Chanel, contributed their names to the *growing* industry. _____

15. France still *produces* some of the most expensive fragrances in the world.   _____

16. To *increase* the size of the market, Americans have extended the industry to men.   _____

17. There *are* many different categories of perfume, including floral blends, which are the most popular.   _____

18. *Gaining* popularity is the spice-blends category, which consists of aromas like clove, cinnamon, and nutmeg.   _____

19. Men's perfume *derives* from fragrances such as citrus, spice, and lavender.   _____

20. Perfumes are also cleverly used *to hide* undesirable smells common to paints and cleaners.   _____

Identifying Adjectives   EXERCISE **6-5**

Underline all adjectives, except the articles *a*, *an*, and *the*. Write them on the lines to the right.

EXAMPLE The abacus is a <u>useful</u> instrument.

                useful _____   _____

1. It allows people to perform arithmetic calculations.

  _____   _____

2. The most familiar form of the abacus is the Chinese *suan p'an* abacus.

  _____   _____

3. It is made of small beads that are strung on parallel wires.

  _____   _____

4. The wires are in a rectangular frame.

  _____   _____

5. The first abacus was composed of a straight row of shallow grooves in the sand, into which pebbles were placed.

  _____   _____

6. Later models used firm slate or boards, which allowed the entire abacus to be moved.

  _____   _____

7. On the portable abacus, pebbles are arranged in order along the parallel lines.

  _____   _____

8. The value of each pebble is determined by its exact position, not by its unique shape.

  _____   _____

9. The abacus works on the fundamental principle of place-value notation.

  _____   _____

10. With this ingenious system of notation, only a few beads are needed to represent large numbers.

  _____   _____

11. The beads are given numerical values when they are shifted in one direction.

  _____   _____

12. Calculations are made as each bead changes from its previous position.

  _____   _____

13. The bead's first value is erased after it has been moved to a new position.

  _____   _____

14. Moving the beads allows the counter to be reused for other calculations.

   _____   _____

15. The abacus is a memory aid for a person making mental calculations.

   _____   _____

16. The abacus is still widely used today among the Asian peoples, as well as in Russia.

   _____   _____

17. The Japanese culture uses the *soroban* form of the abacus.

   _____   _____

18. Russian society uses the *tschoty* form.

   _____   _____

19. At one time, people in the United States typically used machines to perform their complex calculations.

   _____   _____

20. These machines performed physical calculations rather than the mental calculations that the abacus was used for.

   _____   _____

Identifying Adverbs

Underline all the adverbs and circle all the conjunctive adverbs. Remember that some phrases or clauses can function as adverbs. Write your answers on the lines to the right. If there are no adverbs, write *none* on the line.

		adverb	conj. adverb
EXAMPLE	Chimpanzees, <u>commonly</u> called chimps, belong to the ape family; however, they form the single species, *Pan troglodytes*.	*commonly*	*however*

1. Chimps only inhabit the tropical rain forests of central Africa. _____ _____

2. They are the most intelligent of all apes. _____ _____

3. Chimps are also the most easily taught. _____ _____

4. Typically, except for a white patch near its rump, the chimp's coat of fur is black; however, its face is mostly bareskinned and either black, spotted, or pale. _____ _____

5. Chimpanzee hands, feet, and ears have a more pinkish tone. _____ _____

6. In the forest, chimps are extremely noisy; indeed, they will often shriek scream, and slap the ground. _____ _____

7. However, when humans enter their territory, the chimps usually quiet down. _____ _____

8. While living in the forest, chimps do not just swing from branch to branch to get around. _____ _____

9. They are also quite skilled in the ability to walk on the ground. _____ _____

10. Generally, chimps walk on all fours; still, they do sometimes walk and run in an upright position, much like a human. _____ _____

11. In fact, when standing erect, a chimp stands anywhere from 3.75 to 5.5 feet tall. _____ _____

Identifying Prepositions

Underline all prepositions and circle their objects. Write them on the lines to the right.

	PREPOSITIONS	OBJECTS
EXAMPLE The bicycle has been a form of *local transportation* for years.	*of* *for*	*local transportation* *years*

1. In China, there are over 300 million bicycles on the road.

2. The bicycle began to develop after a French model, the *celerifere*, was created.

3. The *celerifere*, which translates to "wooden horse" had a stationary front wheel, unlike those that followed.

4. Until the 1917 invention of a German baron solved the problem of the stationary front wheel, the *celerifere* could not be steered.

5. Karl von Drais developed the first steerable wheel for this bicycle, called *the draisienne*, which means "dandy horse."

6. Twenty-two years later, in a Scottish workshop, blacksmith Kirkpatrick Macmillan created the first bicycle with pedals.

7. The pedals were attached to the rear wheels and were controlled by means of cranks.

8. During the 1860s, the French *velocipede* was introduced, which had pedals attached to the front wheels.

9. In England in 1879, H.J. Lawson developed a bicycle made with a chain and sprocket that controlled the front wheel.

10. Just six years later, J.K. Stanley
    developed a safety model-bicycle,   _____   _____
    which became the prototype for   _____   _____
    today's bicycle.

11. Instead of a larger front wheel,
    Stanley's bicycle had wheels that   _____   _____
    were equal in size.

12. During the 1880s, pneumatic tires,
    tires filled with compressed air,   _____   _____
    were introduced.   _____   _____

13. The two- and three-speed hub gears,
    along with the derailleur gear, were   _____   _____
    developed in the 1890s.   _____   _____

14. Later developments of the bicycle led
    to attempts to motorize it.   _____   _____

Identifying Conjunctions

Underline all coordinating and subordinating conjunctions. Write them in column 1. Then indicate the type of conjunctions by writing *CC* or *SC* in column 2.

EXAMPLE: Demolition has become an exact science in recent years, <u>and</u> it is all thanks to Jack Loiseaux.

    and   *CC*

1. When Jack Loizeaux was a boy, his father conducted an experiment in the family's Maryland orchard.

2. Instead of digging all the tree-planting holes by hand, he put a half-stick of dynamite in a few of them.

3. The dynamite completed the hard labor of digging in a matter of seconds, and it pulverized the soil too, providing excellent drainage.

4. At year's end, young Jack noted the results: Whereas the hand-dug trees had grown just an inch, the dynamite trees had grown six inches.

5. After graduating college, Jack worked as a forester in Baltimore City.

6. Although his main tool was a chain saw, he still used dynamite – to splinter the tree stumps.

7. Because of his experience with dynamite, Jack was asked to demolish chimneys and, subsequently, buildings.

8. He was intimidated by the switch from trees to man-made structures, but he accepted the challenge nonetheless.

9. Jack's method involved weakening a structure's integrity so that it fell by its own weight – imploding rather than exploding.

10. His demolition of an eight-story apartment building in 1957 was only a qualified success, yet it established implosion as a viable alternative to the wrecking ball.

      _____   _____

11. The first blast brought the building down by only five feet, so more explosives had to be set.

      _____   _____

12. It took three tries before the building finally collapsed.

      _____   _____

13. Jack set up a business, Controlled Demolition Incorporated, and he encouraged his wife and children to become licensed blasters.

      _____   _____

14. Although other companies now use implosion, CDI is arguably the world leader, for it holds records for imploding the tallest building, the longest bridge, and the most buildings in a single sequence.

      _____   _____

15. More than 10 full-length documentaries and 100 TV shows have featured the Loizeaux family, and CDI's work can be seen in movies such as *Lethal Weapon 3*, *Demolition Man*, and *Mars Attacks*.

      _____   _____

Identifying the Parts of Speech: Review

Write the part of speech of each underlined word on the corresponding numbered line.

Chewing[1] gum was discovered[2] in the 1860s during[3] a search for rubber materials.[4] Gum is very much an American product[5] and[6] it is rarely[7] found anywhere outside the United States. The recipe for[8] chewing gum received[9] its[10] first patent in 1869. The basic raw material used[11] for all gum is the natural gum known as chicle. Since[12] it is very expensive and hard to obtain, synthetic[13] materials and other natural gums are often used in place of[14] chicle. Bubble gum differs[15] from regular gum because it is made[16] with[17] rubber latex, a compound that provides[18] the gum with the strength to make a bubble. Sugarless gum is made[19] from[20] sugar alcohols,[21] such as xylitol and mannitol, not[22] from regular sugar. The United States wholesale[23] factory sales of chewing gum have often[24] approached one billion[25] dollars.

1. _____	9. _____	17. _____
2. _____	10. _____	18. _____
3. _____	11. _____	19. _____
4. _____	12. _____	20. _____
5. _____	13. _____	21. _____
6. _____	14. _____	22. _____
7. _____	15. _____	23. _____
8. _____	16. _____	24. _____
		25. _____

Identifying Subjects and Predicates

A: Draw a line in each of these sentences to separate the complete subject from the complete predicate.

EXAMPLE: The ice in a skating rink / does not melt.

1.   Warm air cannot melt the ice.

2.   The temperature beneath the ice is kept very low.

3.   This keeps the ice from melting even in the sun.

4.   The ice at a figure-skating rink is two inches thick.

5.   Ice hockey rinks have slightly thicker layers of ice.

6.   The ice is on a concrete floor.

7.   The concrete contains one-inch pipes located no more than two inches apart.

8.   An Olympic-sized rink has about ten miles of piping.

9.   A very cold liquid, like the antifreeze in cars, circulates through the pipes.

10. The liquid absorbs heat from the concrete.

11. Machinery keeps the liquid at - 5° to -15°F.

12. More and more people are enjoying an afternoon of skating at an ice rink.

B: Draw a single line under the simple subject and a double line under the verb. Be sure to underline the complete verb and all parts of compound subjects and verbs. Write them on the lines to the right.

		SUBJECT	VERB
EXAMPLE	Most <u>Americans</u> brush their teeth daily.	_Americans_	_brush_
1.	The original toothbrushes were simply twigs with one soft, shredded end.	_____	_____
2.	People rubbed these "chew sticks" against their teeth.	_____	_____
3.	The first genuine toothbrushes originated in China 500 years ago.	_____	_____
4.	The bristles came from hogs.	_____	_____
5.	Hogs living in the cold regions of China grew stiff bristles.	_____	_____
6.	During this time, few Europeans brushed their teeth regularly.	_____	_____

7. Horsehair toothbrushes and small sponges were used by some Europeans. _____ _____
_____ _____

8. Many men and women picked their teeth clean after meals. _____ _____
_____ _____

9. The stems of feathers or special toothpicks were employed for this. _____ _____
_____ _____

10. Brass or silver toothpicks were safer than animal-hair toothbrushes. _____ _____

11. Germs developed on animal bristles, leading to frequent infections. _____ _____

12. There was no solution to this problem until the 1930s. _____ _____

13. The discovery of nylon led to a big change in the toothbrush industry and made tooth care easier. _____ _____
_____ _____

14. Nylon was tough and resisted the growth of germs. _____ _____
_____ _____

15. The first nylon-bristle brushes were sold in the United States in 1938. _____ _____

16. Unfortunately, they were very hard on gums. _____ _____

17. Soft gum tissue scratched and bled easily. _____ _____
_____ _____

18. In the 1950s, a new, softer version of the nylon toothbrush was developed. _____

19. It cost five times as much as the old, harder brushes. _____ _____

20. With this development, national dental care improved. _____ _____

21. Dentists and oral surgeons have made some suggestions for dental health. _____ _____
_____ _____

22. Toothbrushes should be used regularly and should be replaced every few months. _____ _____
_____ _____

23. Bent bristles are useless in cleaning teeth and can cut gums. _____ _____
_____ _____

Identifying Objects

Draw a single line under all direct objects and a double line under all indirect objects. Not all sentences have both. Write your answers on the lines to the right.

	DIRECT OBJECT	**INDIRECT OBJECT**
EXAMPLE Indian guests at the first Thanksgiving gave the Pilgrims popcorn.	*popcorn*	*Pilgrims*

1. Colonial parents served their children popcorn with cream and sugar for breakfast.

2. Earlier, West Indians had sold Columbus necklaces made of popcorn.

3. The Aztec Indians of Mexico wore strings of popcorn in their religious ceremonies.

4. By the 1880s, people could buy their friends special machines to pop corn.

5. People had to buy themselves popcorn in 25-pound sacks.

6. Stores charged customers one dollar for such a sack.

7. Americans could buy electric poppers beginning in 1907.

8. By the 1940s, most movie theaters sold their customers popcorn.

9. Another popular food has a more recent origin.

10. In Frankfurt, Germany, butchers sold people hot dogs.

11. Immigrants sold New Yorkers the first American hot dogs at Coney Island in 1871.

12. In 1904 they started giving customers buns to protect their hands.

13. Before that, it was common to lend customers gloves.

14. That must have cost the vendors a fortune.

Identifying Complements

Decide if each italicized word is a subject complement or an object complement. Indicate your answer by writing *SC* or *OC* in column 1. Then indicate if it is a noun or an adjective by writing *N* or *Adj* in column 2.

		1	**2**
EXAMPLE	Chocolate is *delicious*.	SC	Adj
1.	Strawberries are not true *berries*.		
2.	They are an *offshoot* of the rose plant family.		
3.	Strawberries taste *sweet*.		
4.	Harpo Marx was not a *mute*.		
5.	Many considered his silence *charming*.		
6.	In fact, friends have called him *talkative*.		
7.	Many people consider elephants *fearless*.		
8.	However, mice can make them *frantic* with fright.		
9.	Carrots are not a *remedy* for poor eyesight.		
10.	This belief is a *myth*.		
11.	Only for improving night vision are they *helpful*.		
12.	India ink is not *Indian*.		
13.	It is *Chinese*.		
14.	Lions are *cats*, or felids.		
15.	Many people mistakenly call them *the largest cats* in the cat family.		
16.	Yet the largest cat is the *tiger*.		
17.	The Siberian tiger is the *king* of all feilds.		
18.	A rabbit is a *lagomorph*.		
19.	It is not a *rodent*.		
20.	Its distinguishing feature is its *digestive system*.		
21.	People mistakenly consider pigs *dirty*.		
22.	Yet pigs are very *clean*.		
23.	Often, their owners leave pig sties *unclean*.		

Identifying and Using Adjectives and Adverbs

A: Decide if each italicized word is an adjective or an adverb. Write your identification on the lines to the right.

EXAMPLE   Bingo is one of the *most*[a] *frequently*[b] played
games in *several*[c] countries around the world.

a. _____*adverb*_____
b. _____*adverb*_____
c. _____*adjective*_____

1.   *Each*[d] player's chances of winning depend *entirely*[e]
on the numbers that are drawn.

d. _____
e. _____

2.   Because it is so *easily*[f] mastered, the game
attracts *many*[g] players.

f. _____
g. _____

3.   Bingo cards are *universally*[h] designed; they have *five*[i].
rows of five squares each.

i. _____

4.   The letters B-I-N-G-O are *clearly*[j] printed on the top
Of each card; each letter heads a *vertical*[k] row.

j. _____
k. _____

5.   *Any*[l] number from one to seventy-five is placed in a
box on the card, except for the center square, which
is *always*[m] a free square.

l. _____
m. _____

6.   There are seventy-five *corresponding*[n] balls, each
with a letter and a number that is drawn *randomly*[o]
from a bowl or box by the caller.

n. _____
o. _____

7.   The *bingo*[p] caller chooses a ball and *quickly*[q]
announces its letter and number.

p. _____
q. _____

8.   *Those*[r] players who have a square with a number
matching the one that was called must *carefully*[s]
place a marker over the square.

r. _____
s. _____

9.   The *first*[t], player to cover five boxes *vertically*[u] or
horizontally yells, "Bingo!" and wins the game.

t. _____
u. _____

10.   *Usually*,[v] the winner receives a prize: *typically*,[w] a
grand[x] prize is given to the player who can cover the
entire card.

v. _____
w. _____
x. _____

B: Fill in the blanks in each sentence with adjectives or adverbs as needed. Write your answers in column 1, and in column 2 identify each as an adjective or an adverb.

	1	2

EXAMPLE   I had had a _____ day   *terrific*   *adjective*
with my sister.

1. We left very _____ this
    morning.   _____   _____

2. The highway was _____ ,
    so we hit no traffic.   _____   _____

3. Since the sun was _____
    shining we kept the sunroof   _____   _____
    open.

4. Her _____ car is fun to
    drive.   _____   _____

5. We arrived at the museum
    _____ earlier than we   _____   _____
    thought we would.

6. We _____ found a
    _____ parking spot right   _____   _____
    near the main entrance.

7   _____ , since we were both
    so hungry, there was a _____   _____   _____
    cafe right next to the museum that
    was serving breakfast.

8. After strolling around the museum,
    we both knew what we _____   _____   _____
    wanted to do next: visit the
    _____ museum gift shop.

9. We bought a _____ vase
    for our mother's birthday next week;   _____   _____
    _____ , it was on sale.

10. _____ , we headed for home,
    because both of us were   _____   _____
    _____ exhausted from a
    great day out together.

Identifying Appositives

Appositives in these sentences have been italicized. On the lines to the right, write the words or phrases modified by the appositives.

EXAMPLE: The history of the Internet, *the electronic communications network that connects computer networks and organizational computer facilities around the world*, is a fascinating one.

<u>   the Internet   </u>

1   In the 1960s, futurist and author *Sir Arthur C. Clarke* predicted that by 2000 a vast electronic "global library" would be developed.

_____

2.   In fact, the origins of the Internet can be traced back to 1958 when ARPA, *the Advanced Research Projects Agency*, was set up by the U.S. Department of Defense.

_____

3.   However, before ARPA began supporting networking research seriously, Leonard Kleinrock, *an MIT graduate student*, had already invented the technology of the Internet.

_____

4.   Packet switching, *a method of sending data as short, independent units of information*, was far more efficient than the traditional circuit-switched method.

_____

5.   It avoided the long periods of "silence," *as much as 99.9 percent of each transmission*, which occur when data is circuit-switched.

_____

6.   Packet-switching technology was used in the creation of ARPAnet, *the network which laid the foundation for the Internet, in 1969*.

_____

7.   In 1972, Ray Tomlinson, *a computer engineer involved in the ARPAnet project*, invented electronic mail.

_____

8.   E-mail was the Internet's first "killer application," *software so useful that people will buy a computer just to have it*.

_____

9.   As academics and researchers in other fields began to use the network, ARPAnet was taken over by NSF, *the National Science Foundation*.

_____

10.   It had created a similar, parallel network of its own, *NSFNet*.

_____

11. In 1989, scientist *Tim Berners-Lee* proposed the World Wide Web project and a new language for linked computers, *Hyper-Text Markup Language.* _____

12. The Web gives users access to a vast array of documents connected to each other by hyperlinks, *electronic connections that link related pieces of information.* _____

13. The World Wide Web gained rapid acceptance with the creation in 1993 of a Web browser called Mosaic, *a program which allowed users to search the Web using "point-and-click" graphical manipulations.* _____

14. One of the developers of Mosaic, *Marc Andreesen*, went on to create Netscape Navigator, *the first commercially successful Web browser.* _____

Identifying Phrases   EXERCISE **6-15**

A: Identify the underlined phrases, and write on the lines to the right *NP* for a noun phrase, *VP* for a verb phrase, *PP* for a prepositional phrase, and *AP* for an absolute phrase.

Example: Each year, lives are lost when <u>inexperienced</u>   *NP*
<u>swimmers</u> are caught in rip tides.

1.   A rip tide is a <u>dangerous current</u>.   _____

2.   It sucks water <u>away from the shore</u>.   _____

3.   Rips <u>are formed</u> when waves break rapidly in shallow water.   _____

4.   <u>Having accumulated near the shore</u>, the water cannot   _____
easily return.

5.   It seeks out <u>underwater troughs</u> through which to escape.   _____

6.   If there are none, the water <u>will erode</u> a channel for itself.   _____

7.   The effect is similar to bathwater escaping <u>down a drain</u>.   _____

8.   Rip tides <u>should not be confused</u> with undertows.   _____

9.   Undertows <u>are associated</u> with larger surf.   _____

10. <u>Once caught in a rip tide</u>, remain calm.   _____

11. Do not tire yourself by attempting to swim <u>against it</u>.   _____

12. Instead, swim parallel to the shore until you are <u>past the</u>   _____
<u>current</u>.

13. Alternatively, you should tread water until help arrives.   _____

B: Identify the italicized verbal phases and write on the lines to the right in for an infinitive phrase, *part* for a participial phrase, and *ger* for a gerund phrase.

EXAMPLE: *To ensure harmony in the home or office*, consider   _____*inf*_____
applying the principles of Feng Shui.

1.   *Practiced in China for more than 4,000 years*, Feng Shui, or the _____
ancient art of placement, is now becoming popular in the West.

2.   *Literally translated*, Feng Shui means "wind and water."   _____

3.   *Believing that everything in the world constitutes an*   _____
interwoven field of energy or "chi," devotees of Feng Shui pay
close attention to their surroundings.

4.   *Derived from Daoist philosophy*, Feng Shui has three basic   _____
schools: the Land School, the Compass School, and the Black
Sect Tantric Buddhist School.

5.   *To harmonize their lives with the forces of nature*, the farmers   _____
of the Land School evaluated a landscape and its natural
features – trees, rivers, mountains – to determine the best
placement for buildings and crops.

6.   *Utilizing compass points, astrology, and mathematics* rather   _____
than landscape features, the practitioners of the Compass
School developed the ba-gua, an eight-sided chart that is
still used today.

7.   *Founded by Chinese-American master Thomas Lin Yun*   _____
around fifty years ago, the BTB school of Feng Shui uses the
door of a room or building as the main point of reference.

8.   *Using the ba-gua chart*, modern practitioners of Feng Shui   _____
select and arrange objects in a room to create harmony.

9.   *To achieve a positive flow of energy or "chi,"* they follow   _____
principles which may at first seem superstitious.

10. For example, *hanging wind chimes* near the front door is said   _____
to keep money in the house.

11. *Having smooth, round objects* in the home rather than sharp,   _____
pointed ones, is also considered beneficial.

12. *Sleeping with your feet facing the door*, however, is thought to   _____
cause sleepless nights.

13. *To maximize chi*, a person should consider not only how a   _____
building is furnished but where it is situated.

14. *Living too close to jagged rocks*, for example, is not advisable.   _____

15. If you are unable to move, however, *setting a large round rock*   _____
in the yard will help restore harmony.

Identifying Dependent Clauses

Underline all dependent clauses. Write the first and last words of each dependent clause on the lines to the right.

EXAMPLE: <u>When you visit London</u>, be sure   *when*   *visit London*
to take a ride on the London Eye.

1. The London Eye Ferris wheel, which   _____   _____
    was designed as part of London's
    Millennium celebrations, is the largest
    attraction of its kind in the world.

2. The structure, which stands 443 feet   _____   _____
    high, was built by British Airways at a
    cost of 35 million pounds.

3. There was disappointment, however,   _____   _____
    on New Year's Eve 1999, when
    technical problems delayed the
    opening of the wheel.

4. A fault was discovered in the clutch   _____   _____
    mechanism of one of its 32 glass pods,
    which meant the wheel had to be shut
    down.

5. Rather than close just one pod, BA   _____   _____
    decided on a complete overhaul.

6. The 250 people who had been invited   _____   _____
    to ride the wheel that night were given
    a rain check.

7. Although each pod can carry 25   _____   _____
    people, fewer people are admitted in
    hot weather.

8. The wheel does not cause motion   _____   _____
    sickness, as it travels extremely
    slowly.

9. However, when one passenger   _____   _____
    suffered vertigo, the wheel had to
    be reversed to let her off.

10. One thing that most people enjoy   _____   _____
    about the wheel is that it is noiseless.

11   The wheel sold its millionth ticket
in April 2000, which was well ahead
of schedule.

     _____   _____

12. Because of the success of the wheel,
other cities – including Boston and
Toronto – have asked if they can
copy it.

     _____   _____

Using Subordination   EXERCISE 6-17

Using the subordinating conjunction or relative pronoun given in parentheses, join each of these pairs of sentences. You may sometimes need to omit a word, but no major rewordings are required.

EXAMPLE   Eight different species of potatoes are grown.
            Most North Americans know only one kind of potato. (although)
            <u>Although most North Americans know only one kind of potato, eight
            different species are grown.</u>

1.   Potatoes grown from seed may not inherit the parent plant's characteristics.
     Potatoes are usually grown from the eye of a planted piece of
     potato. (since)

     _____

2.   Potato blossoms look like those of the poisonous nightshade plant.
     Centuries ago, Europeans were afraid to eat potatoes. (because)

     _____

3.   Tomatoes, tobacco, and eggplant are all relatives of the potato.
     They do not look alike. (although)

     _____

4.   The sweet potato is not related to the potato.
     Its Indian name, batata, was mistakenly taken to mean "potato" by its
     European "discoverers." (even though)

     _____

5.   The potato skin is a good source of dietary fiber.
     Most people throw it away. (which)

     _____

6.   Thirty-two percent of the U.S. potato crop is eaten fresh.
     Twenty-seven percent is made into frozen products, such as french
     fries. (while)

     _____

7.   Would you believe something?
     Twelve percent of the U.S. crop is made into potato chips. (that)

     _____

8.   There are misinformed people.
     They believe the potato is only a poor person's food. (who)

     _____

9. They overlook something.
   Potatoes have nourished the people of Europe since the eighteenth
   century. (that)

   _____

10. Nutritious potatoes allowed the population to expand until 1845.
    Europe—especially Ireland—was almost destroyed by a disease that killed
    the potato crop. (when)

    _____

11. Potato chips were created in New England.
    A hotel chef became angry with a fussy customer. (because)

    _____

12. The customer sent back his french fries twice, saying they were not crisp
    enough.
    No one else had ever complained. (although)

    _____

13. The chef apparently had a bad temper.
    He decided to teach the man a lesson. (who)

    _____

14. He cut the potatoes paper-thin and fried them.
    They were too crispy to pick up with a fork. (until)

    _____

15. The customer tasted these potatoes.
    He was delighted. (once)

    _____

16. The chef never got his revenge, but he did get his own restaurant.
    These "chips" became very popular. (so that)

    _____

Identifying Different Types of Sentences

EXERCISE 6-18

Underline all subjects once and all verbs twice. Then circle and label all coordinating conjunctions (*CC*), subordinating conjunctions (*SC*), relative pronouns (*RP*), and conjunctive adverbs (*CA*). Finally, on the lines to the right, label each sentence as simple, compound, complex, or compound-complex.

EXAMPLE   <u>Forgetting</u> <u>is</u> the loss of information previously stored in the memory, (and)^{cc} all of us <u>have experienced</u> it.

compound

1.   Forgetting is not always permanent.   _____

2.   Interference sometimes keeps us from remembering.   _____

3.   When this happens, we may not be able to stop thinking about something else even though we know it is wrong.   _____

4.   For example, we may not recall a friend's name, and we may even want to call her by someone else's name.   _____

5.   Other times, we try hard to remember, but our memories may not work at all.   _____

6.   The information seems lost until we receive a clue that helps us remember.   _____

7.   Some scientists believe that memories may completely fade away, and then we can never get them back.   _____

8.   Recent studies show that storing memory changes the brain tissue.   _____

9.   However, no one has shown that these changes can be erased, so the "fading-away" theory of forgetting remains unproven.   _____

10. Scientists who believe in the interference theory of forgetting identify different kinds of interference.   _____

11. Sometimes learning new material is made difficult by conflicting old material.   _____

12. Confusion between the old material and the new makes it hard to remember either one.   _____

13. Coming upon similar material soon after learning something can also interfere.   _____

14. Scientists have shown this in experiments, but everyday experience can convince us too.   _____

15. Anyone trying to learn two similar languages, such as French and Spanish, at the same time knows the feeling of confusion.   _____

Writing Different Types of Sentences

A: Combine these groups of simple sentences according to the directions in parentheses. It will be necessary to add coordinating conjunctions, subordinating conjunctions, or relative pronouns. Sometimes it will be necessary to drop or change a few words. Since most passages can be combined in several ways, take the time to draft a few alternatives and then select the version you like best. Try to use at least one elliptical clause in this exercise.

EXAMPLE   Sometimes people repress their memories. They cannot recall anything about an event. (compound)
Sometimes people repress memories, so they cannot recall anything about an event.

1. Psychoanalysis helps people deal with these forgotten memories.
    Psychoanalysis works at exploring them consciously. (compound)

    _____

    _____

2. Repression can make life difficult.
    Repression is the burying in the unconscious of fearful experiences. (complex)

    _____

    _____

3. People repress frightening thoughts and experiences.
    Then they try to go on living normally. (compound)

    _____

    _____

4. People repress experiences.
    They avoid having to relive them.
    They feel better for a time. (compound-complex)

    _____

    _____

5. Experiments show something.
    People forget bad experiences quickly.
    People forget good experiences less quickly. (complex)

    _____

    _____

6. Repression occurs in the mentally ill.
    It occurs also in mentally healthy people. (compound)

    _____

    _____

7. A certain kind of learning atmosphere leads to better memory.
    This kind of learning atmosphere is the kind where people can
    relax. (complex)

    _____

    _____

8. Any student knows this.
    So does any teacher. (compound)

    _____

    _____

9. People are often distracted in stressful situations.
    They simply do not see everything.
    Therefore, they cannot remember everything. (compound-complex)

    _____

    _____

10. This may explain something.
    Accident victims often do not recall details of their experiences. (complex)

    _____

    _____

11. Many people do not remember much from their childhoods.
    This does not mean that they are repressing bad memories. (compound)

    _____

    _____

12. They may have been too interested in some events to notice any others.
    These other events were happening at the same time.
    Maybe their childhoods were simply too boring to remember. (compound-complex)

    _____

    _____

B: Using independent and dependent clauses, expand each of these simple sentences, making a compound, then a complex, and finally a compound-complex sentence.

EXAMPLE He is always late.
(compound) *He is always late, and his brother is always early.*
(complex) *He is always late because he oversleeps.*
(compound-complex) *He is always late when there is a test, so the teacher is moving him to a later class.*

1. Fast food is not cheap._____
(compound) _____
(complex) _____
(compound-complex) _____

_____

2. The movie theater was crowded.
(compound) _____
(complex) _____
(compound-complex) _____

_____

3. Read contracts before you sign them.
(compound) _____
(complex) _____
(compound-complex) _____

_____

4. Ice cream is a popular dessert.
(compound) _____
(complex) _____
(compound-complex) _____

_____

5. Grocery stores should be open twenty-four hours a day.
(compound) _____
(complex) _____
(compound-complex) _____

_____

Name _____   Date _____

C: Write complete sentences by adding one or more independent clauses to each of these subordinate clauses.

EXAMPLE   if I have a chance
          If I have a chance, I'll learn to draw. _____

1. because she has a pet snake

    _____

2. whoever has the flu

    _____

3. before the union votes on the contract

    _____

4. even though they paid the electric bill

    _____

5. where the keys are

    _____

6. that cost a dollar

    _____

7. who has the prize-winning ticket

    _____

8. since she learned to drive

    _____

9. whether the bus stops on that corner

    _____

10. if the milk is sour

    _____

MODULE 7: VERBS

7a What do verbs do?

Verbs convey information about what is happening, what has happened, and what will happen. In English, a verb tells of an action (*move, juggle, race*), an occurrence (*become, change, happen*), or a state of being (*be, seem, feel, exist*).

Americans **enjoy** sports. [action]
Football **becomes** more popular every year. [occurrence]
Soccer **is** a new favorite of many people. [state of being]

Verbs convey information through their person, number, tense, mood, and voice. Three types of verbs are main verbs, linking verbs, and auxiliary verbs.

VERB FORMS

7b What are the forms of main verbs?

Every main verb has five forms. The **simple form** is also known as the **dictionary form** or the **base form**. The simple form shows action (or occurrence or state of being) taking place in the present for *I, you, we,* and *they: I travel, they explore.*

The **past-tense** form indicates an action or occurrence or state of being completed in the past. The past tense of all regular verbs adds final *-ed* or *-d* to the simple form. Many verbs, however, are irregular. That is, their past-tense forms, and often their past participles as well, either change in spelling or use different words instead of adding *-ed* or *-d: ring, rang, rung; fly flew, flown.* Review your handbook for the principal parts of common irregular verbs. Except for the past tense of *be,* the past tense form of each verb is the same for all persons and numbers.

The **past participle** is the third form. In regular verbs, the past participle has the same form as the past tense. However, for many irregular verbs these forms differ and must be memorized.

To function as a verb, a past participle must combine with an auxiliary verb in a **verb phrase.** Verb phrases formed with past participles make the **perfect** tenses and **passive** constructions: *I have succeeded; they are shocked.*

The present participle adds *-ing* to the simple form. To function as a verb, a present participle combines with a subject and one or more auxiliary verbs. Otherwise, present participles function as adjectives.

The infinitive uses the simple form, usually but not always following *to.* The infinitive functions as a noun, adjective, or adverb, not a verb.

7c What is the -s forms of a verb?

Except for *be* and *have*, all verbs in the present tense add an *-s* or *-es* ending to the simple form when the subject is third person singular: *Everybody likes candy.*

Be and *have*—irregular verbs—do not use their simple forms in the third person singular of the present tense. Instead, *be* uses *is* and *have* uses *has*:

Candy **is** fattening; it **has** a lot of calories.

Some dialects of English use forms such as *candy be* and *it have* for third person singular in the present tense. Academic writing requires *is* and *has*.

Also, if you drop the *-s* or *-es* ending when you speak, you may forget to use it when you write. Be sure to proofread your writing to make sure you have used the *-s* form correctly.

7d What is the difference between regular and irregular verbs?

1 Forming the past tense and past participle of a regular verb by adding *-ed* or *-d*

A **regular verb** is one that forms its simple past and past participle by adding *-ed* or *-d* to the simple form. Most verbs in English are regular: *walk, walked, walked; bake, baked, baked.* Some regular verbs, however, require spelling changes at the end of the simple form: *deny, denied.*

Some speakers omit the *-ed* sound in the past tense. If you are unused to hearing or pronouncing this sound, particularly before a word beginning with a *t* or *d*, you may forget to add it when you write the past tense or past participle. Nevertheless, written English requires the *-ed* ending.

2 Memorizing the principal parts of irregular verbs

About two hundred of the most common verbs in English are **irregular**: They do not add the *-ed* or *-d* to form the past tense or past participle. They form the past tense and past participle in different ways. Some irregular verbs change an internal vowel in the simple form to make the past tense and past participle: *ring, rang, rung.* Some change an internal vowel and add an ending other than *-ed or -d: rise, rose, risen.* Some use the simple form throughout: *cost, cost, cost.*

Unfortunately, a verb's simple form does not indicate whether the verb is irregular or regular. If you do not know the principal parts of a verb you are using, you need to find them in a college dictionary.

Common irregular verbs

SIMPLE FORM	PAST TENSE	PAST PARTICIPLE
arise	arose	arisen
awake	awoke *or* awaked	awaked *or* awoken
be (is, am, are)	was, were	been
beat	beat	beaten
become	became	become
begin	began	begun
bend	bent	bent
bite	bit	bitten *or* bit
blow	blew	blown
break	broke	broken
bring	brought	brought
build	built	built
buy	bought	bought
catch	caught	caught
choose	chose	chosen
come	came	come
cost	cost	cost
creep	crept	crept
cut	cut	cut
deal	dealt	dealt
dig	dug	dug
dive	dived *or* dove	dived
do	did	done
draw	drew	drawn
drink	drank	drunk
drive	drove	driven
eat	ate	eaten
fall	fell	fallen
feel	felt	felt
fight	fought	fought
find	found	found
Flee	fled	fled
fly	flew	flown
forbid	forbade *or* forbad	forbidden
forget	forgot	forgotten *or* forgot
freeze	froze	frozen
get	got	got *or* gotten
give	gave	given
go	went	gone
have	had	had
hear	heard	heard
hide	hid	hidden
hit	hit	hit
hold	held	held
hurt	hurt	hurt →

7d

Common irregular verbs (continued)

Simple Form	Past Tense	Past Participle
keep	kept	kept
know	knew	known
lay	laid	laid
lead	led	led
leave	left	left
lend	lent	lent
let	let	let
lie	lay	lain
lose	lost	lost
make	made	made
mean	meant	meant
meet	met	met
pay	paid	paid
quit	quit	quit
read	read	read
ride	rode	ridden
ring	rang	rung
rise	rose	risen
run	ran	run
say	said	said
see	saw	seen
seek	sought	sought
send	sent	sent
set	set	set
shake	shook	shaken
shoot	shot	shot
sing	sang	sung
sit	sat	sat
sleep	slept	slept
speak	spoke	spoken
spend	spent	spent
spring	sprang *or* sprung	sprung
stand	stood	stood
strike	struck	struck
swim	swam	swum
swing	swung	swung
take	took	taken
teach	taught	taught
tear	tore	torn
tell	told	told
think	thought	thought
throw	threw	thrown
wear	wore	worn
write	wrote	written

7e What are auxiliary verbs?

The verbs *be, do,* and *have* function both as main verbs and as auxiliary (or helping) verbs. *Be*, the most common verb in English, is the most irregular as well.

THE FORMS OF *BE*

Simple Form	be
Past Tense	was, were
Past Participle	been
-s Form	is
Present Participle	being

PERSON	PRESENT TENSE	PAST TENSE
I	am	was
you (singular)	are	were
he, she, it	is	was
we	are	were
you (plural)	are	were
they	are	were

Do and *have* are not as irregular as *be*.

THE FORMS OF *DO* AND *HAVE*

Simple Form	do	**Simple Form**	have
Past Tense	did	**Past Tense**	had
Past Participle	done	**Past Participle**	had
-s Form	does	**-s Form**	has
Present Participle	doing	**Present Participle**	having

When used as main verbs, forms of *be* are **linking verbs.** They join a subject to a **subject complement,** a word or group of words that renames or describes the subject.

Water pollution **is** a danger to many communities. [*is* = linking verb, *water pollution* = subject, *a danger to many communities* = subject complement]

Underground streams **are** sources of well water. [*are* = linking verb, *underground streams* = subject, *sources of well water* = subject complement]

When used alone as main verbs, *have* is transitive and *do* can be transitive. Transitive verbs must be followed by a direct object.

Combined with participles of main verbs, forms of *be* and *have* are **auxiliary verbs**, or **helping verbs**, that help the participles to show tense and mood.

> **I am waiting.** [auxiliary verb *am* + present participle *waiting* = present progressive tense]
>
> The news **has been expected** for days. [auxiliary verb *has* + auxiliary verb *been* + past participle *expected* = present perfect tense in the passive voice]

The auxiliary verbs *will* and *shall* help to create two tenses: the future (*I shall try, you will pass*) and, with *have* and past participles of main verbs, the future perfect (*I shall have tried, you will have passed*). *Will* and *shall* never change form. Formal writing reserves *shall* for the first person (*I, we*) and *will* for other persons (*you, he, she, it, they*).

The verbs *can, could, may, might, should, would, must,* and *ought to* are called **modal auxiliary verbs**. Modal auxiliary verbs have only one form; they do not change, no matter what constructions they appear in.

Modal auxiliaries add to the main verb a sense of needing, wanting, or having to do something, or a sense of possibility, permission, or ability.

> The ant **can carry** many times its own weight. [ability]
>
> Ants **may be observed** gathering around crumbs on the sidewalk. [possibility]
>
> We **must sweep up** dropped food or we **might attract** ants in our homes. [necessity, possibility]

Always use the simple form of the verb after a modal auxiliary.

7f What are intransitive and transitive verbs?

The difference between *I see clearly* and *I see a fire* is that the first sentence tells *how* the subject does something while the second points to *what* the subject does. In the first sentence, the verb is **intransitive**—it stops with the action. In the second sentence, the verb is **transitive**—the action of the verb carries over whatever is named in the **direct object.** Many verbs in English can be both intransitive and transitive depending upon how they are used in particular sentences.

INTRANSITIVE (NO OBJECT)	TRANSITIVE (WITH AN OBJECT)
The trees **shook** in the wind.	The boys **shook** the apple tree.
The train **leaves** tonight.	The train **leaves** the station.

Three important pairs of verbs are not this flexible. In these pairs—*sit* and *set, lie* and *lay, rise* and *raise*—one verb is intransitive, the other transitive.

VERBS

SUMMARY OF FORMS FOR *SIT, LIE, RISE,* AND *SET, LAY, RAISE*

INTERACTIVE (NO OBJECT)

Simple Form	Past Tense	Past Participle	-s Form	Present Participle
sit	sat	sat	sits	sitting
lie	lay	lain	lies	lying
rise	rose	risen	rises	rising

TRANSITIVE (WITH AN OBJECT)

Simple Form	Past Tense	Past Participle	-s Form	Present Participle
set	set	set	sets	setting
lay	laid	laid	lays	laying
raise	raised	raised	raises	raising

To *sit* means to seat oneself; to *set* means to place something else down.

INTRANSITIVE	I **sit** down. I **sat** down. [*down* = modifier]
TRANSITIVE	I **set** the stapler on the desk [*stapler* = direct object]

To *lie* means to place oneself down or to recline; to *lay* means to place something else down.

INTRANSITIVE	Oscar **lies** on the couch. Oscar **lay** on the coach. [*on the couch* = modifier]
TRANSITIVE	Oscar **lays** bricks for a living. Oscar **laid** bricks for a living. [*bricks* = direct object]

To *rise* means to stand up, to get up out of bed, or to elevate oneself in some other way; to *raise* is to lift up or elevate someone or something else.

INTRANSITIVE	Wendy **rises** every morning at 6:30. Wendy **rose** every morning at 6:30. [*every morning at 6:30* = modifier]
TRANSITIVE	Wendy **raises** the rent. Wendy **raised** the rent. [*the rent* = direct object]

VERB TENSE

7g What is verb tense?

The **tense** of a verb indicates *when* the action, occurrence, or state of being it expresses takes place. Verbs are the only words that change form to express time.

English verb tenses are divided into two general groups: simple and perfect.

The three **simple tenses** divide time into present, past, and future. The **present** tense describes what is happening, what is true at the moment, and what is always true. It uses the simple form and the -*s* form.

I **study** Italian at the university.
Joe **studies** hard all the time.

The **past tense** tells of a completed action or a condition that has ended. It uses the past tense form.

We **joined** the Italian conversation group.
We **hoped** to practice speaking.

The **future tense** indicates action not yet taken. This tense uses the auxiliary verbs *will* or *shall* and the simple form.

We **shall see** an Italian movie at the next meeting.

The second group of tenses are the **perfect tenses**. They also divide time into present, past, and future.

All six tenses also have **progressive forms**, made from the -*ing* form and the verb *to be*.

7h How do I use the simple present tense?

The **simple present tense** describes what is happening or what is true at the moment. It also has special functions, summarized below.

SUMMARY OF USES FOR THE SIMPLE PRESENT TENSE

DESCRIBING WHAT IS HAPPENING NOW, IN THE PRESENT

You **work** efficiently.
The gale **rattles** the windows.

DESCRIBING A HABITUAL OR REGULARLY OCCURRING ACTION

My accounting class **meets** at 10:00 on Tuesdays.
Horror movies **give** him nightmares.

EXPRESSING A GENERAL TRUTH OR WIDELY HELD OPINION

A kilogram **is** roughly 2.2 pounds.
Good fences **make** good neighbors.

DESCRIBING A FIXED-TIME FUTURE EVENT

The semester **ends** on May 30.
The ship **leaves** port at midnight.
His birthday **falls** on a Sunday this year.

DISCUSSING "TIMELESS" EVENTS AND ACTIVITIES AND INTENTIONS OF THOSE WHO CREATE THEM

Jay Gatsby **wants** it all.
Luke Skywalker and Hans Solo repeatedly **save** Princess Leia.
Einstein **speaks** of matter as something that is interchangeable with energy.

7i How do I form and use the perfect tenses?

The perfect tenses usually describe actions or occurrences that have already been completed or that will be completed before another point in time.

The **present perfect tense** shows that an action begun in the past continues into the present, or that an action completed in the past affects the present.

Betty **has applied** for a summer job.

We **have** always **tried** to do our best.

The **past perfect tense** indicates that an action was completed before another one took place.

The blizzard **had trapped** the climbers before they could get down the mountain.

The **future perfect tense** indicates that an action will be complete before some specified or predictable time.

The space craft **will have sent** back pictures of the outer planets before it flies out of the solar system.

7j How do I form and use progressive forms?

The **progressive form** uses the present participle along with the various forms of *be* and other auxiliary verbs. It shows that an action or condition is ongoing. (Another name for progressive forms is *continuous forms*.)

The **present progressive** indicates something taking place at the time it is written or spoken about.

Rents **are rising**.

The **past progressive** shows the continuing nature of a past action.

The fire **was spreading** rapidly when the firefighters arrived.

The **future progressive** shows that a future action will continue for some time.

After vacation, **we shall be returning** to our study of verb tenses.

The **present perfect progressive** describes something that began in the past and is likely to continue in the future.

The kitchen tap **has been dripping** for weeks.

The **past perfect progressive** describes an ongoing condition in the past that has been ended by something stated in the sentence.

The stereo **had been playing** well until the movers dropped it.

The **future perfect progressive** describes an action or condition continuing until some specific future time.

On November 11, **we shall have been going** together for two years.

7k

SUMMARY OF TENSES INCLUDING PROGRESSIVE FORMS

SIMPLE TENSES	REGULAR VERB	IRREGULAR VERB	PROGRESSIVE FORM
Present	I talk	I eat	I am talking, I am eating
Past	I talked	I ate	I was talking, I was eating
Future	I will talk	I will eat	I will be talking, I will be eating
PERFECT TENSES			
Present Perfect	I have talked	I have eaten	I have been talking, I have been eating
Past Perfect	I had talked	I had eaten	I had been talking, I had been eating
Future Perfect	I will have talked	I will have eaten	I will have been talking, I will have been eating

---

7k How do I use tense sequences accurately?

Sentences often have more than one verb, and these verbs often refer to actions taking place at different times. Showing the right time relationships—that is, using accurate tense sequences—is necessary to avoid confusion. The tense of the verb in an independent clause determines the possibilities for verb tense in that sentence's dependent clauses.

SUMMARY OF SEQUENCE OF TENSES

WHEN INDEPENDENT-CLAUSE VERB IS IN THE SIMPLE PRESENT TENSE, FOR THE DEPENDENT-CLAUSE VERB:

Use the present tense to show same-time action.

The director **says** that the movie **is** a tribute to factory workers.
I **avoid** shellfish because I **am** allergic to it.

Use the past tense to show earlier action.

I **am** sure that I **deposited** the check.

Use the present perfect tense to show a period of time extending from some point in the past to the present.

They **claim** that they **have visited** the planet Venus.

SUMMARY OF SEQUENCE OF TENSES *(Continued)*

Use the future tense for action to come.

The book **is** open because I **will be reading** it later.

WHEN INDEPENDENT-CLAUSE VERB IS IN THE PAST TENSE, FOR THE DEPENDENT-CLAUSE VERB:

Use the past tense to show earlier action.

I **ate** dinner before you **offered** to take me out for pizza.

Use the past perfect tense to emphasize earlier action.

The sprinter **knew** she **had broken** the record.

Use the present tense to state a general truth.

Christopher Columbus **discovered** that the world **is** round.

WHEN INDEPENDENT-CLAUSE VERB IS IN THE PRESENT PERFECT OR PAST PERFECT TENSE, FOR THE DEPENDENT-CLAUSE VERB:

Use the past tense.

The milk **has become** sour since I **bought** it last week.

The price of sugar **had** already **declined** when artificial sweeteners first **appeared**.

WHEN INDEPENDENT-CLAUSE VERB IS IN THE FUTURE TENSE, FOR THE DEPENDENT-CLAUSE VERB:

Use the present tense to show action happening at the same time.

You **will be** rich if you **win** the prize.

Use the past tense to show earlier action.

You **will** surely **win** the prize if you **remembered** to mail the entry form.

Use the present perfect tense to show future action earlier than the action of the independent-clause verb.

The river **will flood** again next year unless we have built a better dam by then.

WHEN THE INDEPENDENT-CLAUSE VERB IS IN THE FUTURE PERFECT TENSE, FOR THE DEPENDENT-CLAUSE VERB:

Use either the present tense or the present perfect tense.

Dr. Chang **will have delivered** 5,000 babies by the time she **retires**.

Dr. Chang **will have delivered** 5,000 babies by the time she **has retired**.

MOOD

71 What is "mood" in verbs?

The **mood** of a verb conveys a writer's attitude toward a statement. The most common mood in English is the **indicative mood**. It is used for statements about real things, or highly likely ones, and for questions about fact: *The car started; how much does that jacket cost?* Most statements are in the indicative mood.

The **imperative mood**, which always uses the simple form of the verb, expresses commands and direct requests. The subject is often omitted in an imperative sentence. It is assumed to be *you. Sit down! Please do not smoke in here.*

The **subjunctive mood** expresses conditions including wishes, recommendations, indirect requests, and speculations. The subjunctive mood in English is rare. Therefore, its forms are less familiar than those of the indicative mood and the imperative mood.

7m What are subjunctive forms?

The **present subjunctive** of all verbs except *be* uses the simple form of the verb for all persons and numbers. The present subjunctive of *be* is *be* for all persons and numbers.

It is important that the vandals **be** [not *are*] found.
I am demanding that he **pay** [not *pays*] his bill.

The **past subjunctive** uses the same form as the past indicative. The past subjunctive of *be* for all persons and numbers is the same as the past plural indicative, *were*.

He wishes he **were** [not *was*] richer.
Although the subjunctive is not as common as it once was, it is still used in four situations:

1.   Use the subjunctive in *if* clauses and some *unless* clauses for speculations or conditions contrary to fact.
     Unless a meltdown **were** [not *was*] to take place, the risks from a nuclear power plant are small.

2.   Use the subjunctive for judgments introduced by *as if* or *as though.*
     The runner looks as though he **were** [not *was*] about to collapse.

3.   Use the subjunctive in *that* clauses for wishes, indirect requests, recommendations, and demands.
     I wish that this building **were** [not *was*] air-conditioned.
     Her mechanic recommended that she **look** [not *looked*] for a new car.

4.   Use the subjunctive in certain standard expressions.
     Please let me **be.**   **Come** what may....
     Be that as it may....   Far **be** it from me....

Modal auxiliary verbs like *would, could, might,* and *should* can convey speculations and conditions contrary to fact and are often used with the subjunctive:

If my father **were** [not *was*] here, he **would** gladly cook the fish.

When the independent clause expresses a conditional statement with a modal auxiliary, be sure to use the appropriate subjunctive form, not another modal auxiliary, in the dependent clause.

No   If I **would have studied** for the final, I might have improved my grade.

Yes   If I **had studied** for the final, I might have improved my grade.

VOICE

7n What is "voice" in verbs?

The **voice** of a verb indicates whether a subject does or receives the action named by the verb. English has two voices: active and passive.

In the **active voice**, the subject performs the action.

Roaches **infest** most cities.

In the **passive voice**, the subject is acted upon, and the person or thing doing the action often appears as the object of the preposition *by*.

Roaches **are considered** a nuisance by many people.

The passive voice uses verb phrases. A past participle indicates the action, and a form of *be* specifies person, number, and tense: *is seen, were seen, have been seen.*

7o How do I write in the active, not passive, voice?

The active voice emphasizes the doer of the action, so active constructions have a more direct and dramatic effect. Active constructions also use fewer words than passive constructions. Therefore, use the active voice wherever you can. Most sentences in the passive voice can easily be converted to the active voice.

PASSIVE   Bicycling tours of Canada **are often taken by younger travelers**.
ACTIVE   **Young travelers often take** bicycling tours of Canada

However, the passive voice is useful in two special situations.

1. You should use the passive voice when the doer of the action is unknown or unimportant.

    The painting **was stolen** some time after midnight. [Who stole the painting is unknown.]

2. You can also use the passive voice to focus attention on the action rather than the doer of the action. For example, in a passage about important contributions to the history of biology, you might want to emphasize a doer by using the active voice.

    William Harvey **studied** the human circulatory system.

    However, in a passage summarizing what scientists know about circulation, you might want to emphasize what was done.

    The human circulatory system **was studied** by William Harvey.

7p What are proper uses of the passive voice?

Although the active voice is usually best, in special circumstances you need to use the passive voice. See the following examples for clarification.

Using passive voice when the doer of the action is unknown or unimportant.

The lock **was broken** sometime after four o'clock. [Who broke the lock is unknown.]
In 1899, the year I was born, a peace conference **was held** at The Hague. [The doers of the action—*holders* of the conference—aren't important.]

—E. B. WHITE, "Unity"

Using passive voice to focus attention on the action, not the doer of the action.

Sometimes the action in the sentence is more important than the doer of the action. Conversely, you want to use the passive voice when you're summarizing what is known about the subject.

ACTIVE   Joseph Priestley **discovered** oxygen in 1774. [*Joseph Priestley* is the subject.]

PASSIVE   Oxygen **was discovered** in 1774 by Joseph Priestley. [*Oxygen* is the subject.]

Using active or passive voice in the social and natural sciences.

Traditionally, the social sciences and natural sciences preferred the passive voice. Very recently, the style manuals for these disciplines have been advising writers to use the active voice whenever possible. "Verbs are vigorous, direct communicators," point out the editors of the *Publication Manual of the American Psychological Association*.

Writing Present-Tense Verbs   EXERCISE **7-1**

Fill in the blanks with the third person singular, present tense of the verbs in parentheses.

EXAMPLE   Every driver (to hope) *hopes* to avoid an accident.

1. However, sometimes a cautious driver (to rush) _____ to cross railroad tracks but doesn't make it.

2. Even if the driver (to tie) _____ in the race with the train, he or she loses.

3. A standard diesel locomotive (to weigh) _____ 135 tons.

4. The train engineer (to need) _____ almost one mile to stop a train that is going sixty-five miles per hour.

5. Often, a driver (to attempt) _____ to go around lowered gates at the crossing.

6. A person who (to fail) _____ to obey warning signs, gates, and signals is in great danger.

7. Similarly, a driver who (to start) _____ across the tracks before the gates have been lifted puts all the people in the car in danger.

8. The safety gate (to open) _____ only when both directions of the train's path are clear.

9. If a driver (to wait) _____ for only one train to pass, he or she may not realize that another train may be coming from the opposite direction.

10. Another dangerous situation (to occur) _____ when the slick pavement and excessive speeds cause a driver to skid onto the tracks.

11. A police officer (to report) _____ that many train-related accidents are caused by drivers whose abilities have been impaired by alcohol or drugs.

12. Adverse weather (to affect) _____ driving conditions as well.

13. A safety bulletin (to recommend) _____ that drivers watch carefully for the yellow and black "RR" signs.

14. Such a sign (to warn) _____ drivers to slow down for an oncoming train.

15. A nearby sign (to post) _____ the appropriate speed limit, which should always be observed near a railroad crossing.

16. Because of traffic laws, a school bus (to stop) _____ completely at railroad crossings—even when the gates are not lowered.

17. The law (to require) _____ the same safety procedure for trucks carrying combustible or hazardous materials.

18. When behind a vehicle of this sort, a driver (to know) _____ not to follow too closely or to become impatient.

19. When a driver (to hear) _____ a bell suddenly activate while passing over the tracks, he or she should not panic.

20. The device (to allow) _____ enough time for the driver to cross the tracks before the train arrives.

21. The gate (to remain) _____ raised until the car gets over to the other side.

22. If a driver (to brake) _____ and reverses, he or she may be blocked by a car in the rear.

23. A train (to cause) _____ an accident only when drivers are careless or impatient.

24. A driver (to face) _____ severe penalties in most states for not obeying the warning gates and lights.

25. If a driver (to practice) _____ safety and caution, others will follow, making railroad crossings safer for all other drivers.

Writing Past Tense Verbs

Fill in the blanks with the past tense forms of the verbs in parentheses.

EXAMPLE   Have you ever (to wonder) __*wondered*__ why people fly kites?

1. Malayans (to start) _____ to use kites for ceremonial purposes at least 3000 years ago.

2. In ancient hieroglyphics, Egyptians (to record) _____ legends about kites.

3. Yet kites probably (to develop) _____ first in China.

4. In the Han Dynasty, the emperor (to use) _____ kites to intimidate invaders.

5. He (to insert) _____ bamboo pipes into the kites.

6. When flown above the invaders' camp, the kites (to issue) _____ moaning sounds that (to startle) _____ the men below.

7. Because the night was dark, the men (to perceive) _____ nothing in the sky above them.

8. It is not surprising that they (to jerk) _____ up their tents and immediately (to head) _____ for home.

9. More recently, Benjamin Franklin (to employ) _____ a kite for his experiments with electricity.

10. An Englishman, George Pocock, (to pull) _____ a carriage and passengers with two eight-foot kites.

11. The Wright brothers (to experiment) _____ with kites even after their success with the airplane.

12. And you (to imagine) _____ that people flew kites just for fun!

Writing Irregular Past-Tense Verbs

Fill in the blanks with the correct past-tense forms of the irregular verbs in parenthesis.

EXAMPLE: We (to swear) _swore_ we would never leave the door unlocked again.

1.   The woman (to wake) _____ early and looked at the clock. It was five a.m.

2.   Sensing something was wrong, she (to get) _____ up and opened the door to the utility room, where her dog normally (to sleep) _____.

3.   She (to freeze) _____ at what she saw: the room was empty and the door (to stand) _____ open.

4.   The woman (to shake) _____ her husband awake and (to tell) _____ him that the dog was missing.

5.   Then she (to throw) _____ on some clothes and jumped in the car.

6.   She (to drive) _____ up and down nearby streets looking for her pet.

7.   She even (to swing) _____ by her friend's house two miles away to see if he was there.

8.   However, she (to draw) _____ a blank. Finally she admitted defeat and (to come) _____ home.

9.   When she (to see) _____ her husband, she (to burst) _____ into tears.

10. They both (to think) _____ they would never see their dog again.

11. The woman (to go) _____ to work and (to spend) _____ the entire day wondering if her dog was safe.

12. When she (to get) _____ home, she (to speak) _____ to her neighbor and asked if he had seen the animal.

13. Then she (to hear) _____ a rustling behind her.

14. She (to spin) _____ around, and (to see) _____ the dog cowering in the bushes.

15. At the sound of his name, however, he (to spring) _____ out.

16. He (to shake) _____ his coat, which was muddy and matted.

17. She immediately (to sweep) _____ him up in her arms and (to take) _____ him inside.

18. He (to cling) _____ to her as if traumatized.

19. However, she (to feel) _____ no broken bones, and he (to eat) _____ and (to drink) _____ normally.

20. When her husband (to ring) _____ to say he was on his way home, she (to tell) _____ him the good news.

Conjunction be

The verb *be* has many irregular forms. Fill in the chart with all of its forms. Then check yourself by looking at the irregular verb chart in this module.

Person	Present Tense	Past Tense
Singular		
First	_____	_____
Second	_____	_____
Third	_____	_____
Plural		
First	_____	_____
Second	_____	_____
Third	_____	_____

Present Participle _____   Past Participle _____

Using the Verbs be

Fill in the blanks with appropriate forms of the verb *be*.

For some people a garden _____ a hobby. For others it _____ a necessity. In either case, _____ a gardener is hard work.

The first thing you must do each spring _____ prepare the garden plot with spade, plow, or rototiller. Your muscles _____ sure to ache after a day of turning the soil. Planting and mulching _____ next. I _____ always excited to see new plants coming up. You will _____ too. However, weeds _____ apt to grow faster than the seeds you planted.

Unless your idea of an aerobic workout _____ thirty minutes with a hoe, you should _____ enthusiastic about mulch. Mulch can _____ straw mounded around plants or plastic sheets covering the ground between rows. If you _____ using plastic, _____ sure you have the kind that can breathe. Otherwise, there will _____ inadequate moisture for your plants.

A garden _____ guaranteed to cultivate your patience while you _____ cultivating it. It cannot _____ rushed. If you hope _____ a successful gardener, you must _____ willing to work at it.

Using Helping Verbs

EXERCISE **7-6**

Fill in the blank with the helping verbs from this list. Some sentences have several possible answers, but be sure to use each helping verb at least once.

are	do	is	was
be	does	may	were
can	has	seem	will
could	have	should	would

EXAMPLE   In order for a child to develop into a helpful member of society, the family unit *should* act as a mini-society.

1. Children who volunteer time, first in the home and then in society, _____ destined to develop qualities like self-sacrifice and a strong commitment to the community.

2. President John F. Kennedy, who said, "Ask not what your country can do for you, ask what you can do for your country," _____ partially responsible for getting Americans to give to their society rather than take from it.

3. Volunteerism _____ be defined as the willingness to go beyond self-interest.

4. People who volunteer in their communities _____ contribute freely toward the common good.

5. Without doubt, volunteering _____ require giving more than spare change: it requires energy, time, and commitment.

6. Adults who _____ raised in homes with limits on their behavior have learned that they were not the center of attention.

7. A family _____ act as a mini-society by demanding of the child what society eventually will.

8. Society _____ eventually expect an honest, responsible, and respectful individual to develop.

9. Society _____ most benefit from a member who is willing to share, to help others, and to encourage the growth of the community.

10. The family _____ responsible for instilling in a child these important values at an early age.

11. Parents _____ begin teaching a child about volunteerism as early as the age of three by assigning routine household chores.

12. At first, children _____ merely be expected to pick up after themselves and keep their rooms in order.

13. A few years later, the child _____ be responsible for chores that involve the home, such as mopping and vacuuming the floor or helping with the dishes.

14. Children who _____ participate in family chores learn that family is not only about fun; it is also about cooperation.

15. Giving children money for doing chores _____ be an obstacle in the learning process because money teaches them that they should expect something in return for their efforts.

16. A child can _____ taught the three R's of good citizenship at an early age: respect, responsibility, and resourcefulness.

17. Volunteering _____ become an important part of family values in the United States, both for parents and children.

18. In fact, nearly one-third of all households _____ participated actively in community service at one time or another, thus making each community a better place to be.

Identifying Transitive, Intransitive, and Linking Verbs

Identify each italicized verb by writing *transitive*, *intransitive*, or *linking* on the lines to the right.

EXAMPLE   The platypus of Australia is an unusual animal.   *linking*

1.   Europeans first *saw* the platypus in 1796.   _____

2.   The platypus *is* nocturnal.   _____

3.   Usually it *stays* out of sight.   _____

4.   The Europeans *could* hardly believe their eyes.   _____

5.   The platypus *has* a bizarre appearance.   _____

6.   Its bill *resembles* that of a duck.   _____

7.   However, the bill *is* really a soft snout.   _____

8.   With the bill the platypus *probes* in the mud for food.   _____

9.   The platypus *has* a tail and fur like a beaver.   _____

10.   With its webbed feet it *swims* well.   _____

11.   Nevertheless, the feet *have* claws for digging in river banks.   _____

12.   The platypus *is* a mammal.   _____

13.   Yet it *lays* eggs.   _____

14.   After hatching, the young *nurse*.   _____

15.   No wonder one scientist *named* the platypus paradoxus.   _____

16.   It *is* indeed a paradox.   _____

Writing Sentences with Transitive and Intransitive Verbs

Write two sentences for each of the following verbs, one in which it is transitive and one in which it is intransitive.

EXAMPLE   solved

The mystery was solved quickly and easily.

John solved the math equation without using a calculator.

1. answer

    intransitive: _____

    transitive: _____

2. walk

    intransitive: _____

    transitive: _____

3. prepare

    intransitive: _____

    transitive: _____

4. drives

    intransitive: _____

    transitive: _____

5. paint

    intransitive: _____

    transitive: _____

Distinguishing the Forms of
lie/lay, sit/set, and rise/raise

Fill in the blanks with the verb in parentheses that best suits the meaning of each sentence.

EXAMPLE   (Setting, Sitting) _Sitting_ among coworkers at a formal dinner can make just about anyone nervous.

1. With seven pieces of silverware (lying, laying) _____ in a specific sequence before you, it is easy to become nervous about your table manners.

2. It is important to remember that if the host (rises, raises) _____ from his or her seat to make a toast, you must (rise, raise) _____ your glass.

3. Typically, before the first course begins, the host will tell you where to (set, sit) _____ but if he or she has forgotten, you may find a spot wherever a place has been (sit, set) _____.

4. Before you take a bit of food, you must (lie, lay) _____ the napkin in your lap.

5. The waiter will always (sit, set) _____ your plate down from the left side and pick it up from the right, so be sure to move to the side.

6. Elbows are never allowed on a table, and you can never (lay, lie) _____ your hands on your head.

7. If a smaller fork has not been (laid, lain) _____ to the left of the larger fork when the salad arrives, you may use the large fork; whoever (set, sat) _____ the table may have forgotten.

8. When eating soup, always try to (rise, raise) _____ the spoon away from your-self to prevent spilling the soup on your clothing.

9. When you are finished with your meal, (lie, lay) _____ the fork and knife together on the right side of the plate; if they are (lying, laying) _____ on opposite sides of the dish, it signifies to the waiter that you are taking a break.

10. Finally, if a cup of coffee is (set, sit) _____ before you, do not dunk your doughnut or croissant in it in front of business associates; it is considered to be inappropriate in this (setting, sitting) _____.

Using the Perfect and Progressive Tenses

Fill in the blanks with the verb forms described in parentheses. Be prepared to discuss why each verb is appropriate in its sentence.

EXAMPLE   The aftereffects of kisses (to cause: present perfect) _have caused_ researchers to recommend a daily dose of this sign of affection.

1. German physicians and psychologists (to discover: present perfect) _____ that a kiss can improve a person's health.

2. Spouses who (to kiss: present perfect progressive) _____ their partner each day before work since the beginning of their marriages tend to live healthier, happier, and longer lives than those who don't.

3. Researchers (to begin: present progressive) _____ to understand why.

4. One researcher, Dr. Arthur Sazbo, (to study: present perfect progressive) _____ those who kiss and those who don't.

5. He (to find: present perfect) _____ that those who kiss their spouses in the morning miss fewer workdays because of illness than do those who don't.

6. Furthermore, it turns out that those who kiss (to involve: past perfect progressive) _____ in fewer automobile accidents while on the way to work than those who didn't.

7. It also seems that spouses who start the day with a kiss (to earn: present progressive) _____ 30 percent more than those who do not.

8. Dr. Sazbo (to say: past perfect) _____ that the difference is that spouses who kiss start their day with a more positive attitude, one which allows them to get through their day a bit easier.

9. In fact, kissing (to link: present perfect progressive) _____ to living longer; on average, those who kiss (to live: present progressive) _____ five years longer than those who don't.

10. Why is it that kisses (to have: present perfect progressive) _____ such huge effects on people?

11. Dr. Sazbo (to suggest: present perfect) _____ that since a kiss is a form of approval, those who don't experience one in the morning do not have the same positive feelings and confidence as those who do kiss.

12. With this report, new superstitions (to start: present progressive) _____ to develop already.

13. Perhaps, people all along (to know: present perfect) _____ that a morning kiss is the right way to start the day.

14. But they could not (to understand: present perfect) _____ why this is true until very recently.

15. Certainly, the physicians and psychologists who (to study: present perfect progressive) _____ kisses strongly recommend them for a boost in spirit, health, and happiness.

Identifying Active and Passive Verbs

Underline the entire main verb in each sentence, and then identify it as active or passive on the lines to the right.

EXAMPLE   The Louvre _contains_ some of the
world's most famous art work.   ____active____

1. The Louvre in Paris was not built as an art museum.   _____

2. The original Louvre was constructed in the twelfth
    century as a fortress.   _____

3. Francis I erected the present building as a residence.   _____

4. A gallery connecting it with the Tuileries Palace was
    started by Henry IV and completed by Louis XIV.   _____

5. A second gallery, begun by Napoleon, would have
    enclosed a great square.   _____

6. However, it was not finished until after his abdication.   _____

7. Revolutionaries overthrew the Bastille on July 14, 1789.   _____

8. Just four years later, the art collection of the Louvre was
    opened to the public.   _____

9. The collection can be traced back to Francis I.   _____

10. Francis, an ardent collector, invited Leonardo da Vinci to
    France in 1515.   _____

11. Leonardo brought the *Mona Lisa* with him from Italy.   _____

12. Nevertheless, the royal art collection may have been
    expanded more by ministers than by kings.   _____

13. Cardinals Richelieu and Mazarin can take credit for many
    important acquisitions.   _____

14. Today the Louvre has a new entrance.   _____

15. A glass pyramid in the courtyard was designed by
    I. M. Pei.   _____

16. Pei's name can be added to a distinguished list of
    Louvre architects.   _____

Revising for the Active Voice

A: Change each of the passive sentences you identified in Exercise 7-11 into the active voice. You may need to add words to act as subjects of your new sentences. Use your own paper.

B: On the lines to the right, identify each sentence as active or passive. Then rewrite each passive sentence into the active voice. However, if you think a sentence is better left passive, write your reason on the line instead.

EXAMPLE   Today's country of Zimbabwe was named after   _passive_
           important ruins.
           Patriots named today's country of Zimbabwe
           after important ruins.

1. The ruins were not known by people outside Africa until 1868. _____

    _____

2. The largest of the ruins, Great Zimbabwe, has two main structures. _____

    _____

3. The building on the hill was constructed primarily for defense. _____

    _____

4. Its stones are fitted together without mortar.   _____

    _____

5. A lower, elliptical building is encircled by a thirty-foot wall.   _____

    _____

6. An inner wall forms a passage to a sacred enclosure.   _____

    _____

7. Majestic soapstone sculptures were discovered there.   _____

    _____

8. The enclosure contains towers forty feet high.   _____

    _____

9. Ancestors of the Shona-speaking people maintained   _____
    Great Zimbabwe as a trade center from the twelfth
    through the fifteenth centuries.

    _____

10. Tools for working with gold have been found in the ruins.   _____

    _____

11. The Shona traded gold and ivory with Arab merchants.   _____

    _____

MODULE 8: PROUNOUN CASE AND REFERENCE

8a What does "case" mean?

Case applies in different ways to pronouns and to nouns. For pronouns, case refers to three pronoun forms: the **subjective** (pronoun as a subject), the **objective** (pronoun as an object), and the **possessive** (pronoun used in possessive constructions). For nouns, case refers to only one noun form: the possessive.

8b What are personal pronouns?

Personal pronouns refer to persons or things. Many of the most difficult questions about pronoun case concern who/whom and whoever/whomever.

The plural of *you* is simply *you*. Avoid the nonstandard plural *yous*.

8c How do pronouns work in case?

In the subjective case, pronouns function as subjects.

We were going to get married. [*We* is the subject.]
John and **I** wanted an inexpensive band for our wedding. [*I* is part of the compound subject *John and I.*]
He and I found an affordable one-person band. [*He and I* is the compound subject.]

In the objective case, pronouns function as objects.

We saw **him** perform in a public park. [*Him* is the direct object.]
We showed **him** our budget. [*Him* is the indirect object.]
He wrote down what we wanted and shook hands with **us**. [*Us* is the object of the preposition.]

In the possessive case, nouns and pronouns usually indicate ownership or imply a relationship.

The **musician's contract** was very fair. [The possessive noun *musician's* implies a type of ownership.]
His contract was very fair. [The possessive pronoun *his* implies a type of ownership.]

The **musician's problems** stem from playing cheap instruments. [The possessive noun *musician's* implies a type of relationship.]

Their problems stem from playing with cheap instruments. [The possessive pronoun *their* implies a type of relationship.]

Sometimes, however, the notion of ownership or relationship calls for a major stretch of the imagination in possessive constructions. In such cases, look for the following pattern: noun + the s sound + noun. This means that two nouns work together, one of which does the possessing and the other of which is possessed.

The **musician's arrival** was eagerly anticipated. [The musician neither owns the arrival nor has a relationship with the arrival. Instead, the pattern noun+ the 's' sound + noun is operating.]

ALERT: Never use an apostrophe in personal pronouns: ours, yours, its, his, hers, theirs.

8d Which case is correct when *and* connects pronouns?

When *and* connects pronouns, or nouns and pronouns, the result is a **compound construction**. Compounding, which means "putting parts together as a whole," has no effect on case. Always use pronouns in the subjective case when they serve as the subjects of a sentence; also, always use pronouns in the objective case when they serve as objects in a sentence. Never mix cases.

COMPOUND PRONOUN **SUBJECT** **He and I** saw the solar eclipse. [*He and I* is a compound subject.]

COMPOUND PRONOUN **OBJECT** That eclipse astonished **him and me**. [*Him and me* is a compound object.]

When you're unsure of the case of a pronoun, use the "Troyka test for case" shown in the box below. In this four-step test, you drop some of the words from your sentence so that you can tell which case sounds correct.

When pronouns are in a prepositional phrase, they are always in the objective case. (That is, a pronoun is always the object of the preposition.) This rule holds whether the pronouns are singular or plural. You can also use the test shown in the box to check what is correct.

TROYKA TEST FOR CASE

Subjective case

STEP 1: Write the sentence twice, once using the subjective case, and once using the objective case.

STEP 2: Cross out enough words to isolate the element you are questioning.

~~Janet and~~ me

learned about the moon.

~~Janet and~~ I

→

TROYKA TEST FOR CASE *(continued)*

STEP 3: Omit the crossed-out words and read each sentence aloud to determine which one sounds right.

> **No** **Me** learned about the moon. [This doesn't sound right.]
>
> **YES** **I** learned about the moon. [This sounds right, so the subjective case is correct.]

STEP 4: Select the correct version and restore the words you crossed out.

> **Janet and** I learned about the moon.

Objective case

STEP 1: Write the sentence twice, once using the subjective case, and once using the objective case.

STEP 2: Cross out enough words to isolate the element you are questioning.

> The astronomer taught ~~Janet and~~ I
>
> about the moon.
>
> The astronomer taught ~~Janet and~~ me

STEP 3: Omit the crossed-out words and read each sentence aloud to determine which one sounds right.

> **No** The astronomer taught **I** about the moon. [This doesn't sound right.]
>
> **YES** The astronomer taught **me** about the moon [This sounds right, so the objective case is correct.]

STEP 4: Select the correct version and restore the words you crossed out.

> The astronomer taught **Janet and me** about the moon.

> **No** Ms. Lester gave an assignment *to* **Sam and I**. [The prepositional phrase, which starts with the preposition *to*, cannot use the subjective-case pronoun *I*.]
>
> **YES** Ms. Lester gave an assignment *to* **Sam and me**. [The prepositional phrase, which starts with the preposition *to*, calls for the objective-case pronoun *me*.]

Be especially careful when one or more pronouns follow the preposition **between**.

> **No** The dispute is *between* **Thomas and I**. [The prepositional phrase, which starts with the preposition *between*, cannot use the subjective-case pronoun *I*.]
>
> **YES** The dispute is *between* **Thomas and me**. [The prepositional phrase, which starts with the preposition *between*, calls for the objective –case pronoun *me*.]

8e How do I match cases with appositives?

You can match cases with **appositives** by putting pronouns and nouns in the same case as the word or words the appositive is renaming. Whenever you're unsure about whether to use the subjective or objective case, use the "Troyka test for case."

We (not *Us*) tennis players practice hard. [Here, the subjective-case pronoun *we* matches the noun *tennis players*, which is the subject of this sentence.]

The winners, **she and I** (not *her and me*), advanced to the finals. [The subjective-case pronouns *she and I* match the noun *winners*, which is the subject of this sentence.]

The coach tells **us** (not *we*) tennis players to practice hard. [The objective-case pronoun *us* matches the noun *tennis players*, which is the object in this sentence.]

The crowd cheered the winners, **her and me** (not *she and I*). [The objective-case pronouns *her and me* match the noun *winners*, which is the object in this sentence.]

8f How does case work after linking verbs?

A pronoun that comes after a **linking verb** either renames the subject or shows possession. In both constructions, always use a pronoun in the subjective case. If you're unsure about how to identify a pronoun's case, use the "Troyka test for case."

The contest winner was **I** (not *me*). [*Was* is a linking verb. *I* renames the subject, which is the noun *contest winner*, so the subjective-case pronoun *I* is correct.]

The prize is **mine**. [*Is* is a linking verb. *Mine* shows possession, so the possessive-case pronoun *mine* is correct.]

8g When should I use *who, whoever, whom,* and *whomever*?

The pronouns *who* and *whoever* are in the subjective case. The pronouns *whom* and *whomever* are in the objective case.

Informal spoken English tends to blur distinctions between *who* and *whom*, so with these words some people can't rely entirely on what "sounds right." Whenever you're unsure of whether to use *who* or *whoever* or to use *whom* or *whomever*, apply the "Troyka test for case." If you see *who* or *whoever*, test by temporarily substituting *he, she,* or *they*. If you see *whom* or *whomever*, test by temporarily substituting *him, her,* or *them*.

My father tells the same story to **whoever/whomever** he meets.

My father tells the same story to ~~she/~~her. [*Note:* When substituting, stop at *she/her*. The objective case *whomever* is correct because the sentence works when you substitute *her* for *whoever/whomever*. In contrast, the subjective case *whoever* is wrong because the sentence doesn't work when you substitute *she* for *whoever/whomever*.]

My father tells the same story to **whomever** he meets.

The most reliable variation of the test for *who, whom, whoever, whomever* calls for you to add a word before the substituted wordset. In this example, the word *if* is added.

I wondered **who/whom** would vote for Ms. Wallace.

I wondered **if he/if him** would vote for Ms. Wallace. [The subjective case *who* is correct because the sentence works when you substitute *if he* for *who/whom*. In contrast, the objective case *whom* is wrong because the sentence doesn't work when you substitute *if him* for *who/whom*.]

I wondered **who** would vote for Ms. Wallace.

Another variation of the test for *who, whom, whoever, whomever* calls for you to invert the word order in the test sentence.

Babies **who/whom** mothers cuddle grow faster and feel happier.

Mothers cuddle **they/them**. [Note: When substituting, stop at *she/her*. By inverting the word order in the sentence—that is, by temporarily using *mothers* as the subject of the sentence—and substituting *they/them* for *who/whom*, you see that *them* is correct. Therefore, the objective case whom is correct.]

Babies **whom** mothers cuddle grow faster and feel happier.

At the beginning or end of a question, use *who* if the question is about the subject and *whom* if the question is about the object. To determine which case to use, recast the question into a statement, substituting *he* or *him* (or *she* or *her*).

Who watched the space shuttle liftoff? [*He* (not *Him*) *watched the space shuttle liftoff* uses the subjective case, so *who* is correct.]

Ted admires **whom**? [*Ted admires him* (not *he*) uses the objective case, so *whom* is correct.]

Whom does Ted admire? [*Ted admires him* (not *he*) uses the objective case, so *whom* is correct.]

To **whom** does Ted speak about becoming an astronaut? [*Ted speaks to them* (not *they*) uses the objective case, so *whom* is correct.]

8h What pronoun case comes after *than* or *as*?

When *than* or *as* is part of a sentence of comparison, the sentence sometimes doesn't include words to complete the comparison outright. Rather, by omitting certain words, the sentence implies the comparison. For example, *My two-month-old Saint Bernard is larger than most full-grown dogs [are]* doesn't need the final word *are*.

When a pronoun follows *than* or *as*, the meaning of the sentence depends entirely on whether the pronoun is in the subjective case or the objective case. Here are two sentences that convey two very different messages, depending on whether the subjective case (*I*) or the objective case (*me*) is used.

1. My sister loved that dog more **than** *I*.
2. My sister loved that dog more **than** *me*.

In sentence 1, because *I* is in the subjective case, the sentence means *My sister loved that dog more than I [loved it]*. In sentence 2, because *me* is in the objective case, the sentence means *My sister loved that dog more than [she loved] me*. In both situations, you can check whether you're using the correct case by supplying the implied words to see if they make sense.

8i How do pronouns work before infinitives?

Most **infinitives** consist of simple forms of verbs that follow *to*: for example, *to laugh, to sing, to jump, to dance*. (A few exceptions occur when the *to* is optional: *My aunt helped the elderly man (to) cross the street*; and when the *to* is awkward: *My aunt watched the elderly man (to) get on the bus*. For both the **subjects** of infinitives and the **objects** of infinitives, use the objective case.

> Our tennis coach expects **me** *to serve*. [Because the word *me* is the subject of the infinitive *to serve*, the objective-case pronoun is correct.]

> Our tennis coach expects **him** *to beat* me. [Because the word *him* is the subject of the infinitive *to beat*, and *me* is the object of the infinitive, the objective-case pronoun is correct.]

8j How do pronouns work with *–ing* words?

When a verb's *–ing* form functions as a noun, it's called a **gerund**. *Brisk walking is excellent exercise*. When a noun or pronoun comes before a gerund, the possessive case is required. *His brisk walking built up his stamina*. In contrast, when a verb's *–ing* form functions as a modifier, it requires the subjective case for the pronoun, not the possessive case. *He, walking briskly, caught up to me*.

1. The detective noticed the **man** *staggering*.
2. The detective noticed the **man's** *staggering*.

Sentence 1 means that the detective noticed the *man*; sentence 2 means that the detective noticed the *staggering*. The same distinction applies to pronouns: When *the man* is replaced by either *him* or *his*, the meaning is the same as in sentences 1 and 2.

1. The detective noticed **him** *staggering*.
2. The detective noticed **his** *staggering*.

In conversation, such distinctions are often ignored, but use them in academic writing.

8k What case should I use for *–self* pronouns?

Two types of pronouns end in *–self*: reflective pronouns and intensive pronouns.

A **reflexive pronoun** reflects back on the subject, so it needs a subject in the sentence to be reflected back on. Without a subject, the reflective pronoun cannot operate correctly.

> The **detective** disguised *himself*. [The reflexive pronoun *himself* reflects back on the subject *detective*.]

Never use a reflexive pronoun to replace a personal pronoun in the subjective case.

> **No** My teammates and **myself** will vote for a team captain.

> **Yes** My teammates and **I** will vote for a team captain.

Also, never use a reflexive pronoun to replace a personal pronoun in the objective case. The only exception is when the object restates the subject.

No That decision is up to my teammates and **myself**.

Yes That decision is up to my teammates and **me**.

Intensive pronouns, which reflect back in the same way as reflexive pronouns, provide emphasis by making the message of the sentence more intense in meaning.

The detective felt that **his career *itself*** was at risk. [*Itself* intensifies the idea that the detective's career was at risk.]

8l What is pronoun reference?

The word or group of words that a pronoun replaces is called its **antecedent**. In order for your writing to communicate its message clearly, each pronoun must relate precisely to an antecedent.

I knew a **woman**, lovely in **her** bones/When small **birds** sighed, she would **sigh** back at **them**.

—Theodore Roethke, "I Knew a Woman"

8m What makes pronoun reference clear?

Pronoun reference is clear when your readers know immediately to whom or what each pronoun refers. The box lists guidelines for using pronouns clearly, and the section in parentheses is where each is explained.

GUIDELINES FOR CLEAR PRONOUN REFERENCE

- Place pronouns close to their ANTECEDENTS.
- Make a pronoun refer to a specific antecedent.
- Do not overuse *it*.
- Reserve *you* only for DIRECT ADDRESS.
- Use *that*, *which*, and *who* correctly.

8n How can I avoid unclear pronoun reference?

Every pronoun needs to refer to a specific, nearby antecedent. If the same pronoun in your writing has to refer to more than one antecedent, replace some pronouns with nouns.

No In 1911, **Roald Amundsen** reached the South Pole just thirty-five days before **Robert F. Scott** arrived. **He** [who? Amundsen or Scott?] had told people that **he** [who? Amundsen or Scott?] was going to sail for the Arctic, but **he** [who? Amundsen or Scott?] was concealing **his** [whose? Amundsen's or Scott's?] plan. Soon, **he** [who? Amundsen or Scott?] turned south for the Antarctic. On the journey home, **he** [who? Amundsen or Scott?] and **his** [whose? Amundsen's or Scott's] **party** froze to death just a few miles from safety.

YES   In 1911, **Roald Amundsen** reached the South Pole just thirty-five days before **Robert F. Scott** arrived. **Amundsen** had told people that **he** was going to sail for the Arctic, but **he** was concealing **his** plan. Soon, **Amundsen** turned south for the Antarctic. Meanwhile, on **their** journey home, **Scott** and his party froze to death just a few miles from safety.

ALERT: Be careful with the verbs *said* and *told* in sentences that contain pronoun reference. To maintain clarity, use quotation marks and slightly reword each sentence to make the meaning clear.

No   **Her** mother told **her she** was going to visit **her** grandmother.

YES   **Her** mother told **her**, "**You** are going to visit your grandmother."

YES   **Her** mother told **her**, "**I** am going to visit your grandmother."

Further, if too much material comes between a pronoun and its antecedent, readers can lose track of the meaning.

Alfred Wegener, a German meteorologist and professor of geophysics at the University of Graz in Austria, was the first to suggest that all the continents on earth were originally part of one large landmass. According to his theory, the supercontinent broke up long ago and the fragments drifted

apart. ~~He~~ named this supercontinent Pangaea.
Wegener

[*He* can only refer to Wegner, but material about Wegener's theory intervenes, so using *Wegener* again instead of *he* jogs the reader's memory and makes reading easier.]

When you start a new paragraph, be cautious about beginning it with a pronoun whose antecedent is in a prior paragraph. You're better off repeating the word.

---

80 How do pronouns work with *it, that, this,* and *which*?

When you use *it, that, this,* and *which,* be sure that your readers can easily understand what each word refers to.

No   Comets usually fly by the earth at 100,000 mph, whereas asteroids sometimes collide with the earth. **This** interests scientists. [Does *this* refer to the speed of the comets, to comets flying by the earth, or to asteroids colliding with the earth?]

YES   Comets usually fly by the earth at 100,000 mph, whereas asteroids sometimes collide with the earth. **This difference** interests scientists. [Adding a noun after *this* or *that* clarifies the meaning.]

No   I told my friends I was going to major in geology, **which** made my parents happy. [Does *which* refer to telling your friends or to majoring in geology?]

YES   My parents were happy **because I discussed my major with my friends**.

YES   My parents were happy **because I chose to major in geology**.

Also, the title of any piece of writing stands on its own. Therefore, in your introductory paragraph, never refer to your title with *this* or *that*. For example, if an essay's title is "Geophysics as a Major," the following holds for the first sentence:

No   **This subject** unites the sciences of physics, biology, and paleontology.

YES   **Geophysics** unites the sciences of physics, biology, and paleontology.

8p How do I use *they* and *it* precisely?

The expression *they say* cannot take the place of stating precisely who is doing the saying. Your credibility as a writer depends on your mentioning a source precisely.

No   **They say** that earthquakes are becoming more frequent. [*They* doesn't identify the authority who made the statement.]

Yes   **Seismologists** say that earthquakes are becoming more frequent.

The expressions *it said* and *it is said that* reflect imprecise thinking. Also, they're wordy. Revising such expressions improves your writing.

No   **It said** in the newspaper that California has minor earthquakes almost daily. [*It is said in the newspaper that* is wordy.]

Yes   **The newspaper reported** that California has minor earthquakes almost daily.

8q How do I use *it* to suit the situation?

The word *it* has three different uses in English. Here are examples of correct uses of *it*.

1. PERSONAL PRONOUN: Ryan wants to visit the 18-inch Schmidt telescope, but **it** is on Mount Palomar.
2. EXPLETIVE (sometimes called a *subject filler*, it delays the subject): **It** is interesting to observe the stars.
3. IDIOMATIC EXPRESSION (words that depart from normal use, such as using *it* as the sentence subject when writing about weather, time, distance, and environmental conditions): **It** is sunny. **It** is midnight. **It** is not far to the hotel. **It** is very hilly.

All three uses above are correct, but avoid combining them in the same sentence. The result can be an unclear and confusing sentence.

No   Because our car was overheating, **it** came as no surprise that **it** broke down just as **it** began to rain. [*It* is overused here, even though all three uses—2, 1, and 3 on the above list, respectively—are acceptable.]

Yes   **It** came as no surprise that our overheating car broke down just as the rain began. [The word order is revised so that *it* is used once.]

8r When should I use *you* for direct address?

Reserve *you* for **direct address**, writing that addresses the reader directly. For example, I use *you* in this handbook to address you, the student. *You* is not a suitable substitute for specific words that refer to people, situations, or occurrences.

No   Prison uprisings often happen **when you allow** overcrowding. [The reader, *you*, did not allow the overcrowding.]

Yes   Prison uprisings often happen **when prisons are** overcrowded.

No   In Russia, **you** usually have to stand in long lines to buy groceries. [Are *you*, the reader, planning to do your grocery shopping in Russia?]

Yes   **Russian consumers** usually have to stand in long lines to buy groceries.

8s When should I use *that*, *which*, and *who*?

To use the pronouns *that* and *which* correctly, you want to check the context of the sentence you're writing. *Which* and *that* refer to animals and things. Only sometimes do they refer to anonymous or collective groups of people. This box shows how to choose between that and which.

CHOOSING BETWEEN *THAT* AND *WHICH*

Choice: Some instructors and style guides use either *that* or *which* to introduce a **restrictive clause** (**a dependent clause** that is essential to the meaning of the sentence or part of the sentence). Others may advise you to use only *that* so that your writing distinguishes clearly between restrictive and nonrestrictive clauses. Whichever style you sue, be consistent in each piece of writing.

The zoos **that** (or **which**) *most children like* display newborn and baby animals. [The point in this sentence concerns children's preferences. Therefore, the words *most children like* are essential for delivering the meaning and make up a restrictive clause.]

No choice: You are required to use *which* to introduce a nonrestrictive clause (a dependent clause that isn't essential to the meaning of the sentence or part of the sentence).

Zoos, **which most children like**, attract more visitors if they display newborn and baby animals. [The point in this sentence concerns attracting more visitors to zoos. Therefore, the words *most children like* are not essential to the meaning of the sentence and make up a nonrestrictive clause.]

Who refers to people and to animals mentioned by name.

John Polany, who was awarded the Nobel Prize in chemistry, speaks passionately in favor of nuclear disarmament. [*John Polany* is a person.]

Lassie, who was known for her intelligence and courage, was actually played by a series of male collies. [*Lassie* is the name of an animal.]

Many professional writers reserve *which* for nonrestrictive clauses and *that* for restrictive clauses. Other writers have begun to use *that* and *which* interchangeably. Current practice allows the use of either as long as you're consistent in each piece of writing. However, for academic writing, your instructor might expect you to maintain the distinction.

ALERT: Use commas before and after a nonrestrictive clause. Don't use commas before and after a restrictive clause.

Knowing the Personal Pronouns

The personal pronouns change form to show whether they are being used as subjects, objects, or possessives and to match the person and number of their antecedents. Fill in this chart with the appropriate forms of the personal pronouns. Then check yourself by looking at the chart at the beginning of this chapter.

Person	Subject Case	Objective Case	Possessive Case
Singular	_____	_____	_____
First	_____	_____	_____
Second	_____	_____	_____
Third	_____	_____	_____
Plural	_____	_____	_____
First	_____	_____	_____
Second	_____	_____	_____
Third	_____	_____	_____

Identifying Pronoun Case

Underline the personal pronouns. Then on the lines to the right indicate their cases.

EXAMPLE <u>I</u> recently read an article about <u>my</u> least favorite animal.   _____subjective_____   _____possessive_____

1. Just thinking about cockroaches makes me uncomfortable.   _____   _____

2. How do they affect you?   _____   _____

3. The author of the article says that the cockroach is his enemy.   _____   _____

4. He is a pest-control specialist.   _____   _____

5. According to him, cockroaches have been around since before the dinosaurs.   _____   _____

6. Roaches have lasted this long because their bodies are perfect for what they do.   _____   _____

7. They can eat almost anything and can survive on very little.   _____   _____

8. A dozen of them can live for a week on the glue of one postage stamp.   _____   _____

9. One variety can live for a month without food as long as it has water.   _____   _____

10. They reproduce very quickly, 100,000 offspring a year from a single pair.   _____   _____

11. A scientist who has spent ten years studying roaches says each one has its own personality.   _____   _____

12. She learned this by studying their nighttime behavior.   _____   _____

13. Research shows that they learn from experience and change their behavior to escape danger.   _____   _____

14. No place is free from them—even submarines.   _____   _____

15. One roach destroyed a $975,000   _____   _____
    computer by getting inside and
    eating its wires.

16. Roaches can also harm us because   _____   _____
    they may carry dangerous bacteria.

17. Our best defense against roaches   _____   _____
    may be new chemicals that stop
    them from reproducing.

18. In the meantime, we may have to   _____   _____
    continue sharing our planet with them.

Using Personal Pronouns   EXERCISE 8-3

Select the correct pronoun from the choice in parentheses. Write your answers on the lines to the right. If two choices are needed, use a comma to separate them on the answer line.

EXAMPLE   My friend and (I, me) visited Washington, D.C.,   _____ I _____
           last spring.

1. Other tourists and (we, us) were delighted   _____
    by what (we, us) saw.

2. (It, Its) is a beautiful city.   _____

3. By the end of the week, each of (us, ours)   _____
    had a favorite place.

4. My little brother was impressed by what (he, his) saw at the   _____
    Bureau of Engraving and Printing.

5. (He, Him) and (I, me) took a tour of the Bureau.   _____

6. We could not believe (our, ours) eyes when we saw   _____
    people actually making money.

7. As (I, me) and (he, him) watched people printing paper money,   _____
    my brother said it was a great job because the people
    could keep some money for (them, themselves).

8. I told (he, him) that he was kidding (him, himself) if   _____
    he really believed that.

9. Employees have security people watching   _____
    (them, themselves) and the money (it, itself) is counted
    and recounted to prevent theft.

10. I wondered if (them, their) working around money all day might _____
    make money less exciting to these people after a while.

11. Still, it was fascinating for (we, us) to watch all that _____
    money being printed.

12. The Lincoln Memorial was (me, my) favorite place. _____

13. The Memorial is a simple statue of Abraham Lincoln _____
    (hisself, himself), seated looking out over the capital.

14. Standing near that huge statue made my sister
    and (I, me) feel very calm, as if Lincoln were
    watching out for (us, ourselves). _____

15. My sister said that the most exciting place for _____
    (she, her) was the National Air and Space Museum.

16. This is probably because of (her, hers) _____
    desire to be an astronaut.

17. If (you, yous) go to Washington, D.C., visit the _____
    National Air and Space Museum even if (you, your)
    are not planning to be a pilot or an astronaut.

18. Children will especially enjoy the chance the Museum _____
    gives (they, them) to see and sometimes touch
    famous old airplanes.

19. While there, they can also see for _____
    (theirselfs, themselves) copies of space vehicles.

20. Now that I have told you about my family's favorite places in _____
    Washington, D.C., will you tell me about (your, yours)?

Identifying and Using Personal Pronouns as Appositives and Complements

A: Underline all personal pronouns used as appositives or complements. Then draw an arrow connecting each to its antecedent. Be prepared to explain why each pronoun takes the case it does.

EXAMPLE The winner of the talent contest is _I_.

1. The comediens, he and she, have been together for years.

2. A comic legend in his own time is he.

3. The judges selected the best comedy act, ours.

4. The first ones in the audience to laugh were they.

5. The job offer reached the comedian, me, the same day.

B: Select the correct pronoun for formal situations from the choices in parentheses. Write your answers on the lines to the right.

EXAMPLE The smartest couple, you and (I, me) _____   _____/_____
will appear on TV.

1. If anyone deserves a job, it is (she, her) _____   _____

2. Our agent has booked a grueling nightclub tour for us,   _____
just you and (I, me) _____.

3. The winner of the standup comic award was (he, him) _____ _____

4. I saw the actors, (he, him) _____ and his brother.   _____

5. Comediens, (I, me) _____ for one, sometimes get the lead
parts in films.   _____

Using who, whoever, whom, *and* whomever

Select the correct relative or interrogative pronoun (*who, whom, whoever,* or *whomever*) from the choices in parentheses. Write your answers on the lines to the right.

EXAMPLE   The number of children (who, whom) are in a family   *who*
           may affect the intelligence of all the children.

1. Researchers (who, whom) studied over 350,000 men   _____
   in the 1940s found that IQ fell as family size increased.

2. Children (who, whom) were born into a family later   _____
   tended to have lower IQs.

3. Recent research supports the theory that (whoever,   _____
   whomever) is born first has an advantage.

4. Children (who, whom) researchers checked for IQ and   _____
   school performance did better if they were the oldest
   in small families.

5. (Whoever, Whomever) was an only child, however,   _____
   scored like a younger child.

6. (Who, Whom) can be sure why these trends occur?   _____

7. It may be that younger children receive less mental   _____
   stimulation because their brothers and sisters (who, whom)
   teach them are immature.

8. Only children, (who, whom) are usually considered lucky,   _____
   may miss out because they never have a chance to grow
   by teaching their own younger brothers and sisters.

9. Perhaps parents' attention, no matter to (who, whom) it is   _____
   given, is limited, so there is simply more of it per child
   in smaller families.

10. Of course, there are highly intelligent and successful   _____
    people (who, whom) are born into large families.

11. Teachers and parents of young children should be   _____
    careful about (who, whom) they make judgments.

12. We cannot use these studies to predict the future of   _____
    (whoever, whomever) we please, because in the end success
    depends on a lot more than birth order and family size.

13. Few successful people (who, whom) have been asked   _____
    the secret of their success talk about birth order.

14. Often, successful people give credit to their drive to achieve something and to the people (who, whom) supported them.   _____

15. For example, listen to the speeches at any awards ceremony and you will hear people thanking the parents, teachers, and friends without (who, whom) they could not have succeeded.   _____

16. (Who, Whom) would you thank if you were giving such a speech?   _____

Choosing Pronoun Cases Carefully   EXERCISE 8-6

Select the correct pronoun from the choices in parentheses. Write your answers on the lines to the right.

EXAMPLE   J. Edgar Hoover changed the way FBI agents worked from the moment he was appointed to lead (they, them) in 1924.   *them*

1. After he proved (him, himself) as a special assistant to the U.S. Attorney General, Hoover was named director of the Bureau of Investigation.   _____

2. The government wanted (he, him) to reorganize the Bureau, which had been filled with scandal.   _____

3. As head of the Bureau, Hoover set new standards for (it, its) recruiting and training of agents.   _____

4. Some nations were reorganizing their police files to keep better track of criminals; Hoover established a fingerprint file that was bigger than any of (them, theirs).   _____

5. He set up a scientific crime lab to help (he, him) and his agents analyze evidence.   _____

6. One of his greatest contributions was (him, his) opening of the FBI National Academy, to which law officers from all over the country are still sent for training.   _____

7. In those early years, the FBI concentrated on fighting organized crime, but to many people the gangsters (they, themselves) were romantic figures.   _____

8. Hoover responded by setting up a publicity campaign
    for the agents to make (they, them) glamorous in the
    public's eyes.

    _____

9. (Him, His) heading the FBI made Hoover a world figure.

    _____

10. People, in comparing his agency to other crime-fighting
    units, said the others were not as free of political control
    as (he, his) was.

    _____

11. Unfortunately, in his later years as director, he and the
    Bureau (it, itself) came under attack for suspicious actions.

    _____

12. Some even said that presidents agreed to keep (he, him)
    in power because of the files he had on them.

    _____

13. However, these charges against Hoover were not proven,
    and (him, his) dying in office in 1972 closed a long
    and eventful career.

    _____

14. Several people have served as FBI directors since
    Hoover's death, but none has been as powerful as (he, him).

    _____

15. The FBI continues to protect (we, us) Americans, but in
    a less dramatic way than when Hoover was its leader.

    _____

Using Pronouns to Refer to a Single Nearby Antecedent

Underline the pronouns in these passages. Then, if the antecedents are clear and close enough to their pronouns, copy the sentences onto the lines. If the antecedents are unclear or too far away, use the lines to revise the sentences.

EXAMPLE   Henry C. Wallace and <u>his</u> son Henry A. Wallace held the same cabinet post. <u>He</u> was the Secretary of Agriculture under Harding and Coolidge, and <u>he</u> was Secretary of Agriculture under Franklin Roosevelt. *Henry C. Wallace and his son Henry A. Wallace held the same cabinet post. Henry C. Wallace was the Secretary of Agriculture under Harding and Coolidge, and Henry A. Wallace was the Secretary of Agriculture under Franklin Roosevelt.*

1. House of Representative and Senate members work with young people called pages. They run errands for them.

   _____

   _____

   _____

2. The longest filibuster in the U.S. Senate was delivered by Senator Wayne Morse of Oregon. However, Texas State Senator Mike McKool spoke far longer. He spoke for 42 hours and 33 minutes.

   _____

   _____

   _____

3. For religious reasons, Zachary Taylor refused to take the presidential oath of office on a Sunday, so David Rice Atchison (president of the Senate) was president for a day. He spent the day appointing his temporary cabinet.

   _____

   _____

   _____

4. Calvin Coolidge was sworn into office by his own father.

   _____

5. An American Indian, Charles Curtis, became vice president when Herbert Hoover was elected president in 1928. He was one-half Kaw.

   _____

   _____

6. William DeVance King, vice president under Franklin Pierce, was in Cuba during the election and had to be sworn in by an act of Congress, never bothering to return to Washington. A month later, never having carried out any official duties, he died.

_____

_____

_____

7. The Republicans got their elephant and the Democrats got their donkey as symbols from political cartoonist Thomas Nast.

_____

_____

8. The first woman presidential candidate was Victoria Woodhull. Years before Geraldine Ferraro ran for vice president, she was on the Equal Rights Party ticket— in 1872.

_____

_____

9. President Grover Cleveland installed the first telephone in the White House in the late 1880s. Whenever it rang, he answered it himself.

_____

_____

10. As a child, president-to-be Andrew Johnson was sold as an indentured servant to a tailor. He was supposed to work for seven years, but he ran away.

_____

_____

11. President William McKinley had a pet parrot. Whenever he whistled the beginning of "Yankee Doodle," it would complete it.

_____

_____

Using Pronouns to Refer to
Definite Antecedents

Revise these vague passages so that all pronouns have definite antecedents. Be alert for implied antecedents and the misuse of *it, they,* and *you.*

EXAMPLE   Researchers say that ordinary people could soon be living and working aboard space stations. They are unusual but quite safe. *Researchers say that ordinary people could soon be living and working aboard space stations. The stations are unusual but quite safe.*

1.   A California company called the Space Island Group is planning to recycle one of the shortest-lived components of the space shuttle. It is ingenious.

_____

_____

2.   Engineers at SIG plan to construct dozens of wheel-shaped space stations using empty shuttle fuel tanks. They are eminently suited to the task.

_____

_____

3.   A shuttle's fuel tanks are huge. Each one is 28 feet in diameter and nearly 160 feet long – approximately the size of a jumbo jet. It jettisons them just before it reaches orbit, leaving them to burn up and crash into the ocean.

_____

_____

4.   Over 100 of these tanks, known as ETs, have been used and destroyed since the first shuttle launch in 1981. So you can see how much hardware has gone to waste.

_____

_____

5.   Using ETs to form manned space stations – and developing passenger shuttles to take people to them – was originally NASA's idea. At first, they were enthusiastic about this possibility.

_____

_____

6.   However, it would have taken too long for NASA to develop and test passenger shuttles, so it was dropped.

_____

_____

7. SIG's plan is to build the passenger shuttles and lease them to commercial airlines. They believe that this is the fastest way to get ordinary people into space.

    _____

    _____

8. The space stations will also be leased – at a rate of $10-$20 per cubic foot per day – to anyone wishing to run a business in space. You simply take the shuttle, transfer to the space station, and set up your office.

    _____

    _____

9. While the space stations have a projected life of 30 years, they claim that tenants would fully pay for them within 2-3 years. This means that the passenger shuttle program could actually operate at a profit.

    _____

    _____

Revising to Eliminate Misuse of you   EXERCISE 8-9

Revise this paragraph to eliminate the inappropriate use of *you*, Begin by changing "You have to be careful" to "Everyone has to be careful." Then change further uses of *you* to suitable nouns or pronouns. It may be necessary to change some verbs in order to have them agree with new subjects.

You have to be careful when buying on credit. Otherwise, you may wind up so heavily in debt that it will take years to straighten out your life. Credit cards are easy for you to get if you are working, and many finance companies are eager to give you installment loans at high interest rates. Once you are hooked, you may find yourself taking out loans to pay your loans. When this happens, you are doomed to being forever in debt.

There are, of course, times when using credit makes sense. If you have the money (or will have it when the bill comes), a credit card can enable you to shop without carrying cash. You may also want to keep a few gasoline credit cards with you in case your car breaks down on the road. Using credit will allow you to deal with other emergencies (tuition, a broken water heater) when you lack the cash. You can also use credit to take advantage of sales. However, you need to recognize the difference between a sale item you need and one you want. If you cannot do this, you may find yourself dealing with collection agents, car repossessors, or even bankruptcy lawyers.

MODULE 9: AGREEMENT

9a What is agreement?

Agreement means you need to match SUBJECTS and VERBS, and you also need to match PRONOUNS and ANTECEDENTS. For example, when you start a new paragraph in a piece of writing, be cautious about beginning it with a pronoun whose antecedent is in a prior paragraph. You're better off repeating the name.

9b What is subject-verb agreement?

Subject-verb agreement occurs at least once per sentence. To function correctly, subjects and verbs must match in number (singular or plural) and in person (first, second, or third).

The human **brain weighs** about three pounds. [brain = singular subject in the third person; weighs = singular verb in the third person]

Human **brains weigh** about three pounds. [brains = plural subject in the third person; weigh = plural verb in the third person]

A QUICK REVIEW OF PERSON FOR AGREEMENT

The **first person** is the speaker or writer. _I_ (singular) and _we_ (plural) are the only subjects that occur in the first person.

Singular	_I_ see a field of fireflies.
Plural	_We_ see a field of fireflies.

The **second person** is the person spoken or written to. _You_ (both singular and plural) is the only subject that occurs in the second person.

Singular	_You_ see a shower of sparks.
Plural	_You_ see a shower of sparks.

The **third person** is the person or thing being spoken or written of. Most rules for subject-verb agreement involve the third person. A subject in the third person can vary widely—for example, _student_ and _students_ (singular and plural people), _table_ and _tables_ (singular and plural things), and _it_ and _they_ (singular and plural pronouns).

Singular	The **scientist sees** a cloud of cosmic dust. **She (he, it) sees** a cloud of cosmic dust.
Plural	The **scientists see** a cloud of cosmic dust. **They see** a cloud of cosmic dust.

9c Why is the final -*s* or -*es* in a subject or verb so important?

Subject-verb agreement often involves one letter: *s*. The key is the difference between the -*s* added to subjects and the -*s* added to verbs.

Plural subjects are usually formed by adding -*s* or -*es* to singular nouns.

Singular verbs in the present tense of the third person are formed by adding -*s* or -*es* to the simple form—with the exceptions of *be* (*is*) and *have* (*has*).

Visualizing how the *s* works in agreement can help you remember when it is needed. The -*s* (or -*es* when the word already ends in -*s*) can take only one path at a time, either the top or the bottom, as in this diagram.

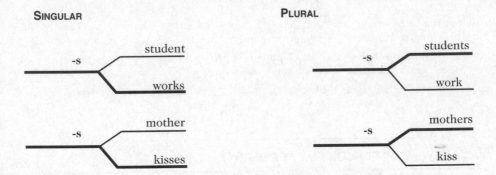

Even though the final -*s* does not appear in some subjects, the principle of the memory device holds. This final -*s* does not appear in the following situations: in subjects that are plural without an -*s* (such as *people, children*); in plural personal pronouns (*we, you, they*); in the plural demonstrative pronouns (*these, those*); and in certain indefinite pronouns when they are used as plurals (*few, some, more, many, most, all*).

A **person** on a diet often **misses** sweets.

People enjoy candy or cake after meals.

They learn to substitute fruit for pastry.

❖ **USAGE ALERT:** Do not add -*s* to the third-person singular main verb after a modal auxiliary verb (a helping verb such as *can, might, must, would*). ❖

9d Can I ignore words between a subject and its verb?

Words that separate the subject from the verb can cause confusion about what the verb should agree with. To locate the subject of the sentence, ignore prepositional phrases or phrases that start with *including, together with, along with, accompanied by, in addition to, except,* or *as well as.*

The best **workers** in the bookkeeping department **have** received raises.

The top-selling sales **representative**, along with her husband, **is going** to visit San Diego as a bonus.

9e How do verbs work when subjects are connected by *and*?

When two or more subjects are joined by *and*, they function as a group; therefore, they need a plural verb.

Soda and iced tea are popular summer drinks.

My friend and I prefer cold milk

However, if the word *each* or *every* precedes objects joined by *and*, use a singular verb.

Each cat and dog in the animal shelter **deserves** a home.

When *each* or *every* follows subjects joined by *and,* however, it does not affect the basic rule: use a plural verb for subjects joined by *and*:

The ASPCA and the Humane Society each **need** our support.

The one exception to the *and* rule occurs when the parts combine to form a single thing or person.

Beans and rice is a popular vegetarian dish.

My husband and business partner keeps our tax records.

9f How do verbs work with *each* and *every*?

The words *each* and *every* are singular even if they refer to a compound subject. Therefore, they take a singular verb.

Each **human hand and foot** *makes* [not *make*] a distinctive print.

To identify lawbreakers, *every* **police chief, sheriff, and federal marshal** *depends* [not *depend*] on such prints.

ALERT: Use one word, either *each* or *every*, not both at the same time. *Each* (not *Each and every*) *robber has been caught.*

9g How do verbs work when subjects are connected by *or*?

When you join subjects with *or* or *nor* or correlative conjunctions, *either . . . or, neither . . . nor, not only . . . but (also)*, make the verb agree with the subject closest to it. Unlike *and*, these conjunctions do not create plurals. For the purpose of agreement, ignore everything before the final subject.

~~Neither Benny Goodman nor~~ **Louis Armstrong is** heard on the radio often.

~~Either the Andrews Sisters or~~ **Frank Sinatra was** my mother's favorite singer.

9h How do verbs work with inverted word order?

In questions, the verb comes before the subject. Be sure to look ahead to check that the subject and verb agree.

Is jazz popular?

Expletive constructions postpone the subject by using *there* or *here* plus a form of the verb *be*. Check ahead in such sentences to identify the subject, and make the form of *be* agree with the subject.

There were many **bands** that played swing in the forties.

There is still a dedicated **audience** for this music.

Introductory *it* plus a form of the verb *be* can be an expletive construction as well, but one that always takes a singular verb.

It is young musicians who strive to capture the sound of the Big Bands.

9i How do verbs work with indefinite pronouns?

Indefinite pronouns do not refer to any particular person, thing, or idea. They take their meanings from context. Indefinite pronouns are usually singular, and therefore they take singular verbs. Here is a list of singular indefinite pronouns:

each	everyone	no one
every	everybody	nobody
one	everything	nothing
either	anyone	someone
neither	anybody	somebody
another	anything	something

Everybody talks about the weather, but **no one does** a thing about it.

No matter what **someone forecasts, something** different **seems** to happen.

Two indefinite pronouns, *both* and *many*, are always plural and require a plural verb.

Both of them **accept** the decision.

A few indefinite pronouns—*none, some, more, most, any,* and *all*—may be either singular or plural, depending on the meaning of the sentence.

All of the weather forecasts we hear **are** based on probabilities.

We hate bad weather, but **some is** inevitable.

9j How do verbs work with collective nouns?

A **collective noun** names a group of people or things: *family, group, audience, class, number, committee, team*. When the group acts as one unit, use a singular verb. When the members of the group act individually, use a plural verb.

The **jury is** hearing evidence. [*Jury* refers to a single unit, so the verb is singular.]

The **jury disagree** on a verdict. [The jury members take separate action, so the verb is plural.]

9k Why does the linking verb agree with the subject, not the subject complement?

Even when the **subject complement** that follows a linking verb differs in number (singular and plural) from the subject, the verb must agree with the subject.

The best **part** of the week **is** Saturday and Sunday.

but

Saturday and Sunday are the best part of the week.

9l What verbs agree with *who, which,* and *that*?

Who, which, and *that* have the same form in singular and plural, so you must find their antecedents before you can decide whether the verb is singular or plural.

The **tenants who move** into this apartment will need to paint it. [*Who* refers to *tenants*, so the verb *move* is plural.]

The **tenant who moves** into this apartment will need to paint it. [*Who* refers to *tenant*, so the verb *moves* is singular.]

Be especially careful to identify the antecedent of *who, which,* or *that* when you see *one of the* or *the only one of the* in a sentence.

George Boyd is one of the **tenants who want** to hire a new janitor. [*Who* refers to *tenants*, so *want* is plural.]

George Boyd is the only **one** of the tenants **who wants** to hire a new janitor. [*Who* refers to *one*, so *wants* is singular.]

9m How do verbs work with amounts, fields of study, and other special nouns?

Subjects that refer to times, sums of money, distance, or measurement are considered singular and take singular verbs.

Seventy-five cents is the toll over the bridge.

One and six-tenths kilometers makes a mile.

Many words that end in -s or -ics are singular in meaning despite their plural appearance. These include *news, ethics, economics, mathematics, physics, politics, sports, statistics* (as a course of study).

Mathematics is necessary for many daily tasks.

Athletics demands total commitment.

In contrast, other words are plural even though they refer to one thing. These include *jeans, pants, scissors, clippers, tweezers, eyeglasses, thanks, riches.*

The **scissors are** on the desk

9n How do verbs work with titles, company names, and words as themselves?

Arm and Hammer is a popular brand of baking soda.

Cats, the musical, is based on a book of poems by T. S. Eliot.

9o What is pronoun-antecedent agreement?

The form of most pronouns depends on what their **antecedents** are, so the connection between a pronoun and its antecedent must be clear. These connections are reflected by agreement in number (singular or plural), person (first, second, or third), and gender (male or female).

Singular pronouns must refer to singular antecedents, and plural pronouns must refer to plural antecedents.

The **ocean** has **its** own plant and animal life.

The **oceans** have **their** own plant and animal life.

First-person pronouns must refer to first-person antecedents, second-person pronouns to second-person antecedents, and third-person pronouns to third-person antecedents.

Beginning **divers** have to watch **their** [third person: not *your*] instructors for directions.

9p How do pronouns work when *and* connects antecedents?

Two or more antecedents joined by *and* require a plural pronoun, even if each antecedent by itself is singular.

Miami and San Francisco are centers of ocean exploration because of **their** coastal locations.

When *each* or *every* precedes singular nouns joined by *and*, use a singular pronoun.

Each scuba diver and sailor hopes to locate a sunken treasure for **herself** or **himself**.

Also when the singular nouns joined by *and* refer to the same person or thing, use a singular pronoun.

Our **captain and diving instructor** warned us to stay near **her**.

9q How do pronouns work when *or* connects antecedents?

When ANTECEDENTS are joined by *or* or by CORRELATIVE CONJUNCTIONS such as *either...or, neither ... nor,* or *not only ... but (also)* the antecedents might mix singulars and plurals. For the purposes of agreement, ignore everything before the final antecedent

~~After the restaurant closes, *either* the resident mice~~ *or* the owner's cat gets **itself** a meal.

~~After the restaurant closes, *either* the owner's cat~~ *or* the resident mice get **themselves** a meal.

9r How do pronouns work when antecedents are indefinite pronouns?

Indefinite pronouns are usually singular. When they are, the pronouns that refer to them should also be singular.

Everyone should know **his or her** Social Security number.

No one can be expected to know **his or her** driver's license number.

9s How do use nonsexist pronouns?

Until about twenty-five years ago the masculine pronoun was used to refer to indefinite pronouns as well as to nouns and pronouns that name general categories to which any person might belong: *Everyone should admit his mistakes.* Today people are more conscious that *he, his, him,* and *himself* exclude women. Many writers try to avoid using masculine pronouns to refer to the entire population.

HOW TO AVOID USING ONLY THE MASCULINE PRONOUN TO REFER TO MALES AND FEMALES TOGETHER

Solution 1   Use a pair—but try to avoid a pair more than once in a sentence or in many sentences in a row.

Everyone hopes that **he or she** will win the scholarship.

A successful doctor knows that **he or she** has to work long hours.

Solution 2   Revise into the plural.

Many people hope that **they** will win the scholarship.

Successful doctors know that **they** have to work long hours.

Solution 3   Recast the sentence.

Everyone hopes to win the scholarship.

Successful doctors should expect to work long hours.

Some indefinite pronouns can be either singular or plural, depending on the meaning of the sentence. When the indefinite pronoun is plural, then the pronouns that refer back to it should be plural.

Many students do not realize they have a talent for mathematics. **Some** have learned this attitude from **their** parents.

9t How do pronouns work when antecedents are collective nouns?

A **collective noun** names a group of people or things: *family, group, audience, class, number, committee, team,* and the like. When the group acts as one unit, use a singular pronoun to refer to it. When the members of the group act individually, use a plural pronoun.

The **committee** has elected **its** new chairperson. [The committee is acting as one unit, so the pronoun is singular.]

The **committee** expressed **their** opinions about the election campaign. [The *committee* is acting as individuals, so the pronoun is plural.]

Making Subjects and Verbs Agree   EXERCISE 9-1

A: Fill in the blanks on the right with the present-tense forms of the verbs in parentheses. Be sure each verb agrees in person and number with the subject of the sentence.

EXAMPLE   The Cuna Indians (to produce) an unusual kind   _produce_
of art.

1. Cuna Indians (to occupy) the San Blas Islands off the coast of   _____
Panama.

2. The outside world (to associate) them with distinctive women's   _____
clothing.

3. Cuna women (to wear) blouses containing two panels of   _____
appliqued cloth.

4. The Cuna word *mola* (to refer) to either a blouse or one   _____
of its panels.

5. The Cuna (to work) their molas in reverse applique.   _____

6. Traditional applique (to consist) of turning under edges   _____
of a piece of fabric and sewing it onto a larger piece.

7. Molas (to use) a different technique.   _____

8. A Cuna woman (to baste) together several layers of cloth of   _____
different colors.

9. She then (to cut) through all but the bottom layer.   _____

10. When turned under, the upper layers (to reveal)   _____
contrasting colors.

B: Fill in the blanks on the right with the appropriate present-tense forms of the verbs in parentheses.

EXAMPLE   Most resources of the earth (to be) not renewable.   _are_

1. Neither coffee grounds nor an apple core (to need) to be   _____
thrown out.

2. Food waste, along with grass clippings, (to make) good   _____
compost.

3. Many items from your garbage (to be) recyclable.   _____

4. Aluminum cans, plastic jugs, and glass bottles (to   _____
deserve) a second life.

5. One of the most tedious jobs (to seem) to be sorting garbage.   _____

6. Yet rewards from such work (to be) immeasurable.   _____

7. Every recycled bottle and can (to mean) a saving of resources. _____

8. Not only an adult but also a child (to be) capable of helping the environment. _____

9. Learning what to recycle, as well as being willing to do it, (to become) necessary. _____

10. You and I each (to be) expected to do our part. _____

C: Circle the subjects and underline the verbs. If the verb does not agree with the subject, cross it out and write the correct form on the line to the right. If the verb does agree, write *correct* on the line.

EXAMPLE   ~~Has~~ you and your family ever, visited the Everglades?   *Have*

1. There are only one place like the Everglades in the entire world. _____

2. The regioun called the Everglades are actually a river. _____

3. There is other names for the Everglades. _____

4. The Native American name Pa-hay-okee meaning grassy water reveal the Native Americans' knowledge of the unusual terrain. _____

5. There is many kinds of wildlife to see in the Everglades. _____

6. It is animals like the Floriday panther that people go to see. _____

7. However, alligators are much more commonly seen than panthers. _____

8. In the Everglades is also found numerous species of birds and fish. _____

9. Now the region of the Everglades are a national park. _____

10. Majorie Stoneman Douglas, an author, deserve a lot of credit for preserving the unique place called the Everglades. _____

D: Fill in the blanks on the right with the present-tense forms of the verbs in parentheses.

EXAMPLE   Most of Chicago's visitors (to be) impressed by its architecture.   *are*

1. The Chicago School (to be) a group of architects at the turn of the century. _____

2 Some (to be) known throughout the world. _____

3. Not everyone in the group (to be) considered a genius. _____

4. Yet all (to have) contributed to the appearance of the city. _____

5. A number of buildings (to be) considered architectural landmarks. _____

6. Many (to share) certain features like Chicago windows. _____

7. One of the most famous styles (to be) Frank Lloyd Wright's Prairie House. _____

8. A tour group visiting Chicago today (to be) sure to enjoy a drive down the Magnificent Mile. _____

9. A family often (to prefer) a walking tour. _____

10. Few (to be) exempt from the charms of a constantly building city. _____

E: Circle the antecedent of each italicized *who, which,* or *that.* Then fill in the blanks on the right with the appropriate present-tense forms of the verbs in parentheses.

EXAMPLE   The *Book of Kells* is one of many (manuscripts) *that* (to belong) to Trinity College, Dublin.   *belong*

1. Its source is a mystery *that* (to continue) to baffle scholars. _____

2. Anyone *who* (to see) it marvels at its brilliant illumination. _____

3. The book, *which* (to be) considered a masterpiece, contains full-page illustrations of the Gospels. _____

4. No one *who* (to study) the book can fail to be impressed by it. _____

5. The paintings, *which* (to be) done in minute detail, retain their vivid colors. _____

6. There is also decoration *that* (to appear) to have no relationship to the text. _____

7. Some of the pictures, *which* (to stem) from unknown origins, seem strange for a religious book. _____

8. One does not expect birds *that* (to wear) ecclesiastical garb. _____

9. Nor does one expect the humor *that* (to pervade) some of the illustrations. _____

10. The text, *which* (to be) written in beautiful script, combines two translations. _____

F: Fill in the blanks on the right with the appropriate present-tense forms of the verbs in parentheses.

EXAMPLE   Most people (to be) interested in learning more about themselves.   *are*

1. Astrology (to seem) to satisfy some people's curiosity about why they are the way they are.

2. Just twelve astrological signs (to show) all the complexities of people's personalities.

3. A friend of mine, a proponent of astrology (to argue) that there is a lot more to it than just the twelve signs.

4   People who are more scientifically inclined (to look) to the Myers-Briggs Type Indicator (MBTI) to learn more about their personalities.

5.   The founders of the MBTI (to belong) to no particular school of psychology, but their findings are similar to those of Carl Jung.

6.   The MBTI (to make) sense to most people who take the test to learn about their personality types.

7.   Numerous companies (to publish) books about personality types.

8.   A psychologist (to deal) with issues of personality in a number of ways.

9.   But the average person (to get) some useful personal insight by taking some psychological tests published in self-help books.

10. If you're curious about your personality traits, there's one way to find out about them. (To ask) a friend.

G: Fill in the blanks on the right with the appropriate present-tense forms of the verbs in parentheses.

EXAMPLE   Everyone (to dream) during sleep.   _____dreams_____

1.   No one (to know) why we (to dream).   _____

2.   Dreams (to occur) during a special kind of sleep, known
     as REM.   _____

3.   REM (to stand) for Rapid Eye Movement.   _____

4.   A total of about two hours a night (to get) spent in this
     dream state.   _____

5.   There (to be) many theories about why people dream
     and what the rapid movement of our eyeballs (to mean).   _____

6.   Some (to suggest) that REM sleep occurs when the brain
     rids itself of unnecessary images.   _____

7.   According to this theory, dreams (to represent) random signals.   _____

8.   Others (to believe) that dreaming helps the brain establish
     patterns for thinking.   _____

9.   Human newborns, they say, (to spend) about half their sleep
     time dreaming.   _____

10. The babies, who (to receive) huge amounts of new
     information very day, may be developing plans for
     processing what they see and hear.   _____

11. In contrast, the elderly (to devote) only fifteen percent of
     their sleep time to dreaming.   _____

12. Why we dream and what dreams mean (to form) a big
     mystery.   _____

13   Psychologists (to think) dreams help people deal with
     emotional issues.   _____

14. The population often (to lack) the time necessary to cope
    with complicated emotional situations.   _____

15. For example, people in the middle of divorce often (to have)
    long, detailed dreams.   _____

16. In contrast, people with peaceful lives generally (to claim)
    their dreams are dull.   _____

17. Sigmund Freud said that dreams (to protect) us from painful
    truths.   _____

18. There (to exist) a radical new theory which (to propose) that
    dreams do something entirely different.   _____

19. While awake, people (to learn) about the environment, but in
    dreams the flow of new information about the world is cut off. _____

20. Each dream (to combine) new information with information
    already in the brain, and new ways of dealing with the world
    (to be) rehearsed.   _____

Making Pronouns
and Antecedents Agree

Select a personal pronoun that agrees with the subject of each of these sentences. Write your answers on the lines to the right. Some items have more than one correct answer.

EXAMPLE   A good book never loses _____ appeal.   _____*its*_____

1.   Both dreams and books contain _____ own worlds.   _____

2.   No matter what genre people enjoy, they can find a book to suit   _____
     _____ tastes.

3.   People should take care of library books because _____   _____
     belong to everyone.

4.   Anyone who wants to annotate a book should buy _____   _____
     own copy.

5.   Remember the saying "You can't tell a book by _____   _____
     cover"?

6.   But book covers may actually tell something about the books   _____

7.   For example, the public library's copy of Dicken's   _____
     Great Expectations may be quite worn, showing
     _____ age and propularity.

8.   Then again, the covers of a friend's copy of *War and Peace* may   _____
     say more about _____ good intentions
     than about the book.

9.   And with the title *Looking Backward* on _____ cover,   _____
     you might not guess that Edward Bellamy's story takes place
     in the future.

10. The way people arrange _____ books is often surprising.   _____

11. One family I know has _____ books carefully color coded.   _____

12. Either the man or his wife had _____ way about   _____
     arranging the books by color.

13. A more suitable arrangement for other people is to arrange   _____
     _____ books by height.

14. Books have had a tremendous influence on _____   _____
     readers.

15. *Common Sense, Addressed to the Inhabitants of America* by Thomas Paine influenced many Americans to give _____ support to the American Revolution.   _____

16. President Lincoln greeted Harriet Beecher Stowe as the little woman who started the big war because of the tremendous influence of _____ book *Uncle Tom's Cabin*.   _____

17. After Rachel Carson wrote _____ book *Silent Spring*, the environmental movement began.   _____

18. An author's audience lets _____ pleasure be known by the number of books bought.   _____

19. In spite of all the distractions of modern life, books still hold an important place in _____ lives.   _____

20. Even though books are inatimate objects, many people refer to them as _____ friends.   _____

Pronoun-Antecedent Agreement

Revise each of these passages so that all pronouns agree with their antecedents in person, number, and gender. You may also have to change verbs or other words. Some sentences can be revised in more than one way. Take the time to try several, and select the version you like best.

EXAMPLE: In our society, a person's success is often defined by what they do and what they own.
In our society, a person's success is often defined by what he or she does and what he or she owns.

1. Many people assume that a person who makes a lot of money has their happiness guaranteed.

    _____
    _____

2. However a person who owns a lot of things is not necessarily as happy as they would like to be.

    _____
    _____

3. An individual who isn't able to buy much beyond life's necessities may not be happy with their life either.

    _____
    _____

4. How do most people define happiness and how can he or she achieve it?

    _____
    _____

5. The answer is that everyone has their own idea of what makes them happy.

    _____
    _____

6. Therefore, each individual should take time to reflect on what makes them happy.

    _____
    _____

7. One of the oldest and wisest sayings is "Know yourself." That is the only way to know what makes him or her happy.

    _____
    _____

8. It's also important to understand that no matter how much somebody may care for you, they are not responsible for your happiness. You are responsible for your own happiness.

    _____
    _____

9. To be happy, it seems that most people need more than just life's necessities, but he or she does not need nearly as much as he or she may think.

    _____
    _____

MODULE 10: ADJECTIVES AND ADVERBS

10a What are the differences between adjectives and adverbs?

Both **adjectives** and **adverbs** are **modifiers**—words or groups of words that describe other words. Because adjectives and adverbs function similarly in sentences, distinguishing between them is sometimes difficult.

Adjective   The **quick** messenger delivered the payroll.

Adverb   The messenger **quickly** delivered the payroll.

The key to distinguishing between adjectives and adverbs is that they modify different types of words or groups of words.

SUMMARY OF DIFFERENCES BETWEEN ADJECTIVES AND ADVERBS	
WHAT ADJECTIVES MODIFY	**EXAMPLE**
nouns	The **busy** *lawyer* rested.
pronouns	*She* felt **triumphant**.
WHAT ADVERBS MODIFY	**EXAMPLE**
verbs	The lawyer *spoke* **quickly**.
adverbs	The lawyer spoke **very** *quickly*.
adjectives	The lawyer was **extremely** *busy*.
independent clauses	**Therefore**, *the lawyer rested*.

Adjectives and adverbs are sometimes confused because of the *-ly* ending. In many cases, an adverb is formed by adding *-ly* to an adjective: *soft, softly; grand, grandly; beautiful; beautifully*. However, even though many adverbs end in *-ly*, some do not: *well, very, worse*. Also some words that end in *-ly* are adjectives: *lively, friendly*. The *-ly* ending, therefore, is not a foolproof way to identify adverbs.

To determine whether an adjective or an adverb is called for, see how the word functions in its sentence. If a noun or pronoun is being modified, use an adjective. If a verb, adjective, or other adverb is being modified, use an adverb.

10b When should I use adverbs—not adjectives— as modifiers?

Only adverbs modify verbs. You should avoid the nonstandard use of adjectives in the place of adverbs.

No	It snowed **heavy** last night. [Adjective *heavy* cannot modify verb *snowed*.]
Yes	It snowed **heavily** last night. [Adverb *heavily* modifies the verb *snowed*.]

Good—well: The words *good* and *well* can be confusing. As an adjective, *good* can modify nouns or noun substitutes.

The **good** news spread. [Adjective *good* modifies noun *news*.]

The reopened factory would be **good** for the town. [Adjective *good* modifies noun phrase the *reopened* factory.]

Good cannot modify verbs. Only *well*, an adverb, can modify verbs.

No	The project started off **good**. [Adjective *good* cannot modify verb started *off*.]
Yes	The project started off **well**. [Adverb *well* modifies verb started *off*.]
Yes	The **good** project started off **well**.

One exception exists: *well* is used as an adjective to describe conditions of health.

I don't feel **well**.

The patient is **well**.

Only adverbs modify adjectives and other adverbs.

No	This is a **true fattening** dessert. [Adjective *true* cannot modify adjective *fattening*.]
Yes	This is a **truly fattening** dessert. [Adverb *truly* modifies adjective *fattening*.]

10c What is wrong with double negatives?

A **double negative** is a statement that contains two negative modifiers. Negative modifiers include *no, never, not, none, nothing, hardly, scarcely,* and *barely*. They should not occur in the same sentence.

No	Some people do **not** have **no** pity for the needy.
Yes	Some people do **not** have any pity for the needy.
No	They **never** donate **no** food.
Yes	They **never** donate food.
No	She could **not hardly** pay the rent.
Yes	She could **hardly** pay the rent.

10d Do adjectives or adverbs come after linking verbs?

Linking verbs indicate a state of being or a condition. They serve to connect the subject to a word that renames or describes it. If the subject is being described after a linking verb, an adjective is needed. If, however, the verb is being described, an adverb is needed.

The bee was **angry**. [Adjective *angry* describes the subject *bee* after linking verb *was*.]

The bee attacked **angrily**. [Adverb *angrily* describes the action verb *attacked*.]

Bad—badly: The words *bad* (adjective) and *badly* (adverb) are often misused with linking verbs, especially verbs related to the senses, such as *feel.* Only the adjectives *bad* or *good* are correct when a verb is operating as a linking verb.

FOR DESCRIBING A FEELING	The coach felt **bad**. [not *badly*]
FOR DESCRIBING A SMELL	The locker room smelled **bad**. [not *badly*]
FOR DESCRIBING A SOUND	The half-time band sounded **good**. [not *well*]

10e What are comparative and superlative forms?

By using special forms of adjectives and adverbs, you can make comparisons. Most adjectives and adverbs show degrees of comparison by means of *-er* and *-est* endings or by being combined with the words *more* and *most*. (All adjectives and adverbs show diminishing or negative comparison by combining with the words *less* and *least: less jumpy, least jumpy; less surely, least surely.*

FORMS OF COMPARISON FOR REGULAR ADJECTIVES AND ADVERBS	
FORM	FUNCTION
POSITIVE	Used for a statement when nothing is being compared
COMPARATIVE	Used when only two things are being compared—with *-er* endings or *more* (or *less*)
SUPERLATIVE	Used when three or more things are being compared—with *-est* ending or *most* (or *least*)

On the following page is a list that contrasts the three forms. Consider the messages of comparison in the sentences after the list.

POSITIVE	COMPARATIVE	SUPERLATIVE
green	greener	greenest
happy	happier	happiest
selfish	less selfish	least selfish
beautiful	more beautiful	most beautiful

Her tree is **green**.
Her tree is **greener** than his tree.
Her tree is the **greenest** one on the block.

The choice of whether to use *-er/-est* or *more/most* depends largely on the number of syllables in the adjective or adverb. With **one-syllable words**, the *-er/-est* endings are most common: *large, larger, largest* (adjective); *far, farther, farthest* (adverb). With **words of three or more syllables**, *more/most* are used: *energetic, more energetic, most energetic*. With adverbs of two or more syllables, *more/most* are used: *easily, more easily, most easily*. With **adjectives of two syllables**, practice varies. Often you will form comparatives and superlatives intuitively, based on what you have heard or read for a particular adjective. If neither form sounds natural for a given adjective, consult your dictionary for the recommended form.

Be careful not to use a **double comparative** or **double superlative**. The words *more* or *most* cannot be used if the *-er* or *-est* ending has been used.

Some comparative and superlative forms are irregular. Learn this short list.

IRREGULAR COMPARATIVES AND SUPERLATIVES		
POSITIVE (1)	COMPARATIVE (2)	SUPERLATIVE (3+)
good (adjective)	better	best
well (adjective and adverb)	better	best
bad (adjective)	worse	worst
badly (adverb)	worse	worst
many	more	most
much	more	most
some	more	most
little	less	least

10f Why avoid a long string of nouns as modifiers?

Sometimes nouns can modify other nouns: *bird watching, fishing pole, fire drill*. These terms create no problems, but when nouns pile up in a list of modifiers, it can be difficult to know which nouns are being modified and which nouns are doing the modifying.

No	I misplaced my **electric garage door opener rebate coupon**.
Yes	I misplaced **the coupon needed to get a rebate on the electric opener for my garage door**.

Identifying Adjectives and Adverbs EXERCISE 10-1

On the lines to the right, identify each of the italicized words as an adjective or adverb. (Following common usage, the titles of books also appear in italics; however, these are nouns, never adjectives or adverbs.)

EXAMPLE Sinclair Lewis was the *first* American to win the
Nobel Prize for Literature.   *adjectives*

1. Agatha Christie is famous for her *mystery* novels.   _____

2. She *also* wrote romantic novels, under a pen name.   _____

3. Joseph Conrad was a *highly* respected English writer.   _____

4. His *native* language was Polish.   _____

5. He *always* had trouble speaking but not writing English.   _____

6. *Gone with the Wind* was Margaret Mitchell's *only* book.   _____

7. Upton Sinclair wrote *The Jungle* hoping to improve
conditions in the *Chicago* stockyards.   _____

8. In *his* book he called for large social and economic reforms. _____

9. Sinclair's work led *directly* to regulations governing food purity. _____

10. Each year, U.S. publishers introduce about 30,000
different books.   _____

11. The *typical* American book author earns less than
$5,000 a year from writing.   _____

12. The U.S. Government Printing Office is a *major* publisher.   _____

13. It has *6,300* employees.   _____

14. Only *recently* have women authors been widely accepted.   _____

15. Many nineteenth-century English female authors
became *widely* popular writing under men's names.   _____

16. George Eliot was *really* Mary Anne Evans, while
Charlotte Brontë wrote as Currer Bell and her sister   _____
Emily Brontë wrote as Ellis Bell.

17. *Other* famous writers have also used pen names.   _____

18. George Orwell was *actually* the pen name of
Englishman Eric Arthur Blair.   _____

19. Popular *romance* novelist Barbara Cortland also
publishes under the name Barbara Hamilton McCorquodale.   _____

20. Even Agatha Christie *sometimes* chose a pseudonym:
Mary Westmacott.   _____

Distinguishing Adjectives From Adverbs

From the choices in parentheses, select the correct modifier for each sentence. Write your answers on the lines to the right.

EXAMPLE   Aspirin can cause a (severe, severely) upset   _severely_
           stomach in some people.

1. Pain sufferers (annual, annually) spend a quarter of a   _____
    billion dollars on aspirin.

2. Over 200 kinds of headache medicines containing aspirin   _____
    are (available, availably).

3. Many of us feel taking aspirin can make us (good, well).   _____

4. However, aspirin has many (serious, seriously) side effects.   _____

5. Aspirin (common, commonly) causes bleeding in the stomach.   _____

6. This can make us feel (bad, badly).   _____

7. Bleeding occurs when an undissolved aspirin tablet lies   _____
    on the (delicate, delicately) stomach wall.

8. For most of us, the amount of blood lost is not   _____
    (dangerous, dangerously).

9. However, some (slow, slowly) dissolving tablets can   _____
    cause prolonged bleeding, leading to great discomfort.

10. (High, Highly) quality aspirin dissolves more quickly and   _____
    is less likely to cause a problem.

11. Aspirin has a (lengthy, lengthily) history.   _____

12. Our (ancient, anciently) ancestors chewed the leaves   _____
    and bark of the willow tree.

13. They contain a substance (chemical, chemically) related   _____
    to aspirin.

14. Aspirin itself was introduced as a painkiller and fever   _____
    reducer more (recent, recently).

15. Coming on the market in 1899, it (quick, quickly)   _____
    became the best-selling nonprescription drug in the world.

16. The tablet form so (popular, popularly) today was   _____
    introduced by Bayer in 1915.

17. Taking an aspirin a day has (late, lately) been claimed   _____
    to be good for the heart.

18. Some research shows that men who take aspirin
    (regular, regularly) after a heart attack are less likely
    to have another attack.   _____
    _____

19. No one knows why this is so, but some healthy people
    have been (quick, quickly) to start taking aspirin daily.   _____

20. Doctors advise us to think (careful, carefully) before we
    do this because there is no evidence that aspirin prevents
    first heart attacks.   _____

Using Comparatives and Superlatives

EXERCISE 10-3

A: Fill in the comparative and superlative forms of the adjectives and adverbs listed on the left.

		Comparative	Superlative
EXAMPLE	tall	taller	tallest
1.	bad		
2.	badly		
3.	forgiving		
4.	free		
5.	good		
6.	gracefully		
7.	handsome		
8.	hot		
9.	little		
10.	loudly		
11.	many		
12.	much		
13.	powerfully		
14.	pretty		
15.	quickly		
16.	some		
17.	sweetly		
18.	sympathetically		
19.	talented		
20.	well		

B: Use the adjectives and adverbs above in sets of sentences that show how the three forms are related to changes in meaning. Use your own paper.

EXAMPLE   I am tall. (positive)
I am taller than my sister. (comparative)
I am the tallest person in my family. (superlative)

Writing with Adjectives

Write a paragraph describing someone, something, or someplace wonderful. Some suggestions: your favorite restaurant, your favorite movie star, an exciting amusement park, your most treasured possession.

Be sure to have a topic sentence. Develop your idea with four to six sentences, each containing strong and appropriate adjectives and adverbs. Try not to use so many modifiers in any one sentence that the main idea gets lost. Use your own paper.

MODULE 11: SENTENCE FRAGMENTS

11a What is a sentence fragment?

A **sentence fragment** is part of a sentence punctuated as though it were a complete sentence. You can avoid writing sentence fragments if you recognize the difference between a fragment and a complete sentence.

11b How can I recognize a sentence fragment?

If you write sentence fragments frequently, you need a system to check that your sentences are complete. Here is a test to use if you suspect that you have written a sentence fragment.

TEST FOR SENTENCE COMPLETENESS

1. **Is there a verb?** If not, there is a sentence fragment.

2. **Is there a subject?** If not, there is a sentence fragment.

3. **Do the subject and verb start with a subordinating word—and lack an independent clause to complete the thought?** If they do, there is a sentence fragment.

QUESTION 1: Is there a verb?

If there is no verb, you are looking at a sentence fragment.

FRAGMENT	Yesterday the math lab hiring tutors.
REVISED	Yesterday the math lab **was** hiring tutors.
FRAGMENT	Today the math lab hiring tutors.
REVISED	Today the math lab **is** hiring tutors.
FRAGMENT	Chosen for their math ability.
REVISED	The tutors **are** chosen for their math ability.
REVISED	Chosen for their math ability, the tutors also **work** well with other students.
FRAGMENT	Each tutor to work with eight students.
REVISED	Each tutor **works** with eight students.
REVISED	Each tutor **is assigned** to work with eight students.

QUESTION 2: Is there a subject?

If there is no subject, you are looking at a sentence fragment. To find a subject, ask "who?" or "what?" question about the verb.

FRAGMENT   Worked in the library. [Who worked? Unknown]

REVISED   The **students** worked in the library.

Every sentence must have its own subject. A sentence fragment without a subject often results when the missing subject is the same as the subject in the previous sentence.

NO   In September, the new dormitories were opened. **Were occupied immediately**.

YES   In September, the new dormitories were opened. **They were occupied immediately**.

Imperative statements—commands and some requests—are an exception. Imperative statements imply the word you as the subject.

Sit down! = (You) sit down!

QUESTION 3: Do the subject and verb start with a subordinating word—and lack an independent clause to complete the thought?

If the answer is yes, you are looking at a sentence fragment. Clauses that begin with subordinating words are called **dependent clauses**. To be part of a complete sentence, a dependent clause must be joined to an independent clause.

One type of subordinating word is a **subordinating conjunction**. Some of the most frequently used are *after, although, because, if, when, where,* and *until.*

FRAGMENT   **If** I see him.

REVISED   **If** I see him, I'll give him your message.

FRAGMENT   **Where** the park is.

REVISED   The city will build a hospital **where** the park is.

✤ PUNCTUATION ALERT: When a dependent clause starting with a subordinating conjunction comes before an independent clause, a comma always separates the clauses. ✤

Another type of subordinating word is a **relative pronoun**. The most common relative pronouns are *who, which,* and *that.*

FRAGMENT   The class **that** we wanted.

REVISED   The class **that** we wanted was full.

FRAGMENT   The students **who** registered early.

REVISED   The students **who** registered early got the classes they wanted.

Questions are an exception—they can begin with words such as *when, where, who,* and *which* without being sentence fragments.

When is the meeting?

Who is your favorite author?

11c What are major ways of correcting fragments?

To correct a dependent clause punctuated as a sentence, you can do one of two things: (1) You can join the dependent clause to an independent clause that comes directly before or after—sometimes you will need to add words so that the combined sentence makes sense. (2) You can drop the subordinating conjunction or relative pronoun and, if necessary, add words to create an independent clause.

FRAGMENT	Students often change their majors. **When they start taking courses.**
REVISED	Students often change their major when they start taking courses. [joined into one sentence]
REVISED	Students often change their majors. They start taking courses and realize they are unhappy. [subordinating conjunction dropped to create an independent cause]
FRAGMENT	The chemistry major is looking for a lab partner. **Who is dependable.**
REVISED	The chemistry major is looking for a lab partner who is dependable. [joined into one sentence]

To correct a phrase punctuated as a sentence, either you can rewrite it to become an independent clause by adding the missing subject or verb, or you can join it to an independent clause that comes directly before or after.

A phrase containing a **verbal** (a *gerund*, an *infinitive*, a *past participle*, or a *present participle*) but no verb is not a sentence.

FRAGMENT	The college administration voted last week. **To offer a new program in nursing.**
REVISED	The college administration voted last week to offer a new program in nursing. [joined into one sentence]
REVISED	The college administration voted last week. The members decided to offer a new program in nursing. [rewritten]
FRAGMENT	**Speaking to the students.** The dean explained the new program.
REVISED	Speaking to the students, the dean explained the new program. [joined into one sentence]
REVISED	The dean spoke to the students. She explained the new program. [rewritten]
FRAGMENT	**Seated in the auditorium.** The students listened carefully.
REVISED	Seated in the auditorium, the students listened carefully. [joined into one sentence]
REVISED	The students were seated in the auditorium. They listened carefully. [rewritten]

A **prepositional phrase** contains a preposition, its object, and any modifiers.

FRAGMENT	She planned to take Biology 102. **During summer session.**
REVISED	She planned to take Biology 102 during summer session. [joined into one sentence]
REVISED	She planned to take Biology 102. It was offered in summer session. [rewritten]

An **appositive** is a word or word group that renames a noun or group of words functioning as a noun.

FRAGMENT	Many students liked the biology professor. **A teacher of great skill and patience.**
REVISED	Many students liked the biology professor, a teacher of great skill and patience. [joined into one sentence]
REVISED	Many students liked the biology professor. She was a teacher of great skill and patience. [rewritten]

11d How can I fix a fragment that is part of a compound predicate?

Compound predicates contain two or more verbs, plus their objects and modifiers, if any. To be part of a complete sentence, a predicate must have a subject. If the second half of a compound predicate is punctuated as a sentence, it is a sentence fragment.

FRAGMENT	The professor was always available for conferences. **And answered students' questions clearly.**
REVISED	The professor was always available for conferences and answered students' questions clearly. [joined into one sentence]
REVISED	The professor was always available for conferences. And she always answered students' questions clearly. [rewritten]

11e What are the two special fragment problems?

The two special fragment problems sometimes come up when people write lists and examples. Lists and examples must be part of a complete sentence, unless they are formatted as a column.

You can connect a list fragment by attaching it to the preceding independent clause by using a COLON or DASH. You can correct an example fragment by attaching it to an independent clause (with or without punctuation, depending on the meaning) or by rewriting it as a complete sentence.

FRAGMENT	You have a choice of desserts. **Carrot cake, chocolate silk pie, or apple pie.** [The list cannot stand on its own as a sentence.]
CORRECT	You have a choice of desserts: carrot cake, chocolate silk pie, or apple pie. [Colon joins the two sentences.]
CORRECT	You have a choice of desserts—carrot cake, chocolate silk pie, or apple pie. [Dash joins the two sentences.]
FRAGMENT	There are several good places to go for lunch. **For example, the restaurants The Big Red Tomato and Smoke.** [Examples can't stand on their own as a sentence.]
CORRECT	There are several good places to go for brunch, for example, the restaurants The Big Red Tomato and Smoke.
CORRECT	There are several good places to go for brunch. For example, there are the restaurants The Big Red Tomato and Smoke.

11f How can I recognize intentional fragments?

Professional writers sometimes intentionally use fragments for emphasis and effect.

But in the main, I feel like a brown bag of miscellany propped against a wall. Pour out the contents, and there is discovered a jumble of small things priceless and worthless. **A first-water diamond, an empty spool, bits of broken glass, lengths of string, a key to a door long since crumbled away, a rusty knife-blade, old shoes saved for a road that never was and never will be, a nail bent under the weight of things too heavy for any nail, a dried flower or two still a little fragrant.**

—ZORA NEALE HURSTON, *How It Feels to Be Colored Me*

For academic writing, most instructors don't accept sentence fragments in student writing until a student demonstrates a consistent ability to write well-constructed, complete sentences. As a rule, avoid sentence fragments in academic writing.

Revising Fragments

A. Explain what is wrong with each fragment and then rewrite it as a complete sentence.

EXAMPLE Celebrating the summer solstice.
There is no subject, and celebrating' is not a conjugated verb.
Many people will be celebrating the summer solstice.

1. When March 21st arrives

    _____

2. whichever participant arrives first

    _____

3. joins the other dancers

    _____

4. in the spring

    _____

5. Happily, the dancers participating

    _____

6. known to be the longest day of the year

    _____

7. that most people like to celebrate

    _____

8. many people's favorite event

    _____

9. visiting with my family, friends and neighbors

    _____

10. and write love letters

    _____

B. Write two corrected versions of each fragment. Be sure to use the fragment differently in each and identify how you have used it (as illustrated in the parentheses below).

EXAMPLE   preparing a lecture
            Preparing lectures / takes muck of the professor's time. (subject)
            The professor / who was preparing lectures / stayed up most of the night.
            (adjective)

1.   gets to class on time

     _____

2.   entered in the literary contest

     _____

3.   to buy a new textbook

     _____

4.   when I take the exam

     _____

5.   working to pay for college

     _____

6.   studying for exams during spring break

     _____

7.   Administrators, faculty, staff, and students

     _____

8.   The power going off suddenly

     _____

9.   who attends night classes

     _____

10. in the writing center

     _____

Revising Fragments within Passages

There is one fragment in each passage below. Find it and correct it in whatever way you feel is most appropriate.

EXAMPLE   James is a very quiet four-year-old. Who was born addicted to cocaine.
Rarely does he speak a word to anyone.
James is a very quiet four-year-old who was born addicted to cocaine.
Rarely does he speak a word to anyone.

1. When he first met with Mary Burch, a Tallahassee-based therapist. Jason sat listlessly and expressionless in her office. After that first meeting, Burch decided to bring a visitor to the next meeting.

    _____

    _____

2. The surprise visitor was Burch's Border collie. During their fifth session, Jason began speaking to the dog. And eventually began to open up to Burch.

    _____

    _____

3. Burch is heavily involved in a pet therapy program. Which is designed to help children who were born addicted to cocaine. It is the only program of its kind in the United States.

    _____

    _____

4. Why animals have such blatant effects on human health is still largely unknown. Yet in recent years, scientists have found proof of such connections. Allowing them to confirm what people have suspected to be true for centuries.

    _____

    _____

5. In fact, at a Quaker retreat in York, England, in 1790. Patients were encouraged to spend time with the animals. Leaders suspected that this would help improve their patients' states of mind.

    _____

    _____

6. Recent evidence suggests that the human bond with animals is uniquely helpful to human health. Many organizations across the country have begun donating time and funds for further research. As a result of this evidence.

    _____

    _____

7. Many jails, hospitals, and nursing homes have also begun to support the human-animal connection. By allowing pet visitation and therapy programs.

_____

_____

8. Scientists suspect that the relationship between humans and animals is so helpful. Because it is so uncomplicated. Animals offer comfort, love, and affection without criticism or judgment.

_____

_____

9. Family and friends who visit loved ones at nursing homes get more of a response when they arrive with a pet. Than do those who come alone.

_____

_____

10. According to research conducted by Suzanne Robb, elderly people in nursing homes smile more. When they are exposed to the company of animals. They are even more alert around animals than when not.

_____

_____

11. For children who are mentally challenged. The effects of animals are even more positive than they are with the elderly. College students at the Julia Dyckman Andrus home in Yonkers, New York, can attest to that.

_____

_____

12. For eight weeks, these students made weekly trips to visit emotionally disturbed children. Each accompanied by a cat or a dog. The students discovered that the children misbehaved less after spending time with the animals.

_____

_____

13. The leader of this experiment was Stephen Daniel. Who is a psychologist at Mercy College. Even he was surprised by the results.

_____

_____

14. Daniel suggests that animals increase a child's self-control. By acting in a pre-dictable manner. The child, it seems, mimics the calm actions of the animals.

_____

_____

15. Although just the presence of an animal is enough to heal children. Nurturing it helps children even more. Nursing an animal back to health nurses a sick child back to health as well.

_____

_____

16. Most children delight in seeing an animal recover. Since the children themselves can identify with the injured animal. When children see that an animal can survive with a physical disability, they believe that they can survive as well.

_____

_____

17. Animals affect humans on a physical level as well. There are confirmed reports. That say the heart rate is lowered when people sit in the presence of an animal.

_____

_____

18. Elderly people living at home also benefit from animals. Those elderly who live with pets visit the doctor less frequently. Than do those without pets.

_____

_____

19. Doctors aren't sure why animals have these effects on humans. Yet scientists do suggest that with an animal present. People feel less lonely and enjoy having an understanding and loving companion.

_____

_____

20. Whether scientifically proven or not, animals are a sure way to help relieve physical and emotional problems. While making a friend at the same time.

_____

_____

Circle the number of any fragments. Then correct each fragment by connecting it to a main clause or by adding words to complete it. Use your own paper.

A.   ¹The Blue Ridge Parkway runs 469 miles. ²Along the crest of mountains in the Appalachian chain. ³It connects two parks. ⁴Shenandoah National Park and Great Smoky Mountains National Park. ⁵The parkway starts in Virginia. ⁶And ends in North Carolina. ⁷Begun by the Works Progress Administration in 1935. ⁸The parkway was completed. ⁹Except for a section around privately owned Grandfather Mountain. ¹⁰Concerned about environmental impact. ¹¹The owner refused to allow any blasting on the mountain. ¹²It was 1987 before the final section, the Linn Cove Viaduct. ¹³Using the latest engineering technology. ¹⁴The viaduct goes around, not over, Grandfather Mountain. ¹⁵Those who drive the parkway. ¹⁶Are not bothered by the speed limit of 45 miles per hour. ¹⁷Driving slowly allows them to appreciate the scenery. ¹⁸To see the many cascades and other natural wonders. ¹⁹One beautiful vista after another. ²⁰ In places the distant mountains seem stacked in layers. ²¹Along some stretches of the parkway can be seen catawba rhododendron and mountain laurel. ²²Along others, various wildflowers. ²³In the autumn traffic almost stops on the parkway. ²⁴As people come to enjoy the fall foliage. ²⁵Although most people drive the parkway for the view. ²⁶There are many who come for camping. ²⁷Or for hiking, biking, or studying the wildlife. ²⁸One attraction is Mount Mitchell. ²⁹At 6,684 feet, the highest point east of the Mississippi River. ³⁰It is not surprising. ³¹That visitors return to the parkway year after year.

B.   ¹The striped barber pole is a symbol left over from the times. ²When barbers doubled as surgeons. ³As early as the fifth century. ⁴Roman barbers pulled teeth, treated wounds. ⁵And bled patients. ⁶Records show that in 1461 the barbers of London were the only people practicing surgery. ⁷In the city. ⁸However, under Henry VIII, less than a hundred years later. ⁹Parliament passed a law limiting barbers to minor operations. ¹⁰Such as blood letting and pulling teeth. ¹¹While surgeons were prohibited from barbery and shaving. ¹²The London barbers and surgeons were considered one group until 1745. ¹³In France and Germany, barbers acted as surgeons. ¹⁴Until even more recent times.

    ¹⁵Barbers usually bled their patients. ¹⁶To cure a variety of ailments. ¹⁷Because few people could read in those days. ¹⁸Pictures were commonly used as shop signs. ¹⁹The sign of the barber was a pole painted with red and white spirals. ²⁰From which was suspended a brass basin. ²¹The red represented the blood of the patient. ²²The white the bandage. ²³And the basin the bowl used to catch the blood. ²⁴In the United States, the bowl is often omitted. ²⁵But it is still common on British barber poles. ²⁶Some American barbers added a blue stripe. ²⁷Probably to make the colors match the flag.

MODULE 12: COMMA SPLICES AND RUN-ON SENTENCES

12a What are comma splices and run-on sentences?

A **comma splice**, also known as a **comma fault**, occurs when a single comma joins independent clauses. A comma is correct between two independent clauses only when it is followed by a coordinating conjunction.

COMMA SPLICE   The car skidded, it hit a mailbox.

A **run-on sentence**, also known as a **run-together sentence** or a **fused sentence**, occurs when two independent clauses are not separated by punctuation nor joined by a comma with a coordinating conjunction.

RUN-ON   The car skidded it hit a mailbox.
SENTENCE

Comma splices and run-on sentences are two versions of the same problem: incorrect joining of two independent clauses. If you tend to write comma splices and run-on sentences, it may be because you don't recognize them.

HOW TO FIND AND CORRECT COMMA SPLICES AND RUN-ON SENTENCES

FINDING COMMA SPLICES AND RUN-ON SENTENCES

1. Look for a pronoun starting the second independent clause.

No Thomas Edison was a productive inventor, **he** held over 1,300 U.S. and foreign patents.

2. Look for a conjunctive adverb or other transitional expression starting the second independent clause.

No Thomas Edison was a brilliant scientist, **however**, his schooling was limited to only three months of his life.

3. Look for a second independent clause that explains or gives an example of information in the first clause.

No Thomas Edison was the genius behind many inventions, the phonograph and the light bulb are among the best known.

FIXING COMMA SPLICES AND RUN-ON SENTENCES

1. Use a period or a semicolon between clauses.
2. Use a comma and a coordinating conjunction between clauses.
3. Use a semicolon and a conjunctive adverb between clauses.

12b How can I recognize comma splices and run-on sentences?

To recognize comma splices and run-on sentences, you need to be able to recognize an independent clause. An **independent clause** contains a subject and a predicate. An independent clause can stand alone as a sentence because it is a complete grammatical unit. A sentence may contain two or more independent clauses only if they are joined properly (with a comma and coordinating conjunction or with a semicolon).

12c How can I correct comma splices and run-on sentences?

A **period** can separate the independent clauses in a comma splice or run-on sentence. A **semicolon** can separate independent clauses that are closely related in meaning.

COMMA SPLICE	In the 1880s, Sir Francis Galton showed that fingerprints are unique for each person, he was an English anthropologist.
CORRECTED	In the 1880s, Sir Francis Galton showed that fingerprints are unique for each person. He was an English anthropologist.
RUN-ON SENTENCE	Mark Twain used fingerprints to solve murders in *Life on the Mississippi* and *Pudd'nhead Wilson* these were popular books.
CORRECTED	Mark Twain used fingerprints to solve murders in *Life on the Mississippi* and *Pudd'nhead Wilson*; these were popular books.

Conjunctive adverbs and other transitional expressions link ideas between sentences. Remember, however, that these words are *not* coordinating conjunctions, so they cannot work with commas to join independent clauses. Conjunctive adverbs and other transitional expressions require that the previous sentence end in a period or semicolon.

When ideas in independent clauses are closely related, you might decide to connect them with a coordinating conjunction that fits the meaning of the material. Two independent clauses joined by a coordinating conjunction and a comma form a compound sentence, also known as a coordinate sentence.

❖ PUNCTUATION ALERT: Use a comma before a coordinating conjunction that links independent clauses. ❖

COMMA SPLICE	In 1901, England began fingerprinting criminals, their prints were kept on file with the police.
CORRECTED	In 1901, England began fingerprinting criminals, **and** their prints were kept on file with the police.
RUN-ON SENTENCE	Edward Richard Henry, of London's Metropolitan Police, invented a system of classifying fingerprints the FBI uses a version of this original system.

CORRECTED   Edward Richard Henry, of London's Metropolitan Police, invented a system of classifying fingerprints, **and** the FBI uses a version of this original system.

You can revise a comma splice or run-on sentence by changing one of two independent clauses into a dependent clause. This method is suitable when one idea can be logically subordinated to the other. Sentences composed of one independent clause and one or more dependent clauses are called complex sentences. Inserting an appropriate subordinating conjunction in front of the subject and verb is one way to create a dependent clause.

❖ PUNCTUATION ALERT: Do not put a period after a dependent clause that is not attached to an independent clause, or you will create a sentence fragment. ❖

COMMA SPLICE   Immigrants are fingerprinted, most have done nothing wrong.

CORRECTED   Immigrants are fingerprinted **although most have done nothing wrong**.

RUN-ON SENTENCE   The government wants to identify dangerous criminals they enter the country.

CORRECTED   The government wants to identify dangerous criminals **before they enter the country**.

A relative pronoun can also be used to correct a comma splice or run-on sentence by creating a dependent clause.

COMMA SPLICE   Government employees are also fingerprinted, they work on sensitive projects.

CORRECTED   Government employees *who work on sensitive projects* are also fingerprinted. [restrictive dependent clause]

12d How can I correctly use a conjunctive adverb or other transitional expression between indepndent clauses?

Conjunctive adverbs include such words as *however, therefore, also, next, the, thus, furthermore,* and *nevertheless*.

COMMA SPLICE   Many people object to being fingerprinted, **nevertheless**, fingerprinting remains a requirement for certain jobs.

CORRECTED   Many people object to being fingerprinted. **Nevertheless**, fingerprinting remains a requirement for certain jobs.

Transitional words include *for example, for instance, in addition, in fact, of course,* and *on the other hand* (see 3g for a fuller list).

RUN-ON SENTENCE   Not everyone disapproves of fingerprinting in fact, some parents have their children fingerprinted as a safety measure.

CORRECTED   Not everyone disapproves of fingerprinting. In fact some parents have their children fingerprinted as a safety measure.

A conjunctive adverb or other transitional expression can appear in various locations within an independent clause. In contrast, a coordinating conjunction can appear only between the independent clauses it joins.

Many people object to being fingerprinted. Fingerprinting, **nevertheless,** remains a requirement for certain jobs.

Many people object to being fingerprinted. Fingerprinting remains, **nevertheless,** a requirement for certain jobs.

Many people object to being fingerprinted. Fingerprinting remains a requirement for certain jobs, **nevertheless.**

Many people object to being fingerprinted, **but** fingerprinting remains a requirement for certain jobs.

Revising Comma Splices and Run-On Sentences

A: Correct each comma splice or run-on sentence in any of the ways shown in this chapter.

EXAMPLE   There's a reason why people are so fond of salt they can't live without it.
           There's a reason why people are so fond of salt. They can't live without it.

1. The average person contains about eight ounces of salt without it a person would die.

   _____

   _____

2. When people began to farm obtaining the salt their bodies required became difficult, they began to seek sources of salt.

   _____

   _____

3. Salt has been used just like money, it was a medium of exchange.

   _____

   _____

4. The world's oceans are very salty, there's enough salt in them to bury the entire United States a mile deep.

   _____

   _____

5. Only five percent of salt is used as a seasoning most of the rest is used in industry.

   _____

   _____

6. We get some salt from the oceans most of it comes from salt mines.

   _____

   _____

7. People used to crave salt now so much is used in food production that we need to be careful not to consume too much of it.

    _____

    _____

B: Correct each comma splice or run-on sentence in the way indicated.

EXAMPLE   Salt can be deadly too much of it can kill fish and keep plants from growing.
           (Make into two separate sentences.)
           Salt can be deadly. Too much of it can kill fish and keep plants from growing.

1. Salt is a major ingredient in pesticides and herbicides, they kill insects and plants.
    (Turn one part into a dependent clause.)

    _____

    _____

2. The Romans destroyed the city of Carthage they plowed the ground with salt and made the area uninhabitable.
    (Make into two separate sentences.)

    _____

    _____

3. Constructive or destructive, salt has many uses it is used far more than any other mineral.
    (Add a semicolon and a conjunctive adverb.)

    _____

    _____

4. The Romans knew the value of salt as a commodity they named their major highway Via Salaria, Salt Road.
    (Add a semicolon.)

    _____

    _____

5. The word _salary_ comes from the word _salarium_ it meant money used to pay soldiers so they could buy salt.
    (Turn one part into a dependent clause.)

    _____

    _____

6. Salt has long been used to perserve food the expression "salted away" means to keep for a future time.
    (Add a comma and a coordinating conjunction.)

    _____

    _____

7. Salt may become even more important to us than it already is we may be able to use it to bury radio-active waste.
    (Add a semicolon.)

    _____

    _____

C: Correct each comma splice or run-on sentence in four ways: (1) make each into two separate sentences by inserting a period; (2) add a semicolon; (3) add a coordinating conjunction to create a compound sentence—you will also need to add a comma unless the clauses are very short; (4) add a subordinating conjunction or relative pronoun—you may need to drop a word-to create a complex sentence.

EXAMPLE   The tallest creatures in the world are giraffes, they can grow to be 15 to 17 feet tall.
            1. giraffes. They can grow . . .
            2. giraffes; they can grow . . .
            3. giraffes, for they can grow . . .
            4. giraffes that can grow

1. Giraffes spend much of their time eating their favorite food, the whistling-thorn acacia tree, it satisfies their hunger and thirst.

    _____

    _____

    _____

    _____

2. To most people giraffes appear awkward and ungainly, they an race along at speeds up to 35 miles per hour.

    _____

    _____

    _____

    _____

3. People have greatly reduced the number of remaining giraffes, they need more protection from poachers.

_____

_____

_____

_____

4. To establish identity, people have fingerprints, giraffes have distinctive patches of brown on their bodies.

_____

_____

_____

_____

5. Introduced to Rome by Julius Caesar in 46 BCE, the giraffe was billed as a camel leopard, its scientific name became Giraffa camelopardalis.

_____

_____

_____

_____

Revising Comma Splices and
Run-On Sentences within Passages

EXERCISE 12-2

Find the comma splice or run-on sentence in each passage. Correct each in any way shown in this chapter.
You may need to change punctuation or wording, but try to keep the meaning of the original passage.

EXAMPLE   Some of the most beautiful temples in the world are those of Angkor.
Angkor is a Cambodian region it served as the capital of the ancient Khmer
empire between the 9th and 15th centuries. The empire once extended into
what are today Vietnam, Laos, and Thailand.

Some of the most beautiful temples in the world are those of Angkor.
Angkor is a Cambodian region that served as the capital of the ancient
Khmer empire between the 9th and 15th centuries. The empire once
extended into what are today Vietnam, Laos, and Thailand.

1.   The king Jayavarman II introduced into the empire an Indian royal cult. The cult held
that the king was related spiritually to one of the Hindu gods, consequently, the king
was thought to fill on earth the role the gods had in the universe.

_____

_____

2.   Each king was expected to build a stone temple. The temple, or wat, was dedicated
to a god, usually Shica or Vishnu, when the king died, the temple became a monument to him as well.

_____

_____

3.   Over the centuries the kings erected more than seventy temples within seventy-five
square miles. They added towers and gates they created canals and reservoirs for
an irrigation system.

_____

_____

4.   The irrigation system made it possible for farmers to produce several rice crops a
year. Such abundant harvests supported a highly evolved culture, the irrigation system and the rice production were what we would call labor-intensive.

_____

_____

5. The greatest of the temples in Angkor Wat, it was built by Suryavarman II in the 12th century. Like the other temples, it represents Mount Meru, the home of the Hindu gods. The tower represent Mount Meru's peaks while the walls represent the mountains beyond.

_____

_____

6. The gallery walls are covered with bas-reliefs they depict historical events. They show the king at his court, and they show him engaging in activities that brought glory to his empire.

_____

_____

7. The walls also portray divine images. There are sculptures of *apsarases*, they are attractive women thought to inhabit heaven. There are mythical scenes on the walls as well.

_____

_____

8. One scene shows the Hindu myth of the churning of the Sea of Milk. On one side of the god Vishnu are demons who tug on the end of the long serpent, on the other are heavenly beings who tug on the other end. All the tugging churns the water.

_____

_____

9. Vishnu is the god to whom Angkor Wat is dedicated. In Hindu myth he oversees the churning of the waters, that churning is ultimately a source of immortality.

_____

_____

10. Another temple is the Bayon, it was built by Jayavarman VII around 1200 A.D. Jayavarman VII was the last of the great kings of Angkor. He built the Bayon in the exact center of the city.

_____

_____

11. The Bayon resembles a step pyramid. It has steep stairs which lead to terraces near the top around its base are many galleries. Its towers are carved with faces which look out in all directions.

_____

_____

12. Jayavarman VII was a Buddhist, the representations on Bayon are different from those on earlier temples. Some scholars think they depict a Buddhist deity with whom the king felt closely aligned.

    _____

    _____

13. To build each temple required thousands of laborers they worked for years. After cutting the stone in far-off quarries, they had to transport it by canal or cart. Some stone may have been brought in on elephants.

    _____

    _____

14. Once cut, the stones had to be carved and fitted together into lasting edifices, thus, in addition to requiring laborers, each project needs artisans, architects, and engineers. Each temple was a massive project.

    _____

    _____

15. Angkor was conquered by the Thais in the 1400s, it was almost completely abandoned. The local inhabitants did continue to use the temples for worship, however, and a few late Khmer kings tried to restore the city.

    _____

    _____

16. The Western world did not learn about Angkor until the nineteenth century, a French explorer published an account of the site. French archaeologists and conservators later worked in the area and restored some of the temples. More recent archaeologists have come from India.

    _____

    _____

17. Today the Angkor Conservancy has removed many of the temple statues. Some of the statues need repair, all of them need protection from thieves. Unfortunately, traffic in Angkor art has become big business among people with no scruples. There is even a booming business in Angkor fakes.

    _____

    _____

18. Theft is just one of the problems Angkor faces today, political upheaval has taken its toll. Although Angkor mostly escaped Cambodia's civil war, some war damage has occurred.

_____

_____

19. More damage has been done by nature, however, trees choke some of the archways, vines strangle the statues, and monsoons undermine the basic structures.

_____

_____

20. Today many Cambodians do what they can to maintain the temples of Angkor. They clean stones or sweep courtyards or pull weeds. No one pays them, they do it for themselves and their heritage.

_____

_____

MODULE 13: MISPLACED AND DANGLING MODIFIERS

13a What is a misplaced modifier?

A **misplaced modifier** is a description incorrectly positioned within a sentence, resulting in distorted meaning. Always check to see that your modifiers are placed as close as possible to what they describe. The various kinds of misplaced modifiers are discussed below.

An **ambiguous placement** means that a modifier can refer to two or more words in a sentence. Little limiting words (such as *only, just, almost, ever, hardly, nearly, exactly, merely, scarcely, simply*) can change meaning according to where they are placed. Consider how the placement of *only* changes the meaning of this sentence: *Scientists say that the space program is important.*

> **Only** scientists say that the space program is important.
> Scientists **only** say that the space program is important.
> Scientists say **only** that the space program is important.
> Scientists say that **only** the space program is important.

Squinting modifiers also cause ambiguity. A squinting modifier appears to describe both what precedes and what follows it.

No	The dock that was constructed **partially** was destroyed by the storm. [What was partial—the construction or the destruction?]
Yes	The dock that was **partially** constructed was destroyed by the storm.
Yes	The **partially** constructed dock was destroyed by the storm.
Yes	The dock that was constructed was **partially** destroyed by the storm.

Wrong placement means that the modifiers are far from the words they logically modify.

No	The British Parliament passed a law forbidding Scots to wear kilts **in 1746**. [This sentence says kilts could not be worn only in 1746.]
Yes	**In 1746**, the British Parliament passed a law forbidding Scots to wear kilts.
No	This was an attempt, **of which the kilt was a symbol**, to destroy Scottish nationalism. [This sentence says the kilt represented the destruction of Scottish nationalism.]
Yes	This was an attempt to destroy Scottish nationalism, **of which the kilt was a symbol**.

13b How can I avoid split infinitives?

An **awkward placement** is an interruption that seriously breaks the flow of the message. A **split infinitive** is a particularly confusing kind of awkward placement. An infinitive is a verb form that starts with *to*: *to buy, to sell*.

No	The herb sweet basil was thought **to**, in medieval Europe, **have** strange effects on people who ate it.
Yes	In medieval Europe, the herb sweet basil was thought **to have** strange effects on people who ate it.

Generally, avoid interruptions between subject and verb, between parts of a verb phrase, and between verb and object.

13c How can I avoid other splits in my sentences?

When too many words split—that is, come between—a SUBJECT and VERB or between VERB and its OBJECT, the result is a sentence that lurches instead of flowing.

No   The **announcer**, because the script, which Welles himself wrote, called for perfect imitations of emergency announcements, **opened** with a warning that included a description of the "invasion." [The subject announcer is placed too far away from the verb opened, so this split is too large.]

Yes   Because the script, which Welles himself wrote, called for perfect imitations of emergency announcements, the **announcer opened** with a warning that included a description of the "invasion." [The subject and verb *announcer opened* aren't split.]

13d How can I avoid dangling modifiers?

A **dangling modifier** modifies what is implied but not actually stated in a sentence. Dangling modifiers can be hard for a writer to spot because the writer's brain tends to supply the missing information, but the reader cannot supply it, and confusion results.

No   **Learning about bamboo, the plant's versatility** amazed me. [This sentence says the plant's versatility is learning.]

13e How can I proofread successfully for misplaced and dangling modifiers?

You can correct a dangling modifier by revising the sentence so that the intended subject is expressed.

Yes   **Learning about bamboo,** I was amazed by the plant's versatility.

Yes   **I learned about bamboo** and was amazed by its versatility.

Eliminating Misplaced and Dangling Modifiers

A: Underline all misplaced and dangling modifiers in this paragraph. Then revise the paragraph to eliminate them. You can change or add words and otherwise revise to make the material sensible.

[1]The art of carving or engraving marine articles, sailors developed scrimshaw while sailing on long voyages. [2]Practiced primarily by whalermen, sperm whale teeth were the most popular articles. [3]Baleen was another popular choice which was also called whalebone. [4]A sailor needed something to occupy his time with whaling voyages taking several years. [5]Imagination or available material only limited scrimshaw. [6]All kinds of objects were produced by the scrimshander, canes, corset busks, cribbage boards. [7]From whaling scenes to mermaids the sailor used everything to decorate his work. [8]A sailor doing scrimshaw often drew his own ship. [9]The most frequently depicted ship, the *Charles W. Morgan*, is, at present, a museum ship at Mystic Seaport. [10]It is possible to easily see it on a visit to Connecticut.

Eliminating Misplaced and Dangling Modifiers

A: Underline each misplaced modifier. Then revise the sentence, placing the modifier where it belongs.

EXAMPLE   Inexperienced people are afraid to paint their own homes often.
*Inexperienced people are **often** afraid to paint their own homes.*

1. To paint one's house frequently one must do it oneself.

    _____

2. All homeowners almost try to paint at one time or another.

    _____

3. They try to usually begin on a bedroom.

    _____

4. They think no one will see it if they botch the job by doing so.

    _____

5. Most people can learn to paint in no time.

    _____

6. The uncoordinated should only not try it.

    _____

7. People have a distinct advantage that have strong arm muscles.

    _____

8. Prospective painters can always exercise lacking strength.

    _____

9. Novices need to carefully purchase all supplies, such as brushes, rollers, and drop cloths.

    _____

10. They must bring home paint chips exactly to match the shade desired.

    _____

11. It takes as much time nearly to prepare to paint as it does to do the actual job.

    _____

12. Painters are in for a surprise who think they are done with the last paint stroke.

    _____

13   Painters need to immediately clean their own brushes and put away all equipment.

_____

14   They can be proud of their accomplishment in the long run.

_____

15   Then can they enjoy only the results of their labor.

_____

16.   Painting one's own home can, when all is said and done, be extremely satisfying.

_____

B: Revise each sentence to eliminate dangling modifiers. You may have to add or change a few words. If a sentence is acceptable as written, write *correct* on the line.

EXAMPLE   Advising a group of young women in his neighborhood, many discussions focusing on love problems were led by Samuel Richardson.
Advising a group of young women in his neighborhood, Samuel Richardson led many discussions focusing on love problems.

1.   Playing the role of a caring and wise father, the girls were told by Richardson how to handle various situations.

_____

_____

2.   To help the girls, letters to their suitors were sometimes written for them by Richardson.

_____

_____

3   After writing a number of successful letters, the idea of writing a book of model letters occurred to Richardson.

_____

_____

4.   To prepare the book, it included letters written as if from adults to sons, daughters, nieces, and nephews.

_____

_____

5   When ready to send advice, a letter was copied out by a parent, and just the names changed.

_____

_____

6. Bought by many, Richardson was a successful author.

_____

_____

7. While working on one letter, enough ideas for a whole book occurred to Richardson.

_____

_____

8. By writing a series of letters between a girl and her faraway parents, young readers would be entertained and instructed.

_____

_____

9. Upon finishing *Pamela*, or *Virtue Rewarded* in 1740, a new form of literature had been invented by Richardson.

_____

_____

10. After years of development, we call this form the novel.

_____

_____

11. Being a nasty person, Horace Walpole's only novel wasn't very attractive either.

_____

_____

12. Imitated by others for over 200 years, his *The Castle of Otranto* was the first gothic novel.

_____

_____

13. Although badly written, Walpole invented the themes, atmosphere, mood, and plots that have filled gothic novels ever since.

_____

_____

14. Featuring gloomy castles filled with dark secrets, people are entertained by gothic movies too.

_____

_____

MODULE 14: SHIFTING AND MIXED SENTENCES

SHIFTING SENTENCES

14a What is a shifting sentence?

A sentence can seem correct at first glance but still have flaws that keep it from delivering a sensible message. Sentences may be sending unclear messages because of shifts in person and number, in subject and voice, in tense and mood, and between direct and indirect discourse; misplaced modifiers; dangling modifiers; mixed structures; or incomplete structures.

Unless the meaning or grammatical structure of a sentence requires it, do not shift person and number, subject and voice, and tense and mood. Also, do not shift from indirect to direct discourse within a sentence without using punctuation and grammar to make the changes clear.

14b How can I avoid shifts in person and number?

Person in English includes the **first person** (*I, we*), who is the speaker; the second person (*you*), who is the person spoken to; and the third person (*he, she, it, they*), who is the person or thing being spoken about. Do not shift person within a sentence or a longer passage unless the meaning calls for a shift.

No   We need to select a college with care. **Your** future success may depend upon **your** choice. [*We* shifts to *your*.]

Yes   We need to select a college with care. **Our** future success may depend upon **our** choice.

Number refers to one (singular) and more than one (plural). Do not start to write in one number and then shift suddenly to the other.

No   A college **freshman** has to make many adjustments. **They** have to work harder and become more responsible. [The singular *freshman* shifts to the plural *they*.]

Yes   College **freshmen** have to make many adjustments. They have to work harder and become more responsible.

A common source of confusion in person and number is a shift to the second person *you* from the first-person *I* or a third-person noun such as *person*, or *people*. You can avoid this error if you remember to reserve *you* for sentences that directly address the reader and to use third-person pronouns for general statements.

No   The French **president** serves for seven years. **You** can accomplish much in such a long term. [*President*, third person, shifts to *you*, second person.]

Yes   The French **president** serves for seven years. He can accomplish much in such a long term.

NO	I would be afraid to give someone such power for so long a time. **You** might decide **you** disliked his policies. [*I*, first person, shifts to *you*, second person.]
YES	I would be afraid to give someone such power for so long a time. I might decide **I** disliked his policies.

14c How can I avoid shifts in subject and voice?

The **subject** of a sentence is the word or group of words that acts, is acted upon, or is described: *The bell rings*. The **voice** of a sentence is either active (*The bell rings*) or passive (*The bell is rung*). Whenever possible, use the active voice.

NO	The chemistry **student lit** a match too near the supplies, and some pure **oxygen was ignited.** [The subject shifts from *student* to *oxygen,* and the voice shifts from active to passive.]
YES	The chemistry **student lit** a match too near the supplies, and **he ignited** some pure oxygen.
NO	When **people heard** the explosion, **the hall was filled.**
YES	When **people heard** the explosion, **they filled** the halls.
YES	**People**, hearing the explosion, **filled** the halls.

14d How can I avoid shifts in tense and mood?

Tense refers to the ability of verbs to show time. Tense changes are required when time movement is described: *I expect the concert will start late*. If tense changes are illogical, the message becomes unclear.

NO	Traffic accidents **kill** between forty and fifty thousand people as they **drove** on U.S. highways each year. [The tense shifts from the present *kill* to the past *drove*.]
YES	Traffic accidents **kill** between forty and fifty thousand people as they **drive** on U.S. highways each year.
NO	India **loses** few people in traffic accidents. Unfortunately, ten thousand people a year **died** of cobra bites. [The shift occurs between sentences. The present tense *loses* shifts to the past tense *died*.]
YES	India **loses** few people in traffic accidents. Unfortunately, ten thousand people a year **die** of cobra bites.

14e How can I avoid shifts between indirect and direct discourse?

Indirect discourse *reports* speech or conversation; it is not enclosed in quotation marks. **Direct discourse** *repeats* speech or conversation exactly and encloses the spoken words in quotation marks. Sentences that mix direct and direct discourse without quotation marks and other markers confuse readers.

NO	The recruiter said I could advance in the Air Force, but do you really want to enlist? [The first clause is indirect discourse; the second shifts to unmarked direct discourse.]
YES	The recruiter said I could advance in the Air Force, but asked, whether I really wanted to enlist. [indirect discourse]

YES   The recruiter said I could advance in the Air Force, but asked, "Do you really want to enlist?" [This revision uses direct and indirect discourse correctly.]

MIXED SENTENCES

14f What is a mixed sentence?

A **mixed sentence** has two or more parts that do not make sense together. In a **mixed construction**, a sentence starts out taking one grammatical form and then changes, confusing the meaning.

No   When the Pony Express's riders included Wild Bill Hickok and Buffalo Bill Cody became folk heroes. [The opening dependent clause is fused with the independent clause that follows.]

YES   The Pony Express's riders included Wild Bill Hickok and Buffalo Bill Cody, who became folk heroes. [*When* has been dropped, making the first clause independent; and *who* has been added, making the second clause dependent and logically related to the first.]

No   To novelists, such as Ned Buntline, romanticized their adventures. [A prepositional phrase, such as to novelists, cannot be the subject of a sentence.]

YES   Novelists, such as Ned Buntline, romanticized their adventures. [Dropping the preposition *to* clears up the problem.]

YES   To novelists, such as Ned Buntline, their adventures were romantic. [Inserting a logical subject, *their adventures*, clears up the problem; an independent clause is now preceded by a modifying prepositional phrase.]

14g How can I correct a mixed sentence due to faulty predication?

In **illogical predication**, sometimes called **faulty predication**, the subject and predicate do not make sense together.

No   The **job** of the Pony Express riders **delivered** the mail from Saint Joseph, Missouri, to Sacramento, California.

YES   The Pony Express **riders delivered** the mail from Saint Joseph, Missouri, to Sacramento, California.

YES   The job of the Pony Express riders **was to deliver** the mail from Saint Joseph, Missouri, to Sacramento, California.

Illogical predication is the problem in several common, informal constructions: *is when, is where,* and *reason is because.* Avoid these constructions in academic writing.

No   Across dangerous territory **is where** the riders traveled.

Yes   The riders traveled across dangerous territory.

No   **One reason** the Pony Express was so popular **was because** usual mail delivery took six weeks.

YES   **One reason** the Pony Express was so popular **was that** usual mail delivery took six weeks.

YES   The Pony Express was so popular **because** usual mail delivery took six weeks.

14h What are correct elliptical constructions?

An **incomplete sentence** is missing words, phrases, or clauses necessary for grammatical correctness or sensible meaning. Do not confuse an incomplete sentence with an elliptical construction. An **elliptical construction** deliberately leaves out words that have already appeared in the sentence: *I have my book and Joan's [book]*. The chief rule for an elliptical comparison is that the words left out must be exactly the same as the words that do appear in the sentence.

No   When migrating, most **birds travel** 25 to 30 miles per hour, but **the goose** 60 miles per hour. [The word *travel* cannot take the place of *travels*, needed in the second clause.]

YES   When migrating, most **birds travel** 25 to 30 miles per hour, but the **goose travels** 60 miles per hour.

No   Flying **in fog** and **water**, many migrating birds perish.

YES   Flying **in fog** and **over water**, many migrating birds perish.

14i What are correct comparisons?

In writing a comparison, be sure to include all words needed to make clear the relationship between the items or ideas being compared.

No   Young people learn languages faster. [*Faster* indicates a comparison, but none is stated.]

YES   Young people learn languages faster than adults do.

No   Some employers value bilingual employees more than people who speak only English. [not clear: Who values whom?]

YES   Some employers value bilingual employees more than they value people who speak only English.

No   A French speaker's enjoyment of Paris is greater than a nonspeaker. [*Enjoyment* is compared with a *nonspeaker*, a thing cannot be compared logically with a person.]

YES   French speaker's enjoyment of Paris is greater than a nonspeaker's.

No   Unfortunately, foreign languages have such a reputation for difficulty. [In academic writing, comparisons begun with *such*, *so*, and *too* must be completed.]

YES   Unfortunately, foreign languages have such a reputation for difficulty that many students are afraid to try to learn one.

14j How can I proofread successfully for little words I forget to use?

Small words—articles, pronouns, conjunctions, and prepositions—that are needed to make sentences complete sometimes slip into the cracks. If you tend accidentally to omit words, proofread your work an extra time solely to find them.

No   Naturalists say squirrel can hide as much twenty bushels food dozens of spots, but it rarely remembers where most of food is hidden.

YES   Naturalists say **a** squirrel can hide as much **as** twenty bushels **of** food **in** dozens of spots, but it rarely remembers where most of its food is hidden.

Revising to Eliminate Shifts   EXERCISE 14-1

A: Revise this paragraph to eliminate shifts in person and number. The first sentence should become "If you ever visit Miami, you will want to see Vizcaya." Use your own paper.

If I ever visit Miami, I will want to see Vizcaya. The estate was one of the homes of James Deering. He hired three young geniuses to build them: Hoffman, the architect; Chalfin, the artistic director; and Suarez, the landscape architect. Together, he built Deering's winter home on the shore of Bixcayne Bay. As the estate was built, they took almost ten percent of Miami's 1913 population to work on them. Deering was able to spend their first winter at Vizcaya in 1916. Other extremely wealthy people have also built great estates, but he didn't have the exquisite taste of Deering and his geniuses. Today, Vizcaya is a museum of the European decorative arts, a place they won't want to miss.

Sign language differs from the signage used by hearing-impaired people. For instance, he indicates the forehead to mean think while a Sioux pointed to the heart. You also use extensive facial expression in speaking to someone with a hearing loss while Native Americans maintained a stoic countenance. She believed the signs could speak for itself. Ideally you made the signs in round, sweeping motions. They tried to make conversation beautiful.

B: Revise this paragraph to eliminate shifts in verb tense. The first sentence should read "No one knows why sailors wear bell-bottom pants." Use your own paper.

No one knows why sailors wore bell-bottom pants. However, three theories were popular. First, bell-bottoms will fit over boots and keep sea spray and rain from getting in. Second, bell-bottoms could be rolled up over the knees, so they stayed dry when a sailor must wade ashore and stayed clean when he scrubbed the ship's deck. Third, because bell-bottoms are loose, they will be easy to take off in the water if a sailor fell overboard. In boot camp, sailors were taught another advantage to bell-bottoms. By taking them off and tying the legs at the ends, a sailor who has fallen into the ocean can change his bell-bottom pants into a life preserver.

C: Identify the shift in each passage by writing its code on the line to the right: 1 for a shift in person or number, 2 in subject or voice, 3 in tense, 4 in mood, or 5 in discourse (confusing direct and indirect quotation). Then revise each sentence to eliminate the shift.

EXAMPLE   When people speak of a fisherman knit sweater, you mean one from the
Aran Isles.   _____1_____
When people speak of a fisherman knit
sweater, they mean one from the Aran Isles.

1.   The Aran Isles are situated off the coast of Ireland. Galway is not far from the Isles.

     _____

     _____

2.   An islander has a difficult life. They must make their living by fishing in a treacherous sea.   _____

     _____

3.   They use a simple boat called a *curragh* for fishing. It is also used to ferry their market animals to barges.   _____

     _____

4.   Island houses stood out against the empty landscape. Their walls provide scant protection from a hostile environment.   _____

     _____

5.   In 1898 John Millington Synge first visited the Aran Isles. They are used as the setting for *Riders to the Sea* and other of his works.   _____

     _____

6.   Whether people see the Synge play or Ralph Vaughan Williams' operatic version of *Riders to the Sea*, you will feel the harshness of Aran life.   _____

     _____

7.   The mother Maurya has lost her husband and several sons. They are all drowned at sea.   _____

     _____

8.   When the body of another son is washed onto the shore, his sister identifies it from the pattern knitted into his sweater.   _____

     _____

9.   Each Aran knitter develops her own combination of patterns. The patterns not only produce a beautiful sweater, but they will have a very practical purpose.

     _____

     _____

10. The oiled wool protected the fishermen from the sea spray while the intricate patterns offer symbolic protection as well as identification when necessary. _____

_____

11. When you knit your first Aran Isle sweater, you should learn what the stitches mean. Don't choose a pattern just because it is easy. _____

_____

12. A cable stitch represents a fisherman's rope; winding cliff paths are depicted by the zigzag stitch. _____

_____

13. Bobbles symbolize men in a *curragh* while the basket stitch represented a fisherman's creel and the hope that it will come home full. _____

_____

14. The tree of life signifies strong sons and family unity. It was also a fertility symbol. _____

_____

15. When someone asks you did you knit your Aran Isle sweater yourself, you can proudly say that you did and you also chose the patterns. _____

_____

Eliminating Mixed Constructions, Faulty Predication, and Incomplete Sentences

A: Revise these mixed sentences to eliminate faulty predication and mixed constructions. It may be necessary to change, add, or omit words.

EXAMPLE: Easter is when Russians traditionally exchanged eggs.
            On Easter Russians traditionally exchanged eggs.

1.   When one thinks of Carl Faberge created Easter eggs for the stars.

     _____

2.   Because Faberge was a talented goldsmith was the reason he was able to make exquisite objects.

     _____

3.   Working for the court of Imperial Russia was able to combine craftsmanship and ingenuity.

     _____

4.   The object of Faberge pleased his clients by creating unique works of art.

     _____

5.   When he included gems in his creations but they did not overshadow his workmanship.

     _____

6.   In adapting enameling techniques achieved a level seldom matched by other artisans.

     _____

7.   With buyers in Europe expanded his clietele beyond the Russian royal family.

     _____

8.   Because he had no money worries meant few restrictions on imagination.

     _____

9.   Although Faberge created other examples of the jeweler's art, but it is the Imperial Easter eggs for which he is most remembered.

     _____

10. In the most famous eggs contained surprises inside—a hen, a ship, a coach.

     _____

11. When one egg opened to reveal a model of a palace.

_____

12. Because the most ambitious creation represented an egg surrounded by parts of a cathedral.

_____

13. An artist is when one practices an imaginative art.

_____

14. One reason Faberge is so admired is because he was a true artist.

_____

B: Revise these incomplete sentences to supply any carelessly omitted words or to complete compound constructions and comparisons clearly. Write *correct* if the sentence has no errors.

EXAMPLE   Cuneiform was system of writing with wedgelike marks.
            Cuneiform was a system of writing with wedgelike marks.

1. The use of cuneiform began and spread throughout ancient Sumer.

_____

2. This picture language of the Sumerians is thought to be older than the Egyptians.

_____

3. Like hieroglyphics, early cuneiform used easily recognizable pictures represent objects.

_____

4. When scribes began using a wedge-shaped stylus, greater changes occurred.

_____

5. The new marks were different.

_____

6. They had become so stylized.

_____

7. Early Sumerian tablets recorded practical things such lists of grain in storage.

_____

8. Some tablets were put clay envelopes that were themselves inscribed.

_____

9. Gradually ordinary people used cuneiform as much as official scribes.

_____

10. The Epic of Gilgamesh, written in Akkadian cuneiform, is older than any epic.

_____

11. The Code of Hammurabi recorded in cuneiform a more comprehensive set of laws.

_____

12. No one could decipher cuneiform script until someone discovered the Record of Darius.

_____

13. Because it was written in three languages, it served the same purpose.

_____

14. Today we understand cuneiform as much, if not more than, we understand hieroglyphics.

_____

C: Revise this paragraph, changing, adding, or deleting words as you see best, in order to eliminate mixed and incomplete sentences. Circle the number of the one sentence that contains no errors. Use your own paper.

[1]Although wild rice may be the caviar of grains is not really rice. [2]It is, however, truly wild. [3]One reason is because it needs marshy places in order to thrive. [4]By planting it in manmade paddies can produce abundant crops. [5]Nevertheless, most wild rice grows naturally along rivers and lake shores northern states and Canada. [6]In certain areas only Native Americans are allowed harvest the rice. [7]Connoisseurs think wild rice tastes better than any grain. [8]It is surely the most expensive. [9]Some hostesses serve it with Cornish hens exclusively, but the creative cook, with many dishes. [10]Try it in quiche or pancakes; your guests will be so pleased.

MODULE 15: CONCISENESS

15a What is conciseness?

Conciseness refers to writing that is direct and to the point. In concise writing, every word contributes to the clear presentation of the author's message.

15b What common expressions are not concise?

Imprecise and showy language creates wordiness. Review your handbook for advice on recognizing and avoiding showy (pretentious) language. When a writer tries to write very formally or tries to reach an assigned word limit, **padding** usually results. Sentences are loaded down with **deadwood**—empty words and phrases that add nothing but confusion.

PADDED	The lifeguards, who watch out for the safety of beachgoers, closed the beach near the water when a shark was sighted and seen.
CONCISE	The lifeguards closed the beach when a shark was sighted.
PADDED	After two hours, a fishing boat full of fishermen reported seeing the shark leave the local area of the shore, so the beach was declared reopened to the public.
CONCISE	Two hours later, a fishing boat reported seeing the shark leave the area, so the beach was reopened.

On the next page is a chart showing a few of the most common empty phrases. Before you use one of these, be sure it adds to the meaning of your passage.

GUIDE FOR ELIMINATING EMPTY WORDS AND PHRASES

EMPTY WORD OR PHRASE	WORDY EXAMPLE	REVISION
as a matter of fact	**As a matter of fact,** statistics show that many marriages end in divorce.	Statistics show that many marriages end in divorce.
because of the fact	**Because of the fact that** a special exhibit is scheduled, the museum will be open until ten o'clock.	Because of a special exhibit, the museum will be open until ten o'clock.
in fact	**In fact,** the physicist published her results yesterday.	The physicist published her results yesterday.
in view of the fact that	**In view of the fact that** the rainfall was so heavy, we may have flooding.	Because the rainfall was so heavy, we may have flooding.
seems	It **seems** that the union called a strike over health benefits.	The union called a strike over health benefits.
tendency	The team had a **tendency** to lose home games.	The team often lost home games.

15c What sentence structures usually work against conciseness?

1 Avoiding expletive constructions

An **expletive** postpones the subject by putting *it* or *there* plus a form of the verb *be* before the subject. If you remove the expletive and revise slightly, you place the subject in a position of greater impact—the beginning of the sentence.

No	It is fun to taste foods from other cultures.
Yes	Tasting foods from other cultures is fun.
No	There is a new Greek restaurant opening in town.
Yes	A new Greek restaurant is opening in town.

2 Avoiding the passive voice

For most writing, the active voice adds liveliness as well as conciseness. When a passive construction names the doer of an action, it does so in a phrase starting with *by*. To change a passive sentence into an active sentence, make the noun or pronoun in the *by* phrase the subject of the sentence.

No	The cafeteria was boycotted by students to protest high prices.
Yes	Students boycotted the cafeteria to protest high prices.

You can also revise a sentence from passive to active by finding a new verb. In this technique you keep the same subject but change the verb voice.

Passive	Clint Eastwood **was elected** mayor of Carmel, California.
Active	Clint Eastwood **won** the mayoral election in Carmel, California.

15d How else can I revise for conciseness?

1 Revising to eliminate unplanned repetition

Intentional repetition can create a powerful effect, but unplanned repetition of words or ideas (known as **redundancy**) can make an essay boring.

No	The college is building a new **parking lot** to provide more **parking space.**
Yes	The college is building a new **lot** to provide more **parking space.**
No	The model was **slender in shape** and **tall in height.**
Yes	The model was **slender** and **tall.**

2 Revising by combining sentences

Often when you revise you can combine sentences or reduce a clause to a phrase or a phrase to a single word, making your writing more concise and your original idea clearer.

Combining sentences: Look carefully at sets of sentences in your draft. You may be able to reduce the information in an entire sentence to a group of words that you can include in another sentence.

TWO SENTENCES	In 1985, Mel Fisher found *Nuestra Señora de Atocha* 40 miles west of Key West, Florida. The *Atocha* was a Spanish treasure ship.
COMBINED SENTENCE	In 1985, Mel Fisher found the Spanish treasure ship *Nuestra Señora de Atocha* 40 miles west of Key West, Florida.
TWO SENTENCES	The *Atocha* was heading for Spain in 1622 when it sank in a hurricane. It was loaded with gold and silver.
COMBINED SENTENCE	The *Atocha* was heading for Spain in 1622 when it sank in a hurricane, along with its load of gold and silver.

3 Revising by shortening clauses

Reducing clauses: You can often reduce adjective clauses to phrases, sometimes just by dropping the relative pronoun and its verb.

Earlier, Fisher had found the *Santa Margarita,* **which was the *Atocha's*** sister ship.

Earlier, Fisher had found the *Santa Margarita,* **the *Atocha's*** sister ship.

Sometimes you can reduce the clause to a single word.

Fisher's find will make **people who invested in his company** rich.

Fisher's find will make **investors** rich.

Creating elliptical constructions is another way to reduce clauses, but be sure to omit only strongly implied words.

While they were searching for the *Atocha*, Fisher's son and daughter-in-law drowned.

While searching for the *Atocha*, Fisher's son and daughter-in-law drowned.

4 Revising by shortening phrases and cutting words

Reducing phrases: You may be able to shorten phrases or reduce them to single words.

In 1966, Fisher had begun to search for **the fleet that the *Atocha* was leading.**

In 1966, Fisher had begun to search for **the *Atocha* fleet.**

In twenty years, Fisher found more than a hundred **ships that had been wrecked.**

In twenty years, Fisher found more than a hundred **shipwrecks**.

15e How do verbs affect conciseness?

Your writing will have more impact when you choose strong verbs—verbs that directly convey action—instead of forms of *be* or *have*. Using strong verbs also reduces the number of words in your sentences.

No	The city council **has a plan** to build a new stadium.
Yes	The city council **plans** to build a new stadium.
No	Being home to a professional baseball team **is a way to promote** civic pride.
Yes	Being home to a professional baseball team **promotes** civic pride.

When you look for weak verbs to revise, look too for **nominals**—nouns created from verbs, often by adding suffixes such as *-ance, -ment,* or *-tion.* For clear, concise writing, turn nominals back into verbs.

No	The company **was involved in the importation** of catchers' mitts.
Yes	The company **imported** catchers' mitts.

Eliminating Wordy Sentence Structures

Revise these sentences to eliminate wordy sentence structures. You may need to delete expletives, change passive sentences to the active voice, reduce clauses to phrases or phrases to words, and/or replace weak, heavily modified verbs with strong direct verbs.

EXAMPLE   It is Art Deco which became an international style in the 1920s and 1930s.
Art Deco became an international style in the 1920s and 1930s.

1. Art Deco took its name from an exposition which was held in Paris in 1925.

   _____

2. Art Deco may be defined as a style that used shapes that were bold and stream-lined and that experimented with new materials.

   _____

3. In the 1920s Art Deco was influenced by public fascination with technology and the future.

   _____

4. In addition to architecture, which it dominated, the style could be found in designs for glassware, appliances, furniture, and even advertising art.

   _____

5. The Empire State Building and the Chrysler Building are exemplifications of the dynamic style of Art Deco.

   _____

6. After the crash of the stock market in 1929, Art Deco became less extravagant in its expression of modern ideas and themes.

   _____

7. There was a restraint and austerity in the Art Deco of the Great Depression.

   _____

8. Builders of architecture made use of rounded corners, glass blocks, and porthole windows.

   _____

9. They had a liking for roofs that were flat.

   _____

10. Buildings that had plain exteriors often were decorated with lavish care inside and had furniture to match.

   _____

Revise these sentences to eliminate unneeded words and phrases.

EXAMPLE   It seems that many cultures considered the first of May the official beginning of summer.
Many cultures considered the first of May the official beginning of summer.

1. As a matter of fact, the Romans gave sacrifices to the goddess Maia on the first day of the month named for her.

    _____

2. It seems that the Celts also celebrated May Day as the midpoint of their year.

    _____

3. One of the most important of the May Day celebrations that exist is the Maypole.

    _____

4. In a very real sense, the Maypole represented rebirth.

    _____

5. In Germany a Maypole tree was often stripped of all but the top branches for the purpose of representing new life.

    _____

6. In the case of Sweden, floral wreaths were suspended from a crossbar on the pole.

    _____

7. The English had a different type of tradition.

    _____

8. Holding streamers attached to the top of the Maypole, villagers danced around it in an enthusiastic manner.

    _____

9. In view of the fact that May Day had pagan beginnings, the Puritans disapproved of it.

    _____

10. Thus it never had a tendency to become popular in the United States.

    _____

Eliminating Redundancies

Revise these sentences to eliminate unnecessary repetition of words and redundant ideas. Retain helpful repetition.

EXAMPLE   Stamps are small in size, and it takes many in number to make a good collection.
Stamps are small, and it takes many to make a good collection.

1. Many new collectors express astonished amazement at the number of stamps to be collected.

_____

2. They get excited about each and every new stamp they acquire.

_____

3. They hope to make their collections totally complete.

_____

4. Soon it becomes perfectly clear that a complete collection is impossible.

_____

5. Then they may take the pragmatic approach and be practical.

_____

6. They limit their collections by confining them to one country, continent, or decade.

_____

7. At that point in time, their collections will again provide great satisfaction.

_____

8. It is a consensus of opinion that collecting stamps can be educational.

_____

9. It can teach about past history or the geography of the earth.

_____

10. Nevertheless, a new collector should not become discouraged by overstepping possibility and trying to collect too much.

_____

Revising for Conciseness

Revise these paragraphs to eliminate wordiness, pointless repetitions, and redundancies. Combine sentences as necessary.

A: The city of San Juan, a city in Puerto Rico, is interesting not only because it is a growing and expanding metropolis but also because of its historical roots in the past. It was founded in 1521. San Juan is the oldest city on United States soil. It seems that San Juan was originally enclosed in a seven-square-block walled area. This area was known as Old San Juan. The city experienced a large population explosion in the nineteenth century. As a result, it grew in size. As a matter of fact, by 1898, at the time of the Spanish-American war, parts of the wall had been destroyed and knocked down to allow for the expansion of the city that was growing rapidly. Presently, San Juan today is home to 1.5 million people. San Juan is considered to be very influential in the Puerto Rican community. People consider it to be influential because in addition to being the island's political capital, it seems that it is also known as the island's cultural, financial, and social capital.

B: Auguste Escoffier was the most famous chef at the turn of the century between 1880 and World War I. In a very real sense, he was the leader of the culinary world of his day. Until that point in time, the best chefs were found in private homes. With Escoffier came an era of fine dining at restaurants to which the nobility and wealthy flocked in order to eat well. After Escoffier joined Cesar Ritz, the luxury hotel owner, they worked as a team together to attract such patrons as the Prince of Wales. Ritz had a tendency to make each and every guest feel personally welcome. It was Escoffier who added the crowning touch by preparing dishes made especially for guests. He created dishes for the prince and for celebrities such as those well known in the entertainment world. He concocted a soup which was called consomme favori de Sarah Bernhardt for the actress of the same name. There was an opera singer for whom he created poularde Adelina Patti. As a matter of fact, another singer was fortunate to have more than one dish named for her. When Nellie Melba, an Australian singer, sang in Lohengrin, Escoffier served peaches melba, a combination of poached peaches and vanilla ice cream. To commemorate the swans of Lohengrin, he served the dessert in a swan that was made of ice. Melba toast was created by Escoffier during one of the periods when Melba was trying to diet. Today despite the fact that many people have not heard of Nellie Melba, they are familiar with melba toast. As a young army chef, Escoffier had to prepare horse meat and even rat meat for the purpose of feeding the troops. It is obvious that he left those days far behind him when he became the most renowned chef of his day.

MODULE 16: COORDINATION AND SUBORDINATION

COORDINATION

16a What is coordination of sentences?

A **coordinate** (or **compound**) **sentence** consists of independent clauses joined by a semi-colon or a coordinating conjunction (*and, but, for, nor, or, so,* or *yet*). ✤ PUNCTUATION ALERT: Always put a comma before a coordinating conjunction that joins two independent clauses. ✤

COORDINATE (COMPOUND) SENTENCE
Independent clause   , and / , but / , for / , nor / , or / , so / , yet / ;   independent clause.

Each coordinating conjunction has a specific meaning that establishes the relationship between the ideas in a coordinate sentence.

MEANING OF THE COORDINATING CONJUNCTIONS

CONJUNCTION	MEANING	FUNCTION
and	also, in addition to	to join
but	however	to contrast
for	because	to show cause
nor	an additional negative	to make the second element negative
or	an alternative	to show more than one possibility
so	therefore	to show result
yet	nevertheless	to contrast

Tuition was increasing, **and** the price of the meal plan was going up even more.

Her schedule was tight, **but** she knew she needed to get a job.

16b What is the structure of a coordinate sentence?

Coordinate sentences communicate that the ideas in each independent clause carry equal weight. At the same time, they explain the relationships among those ideas more effectively than a group of separate sentences would.

UNCLEAR RELATIONSHIPS	We planned a picnic. It rained. We had brought a lot of food. We had to make other arrangements. The food would spoil. We went to the ballfield in the park to use the dugout. It was full of water. We all went home.
CLEAR RELATIONSHIPS	We planned a picnic, **but** it rained. We had brought a lot of food, **so** we had to make other arrangements, **or** the food would spoil. We went to the ballfield in the park to use the dugout, **but** it was full of water, **so** we all went home.

16c What meaning does each coordinating conjunction convey?

Coordination can be used to pile up details for dramatic effect. Consider this passage, in which coordinate sentences present an unfolding of events.

Scott woke up before the alarm went off. He was hungry, **but** he skipped breakfast. He raced to the showroom, **and** then he had to stand in the cold for fifteen minutes waiting for the place to open. Finally, the manager arrived, **but** before he could put the key in the lock Scott blurted out, "I got this card; it says my car has arrived."

16d How can I avoid misusing coordination?

Coordination is illogical when ideas in the joined independent clauses are not related and when ideas do not unfold in a purposeful sequence. Avoid illogically coordinated sentences.

No   Bicycles are becoming a popular means of transportation, **and** they are dangerous on city streets. [Each independent clause is true, but the ideas are not related.]

Yes   Bicycles are becoming a popular means of transportation, **yet** the crowded conditions on city streets can make riding them dangerous.

Like all good techniques, coordination can be used too often. Overused coordination can result from writing down whatever comes into your head and not revising later. Avoid overusing coordination.

No   Hawaii is famous for its coral, **and** some of it is very shiny and hard, **so** it can last indefinitely. Some Hawaiian coral is black, **and** some is gold or pink, **and** Hawaii has $10 million a year in coral sales, **but** worldwide sales are $500 million a year.

Yes   Hawaii is famous for its coral. Some of it is very shiny and hard enough to last indefinitely. Hawaiian coral comes in black, gold, and pink. Although Hawaii has $10 million a year in coral sales, worldwide sales are $500 million a year.

No   Laughter seems to help healing, **so** many doctors are prescribing humor for their patients, **and** some hospitals are doing the same. Comedians have donated their time to several California hospitals, **and** the nurses in one large hospital in Texas have been trained to tell each patient a joke a day.

Yes   Laughter seems to help healing. Many doctors and hospitals are prescribing humor for their patients. Comedians have donated their time to several California hospitals, and the nurses in one large hospital in Texas have been trained to tell each patient a joke a day.

SUBORDINATION

16e What is subordination in sentences?

A sentence that uses subordination contains at least two clauses: (1) an **independent clause**, which can stand on its own as a sentence, and (2) a **dependent clause**, which cannot stand alone. Subordination joins related but separate items so that one is featured—the one in the independent clause.

Some dependent clauses start with **subordinating conjunctions**, words such as *after, before, until, when, so that* and *although*. ❖ PUNCTUATION ALERTS: (1) When a dependent clause that starts with a subordinating conjunction occurs before the independent clause, separate the clauses with a comma. (2) When such a clause follows the independent clause, separate the clauses with a comma *unless* the dependent clause is essential to the meaning of the independent clause. ❖

While tuition had increased, the price of the meal plan had gone up even more.
Although her schedule was tight, she knew she needed to get a job.

Some dependent clauses start with **relative pronouns**, such as *who, which,* and *that*. Dependent clauses that begin with relative pronouns are called **relative clauses** (or **adjective** clauses). They either follow or interrupt the independent clauses they modify. ❖ PUNCTUATION ALERT: When an adjective clause is nonrestrictive—that is, when the clause is not essential to the meaning of the sentence—separate it from the independent clause with commas. ❖

Tuition, **which was high**, increased again.

The student, **who was already on a tight schedule**, needed to get a job.

16f What is the structure of a subordinate sentence?

To use subordination in your sentences, start the **dependent clause** with either a subordinating conjunction, or a relative pronoun (*which, that, who, whom, whose*).

If they are very lucky, the passengers may glimpse dolphins breaking water playfully near the ship.

—ELIZABETH GRAY, *student*

Pandas are solitary animals, **which** means they are difficult to protect from extinction.

—JOSE JOSE SANTOS, *student*

Dependent clauses are of two types: **adverb clauses** and **adjective clauses**. An adverb clause starts with a subordinating conjunction. Each subordinating conjunction has a specific meaning that expresses a relationship between the dependent clause and the independent clause. An adjective clause starts with a **relative pronoun** (*that, which, who, whom, whose*).

16g What meaning does each subordinating conjunction convey?

Each subordinating conjunction expresses a different relationship between the major and minor ideas in the subordinate sentences.

SUBORDINATING CONJUNCTIONS AND THE RELATIONSHIPS THEY IMPLY	
Time	*after, before, once, since, until, when, whenever, while*
Reason or Cause	*as, because*
Result or Effect	*in order that, so that*
Condition	*if, even if, provided that unless*
Concession	*although, even though, though*
Location	*where, wherever*
Choice	*rather than, than, whether*

Notice how a change in the subordinating conjunction can change your meaning.

After you have been checked in, you cannot leave the security area without a pass. [time limit]

Because you have been checked in, you cannot leave the security area without a pass. [reason]

Unless you have been checked in, you cannot leave the security area without a pass. [condition]

Although you have been checked in, you cannot leave the security area without a pass. [concession]

16h How can I avoid misusing subordination?

Subordination directs your reader's attention to the idea in the independent clause, while using the ideas in the dependent clause to provide context and support. Subordination communicates relationships among ideas more effectively than a group of separate sentences does.

UNCLEAR RELATIONSHIPS	I waited at the bus station. I thought I saw Marcia. She was my baby-sitter fifteen years ago. I was gathering the courage to approach her. She boarded a bus and was gone.
CLEAR RELATIONSHIPS	As I waited at the bus station, I thought I saw Marcia, who was my baby-sitter fifteen years ago. While I was gathering the courage to approach her, she boarded a bus and was gone.

Subordination is illogical when the subordinating conjunction does not make clear the relationship between the independent and dependent clauses. Avoid illogical subordination.

No	Before some states made wearing seat belts mandatory, the number of fatal automobile accidents fell. [illogical: The fatality rate fell as a result of, not prior to, the seat belt laws.]
YES	After some states made wearing seat belts mandatory, the number of fatal automobile accidents fell.
No	Because he was deaf when he wrote them, Beethoven's final symphonies were masterpieces. [illogical: It was not Beethoven's deafness that led to his writing symphonic masterpieces.]
YES	Although Beethoven was deaf when he wrote his final symphonies, they are musical masterpieces.

Like all good writing techniques, subordination can be overused. Overusing subordination means crowding together too many images or ideas, so that readers become confused and lose track of the message. Avoid overusing subordination.

No	As a result of water pollution, many shellfish beds, which once supported many families that had lived in the areas for generations, are being closed, which is causing hardships for these families.
YES	As a result of water pollution, many shellfish beds are being closed. This is causing hardships for the many families that have supported themselves for generations by harvesting these waters.
No	A new technique for eye surgery, which is supposed to correct nearsightedness, which previously could be corrected only by glasses, has been developed, although many doctors do not approve of it because it can create unstable eyesight.

YES A new technique for eye surgery, which is supposed to correct nearsightedness, has been developed. Previously, nearsightedness could be corrected only by glasses. Because it can create unstable eyesight, many doctors do not approve of it, however.

16i How can I effectively use coordination and subordination together?

Coordination and subordination are not always used in separate sentences. **Compound-complex sentences** combine coordination with subordination to make sentences that flow.

Since only a few people are supposed to have this mathematical mind, part of what makes us so passive in the face of our difficulties in learning mathematics is that we suspect all the while we may not be one of "them," and we spend our time waiting to find out when our nonmathematical minds will be exposed.

—SHEILA TOBIAS, *Overcoming Math Anxiety*

Name _____   Date _____

Combining Sentences with Coordination

Combine these sentences using coordination. For the first five sentences, use the coordinating conjunction given; for the rest, use whatever coordinating conjunction you feel is most appropriate. It may be necessary to add or change a few words, but major rewriting is not needed.

EXAMPLE   *TV Guide* was not the first television magazine with local listings. It has become the most popular. (but)
    TV Guide *was not the first television magazine with local listings,* *but it has become the most popular.*

1. In 1952 publisher Walter H. Annenberg heard that someone was considering starting a national television magazine.
    He became interested in the idea himself. (and)

    _____

    _____

2. He wanted to learn about his competition.
    He had one of his assistants find out if such magazines already existed. (so)

    _____

    _____

3. The assistant found local television magazines being published in New York, Philadelphia, Chicago, and Los Angeles.
    Annenberg bought them all. (;)

    _____

    _____

4. Articles to appear in the first issue were written quickly.
    There was no supply of already completed work to rely on. (for)

    _____

    _____

5. One of the first people hired was sportswriter Red Smith.
    This was before he won a Pulitzer Prize for sports reporting. (but)

    _____

    _____

6. Starting the magazine was hard work.
    One decision was not hard at all.

    _____

    _____

7. *I Love Lucy* was the most popular show on the air in 1953.
    The star, Lucille Ball, had just given birth to a baby boy.

    _____

    _____

8. The whole country had followed Lucy's pregnancy.
The editors decided to take advantage of this interest and to feature the baby, Desi Arnaz, Jr.

_____

_____

9. They could not ignore the baby's popularity.
They could not ignore Lucy's popularity.

_____

_____

10. The cover had a big picture of Desi Jr.
It had a smaller picture of Lucy in the upper right-hand corner.

_____

_____

11. From the beginning *TV Guide* has been a national magazine.
It has different editions, giving local listings.

_____

_____

12. Sales fell soon after the first, successful issue.
Summer had come.
People preferred to sit outside in the cool night air rather than watch television in their hot living rooms.

_____

_____

13. The editors had to have a sudden great idea.
The magazine would fail.

_____

_____

14. They needed to increase interest in their subject.
They decided to devote one issue to the new shows scheduled for the 1953-54 season.

_____

_____

15. That first Fall Preview issue sold out.
It started a tradition that is repeated at the start of every new television season.

_____

_____

Combining Sentences
with Subordination

EXERCISE 16-2

Combine these sentences using subordination. For the first five sentences, use the subordinating conjunction or relative pronoun given; for the rest, use whatever subordinating conjunction or relative pronoun you feel is most appropriate. Some items have more than one correct answer, but most make sense only one way, so decide carefully which sentence comes first and where to place the subordinating conjunction or relative pronoun. It may sometimes be necessary to add or change a few words, but major rewriting is not needed.

EXAMPLE   Many countries around the world started using fragrances.
Researchers found that fragrances have a stimulating effect on people. (after)
Many countries around the world started using fragrances after researchers found that fragrances have a stimulating effect on people.

1. A company in Toronto, Canada, was one of the first ones to install a fragrancing unit in its office ventilation system. It was installed to control employee behavior. (in order to)

    _____

    _____

2. The company was careful about which fragrances it introduced into the workplace. Some fragrances rev people up, and some calm them down. (because)

    _____

    _____

3. The scents were designed by Toronto-based Aromasphere, Inc. The company created a time-release mechanism to send the scents directly into the work area. (which)

    _____

    _____

4. Bodywise Ltd. in Great Britain received a patent for a fragrance. It began to market its scent, which contains adrostenone, an ingredient of male sweat. (once)

    _____

    _____

5. The scent was adopted by a U.S. debt-collection agency. Another agency in Australia reported that chronic debtors who receive scented letters were 17 percent more likely to pay than were those who received unscented letters. (after)

    _____

    _____

6. Researchers have recently discovered how much odor can influence behavior. Smell is still the least understood of the five senses.

    _____

    _____

7. Aromasphere's employees have been asked to keep logs of their moods. They are in the workplace.

_____

_____

8. Researchers have raised many concerns about trying to change human behavior. They feel that this kind of tampering may lead to too much control over employees.

_____

_____

9. Smells can have an effect on people. They may be completely unaware of what is happening.

_____

_____

10. Employees are forewarned, however, that they will be exposed to mood-altering fragrances. Such employees may protest against the introduction of such scents in the workplace.

_____

_____

11. Even psychiatric wards emit a scent. It makes the patients calm.

_____

_____

12. International Flavors and Fragrances of New York is the world's largest manufacturer of artificial flavors and aromas. It has developed many of the scents commonly used today.

_____

_____

13. It has even created a bagel scent. Bagels lose their aroma when they are contained in plexiglass.

_____

_____

14. There wasn't a true commercial interest in these products. Researchers began to understand somewhat the anatomy of smell.

_____

_____

15. It turns out that olfactory signals travel to the limbic region of the brain. Hormones of the automatic nervous system are regulated.

_____

_____

Expanding Sentences with Coordination and Subordination

Add to each sentence below in two ways. First add an independent clause, using a coordinating conjunction. Then add a dependent clause beginning with either a subordinating conjunction or a relative pronoun.

EXAMPLE   Living in Northern California can be challenging.
Living in Northern California can be challenging, but the residents don't seem to mind.
Living in Northern California can be challenging as people who live there will tell you.

1.   There are severe winter storms.

_____

_____

2.   The electricity often goes out.

_____

_____

3.   Flooding occurs.

_____

_____

4.   Roads may be blocked by landslides.

_____

_____

5.   Wind and surf advisories are frequent.

_____

_____

6.   Summers are cool and foggy.

_____

_____

7.   The average ocean temperature is about 55 degrees.

_____

_____

8.   Large rogue waves thunder onto beaches and jetties.

_____

_____

9.   Shaking from earthquakes can be unnerving.

_____

_____

10.   The area's natural beauty is worth the many challenges of living there.

_____

_____

Using Coordination and Subordination in a Paragraph

These paragraphs are full of choppy sentences. Revise them using coordinating and subordinating conjunctions so that the sentences are smoother and more fully explain the relationships between ideas. Many correct versions are possible. Take the time to try several, and select the version you like best.

Senet is a game. It was played by ancient Egyptians. It was very popular. Egyptians began putting senet boards into tombs as early as 3100 B.C. Tomb objects were intended for use in the afterlife. They give us a good idea of daily life.

Many senet boards and playing pieces have been found in tombs. The hot, dry air of the tombs preserved them well. Tomb paintings frequently show people playing the game. Hieroglyphic texts describe it. Numerous descriptions of the game survive. Egyptologists think it was a national pastime.

Senet was a game for two people. They played it on a board marked with thirty squares. Each player had several playing pieces. They probably each had seven. The number did not matter as long as it was the same for both. Opponents moved by throwing flat sticks. The sticks were an early form of dice. Sometimes they threw pairs of lamb knuckles instead. Players sat across from each other. They moved their pieces in a backward S line. The squares represented houses. They moved through the houses.

By the New Kingdom the game began to take on religious overtones. The thirty squares were given individual names. They were seen as stages on the journey of the soul through the netherworld. New Kingdom tomb paintings showed the deceased playing senet with an unseen opponent. The object was to win eternal life. The living still played the game. They played it in anticipation of the supernatural match to come.

MODULE 17: PARALLELISM

17a What is parallelism?

Parallelism is related to the concept of parallel lines in geometry. In writing, parallelism calls for the use of equivalent grammatical forms to express equivalent ideas. Parallel forms match words with words in the same form, phrases with similar phrases, or clauses with other clauses composed of the same verb forms and word orders.

Parallelism helps you communicate that two or more items in a group are equally important and makes your writing more graceful. For this reason, it is a good idea to avoid the error of faulty **parallelism**—using nonequivalent grammatical patterns.

PARALLEL WORDS	A triathlon includes **running, swimming**, and **cycling**. [The *-ings* are parallel in form and equal in importance.]
PARALLEL PHRASES	Training requires **an intense exercise program** and a **carefully regulated diet**. [The phrases are parallel in structure and equal in importance.]
PARALLEL CLAUSES	Most people prefer to watch the triathlon rather than participate **because the triathlon is so difficult** and **because their couches are so comfortable**. [The clauses starting with because are parallel in structure and equal in importance.]

17b What is a balanced sentence?

Words in lists or other parallel structures must occur in the same grammatical form. Be sure to use such matching forms for parallel items.

No	The warm-up includes **stretches, sit-ups**, and **sprinting**.
YES	The warm-up includes **stretches, sit-ups**, and **sprints**.
YES	The warm-up includes **stretching, doing sit-ups**, and **sprinting**.
No	The strikers had tried **pleading, threats**, and **shouting**.
YES	The strikers had tried **pleading, threatening**, and **shouting**.
YES	The strikers had tried **pleas, threats**, and **shouts**.

17c How do words, phrases, and clauses work in parallel form?

Phrases and clauses in parallel structures must occur in the same grammatical form. Be sure to use such matching forms for parallel items.

No	The kitchen crew **scraped the grill**, the salt shakers were refilled, and were taking out the trash.
Yes	The kitchen crew **scraped the grill**, **refilled the salt shakers**, and **took out the trash**.

17d How does parallelism deliver impact?

Parallel structures characterized by balance serve to emphasize the meaning that sentences deliver. Balanced, parallel structures can be words, phrases, clauses, or sentences.

Deliberate, rhythmic repetition of parallel, balanced word forms and word groups reinforces the impact of a message. Consider the impact of this famous passage:

> **Go back** to Mississippi, **go back to** Alabama, **go back to** South Carolina, **go back to** Georgia, **go back to** Louisiana, **go back to** the slums and ghettos of our northern cities, knowing that somehow this situation can and will be changed.
>
> —Martin Luther King Jr., "I Have a Dream"

King's structures reinforce the power of his message. An ordinary sentence would have been less effective: "Return to your homes in Mississippi, Alabama, South Carolina, Georgia, Louisiana, or the cities, and know that the situation will be changed."

A **balanced sentence** has two parallel structures, usually sentences, with contrasting content. A balanced sentence is a coordinate sentence, characterized by opposition in the meaning of the two structures, sometimes with one cast in the negative: *Mosquitos do not bite, they stab.*

Parallel sentences in longer passages provide coherence. The carefully controlled repetition of words and word forms creates a pattern that enables readers to follow ideas more easily.

17e How can I avoid faulty parallelism?

Whenever you join words, phrases, or clauses with coordinating conjunctions or correlative conjunctions, be sure that they occur in parallel form.

Happiness is good health **and** a bad memory.

> —Ingrid Bergman

We are the carriers of health and disease—**either** *the divine health of courage and nobility* **or** *the demonic disease of hate and anxiety.*

> —Joshua Loth Liebman

Absence *diminishes little passions* **and** *increases great ones,* **as** wind *extinguishes candles* **and** *fans a fire.*

> —Francois de La Rochefoucauld

To strengthen the effect of parallelism, repeat words that begin parallel phrases or clauses. Such words include prepositions, articles (*a, an, the*), and the *to* of an infinitive.

To *find* a fault is easy; **to** *do* better may be difficult.

—PLUTARCH

Use parallel clauses beginning with *and who, and whom,* or *and which* when they follow clauses beginning with *who, whom,* or *which.*

I have in my own life a precious friend, a woman of 65 who has lived very hard, who is wise, who listens well, who has been where I am and can help me understand it; and who represents not only an ultimate ideal mother to me but also the person I'd like to be when I grow up.

—JUDITH VIORST, "Friends, Good Friends—and Such Good Friends"

17f How does parallelism work in outlines and lists?

Items in formal outlines and lists should be in parallel structure. Without parallelism, the information may not be clear to the reader and may not communicate that the items are equally important.

Outline not in parallel form

TYPES OF FIRE EXTINGUISHER

I.   The Class A Type
  A.   Contains water or water-chemical solution
  B.   For fighting wood, paper, or cloth fires
II. Class B
  A.   Foam, dry chemicals, or carbon dioxide "snow"
  B.   Use against grease or flammable-liquid fires
III. Class C
  A.   Containing dry chemicals
  B.   Electrical fires

Outline in parallel form

TYPES OF FIRE EXTINGUISHER

I.   **Class A**
  A.   **Contains** water or water-chemical solution
  B.   **Fights** wood, paper, or cloth fires
II. **Class B**
  A.   **Contains** foam, dry chemicals, or carbon dioxide "snow"
  B.   **Fights** grease or flammable-liquid fires
III. **Class C**
  A.   **Contains** dry chemicals
  B.   **Fights** electrical fires

List not in parallel form

HOW TO ESCAPE A FIRE

1. Feel the door for heat, and don't open it if it is hot.
2. You should open the door slowly.
3. Smoke?
4. If there is smoke, close the door and leave by another door or window.
5. If there is no other exit—try crawling under the smoke.
6. Be sure to use the stairs; the elevator should be avoided.
7. The fire department.
8. Reenter the building? No!

List in parallel form

HOW TO ESCAPE A FIRE

1. **Feel** the door for heat; **do** not **open** it if it is hot.
2. **Open** the door slowly.
3. **Check** the hall for smoke.
4. **If there is** smoke, **close** the door and **leave** by another door or window.
5. **If there is** no other exit, **crawl** under the smoke.
6. **Use** stairs, never an elevator.
7. **Call** the fire department.
8. **Do** not **reenter** the building.

Identifying Parallel Elements   EXERCISE 17-1

Underline parallel words, phrases, and clauses.

EXAMPLE   Many ancient writers <u>in Greece</u> and <u>in Rome</u> wrote about underwater ships.

1.   They hoped these ships would be used for exploration and travel.

2.   Leonardo Da Vinci felt that humanity would be destroyed by a great flood because of its proud and evil ways.

3.   Therefore, just as earlier he had made plans for a helicopter, he made plans for an underwater ship.

4.   However, the first working submarine was designed by a British mathematician and built by a Dutch inventor.

5.   It was designed in 1578, built in 1620, and successfully tested from 1620 to 1624.

6.   This submarine was equipped with oars, so it could be used either on the surface or below the surface.

7.   King James I of England actually boarded the submarine and took a short ride.

8.   James's praise soon made submarines the talk of the town and the focus of scientific investigation.

9.   A much later model featured goatskin bags attached to holes in the bottom of the ship. When the vessel was to submerge, the bags would fill with water and pull the ship downward; when the vessel was to rise, a twisting rod would force water from the bags, and the lightened ship would surface.

10.   David Bushnell, a student at Yale during the American Revolution, designed and built a war-submarine, the Turtle.

11.   It was intended to sneak up on British warships and attach explosives to their hulls.

12.   Despite successful launching and steering, the Turtle failed on its only mission when the pilot was unable to attach the explosives to the British target ship.

13.   The first successful wartime submarines were developed by the South in the Civil War: small, four-person ships called "Davids" and a full-sized submarine called the "Hunley."

14.   New submarines were designed throughout the nineteenth century, but providing dependable power and seeing to navigate remained problems for years.

15.   The development of the gasoline engine and the invention of the periscope solved these problems before the beginning of World War I.

Writing Parallel Elements

Fill in the blanks with words, phrases, or clauses, as appropriate.

EXAMPLE   Many people enjoy watching TV once in awhile, especially when they are
physically, and _mentally_, exhausted.

1   Sometimes after a demanding day at work, it's relaxing to turn on the TV,
_____, and _____.

2.   TV shows can be _____ and _____.

3.   Because there are more channels than ever before, channel surfing can be
_____ or _____.

4.   _____ and _____ are ways some people describe TV viewing.

5.   Others describe TV viewing as _____ and _____.

6.   Those people claim that finding a _____ TV show is much more difficult
than finding a _____ one.

7.   But the wonderful range of programs now available means that people of all
_____ and _____ can find something they want to watch on TV.

8.   Like anything else, watching too much TV may cause _____ , and
_____ problems.

9.   Just be sure to balance TV viewing with physical activities such as _____
and _____.

10. Also be sure to balance TV viewing with mental activities such as _____
or _____ a puzzle.

11. It an be upsetting when your favorite TV show is scheduled while you are away from
home either _____ or _____ errands.

12. However, many people are adept at recording the TV shows they want to
_____ or can't bear to _____.

13. TV is especially important for people who live in rural areas where live _____
and sports _____ are rare.

14. These people can enjoy an evening at the New York Metropolitan Opera or at
Yankee Stadium in the _____ and _____ of their own homes.

15. In spite of what naysayers may think of TV, I would rather _____ one than
not _____ one.

MODULE 18: VARIETY AND EMPHASIS

18a What are variety and emphasis in writing?

Your writing style has **variety** when your sentence lengths and patterns vary. Your writing style has **emphasis** when your sentences are constructed to reflect the relative importance of your ideas. Variety and **emphasis** are closely related. They represent the joining of form and meaning.

18b How do different sentence lengths create variety and emphasis?

If you vary your sentence length, you signal distinctions among your ideas so that your readers can understand the focus of your material. Also you avoid the monotony created by an unvarying rhythm.

Strings of too many short sentences rarely establish relationships and levels of importance among ideas. Such strings suggest that the writer has not thought through the material and decided what to emphasize.

No   Ants are much like human beings. It is embarrassing. They farm fungi. They raise aphids as livestock They launch armies into wars. They use chemical sprays to alarm and confuse enemies. They capture slaves.

YES   Ants are so much like human beings as to be an embarrassment. They farm fungi, raise aphids as livestock, launch armies into wars, use chemical sprays to alarm and confuse enemies, capture slaves.

—LEWIS THOMAS, *"On Societies as Organisms"*

Too often, compound sentences are only short sentences strung together with *and* or *but*, without consideration of the relationships among the ideas. Consider this passage, which babbles along.

No   Sodium is an element and some people think it is the same as salt, but sodium is just one element in salt, and it also contains chlorine.

YES   Sodium is an element. Some people think it is the same as salt; however, sodium is just one element in salt. In fact, salt also contains chlorine.

As can be seen in the passage below, you can emphasize one idea among many others by expressing it in a sentence noticeably different in length or structure from the sentences surrounding it.

> Mistakes are not believed to be part of the normal behavior of a good machine. **If things go wrong, it must be a personal, human error, the result of fingering, tampering, a button getting stuck, someone hitting the wrong key.** The computer, at its normal best, is infallible. I wonder whether this can be true.
>
> —Lewis Thomas, "To Err is Human"

18c How do occasional questions, commands, or exclamations create variety and emphasis?

To vary your sentence structure and to emphasize material, you can call on four basic sentence types. The most typical English sentence is **declarative**: it makes a statement—it declares something. A sentence that asks a question is called **interrogative**. Occasional questions help you involve your reader. A sentence that issues a mild or strong command is called **imperative**. Occasional mild commands are particularly helpful for gently urging your reader to think along with you. A sentence that makes an exclamation is called **exclamatory**.

Consider the following examples from *Change!* by Isaac Asimov.

QUESTION	The colonization of space may introduce some unexpected changes into human society. **For instance, what effect will it have on the way we keep time?** Our present system of time keeping is a complicated mess that depends on accidents of astronomy and on 5,000 years of primitive habit.
MILD COMMAND	**Consider the bacteria.** These are tiny living things made up of single cells far smaller than the cells in plants and animals.
EXCLAMATION	**The amazing thing about the netting of the coelacanth was that till then zoologists had been convinced the fish been extinct for 60 million years!** Finding a living dinosaur would not have been more surprising.

18d How can modifiers create variety and emphasis?

Sometimes you may want a very short sentence for its dramatic effect, but you usually need to modify simple subjects and verbs. (The parentheses below tell where in the workbook you can find the definitions of each term.)

BASIC SENTENCE	Traffic stopped.
ADJECTIVE	**Rush-hour** traffic stopped.
ADVERB	Traffic stopped **suddenly**.
PREPOSITIONAL PHRASE	**In the middle of rush hour**, traffic stopped **on the bridge**.
PARTICIPIAL PHRASE	**Blocked by an overturned tractor-trailer**, traffic stopped, **delaying hundreds of travelers**.

ABSOLUTE PHRASE	**The accident blocking all lanes,** traffic stopped.
ADVERB CLAUSE	**Because all lanes were blocked,** traffic stopped **until the trailer could** be removed.
ADJECTIVE CLAUSE	Traffic, **which was already slow,** stopped.

18e How does repetition affect variety and emphasis?

Repeating carefully chosen words can help you to emphasize your meaning, but choose for repetition only those words that contain a main idea or that use rhythm to focus attention on a main idea.

> **Happiness** is never more than partial. There are no pure states of mankind. Whatever else **happiness** may be, it is neither in having nor in being, but in becoming. What the Founding Fathers declared for us as an inherent right, we should do well to remember, was not **happiness** but the *pursuit* of **happiness**.
>
> —JOHN CIARDI, "Is Everybody Happy?"

18f How else can I create variety and emphasis?

Changing word order

Standard word order in English places the SUBJECT before the VERB.

The **mayor** *walked* into the room. [*Mayor* is the subject, which comes before the verb *walked*.]

Any variation from standard word order creates emphasis. For example, **inverted word order** places the verb before the subject.

Into the room *walked* the **mayor**. [*Mayor* is the subject, which comes after the verb *walked*.]

Changing a sentence's subject

The subject of a sentence establishes the focus for that sentence. To create the emphasis you want, you can vary each sentence's subject. All the sample sentences below express the same information, but the focus changes in each according to the subject (and its corresponding verb).

Our study *showed* that 25 percent of college students' time is spent eating or sleeping. [Focus is on the study.]

College students *eat or sleep* 25 percent of the time, according to our study. [Focus is on the students.]

Eating or sleeping *occupies* 25 percent of college students' time, according to our study. [Focus is on eating and sleeping.]

Twenty-five percent of college students' time *is spent* eating or sleeping, according to our study. [Focus is on the percentage of time.]

Using a periodic sentence among cumulative sentences

The **cumulative sentence** is the most common sentence structure in English. Its name reflects the way information accumulates in the sentence until it reaches a period. Its structure starts with a SUBJECT and VERB and continues with modifiers. Another term for cumulative sentence is *loose sentence* because it lacks a tightly planned structure.

For greater impact, you might occasionally use a **periodic sentence**, also called a *climactic sentence*, which reserves the main idea for the end of the sentence. This structure tends to draw in the reader as it moves toward the period. If overused, however, periodic sentences lose their punch.

CUMULATIVE A car hit a shoulder and turned over at midnight last night on the road from Las Vegas to Death Valley Junction.

PERIODIC At midnight last night, on the road from Las Vegas to Death Valley Junction, a car hit a shoulder and turned over.

                    —JOAN DIDION, "On Morality"

Varying Sentence Beginnings by Varying Subjects

Revise each sentence so that it begins with the word or words given.

EXAMPLE   For many people, <u>building a house</u> is challenging and rewarding.
<u>Building a house: Building a house is challenging and rewarding for many people.</u>

1. Choosing a house plan is the first task.
    <u>The first task:</u> _____

2. It's difficult to choose just the right plan among all the architectural styles and floor plans.
    <u>To choose:</u> _____

3. Next people can get their finances in order by talking to loan officers at different banks.
    <u>By talking:</u> _____

4. The bank that gives the lowest interest rate is the bank most people want to borrow from.
    <u>Most people:</u> _____

5. A contractor who is trustworthy and competent is every homeowner's dream come true.
    <u>Every homeowner's:</u> _____

6. It's time to begin building the house once all the permits have been signed by city and county officials.
    <u>Once all:</u> _____

7. As the contract clears the lot and lays the foundation, the homeowners get a little break.
    <u>The homeowners:</u> _____

8. For the homeowners, choosing all the materials and colors to use in a new home is exciting and demanding.
    <u>Choosing:</u> _____

9. People who are building a new home should do lots of shopping before the contractor calls and asks if they have their flooring, counters, cabinets, and paint colors picked out.
    <u>Before the contractor:</u> _____

10. What went right, what changes they made, and what they would do differently if they could go back in time and build their house again are stories people enjoy telling their friends.
    <u>Stories people enjoy telling:</u> _____

Expanding Sentences with Modifiers

A: Expand these simple sentences in the ways stated in parentheses.

EXAMPLE   The city seems busy.
           (prepositional phrase) *The city seems busy in the mornings.*

1. The children walk to school.

    (adjective)_____

    (adverb clause) _____

    (participial phrase) _____

2. Shopkeepers open their stores.

    (adverb) _____

    (adjective clause) _____

    (absolute phrase) _____

3. People go shopping.

    (prepositional phrase) _____

    (adjective)_____

    (adverb clause) _____

4. Delivery trucks are seen.

    (participial phrase) _____

    (adverb) _____

    (adjective clause) _____

5. The coffee shops are crowded.

    (absolute phrase) _____

    (prepositional phrase) _____

    (adjective)_____

B: Add the several elements given to each of the following sentences.

EXAMPLE   The astronaut was welcomed home.
(adjective modifying *astronaut*; adverb modifying *was welcomed*; prepositional phrase modifying *home*)
The *brave* astronaut was *warmly* welcomed home *from* space.

1.   The celebration included a parade.
(adjectives modifying *celebration* and *parade*; prepositional phrase modifying
parade)

_____

2.   The crowd was dressed in shorts and shirts.
(absolute phrase; adjective modifying *shirts*)

_____

3.   The mayor stopped traffic.
(adjective clause modifying *mayor*; adverb clause)

_____

4.   The astronaut rode in a car.
(adjectives modifying *astronaut* and *car*; adverb modifying *rode*)

_____

5.   Youngsters tried to get autographs.
(adverb clause; adjective clause modifying *youngsters*)

_____

6.   The mayor gave a speech.
(absolute phrase; two adjectives modifying *speech*)

_____

7.   Everyone cheered.
(two adverb clauses)

_____

8.   The celebration ended.
(prepositional phrase modifying *ended*)

_____

9.   Everyone headed home.
(participial phrase modifying *everyone*)

_____

10.   The street cleaners came out.
(prepositional phrase modifying *came out*; adverb clause)

_____

Revising to Emphasize the Main Idea

Using sentence combining, revise each passage into one or two sentences that emphasize the main idea. To do this, select the most effective subject for the sentence, stay in the active voice whenever possible, use a variety of sentence types (simple, compound, complex, compound-complex) and modifiers, and change clauses into phrases where practical.

EXAMPLE   Retail chain stores are closing outlets. Firms are laying off many employees. There is a shift from intimidation to collaboration among workers and their bosses.
Because retail chain stores are closing outlets and firms are laying off many employees, there is a shift from intimidation to collaboration among workers and their bosses.

1.   There is a new emphasis on teamwork. There is a new emphasis on trust in the workplace. Managers hope that the new shift in attitude will increase the quality of businesses in the United States.

_____

_____

2.   Companies are trying to make a difference. They are experimenting with group talks among employees. These groups discuss issues dealing with workers as individuals and as team members.

_____

_____

3.   The talks are very helpful for managers. The workers involved are those who are still with the company. They have survived the massive cutbacks and need a boost in morale.

_____

_____

4.   These experimental groups also break down barriers in the workplace. These barriers tend to separate one department from another. This separation takes away any feelings of teamwork and cooperation.

_____

_____

5.   Teamwork is critical for companies that want to regain competitiveness. These groups strive to remove obstacles that prevent communication and respect among workers. Teamwork is a necessary step in the right direction.

_____

_____

MODULE 19: THE IMPACT OF WORDS

19a What is American English?

Evolving over centuries into a rich language, **American English** is the variation of English spoken in the United States. It demonstrates that many cultures have created the U.S. melting-pot society. Food names, for example, reflect that Africans brought the words *okra, gumbo,* and *goober* (peanut); Spanish and Latin American peoples contributed *tortilla, taco,* and *burrito.* Greek gave us *pita,* Cantonese *chow,* and Japanese *sushi.*

The meanings of some words change with time. For example, W. Nelson Francis points out in *The English Language* that the word nice "has been used at one time or another in its 700-year history to mean: *foolish, wanton, strange, lazy, coy, modest, fastidious, refined, precise, subtle, slender, critical, attentive, minutely accurate, dainty, appetizing, agreeable.*"

19b What are levels of formality in language?

Good writers pay special attention to **diction** (word choice), making certain that the words they use communicate their meaning as clearly and convincingly as possible.

Informal levels and highly formal levels of writing use different vocabulary and sentence structures, and the two differ clearly in **tone**. Tone reflects the attitude of the writer toward the subject and audience. It may be highly formal, informal, or in between. Different tones are appropriate for different audiences, subjects, and purposes. An **informal** tone occurs in casual conversation or letters to friends. A highly **formal** tone, in contrast, occurs in public and ceremonial documents, such as proclamations and treaties. Informal language, which creates an informal tone, may use slang, colloquialisms, and regionalisms. In addition, informal writing may include sentence fragments, contractions, and other casual forms. Medium-level language uses general English—not too casual, not too scholarly. Unlike informal language, medium-level language is acceptable for academic writing. This level uses standard vocabulary (for example, *learn* instead of the informal *wise-up*), conventional sentence structure, and few or no contractions. Highly formal language uses many long words derived from Latin and a flowery style. Academic writing and most writing for general audiences should range from medium to somewhat formal levels of language.

19c What is edited American English?

The language standards you are expected to use in academic writing are those of a book like this workbook. Such language is called **standard English**, because it follows established rules of grammar, sentence structure, punctuation, and spelling. This language is also called **edited American English**. Standard English is not a fancy dialect for the elite. It is a practical set of rules about language use that most educated people observe.

To communicate clearly, choose words that demonstrate your fairness as a writer. When you are talking about a subject on which you hold strong opinions, do not slip into biased or emotionally loaded language. Suppose you were arguing against a proposed increase in tuition. If you write that the president of the college is "a blood-sucking dictator out to destroy the lives of thousands of innocent young people," a neutral audience will doubt your ability to think rationally and write fairly about the subject.

19d What is figurative language?

Figurative language uses one idea or image to explain another by creating comparisons and connections. The most common figures of speech are similes and metaphors.

A **simile** states a direct comparison between two otherwise dissimilar things. It sets up the comparison by using the words *like* or *as*. A disagreeable person might be said to *be as sour as unsweetened lemonade*.

A **metaphor** implies a comparison between otherwise dissimilar things without using *like* or *as*. *The new tax bill bled lower-income families of their last hope.*

Be careful not to create an inappropriate and silly image, such as in *The rush hour traffic bled out of all the city's major arteries*. Cars are not at all like blood and their movement is not similar to the flow of blood, so the metaphor ends up confusing rather than explaining. Also be careful not to create **mixed metaphors**, illogical combinations of images: *Milking the migrant workers, the supervisor bled them dry*. Here the initial image is of taking milk from a cow, but the final image is of blood, not milk.

19e How can using exact diction enhance my writing?

Careful writers pay close attention to **diction**—word choice. To choose the most appropriate and accurate word, a writer must understand the word's connotation and denotation.

Connotation refers to the ideas implied but not directly indicated by a word. Connotations convey emotional overtones beyond a word's direct definition. What first comes to mind when you see the word *blood*? To some people *blood* represents war or injury while to others it is a symbol of family or ethnic identity; to people in the healing professions, *blood* may be interpreted as a symbol of life. Good writers understand the additional layer of meaning connotations deliver to specific audiences.

When you look up a new word in the dictionary to find out exactly what it means, you are looking for its **denotation**. Words with the same general definition may have subtle differences of meaning. These differences enable you to choose precisely the right word, but they also obligate you to make sure you know what meanings your words convey. For example, describing someone as *lean* or *slender* is far different from calling that person *skinny*.

Good dictionaries show how language has been used and is currently being used. Such dictionaries give not only a word's meaning, but also much additional important information.

An individual dictionary entry usually includes the following information: spelling; word division into syllables (syllabication); pronunciation; parts of speech; grammatical forms (plurals, parts of verbs including irregular forms, etc.); word origin; meanings; related words (nouns, adjectives); synonyms; words used in sample sentences; usage labels; and idioms that include the word.

The spelling is given first, with the word usually divided into syllables by centered dots. The pronunciation follows. Here you will sometimes see unusual symbols, such as /ə/, the **schwa** or "uh" sound. These symbols are explained in a pronunciation key, usually located in the dictionary's introduction or at the bottom of each page. The part of speech comes next. It is usually abbreviated, such as *n* for *noun* or *vt* for *transitive verb*. The dictionary also gives the principal parts of each word (for regular verbs, the *-ed* form for past tense and past participle, the *-ing* form for the present participle). The word's history (known as the etymology) usually follows. The word's meanings come next. If a word can be used as more than one part of speech, the meanings are grouped according to the parts of speech. Usage labels give additional important information, indicating which words are *slang*, *poetic*, or *dialect*.

Dictionaries come in several varieties. **Unabridged** ("unshortened") dictionaries have the most in-depth, accurate, complete, and scholarly entries of the various kinds of dictionaries. They give many examples of a word's current uses and changes in meanings over time. They also include infrequently used words that other dictionaries may omit.

Abridged ("shortened") dictionaries contain only the most commonly used words. They are convenient in size and economical to buy. These are the most practical reference books for writers and readers.

A number of specialized dictionaries focus on single areas, such as slang, word origins, synonyms, usage, or almost any other aspect of language. Whatever your interest, a specialized dictionary is probably available. Ask your reference librarian to point out what you need.

19f How can using specific words enhance my writing?

Specific words identify individual items in a group (*grape, orange, apple, plum*), whereas **general** words relate to an overall group (*fruit*). **Concrete** words identify persons and things that can be detected by the senses—seen, heard, tasted, felt, smelled (*the crisp, sweet red apple*). **Abstract** words denote qualities, concepts, relationships, acts, conditions, or ideas (*delicious*). Writers must use all these types of words. Effective writers, however, make sure to supply enough specific, concrete details to breathe life into generalizations and abstractions.

19g What is gender-neutral language?

Sexist language assigns roles or characteristics to people on the basis of sex. Such practices unfairly discriminate against both sexes. Sexist language inaccurately assumes that all nurses and homemakers are female (and therefore refers to them as "she") and that all physicians and wage earners are male (and therefore refers to them as "he"). One of the most widespread occurrences of sexist language is the use of the pronoun *he* to refer to someone of unidentified sex. Although traditionally *he* has been correct in such a general situation, using only masculine pronouns to represent the human species excludes females. You can avoid this problem by using the techniques suggested in the following chart.

HOW TO AVOID SEXIST LANGUAGE

1. Avoid using only the masculine pronoun to refer to males and females together:
   a. Use a pair of pronouns, but try to avoid strings of pairs in a sentence or in several consecutive sentences.

      No   A doctor cannot read much outside **his** specialty.

      YES   A doctor cannot read much outside **his or her** specialty.

   b. Revise into the plural.

      No   A successful doctor knows that **he** has to work long hours.

      YES   Successful doctors know that **they** have to work long hours.

   c. Recast the sentence to omit the gender-specific pronoun.

      No   Everyone hopes that **he will** win the scholarship.

      YES   Everyone hopes **to win** the scholarship.

2. Avoid using man when men and women are clearly intended in the meaning.

   No   **Man** is a social animal.

   YES   **People** are social animals.

3. Avoid stereotyping jobs and roles by gender when men and women are included.

   No   chairman; policeman; businessman; statesman

   YES   chair, chairperson; police officer; businessperson, business executive; diplomat, prime minister, etc.

   No   teacher . . . she; principal . . . he

   YES   teachers . . . they; principals . . . they

4. Avoid expressions that exclude one sex.

   No   mankind; the common man; man-sized sandwich; old wives' tale

   YES   humanity; the average person; huge sandwich; superstition

5. Avoid using degrading and insulting labels.

   No   lady lawyer; gal Friday; career girl; coed

   YES   lawyer; assistant; professional woman; student

19h What other types of language do I want to avoid?

Always try to make what you are saying as clear as possible to your readers. Extremely complex ideas or subjects may require complex terms or phrases to explain them, but in general the simpler the language, the more likely it is to be understood.

Pretentious language is too showy and sometimes silly, calling unsuitable attention to itself with complex sentences and long words: *I had a portion of an Italian comestible for the noontime repast* [Translation: I had a slice of pizza for lunch]. Plain English that communicates clearly is far better than fancy English that makes the reader aware that you are showing off.

Colloquial language is characteristic of casual conversation and informal writing: *The pile-up on Route 23 halted traffic.* **Regional (dialectal) language** is specific to some geographic areas: *They had **nary** a dime to their name.* These usages are not appropriate for academic writing.

19i What is regional language?

Regional language also called *dialectal language*, is specific to certain geographical areas. For example, a *dragonfly* is a *snake feeder* in parts of Delaware, a *darning needle* in parts of Michigan, and a *snake doctor* or an *ear sewer* in parts of the southern United States. Using a dialect in writing for the general reading public tends to shut some people out of the communication. Except when dialect is the topic of the writing, ACADEMIC WRITING rarely accommodates dialect well. Avoid it in ACADEMIC WRITING.

19j What are clichés?

A **cliché** is an overused, worn-out expression that has lost its ability to communicate effectively. Some comparisons that were once clever have grown old and worn out: *dead as a doornail, gentle as a lamb*. Do not take the easiest phrase, the words that come immediately to mind. If you have heard them over and over again, so has your reader. Rephrasing clichés will improve your writing.

19k When is jargon unnecessary?

Jargon is specialized vocabulary of a particular group—words that an outsider would not understand. Whether or not the word is considered jargon depends on purpose and audience. For example, when a sportswriter uses words such as *gridiron* and *sacked*, a football fan understands them with no difficulty. Specialized language evolves in every field: professions, academic disciplines, business, even hobbies. However, using jargon unnecessarily or failing to explain it is showy and artificial.

19l What are euphemisms?

Euphemisms attempt to avoid harsh reality by using pleasant-sounding, "tactful" words. Although they are sometimes necessary to spare someone's feelings, euphemisms drain meaning from truthful writing. People use unnecessary euphemisms to describe socially unacceptable behavior: *Barry bends the rules* instead of *Barry cheats*. They use euphemisms to hide unpleasant facts: *She really likes her liquor* instead of *She is a drunk*. Euphemisms like these fool no one. Except in the rare cases where delicate language is needed—to soften the pain of death, for example—keep your language free of euphemisms.

19m What is bureaucratic language?

Bureaucratic language is confusing. It is carelessly written, stuffy, overblown language, as shown by the following memo:

You can include a page that also contains an Include instruction. The page including the Include instruction is included when you paginate the document but the included text referred to in its Include instruction is not included.

Recognizing Levels of Formality

Different levels of formality are appropriate in different situations. Decide which level (informal, medium, between medium and formal, and formal) best fits each of these situations.

		Level of Formality
EXAMPLE	a letter requesting the list of winners in a sweepstakes	*Medium*
1.	a note to a friend asking him or her to take a package to the post office for you	
2.	a lab report for chemistry	
3.	a petition to have a candidate's name added to the election ballot	
4.	an invitation to a veteran to speak to your daughter's sixth grade class about his experiences in Viet Nam	
5.	the valedictorian's speech at a college graduation ceremony	

Now select three of these documents, each calling for a different level of formality, and write them. Use your own paper.

Understanding Differences in Denotation and Connotation

A: Underline the most appropriate word from the pair given in parentheses. If you are unsure, consult your dictionary's synonymy. (A synonymy is a paragraph comparing and contrasting words.)

EXAMPLE   The sky was (<u>clear</u>, transparent), with not a cloud in sight.

1. The sergeant (instructed, commanded) his men to clean the barracks.

2. The plane remained (complete, intact) after passing through the severe storm.

3. The dictator was (conquered, overthrown) by his own brother.

4. Astronomy calls for great (accuracy, correctness).

5. After he fell into the cesspool, his suit was so (soiled, foul) it could not be cleaned.

6. The inheritance was (divided, doled out) among her sisters.

7. The crowd (dissipated, dispersed) once the ambulance took away the accident victim.

8. The tenants (withheld, kept) their rent in protest over the long-broken boiler.

9. Most fashion models are (lofty, tall).

10. The patient was (restored, renovated) to health by physical therapy.

11. Because of his (immoderate, exorbitant) behavior, the young man was thrown out of the restaurant.

12. The committee voted to (eliminate, suspend) voting on the budget until the missing members could be located.

13. The coach talked to the team in the (capacity, function) of a friend.

14. The family (donated, bestowed) its time to help restore the fire-damaged day-care center.

15. The practical joker (tittered, guffawed) as his victim slipped on a banana peel.

16. The professor (praised, eulogized) the class for its good work on the midterm examination.

17. Sometimes people offer (premiums, rewards) to help capture dangerous criminals.

18. The guest wondered if it would be (impolite, boorish) to ask for a third piece of pie.

19. The man (clandestinely, secretly) took his wife's birthday present into the attic.

20. The lifeguard's (skin, hide) was dry from overexposure to the sun.

B: The following words are synonymous, but not all are equally appropriate in every situation. Check the precise meaning of each word, and then use each in a sentence. Your dictionary may have a synonymy (a paragraph comparing and contrasting all the words) listed under one of the words, so check all the definitions before writing your sentences.

EXAMPLE   laughable   *The travel book was laughable, because the author had never left the tour bus.*

amusing   *We spent an amusing, afternoon riding in an old, horse-drawn carriage.*

droll   *The political commentator had a droll sense of humor.*

comical   *The clowns in the circus were truly comical.*

1. danger _____

peril _____

hazard _____

risk _____

2. rich _____

wealthy _____

affluent _____

opulent _____

274

3. speak _____

    talk _____

    converse _____

    discourse _____

4. think _____

    reason _____

    reflect _____

    speculate _____

    deliberate _____

5. irritable _____

    choleric _____

    touchy _____

    cranky _____

    cross _____

Using Concrete, Specific Language

A: Reorder the words in each list so they move from most general to most specific.

Example   cola   _beverage_

          soda   _soda_

          Coca-Cola   _cola_

          beverage   _Coca-Cola_

1. sandwich   _____

    food   _____

    cheese sandwich   _____

    Swiss cheese on rye _____

2. A&P   _____

    store   _____

    business   _____

    supermarket   _____

3. bill   _____

    record club charges _____

    letter   _____

    mail   _____

4. clothing   _____

    jeans   _____

    pants   _____

    stone-washed jeans _____

5. land _____
   tropical paradise _____
   islands _____
   Hawaii _____
6. cookbook _____
   The Joy of Cooking _____
   how-to book _____
   book _____
7. lion _____
   hunter _____
   cat _____
   animal _____

8. television show _____
   entertainment _____
   family comedy _____
   The Cosby Show _____
9. *The Blue Boy* _____
   painting _____
   art _____
   portrait _____
10. sports _____
   100-yard dash _____
   running _____
   track _____

B: The italicized word or phrase in each sentence below is too abstract or general. Replace it with a word (or words) that is more specific or concrete. Use the lines to the right.

EXAMPLE   The beast escaped from the zoo.   *ferocious leopard*

1.   He's very proud of his new car.   _____

2.   They planted bushes along the edge of the walk.   _____

3.   The milk tasted funny.   _____

4.   Proudly, she walked onto the stage.   _____

5.   My aunt lives in the South.   _____

6.   Somebody asked me to deliver these roses to you. _____

7.   She wrote a book about history.   _____

8.   A bird flew into the classroom.   _____

9.   To be successful, an accountant must be good.   _____

10. The Coast Guard chased the criminals.   _____

11. The dancer hurt her ankle.   _____

12. He received jewelry as a birthday present.   _____

13. The engine made a strange sound.   _____

14. He thought Economics class was a pain.   _____

15. The nurse was very nice to the patients.   _____

16. After practice, we went to a movie.   _____

17. His new dining room set was delivered damaged. _____

18. The building is a mess.   _____

19. I want to get a good job after graduation.   _____

20. The doctor gave everyone a booklet about how to quit
     smoking.   _____

276

Avoiding Slang, Colloquial, and Overly Formal Language

EXERCISE 19-4

Underline the word in each sentence that best suits an academic style. You may need to check your dictionary for usage labels.

EXAMPLE   That academic advisor fails to motivate students because she is (stuck-up, <u>aloof</u>).

1.   My anthropology professor is a brilliant (guy, man).

2.   The food in the main dining hall is barely (edible, comestible).

3.   (Prithee, Please) shut off the lights when leaving classrooms.

4.   The Dean of Faculty will (address, parley with) the audience at graduation.

5.   (Regardless, Irregardless) of the weather, the honors and awards ceremony will be held on Thursday evening.

6.   All students must wear skirts or (britches, slacks) under their graduation robes.

7.   The elevator is reserved for faculty and (educands, students) with passes.

8.   Remind your guests to park their (cars, wheels) in the visitors' lot.

9.   Anyone parking a (motorcycle, chopper) on campus should chain it to the rack in the parking field.

10. Relatives may stay overnight in the (dormitories, dorms) provided they have written in advance and (checked in, touched base) with the house parents before 10 P.M.

Revising Sentences for Appropriate language

EXERCISE 19-5

Revise these sentences using language appropriate for acedemic writing

EXAMPLE   It stinks that I can't go skydiving more often.
           <u>*It's a shame that I can't go skydiving more often.*</u>

1.   Before I tried skydiving, I thought skydivers were nuts.

     _____

2.   It seemed so out there.

     _____

3.   But now I've done it, I think it's a blast.

     _____

4.   The day of the jump, I was totally stoked.

     _____

5. My friends were pretty weirded out on my account, though.

_____

6. But then, they're such wusses.

_____

7. I thought I was going to barf just before I jumped out the plane.

_____

8. But it was great – it blew me away.

_____

9. It has to be way cooler than bungee-jumping, which is, like, blink and you've missed it.

_____

10. Yeah, skydiving definitely rocks.

_____

Revising Slanted Language

Here is the opening paragraph of a very slanted letter to the editor. Revise it, using moderate language. Try to convince the reader that you are a reasonable person with a valid argument.

Dear Editor:

    I just read your ridiculous article on the proposed opening of a hazardous waste storage depot just outside town. Are you crazy? Anyone who would propose such a deadly project has no soul. Those city council members who are sponsoring this monstrous facility obviously have the brains of fruit flies. If they had bothered to do a little research, they would have discovered that dreadful things can happen to any poor community that lets such a depot be forced upon it.

_____

Revising for Appropriate Figurative Language

Revise these sentences by replacing clichéd, inappropriate, or mixed metaphors with fresh, appropriate figures of speech. You may want to reduce the number of figures of speech in a sentence, or you may sometimes feel a message is best presented without any figurative language.

EXAMPLE   In high school, I decided that an actor's life is as good as it gets.

<u>In high school, I decided that I wanted to be an actor. [As good as it gets is a cliché..]</u>

1. Once I began acting, I was bowled over while walking on air.

2. I took to the stage like a duck to water.

3. My lines stuck to my brain like glue.

4. Sometimes the famous lines I spoke filled me with awe and left me speechless.

5. When I danced on stage, I met with success at every turn.

6. My singing was out of sight.

7. At every audition I came out smelling like a rose.

8. In all its days, my high school had never seen an actor like me.

9. Being in a television commercial was the first step in my meteoric rise to fame.

10. The commercial was about a new and improved, never before seen product.

11. After that, my agent's cell phone rang off the hook.

12. My schedule became a constant flow of stops for public appearances.

13. During these public appearances, I had to sign autographs until the cows came home.

14. I soon learned that being rich and famous isn't all it's cracked up to be.

15. Buy my passion for acting is like a tide that never stops rising.

Using Figurative Language

Using new, appropriate figures of speech, write a sentence describing each of the following.

Example   a fast train
Disappearing like the vapor trail of a jet, the train sped into the distance.

1. a graceful horse

2. a run-down shack

3. a terrible dance band

4. greasy french fries

5. being awakened by your alarm clock

6. a professor who requires too much work

7. a salesperson with a phony smile

8. a hot day in the city

9. something that is very late

10. an unpleasant singing voice

Eliminating Artificial Language   EXERCISE 19-9

A: "Translate" these sentences into standard academic English by eliminating inappropriate jargon and euphemisms. You may need to refer to your dictionary.

EXAMPLE   Vernal intermission during the college year is an excellent habitude.
Spring break is a wonderful tradition. _____

1. Every year, scholars across this great nation anticipate this time period.

    _____

    _____

2. Many travel to ensconce themselves in tropical climes to rest and relax.

    _____

    _____

3. Many others recrudesce at home interfacing with their nearest and dearest.

    _____

    _____

4. However, many educatees use this time peiod to get back in the grind.

    _____

    _____

5. No matter how students employ this time, college life without it would be inconceivable.

    _____

    _____

B: Find a piece of published writing that you feel uses pretentious language, unnecessary jargon, unnecessary euphemisms, and/or bureaucratic language. Likely sources are newsletters, business memos and reports, political mailings, solicitations for charity, and sales brochures. Be prepared to say in what ways the language is artificial and what problems that language can create for readers. Then rewrite the piece using appropriate language. Submit the original and your revision to your instructor.

MODULE 20: SPELLING AND HYPHENATION

SPELLING

20a What makes a good speller?

One reason English spelling can be difficult is that our words have come from many sources. We have borrowed words from Latin, Greek, French, Spanish, and many other languages. Because of these various origins, plus differences in the ways English-speaking people pronounce words, it is unwise to rely on pronunciation in spelling a word.

What we can rely on, however, is a system of proofreading, studying, and learning spelling rules. With a little time and effort, English spelling can be mastered.

20b How can I proofread for errors in spelling and hyphen use?

Many spelling errors are not spelling errors at all. They are the result of illegible handwriting, slips of the pen, or typographical errors ("typos"). While you may not be able to change your handwriting completely, you can make it legible enough so that readers know what words you are writing. Careful proofreading is required to catch typos. When you reread your papers, you are likely to read what you meant to write rather than what is actually on the page because the brain tends to "read" what it expects to see. When proofreading for typos, then, try reading the page backwards, from the last sentence to the first. Using a ruler to help you focus on one line at a time is also effective.

If you are unsure how to spell a word but you do know how it starts, look it up in the dictionary. If you do not know how to spell the beginning of a word, think of a synonym, and look that word up in a thesaurus.

When you come across unfamiliar words in a textbook highlight or underline them as you read. Then, after you have finished reading, go back and memorize the correct spelling.

As you discover words you frequently misspell, print each carefully on a card, highlighting the problem area by using larger print, a different-colored ink, or a highlighter.

Mnemonic devices, techniques to improve memory, can also help you to remember the spelling of difficult words:

The princi**pal** is your **pal**. A princi**ple** is a **rule**.

The we**a**ther is cle**a**r. **Whether** is **what**.

PLURALS

20c How are plurals spelled?

Regular plurals: In general, add -*s* to form a plural: *desks, tables.* If a word ends in -*ch, -s, -sh, -x,* or -*z,* add -*es: patches, dresses, flashes, waxes, buzzes.* Words ending in -*o* preceded by a consonant take the -*es* plural: *heroes, tomatoes.* Words ending in -*o* preceded by a vowel take the -*s* plural: *ratios, videos.* There are exceptions to these two rules, many of which are music terms taken from Italian:*contraltos, solos, pianos, tobaccos.* A few words ending in -*o* may take either the -*s* or -*es* plural: *cargoes/cargos, volcanoes/volcanos, zeroes/zeros.*

Words ending in -f or -fe: In general, change the -*f* to -*ve* before adding -*s. leaf/leaves, wife/wives.* There are three exceptions to this rule: *belief/beliefs, motif/motifs, safe/safes.* These exceptions avoid confusion with the singular verbs *believes* and *saves* and the plural noun *motives.* When the word ends in -*ff* or -*ffe,* simply add -*s: giraffe/giraffes, staff/staffs.*

Compound nouns: In general, place the -*s* or -*es* at the end of a compound noun: *attorney generals, capfuls, nurse-midwives.* If, however, the major word in the compound is the first word, add the -*s* or -*es* to the first word: *professors emeritus, passersby, sisters-in-law.*

Internal changes: Some words change internally to form the plural: *man/men, child/children, mouse/mice, foot/feet, ox/oxen.*

Foreign plurals: Words borrowed from other languages usually form their plurals according to the rules of that language. Latin words ending in -*um* or -*on* usually form their plurals by changing the -*um* or -*on* to -*a: curriculum/curricula, medium/media, datum/data, criterion/criteria.* For Latin words ending in -*us,* the plural is -*i: alumnus/alumni, syllabus/syllabi.*

Plurals retaining singular form: Some words are spelled the same in both singular and plural forms. Usually these are the names of animals or grains: *deer, elk, fish, rice, wheat.*

20d How are suffixes spelled?

A **suffix** is an ending added to the basic form of a word, to change either the tense (-*d, -ed*) or the part of speech. Spelling problems arise when different suffixes sound alike or when changes must be made in the base word before the suffix is added.

-able, -ible: These two suffixes cause problems because there are no reliable rules for their use. More words end in -*able: comfortable, probable, treatable.* Still, some common words end in -*ible: irresistible, audible.* The best rule to follow with these two endings is when in doubt, look up the word.

-ally / -ly: Both endings turn words into adverbs: -*ally* is added to words ending in -*ic* (*logically, tragically*); -*ly* is added to words not ending in -*ic* (*quickly, slowly*).

-ance, -ence, -ant, -ent: These endings do not occur according to any rules. Some words end

in -*ance*: *observance, reluctance*. Some words end in -*ence*: *convenience, correspondence*. Once you know whether a noun ends in -*ance* or -*ence*, you will know whether its adjective form ends in -*ant* or -*ent*: *observant, reluctant, convenient, correspondent*.

-*cede*, -*ceed*, -*sede*: Only one word ends in -*sede*: *supersede*. Only three words end in -*ceed*: *exceed, proceed, succeed*. The rest end in -*cede*: *precede, recede, secede*.

-*d* ending: When the -*d* ending is not clearly pronounced at the end of past-tense verbs and adjectives, the wrong form of the word may be written. Watch out for incorrect forms such as 'prejudice person' (instead of *prejudiced person*) and 'use to' (instead of *used to*).

Final *e*: Drop the final *e* before a suffix beginning with a vowel (*arrange* + -*ing* = *arranging*), but keep it if the suffix begins with a consonant (*arrange* + -*ment* = *arrangement*). Often a final *e* "softens" the sound of a preceding *c* or *g* (soft *c* sounds like *s*, soft *g* like *j*). In such cases, the final *e* is retained with suffixes beginning with *a* or *o*, in order to retain the soft sound of the consonant: *service* + -*able* = *serviceable*; *outrage* + -*ous* = *outrageous*. Some words retain the final *e* to prevent confusion with other words: *dye* + -*ing* = *dyeing*, to avoid confusion with dying. For the few exceptions to the basic rule for final *e*, simply memorize their spelling: *argument, awful, truly, wisdom*.

Final *y*: If the final *y* is preceded by a consonant, change the *y* to *i* before adding a suffix unless the suffix begins with *i*: *try* + -*ed* = *tried*; *try* + -*ing* = *trying*. If the final -*y* is preceded by a vowel, retain the -*y* when adding any suffix: *employ* + -*ed* = *employed*; *employ* + -*ing* = *employing*; *employ* + -*er* = *employer*. Common exceptions to this rule are the past tenses of *lay, pay,* and *say*: *laid, paid,* and *said*.

Double final consonants: If a one-syllable word ends in a consonant preceded by a single vowel, double the final consonant before adding a suffix: *flip* + -*ing* = *flipping*. With two-syllable words, an additional rule applies: double the final consonant only if the last syllable of the stem is accented. Thus, adding -*ing* to the word *refer* produces *referring* (final *r* doubled), but adding -*ence* produces *reference* (final *r* not doubled) because in *referring* the accent is on the last syllable of *refer*, while in *reference* the accent is on the first syllable.

20e What is the *ie, ei* rule?

Generally, you can rely on the old rhyme: "*i* before *e*, except after *c*, or when sounded like *ay*, as in *neighbor* and *weigh*": *field, believe, grief; receive, ceiling, conceit; neigh, vein, eight*. There are, however, a few common exceptions that are worth memorizing: *counterfeit, foreign, forfeit, either, neither, leisure, seize, weird, height, sleight, ancient*.

20f How are homonyms and other frequently confused words spelled?

Many words sound similar to or exactly like others (*its/it's, morning/mourning*). Words that sound alike are called **homonyms**. To avoid using the wrong word, look up unfamiliar homonyms in the dictionary, and then use mnemonic devices to help you remember their meanings.

Some expressions may be written either as one word or two, depending on meaning:

An **everyday** occurrence is something that happens **every day**.
The guests were there **already** by the time I was **all ready**.
When we were **all together** there were five of us **altogether**.
We were there for **a while** when the host said dinner would be **awhile** longer.
Maybe the main course will be sushi, but it **may be** tofuburgers.
When we went **in to** dinner, he walked **into** the table.

Two expressions, however, are *always* written as two words: *all right* (not *alright*) and *a lot* (not *alot*).

HOMONYMS AND NEAR SOUNDALIKES

accept / except	hole / whole
advice / advise	human / humane
affect / effect	its / it's
aisle / isle	know / no
already / all ready	later / latter
altar / alter	lead / led
altogether / all together	lessen / lesson
angel / angle	lightning / lightening
are / hour / our	loose / lose
ascent / assent	maybe / may be
assistance / assistants	meat / meet
bare / bear	miner / minor
board / bored	of / off
brake / break	passed / past
breath / breathe	patience / patients
buy / by	peace / piece
capital / capitol	personal / personnel
choose / chose	plain / plane
cite / sight / site	principal / principle
clothes / cloths	quiet / quite / quit
coarse / course	rain / reign / rein
complement / compliment	right / rite / write
conscience / conscious	road / rode
council / counsel	scene / seen
dairy / diary	sense / since
dessert / desert	stationary / stationery
device / devise	than / then
dominant / dominate	there / they're / their
die / dye	through / threw / thorough
dying / dyeing	to / too / two
fair / fare	weak / week
formally / formerly	weather / whether
forth / fourth	where / were / wear
gorilla / guerrilla	which / witch
hear / here	whose / who's
heard / herd	your / you're / yore

20g What are compound words?

A **compound word** consists of two or more words used together to form one word. When a compound acts as a modifier *before* a noun, it is usually hyphenated: *fast-paced lecture, long-term commitment.* When the same modifier comes after the noun, however, there is no hyphen: *The lecture was fast paced.* Some terms have become clear enough that they do not require hyphens: *genetic engineering laboratory, health insurance policy, junior high school, state sales tax.*

The hyphen is omitted in several other situations: when the first word in the compound ends with *-ly,* when the first word is a comparative or superlative, or when the compound is a foreign phrase: *happily married couple, lowest common denominator, ad hoc committee.*

A hyphen is placed between the two parts of a combined unit of measurement: *kilowatt-hours, light-years.*

Most compound titles are not hyphenated (*state senator, vice principal*), but many are. Hyphenated titles usually are national names, actual double titles, or three-word titles: *Italian-American, father-in-law, director-producer.*

Correcting Common
Spelling Errors

Underline the misspelled word in each sentence, and spell it correctly on the line to the right. If a sentence has no misspellings, write correct on the line.

EXAMPLE   Some exceptions to spelling rules are <u>wierdly</u> irregular.   _weirdly_

1.   The letter carrier retired after being biten by the same   _____
      dog for the seventh time.

2.   The counterfeiter pleaded innocent, saying he had been   _____
      frammed.

3.   In the committee's judgment, the fair succeeded because   _____
      of extremely efficient managment.

4.   The scientists received news from a reliable source about   _____
      an important foriegn discovery.

5.   We had hoped to buy a new dinning room set with our   _____
      winnings from the quiz show we competed on last month.

6.   It seems incredable that, after trailing in the polls for weeks,   _____
      our candidate managed finally to win the election.

7.   Running, swimming, and jumping rope are all ways to   _____
      increase the heart's endurance.

8.   Many undocumented aliens have little liesure time because   _____
      they often hold two or even three jobs, all paying illegally low
      salaries.

9.   Because we did not think the payments were affordable,   _____
      we reluctently postponed repairing the leaky ceiling.

10.   The disatisfied customers tried to return the chipped benches   _____
      to the manufacturer, but the factory was permanently closed.

11.   The young man received a commendation from the community   _____
      for his incredibly couragous performance in rescuing disabled
      children from an overturned bus.

12.   When he was layed off from work, he filed a grievance with   _____
      his union representative and then proceeded to the
      unemployment office.

13.   After carefully painting the attic stairs, my brother-in-law   _____
      realized he had closed off his route of escape, and he
      was traped upstairs until the paint dried.

14. When I was younger, I use to want to take drum lessons   _____
    until I realized how tiring practicing the drums could be.

15. The professor stated that she would return illegable papers   _____
    without commenting on them, and she encouraged students
    to type all work carefully.

16. Although the street was usually gloomy, every New Year's Eve   _____
    it magicly transformed itself into a joyful scene for a few hours.

17. According to some philosophies, the world is constantly   _____
    changing and it is pointless to expect anything to be permanant.

18. The neighborhood children voted to coordinate a carwash   _____
    and use the procedes to buy durable playground equipment.

19. The chef advertised in the classified section of the newspaper   _____
    for a relieable dessert-maker.

20. The school aide was payed a bonus for her invaluable   _____
    assistance during the hurricane.

21. In some cultures, it is beleived that the ghosts of ancestors   _____
    take up residence in the family home.

22. One of the most appealing aspects of watching team sports   _____
    is seeing the interaction among the players on the field.

23. The most boring part of working in a department store is   _____
    taking part in periodic inventorys of the available merchandise.

24. Each autumn, people tragically injure themselves in avoidable   _____
    falls on rain-soaked leafs.

25. *Star Wars* was a very well-received and profitible movie,   _____
    and it set the pattern for many imitations.

Writing Plural Nouns

Write the plural forms of these nouns.

EXAMPLE   lamp   ___lamps___
            attorney at law   _attorneys at law_

1. orange   _____
2. kiss   _____
3. stray   _____
4. life   _____
5. radio   _____
6. pair   _____
7. speech   _____
8. fly   _____
9. monkey   _____
10. piano   _____

11. mother-in-law   _____
12. datum   _____
13. ice skate   _____
14. herself   _____
15. echo   _____
16. half   _____
17. child   _____
18. woman   _____
19. phenomenon   _____
20. mouse   _____

Adding Suffixes

A: Combine these suffixes and roots. If in doubt about the spelling, look up the word in your dictionary.

EXAMPLE   awake + ing   ___awaking___

1.   motivate + ion   _____
2.   guide + ance   _____
3.   notice + able   _____
4.   grace + ful   _____
5.   true + ly   _____
6.   accurate + ly   _____
7.   mile + age   _____
8.   argue + ment   _____
9.   drive + ing   _____
10.   outrage + ous   _____

What basic rules govern the combining of roots ending in *e* and suffixes?

_____

_____

B: Combine these suffixes and roots. If in doubt about the spelling, look up the word in your dictionary.

EXAMPLE   carry + ing   ___carrying___

1.   duty + ful   _____
2.   play + ing   _____

3.　　dry + er　　_____

4.　　supply + ed　　_____

5.　　noisy + est　　_____

6.　　stray + ed　　_____

7.　　sloppy + er　　_____

8.　　gravy + s　　_____

9.　　happy + ness　　_____

10.　buy + ing　　_____

What basic rules govern the combining of roots ending in *y* and suffixes?

_____

_____

C: Combine these suffixes and roots. If in doubt about the spelling, look up the word in your dictionary.

EXAMPLE　trap + ed　___*trapped*___

1.　grip + ing　　_____

2.　mend + able　　_____

3.　steam + ed　　_____

4.　begin + er　　_____

5.　plant + ing　　_____

6.　stop + er　　_____

7.　pour + ed　　_____

8.　split + ing　　_____

9.　occur + ence　　_____

10.　refer + ence　　_____

What basic rules govern the doubling of final consonants when a suffix is added?

_____

_____

Distinguishing Between ei and ie　　EXERCISE 20-4

Fill in the blanks with ei or ie. Because there are frequent exceptions to the rule, check your dictionary whenever you are in doubt.

EXAMPLE　　anc_*ie*_nt

1. bel_____ve

2. rec_____ve

3. n_____ther

4. c_____ling

5. for_____gn

6. f_____ld

7. counterf_____t

8. w_____rd

9. fr_____ght

10. n_____ce

Writing Sentences with Homonyms and Commonly Confused Words

Use each word below in a sentence that clearly demonstrates its meaning.

EXAMPLE   its   *Every plan has its disadvantages*.
              it's   *It's too late to go out for pizza.*

1. already _____

    all ready _____

2. its _____

    it's _____

3. than _____

    then _____

4. they're _____

    their _____

    there _____

5. to _____

    two _____

    too _____

6. your _____

    you're _____

7. passed _____

    past _____

8. quiet _____

    quite _____

9. through _____

    threw _____

    thorough _____

10. whose _____

     who's _____

Recognizing Homonyms and Commonly Confused Words

Underline the word within parentheses that best fits each sentence.

EXAMPLE   (Accepting, Excepting) and following some (advise, advice) can make travelling a (hole, whole) lot of fun.

1.   When (your, you're) traveling, the key (to, two, too) enjoying yourself is to relax.

2.   (Weather, Whether) of any kind, (reign, rain, rein), cold, or heat, shouldn't (affect, effect) you.

3.   Pack (cloths, clothes) which are suitable to (wear, where) (where, wear) you'll be staying.

4.   (Buy, By) clothes which don't (weigh, way) (to, two, too) much and (which, witch) remain wrinkle-free.

5.   Whether you're traveling for business or pleasure, you don't want to (waist, waste) time ironing.

6.   When you travel on vacation, pack some (stationary, stationery) so you can (rite, write, right) to your loved ones, and take a (dairy, diary) to record your adventures.

7.   If you're leaving the (county, country), you can't be (already, all ready) until you have your passport.

8.   Of (course, coarse), you should arrive at the airport in plenty of time to (bored, board) the (plain, plane).

9.   Most airline (personal, personnel) are glad to be of (assistants, assistance) to customers, so don't be afraid to ask them questions.

10.   If flying makes you nervous, choose an (aisle, isle) seat and remember to (breath, breathe) deeply and swallow often during the (assent, ascent) and (descent, dissent).

11.   The (affect, effect) of breathing and swallowing is that (you're, your, yore) ears won't hurt as much.

12.   Again, the (hole, whole) idea of traveling is to relax and enjoy it.

13.   Whether you visit a famous (capitol, capital) or a (desert, dessert) resort, allow positive thoughts to (dominate, dominant) your mind.

14.   (Its, It's) often fun to (meat, meet) some of the other guests (where, were) you are staying.

15.   After all, it's only (human, humane) to want to (hear, here) from those who have been (through, threw) exciting adventures and who have (scene, seen) wonderful (cites, sites, sights).

16.   The (presence, presents) of a few friendly faces (there, they're, their) can make it seem as though you've (already, all ready) been to a place before.

17.   Here is some more (council, counsel) regarding traveling that (may be, maybe) helpful: Be prepared to spend money.

18.   It's possible to travel on a tight budget, but to (ensure, insure) a good time, have extra spending money.

19.   You'll (altar, alter) your spending habits when traveling because you"ll spend more on (fares, fairs) for transportation.

20.   You won't need to (break, brake) the bank, but you'll probably want to (by, buy) a few (presents, presence) for your family and friends.

21.   A final (peace, piece) of (advice, advise) regards delays while traveling.

22.   Being (stationary, stationery) while traveling can leave you (quiet, quite) (board, bored) and irritable.

23.   Keep your positive attitude and sense of humor no matter how your (patients, patience) may be tried.

24.   Your (since, sense) of humor may keep other upset passengers from making a (seen, scene).

25.   Once the delay and inconveniece have (passed, past), you'll be more (conscience, conscious) of the (principle, principal) that you cannot control what happens, but you can control your reactions to what happens.

Writing Compound Nouns and Adjectives

Using your dictionary, rewrite each of these compound words as a single word, as a hyphenated word, or as two separate words. If more than one form is correct, be prepared to explain.

EXAMPLE   foot ball   _____football_____

1. open heart surgery   _____
2. free for all   _____
3. high school   _____
4. pear shaped   _____
5. bird house   _____
6. accident prone   _____
7. pot hole   _____
8. bathing suit   _____
9. bread winner   _____
10. hand made   _____

11. head ache   _____
12. head cold   _____
13. head phone   _____
14. head to head   _____
15. head stone   _____
16. free agent   _____
17. free hand   _____
18. free form   _____
19. free spoken   _____
20. free style   _____

MODULE 21: PERIODS, QUESTION MARKS, AND EXCLAMATION POINTS

PERIODS

21a When does a period end a sentence?

Most sentences end with a period.

STATEMENT	Those who cannot remember the past are condemned to repeat it.
	—GEORGE SANTAYANA
MILD COMMAND	Be ready at 6:00.
INDIRECT QUESTION	I wondered how to select a deserving charity. [Compare with direct question.]

21b How do I use periods with abbreviations?

Most abbreviations call for periods, but some do not. Typical abbreviations with periods that are acceptable in academic writing include *Dr., Mr., Mrs., Ms., Ph.D., M.D., RN.,* and *a.m.* and *p.m.* with exact times such as *2:15 p.m.* Abbreviations not requiring periods include postal abbreviations for states, such as *CA* and *NY*; names of some organizations and government agencies, such as *CBS* and *FBI*; and acronyms (initials pronounced as words), such as *NASA* and *CARE*.

❖ PUNCTUATION ALERT: (1) Abbreviations of academic degrees should usually be set off with commas. When they follow city names, abbreviations of states are set off by commas. (2) When the period of an abbreviation falls at the end of a sentence, the period also serves to end the sentence ❖

QUESTION MARKS

21c When do I use a question mark?

In contrast to an **indirect question,** which *reports* a question and ends with a period, a **direct question** *asks* a question and ends with a question mark.

What is the capital of Georgia?
How do I select a deserving charity?

❖ PUNCTUATION ALERT: Do not combine a question mark with a comma, a period, or an exclamation point. ❖

No   She asked, "How are you?."

Yes   She asked, "How are you?"

21d When can I use a question mark in parentheses?

The only time to use a question mark in parentheses (?) is if a date or other number is unknown or doubtful. Never use (?) to communicate that you're unsure of information.

Mary Astell, a British writer of pamphlets on women's rights, was born in 1666 (?) and died in 1731.

The word *about* is often a more graceful substitute for (?): **Mary Astell was born about 1666**.

Also, never use (?) to communicate IRONY or sarcasm. Choose words to deliver your message.

EXCLAMATION MARKS

21e When do I use an exclamation point?

A strong command gives a very firm order, and an emphatic declaration makes a shocking or surprising statement.

Wait!   Sit down!   He lost the rent money!

❖ PUNCTUATION ALERT: Do not combine an exclamation point with a comma, a period, or a question mark. ❖

No   "Halt!," shouted the guard.

YES   "Halt!" shouted the guard.

21f What is considered overuse of exclamation points?

In academic writing your choice of words, not exclamation points, is expected to communicate the strength of your message. Overusing exclamation points can make your writing appear hysterical.

No   Any head injury is potentially dangerous! Go to the doctor immediately in case of bleeding from the ears, eyes, or mouth! Go if the patient has been unconscious!

YES   Any head injury is potentially dangerous. Go to the doctor immediately in case of bleeding from the ears, eyes, or mouth, or if the patient has been unconscious.

Name _____ Date _____

Supplying Appropriate End Punctuation

A: Circle all inappropriate end punctuation: periods, exclamation marks, and question marks. Then on the line to the right, copy the final word of the sentence and add the appropriate end punctuation. If the end punctuation is correct as is, write correct on the line.

EXAMPLE   Many people wonder why nurses wear white?   _____*white.*_____

1. Have you ever wondered why doctors wear blue or green while operating.   _____

2. White is the traditional symbol of purity!   _____

3. It is also easier to keep clean because it shows dirt.   _____

4. Surgeons wore white during operations until 1914?   _____

5. Then one surgeon decided that the sight of red blood against the white cloth was disgusting!   _____

6. He preferred—would you believe?—a spinach green that he felt reduced the brightness of the blood?   _____

7. After World War II, surgeons began using a different shade of green!   _____

8. Called minty green, it looked better under the new lighting used in operating rooms.   _____

9. The latest color is a blue-gray!   _____

10. Why did the doctors change again.   _____

11 Do you believe they did it because this blue shows up better on television than green does.   _____

12. Believe it or not.   _____

13. The surgeons appear on in-hospital television demonstrating new techniques to medical students!   _____

B: Add end punctuation to this paragraph as needed.

   Do you know who Theodor Seuss Geisel was Sure you do He was Dr Seuss, the famous author of children's books After ten years as a successful advertising illustrator and cartoonist, Seuss managed to get his first children's book published *And to Think That I Saw It on Mulberry Street* was published in 1937 by Vanguard Press It had been rejected by 27 other publishers I wonder why They certainly were foolish What's your favorite Dr Seuss book Mine is *The Cat in the Hat,* published in 1957 Everyone has a favorite And I do mean *Everyone* His books have been translated into 17 languages, and by 1984 over a hundred million copies had been sold worldwide In fact, in 1984 Seuss received a Pulitzer Prize for his years of educating and entertaining children How fitting Sadly Dr. Seuss died in 1991 We will all miss him

Writing Sentences with Appropriate End Punctuation

Write a sentence to illustrate each of these uses of end punctuation.

EXAMPLE   an emphatic command
           Wipe that grin off your face! _____

1. an indirect question

   _____

2. a mild command

   _____

3. a direct question

   _____

4. an abbreviation

   _____

5. a declarative sentence containing a direct quotation

   _____

6. an exclamation

   _____

7. a declarative statement

   _____

8. an emphatic command

   _____

9. a declarative sentence containing a quoted direct question

   _____

10. a declarative sentence containing an indirect quotation

    _____

11. a declarative sentence containing a quoted exclamation

    _____

MODULE 22: COMMAS

22a What is the role of the comma?

Commas are the most frequently used marks of punctuation, occurring twice as often as all other punctuation marks combined. A comma must be used in certain places, it must not be used in other places, and it's optional in still other places. This chapter helps you sort through the various rules. The role of the comma is to group and separate parts of a sentence for clarity.

22b How do commas work with coordinating conjunctions?

The coordinating conjunctions—*and*, *but*, *for*, *or*, *nor*, *yet*, and *so*—can link two or more independent clauses to create compound sentences. Use a comma before the coordinating conjunction. ❖ COMMA CAUTION: Do not put a comma *after* a coordinating conjunction that links independent clauses clause. ❖

	and	
	but	
	for	
Independent clause,	or	independent clause.
	nor	
	yet	
	so	

Tea contains caffeine, **but** herbal tea does not.
Caffeine makes some people jumpy, **and** it may even keep them from sleeping.
Caffeine is found in colas, **so** heavy cola drinkers may also have trouble sleeping.

❖ COMMA CAUTION: Do not use a comma when a coordinating conjunction links words, phrases, or dependent clauses. ❖

No   More restaurants now carry decaffeinated coffee, and fruit juice.
Yes   More restaurants now carry decaffeinated coffee and fruit juice.

❖ COMMA CAUTION: To avoid creating a comma splice, do not use a comma to separate independent clauses unless they are linked by a coordinating conjunction. ❖

| **No** | Caffeine occurs naturally in many foods, it is even found in chocolate. [These independent clauses have no linking word. The comma cannot substitute for a linking word.] |
| **Yes** | Caffeine occurs naturally in many foods, and it is even found in chocolate. [A coordinating conjunction and comma link the two independent clauses.] |

When independent clauses containing other commas are linked by a coordinating conjunction, use a semicolon before the coordinating conjunction.

Some herbal teas, such as orange flavored, have become very popular; yet some people, afraid to try anything new, refuse to taste them.

22c How do commas work with introductory clauses, phrases, and words?

When a clause, phrase, or word introduces an independent clause, use a comma to signal the end of the introductory element and the beginning of the independent clause.

Introductory clause,
Introductory phrase, ⟶ independent clause.
Introductory word,

An adverb clause, one type of dependent clause, cannot stand alone as an independent unit. Although it contains a subject and verb, it begins with a subordinating conjunction (7i, 7p). Use a comma to set off an adverb clause that introduces an independent clause.

Whenever it rains, the lake floods local streets.
Because federal loans are hard to get, the community will have to get private help.

When an adverb clause comes after the independent clause, do not use a comma.

The lake floods local streets whenever it rains.
The community will have to get private help because federal loans are hard to get.

A **phrase** is a group of words that cannot stand alone as an independent unit because it lacks a subject, a verb, or both. Use a comma to set off a phrase that introduces an independent clause.

Inside even the cleanest homes, insects thrive. [prepositional phrase]
Carefully using insecticides, we can safely drive the insects out of our homes again. [participial phrase]

Introductory transitional words indicate relationships between ideas in sentences and paragraphs. Use a comma to set off a transitional word or phrase that introduces an independent clause (some writers prefer to omit the comma after single-word transitions).

First, an exterminator must clear the area of pets, fragile plants, and open containers of food.

In addition, he must be careful not to transport insects to new areas when he moves these items.

22d How do commas work with items in a series?

A series is a group of three or more elements—words, phrases, or clauses—that match in grammatical form and have the same importance within a sentence. Use commas between items in a series and before *and* when it is used between the last two items.

> **word, word,** and **word**
>
> **word, word, word**
>
> **phrase, phrase,** and **phrase**
>
> **phrase, phrase, phrase**
>
> **clause, clause,** and **clause**
>
> **clause, clause, clause**

Citrus fruits include **oranges, tangerines,** and **grapefruits.**

There are many varieties of oranges: **the sweet orange, the Jaffa orange, the navel orange, the mandarin.**

Lemons are good for **flavoring cakes, decorating platters,** and **removing stains.**

When the items in a series contain commas or other punctuation, or when the items are long and complex, separate them with semicolons instead of commas.

Oranges are probably native to tropical Asia, but they spread quickly centuries ago because of the Roman conquest of Asia, Europe, and North Africa; the Arab trade routes; the expansion of Islam throughout the Mediterranean, except for France and Italy; and the Crusades.

22e How do commas work with coordinate adjectives?

Coordinate adjectives are two or more adjectives that equally modify a noun or noun group. Separate coordinate adjectives with commas or coordinating conjunctions.

> **coordinate adjective, coordinate adjective** noun

The sweet orange has **broad, glossy** leaves.

Adjectives are coordinate if *and* can be inserted between them or if their order can be reversed without damaging the meaning of the sentence. Meaning does not change when the example sentence says *broad and glossy leaves* or *glossy, broad leaves*. ❖ COMMA CAUTIONS: (1) Don't put a comma after a final coordinate adjective and the noun it modifies—note that no comma comes between *glossy* and *leaves* in the above example. (2) Don't put a comma between adjectives that are not coordinate: *Six large oranges cost two dollars.* ❖

22f How do commas work with nonrestrictive elements?

Restrictive and nonrestrictive elements are kinds of modifiers. A nonrestrictive modifier is also called a nonessential modifier because the information it provides about the modified term is "extra." If a nonrestrictive modifier is dropped, a reader can still understand the full meaning of the modified word. Nonrestrictive modifiers are set off with commas.

Nonrestrictive element, independent clause.

Beginning of independent clause, **nonrestrictive element**, end of independent clause.

Independent clause, **nonrestrictive element**.

Believe it or not, the first daily newspaper was a Roman invention.

The *Acta Diurna*, **whose title means "daily events,"** was available every day.

Scribes made multiple copies of each day's political and social news, **which included senate action and the results of gladiatorial games.**

When the nonrestrictive information in these examples is eliminated, the meaning of the modified terms does not change.

The first daily newspaper was a Roman invention.

The *Acta Diurna* was available every day.

Scribes made multiple copies of each day's political and social news.

In contrast, a **restrictive modifier** (also known as an **essential modifier**) cannot be omitted without creating confusion. No commas are used because the information in these passages is part of the basic message of the sentence. ❖ COMMA CAUTION: A restrictive modifier is not extra. Do not use commas to set it off from the rest of the sentence. ❖

Whoever invented paper is unknown.

The Chinese printed **what are considered the first books.**

They invented a white paper **that was made of wood** and a way to transfer a carved image from stone to paper.

Compare the pairs of restrictive and nonrestrictive modifiers that follow.

NONRESTRICTIVE CLAUSE	The world's oldest surviving book printed from wood blocks was published in A.D. 868 by Wang Chih, **who followed an already long Chinese printing tradition.** [*Who followed an already long Chinese printing tradition* adds information about Wang Chih, but it is not essential to the sentence.]
RESTRICTIVE CLAUSE	Students **who wish to imitate the woodblock method** do not need many materials. [The clause clarifies which students, so it is essential.]

NONRESTRICTIVE CLAUSE	**Before carving,** the student should sketch out a preliminary version of the page. [*Before carving* is a prepositional phrase that explains when to act. However, the sentence is clear without it.]
RESTRICTIVE CLAUSE	Marco Polo introduced woodblock printing **to Europe.** [Prepositional phrase is essential to the message.]

An **appositive** is a word or group of words that renames the noun or noun group preceding it. Most appositives are nonrestrictive. Once the name of something is given, words renaming it are not usually necessary to specify or limit it even more.

> Johann Gutenberg, **a German printer living in France**, was the first European to use movable type.

Some appositives, however, are restrictive and are not set off with commas.

> Mr. Jones **the rare book collector** would pay a fortune to own a Gutenberg Bible. [The appositive is essential for distinguishing this Mr. Jones from other Mr. Joneses.]

22g How do commas set off parenthetical expressions, contrasts, words of direct address, and tag sentences?

Words, phrases, or clauses that interrupt a sentence but—like nonrestrictive elements—do not change its basic meaning should be set off, usually with commas. (Parentheses or dashes also set material off.)

Parenthetical expressions are "asides," additions to sentences that the writer thinks of as extra.

> The Spanish brought the first printing press in the New World to Mexico City in 1534, but, **surprisingly**, the earliest surviving pieces of work are from 1539. [parenthetical expression]

Expressions of contrast are set off with commas.

> An early printing press at Lima turned out Indian- and Spanish-language religious material, **not political or news pamphlets.** [words of contrast]

> The roots of the extensive modern Spanish-language press go back to these two printing centers, **rather than to Spain itself.** [words of contrast]

Words of direct address and tag questions should be set off with commas.

> Did you know, **Rosa**, that your daily Spanish newspaper is part of a 400-year-old tradition? [direct address]

> You are bilingual, **aren't you?** [tag question]

22h How do commas work with quoted words?

Use a comma to set off quoted words from short explanations in the same sentence, such as *she said, they replied, and he answered.*

According to a Chinese proverb, "A book is like a garden carried in the pocket."

"When I stepped from hard manual work to writing," said Sean O'Casey, "I just stepped from one kind of hard work to another."

"I can't write five words, but that I change seven," complained Dorothy Parker.

❖ COMMA CAUTION: When quoted words end with a question mark or an exclamation point, keep that punctuation and do not add a comma even if explanatory words follow. ❖

22i How do commas work in dates, names, addresses, correspondence, and numbers?

RULES FOR COMMAS WITH DATES

1. Use a comma between the date and the year: **November 24,1859**.

2. Use a comma between the day and the date: **Thursday, November 24**.

3. Within a sentence, use commas after the day *and* the year in a full date.
   November 24, **1859**, was the date of publication of Charles Darwin's *The Origin of Species*.

4. Don't use a comma in a date that contains only the month and year or only the season and year.
   Darwin's *The Origin of Species* was published in **winter 1859**.

5. An inverted date takes no commas.
   Charles Darwin's *The Origin of Species* was first published on **24 November 1859**.

RULES FOR COMMAS WITH NAMES, PLACES, AND ADDRESSES

1. When an abbreviated title (M.D., Ph.D.) comes after a person's name, set the abbreviation off with commas.
   The company celebrated the promotion of **Susan Cohen, M.B.A.**, to senior vice president.

2. When you invert a person's name, use a comma to separate the last name from the first: **Cohen, Susan**.

3. Use a comma between a city and state: **Cherry Hill, New Jersey**. In a sentence, use a comma after the state as well.
   Cherry Hill, New Jersey, is not far from Philadelphia.

4. When you write a complete address as part of a sentence, use a comma to separate all the items but the zip code, which follows the state. A comma does not follow the zip code.
   The check from U.R. Stuk, **1313 Erewhon Lane, Englewood Cliffs, New Jersey 07632** bounced.

RULES FOR COMMAS WITH LETTERS

1. For the opening of an informal letter, use a comma: **Dear Betty,**

2. For the close of a letter, use a comma: **Sincerely yours, Love, Best regards, Very truly yours,**

RULES FOR COMMAS WITH NUMBERS

1. Counting from the right, put a comma after every three digits in numbers over four digits: **72,867   156,567,066**

2. In a number of four digits, a comma is optional.
   $1776 or $1,776   1776 miles or 1,776 miles

3. Don't use a comma for a four-digit year—**2001** (but **25,000 B.C.**); or in an address—**12161 Dean Drive**; or in a page number—**see page 1338**

4. Use a comma to separate related measurements written as words: **five feet, four inches**

5. Use a comma to separate a play's scene from an act: **Act II, scene iv**

6. Use a comma to separate a reference to a page from a reference to a line: **page 10, line 6**

22j How do commas clarify meaning?

Sometimes you will need to use a comma to clarify the meaning of a sentence, even though no other rule calls for one.

No	In his will power to run the family business was divided among his children.
Yes	In his will, power to run the family business was divided among his children.
No	People who want to register to vote without being reminded.
Yes	People who want to, register to vote without being reminded.

22k How can I avoid misusing the comma?

Do not overuse commas by inserting them where they do not belong. Comma misuses are discussed throughout this chapter, signaled by ✤ COMMA CAUTION. ✤

Besides the misuses of commas discussed earlier, writers sometimes mistakenly use commas to separate major sentence parts.

No	Snowballs over the last 20 million years, have created the Antarctic ice sheet. [Do not separate a subject from its verb with a single comma.]
Yes	Snowfalls over the last 20 million years have created the Antarctic ice sheet.
No	The massive ice sheet is, 16,000 feet deep. [Do not separate a verb from its complement with a single comma.]
Yes	The massive ice sheet is 16,000 feet deep.

No   The weight of the ice has pushed, the continent 2,000 feet into the water. [Do not separate a verb from its object with a single comma.]

YES   The weight of the ice has pushed the continent 2,000 feet into the water.

No   Therefore, most of the continent lies below, sea level. [Do not separate a preposition from its object with a single comma.]

YES   Therefore, most of the continent lies below sea level.

221 How can I avoid comma errors?

You can avoid most comma errors with these two bits of advice:

As you write or reread what you've written, don't insert a comma simply because you happen to pause to think or take a breath before moving on.

As you're writing, if you're unsure about a comma, insert it and circle the spot. Later, when you're **editing**, check your handbook for the rule that applies.

Using Commas in Compound Sentences

A: Rewrite the following sentences, inserting commas wherever coordinating conjunctions are used to join sentences. If a sentence does not need any additional commas, write *correct* on the line.

EXAMPLE   Some people consider slime molds protozoans but most scientists class them with the fungi.
Some people consider slime molds protozoans, but most scientists class them with the fungi.

1.   Slime molds move by creeping along and sometimes they seem to flow.

     _____

2.   They have a stationary stage, however and then they are more plantlike.

     _____

3.   An observer seldom sees much of the mold's body or plasmodium for it stays beneath decaying matter.

     _____

4.   The main part contains several nuclei but has no cell walls.

     _____

5.   Like an amoeba, its protoplasm moves in one direction and then it goes in another.

     _____

6.   Not only do slime molds come in many colors but they also come in many types.

     _____

7.   Some grow on long stalks while others are stalkless.

     _____

8.   Some kinds are very small and can only be seen through a microscope.

     _____

9.   Most slime molds grow on decaying wood yet some grow directly on the ground.

     _____

10. A mold depends on water so it will dry up if it lacks moisture.

     _____

11. Most mature molds change into sporangia and the sporangia each contain many spores.

   _____

12. Scientists know that the wind carries the spores and that they eventually germinate and form new molds.

   _____

13. The slime-mold species *Fuligo* has the largest sporangia and they dwarf others by comparison.

   _____

14. Either they appear to be large sponges on the ground or they look like dark holes in the grass.

   _____

B: Combine the following sentences by using the coordinating conjunctions given in parentheses. Remember to use a comma before each coordinating conjunction used to join two sentences.

EXAMPLE   Most slime molds live in the woods.
           They like soil with high humus content. (and)
           Most slime molds live in the woods, and they
           like soil with high humus content.

1. Some, however, leave the forest.
   They live on cultivated plants. (and)

   _____

2. They can cause clubroot of cabbage.
   They can create powdery scab of potato. (or)

   _____

3. Slime molds sound disagreeable.
   Some are quite attractive. (yet)

   _____

4. One form produces unappealing stalks.
   The stalks are topped with tiny balls. (but)

   _____

5. The balls appear to be woven.
   They look rather like baskets. (so)

   _____

6. The woven balls are really sporangia.
   They contain spores for distribution. (and)

   _____

7. Another form looks like tiny ghosts.
   Its white molds could be small sheeted figures. (for)

   _____

8. Serpent slime mold is yellow.
   It can look like a miniature snake on top of a decaying log. (and)

   _____

9. One would have to work hard to find it in New England.
   It is most common in the tropics. (for)

   _____

10. After one learns about slime molds, they no longer seem disgusting.
    They do not even seem disagreeable. (nor)

    _____

Using Commas after Introductory Elements

A: Applying the rules regarding commas and introductory elements, rewrite these sentences, inserting commas as needed. If any sentence does not need an additional comma, write *correct* on the line.

EXAMPLE   Known as the Empty Quarter the Rub al-Khali is the largest of the deserts in Saudi Arabia.
Known as the Empty Quarter, the Rub al-Khali is the largest of the deserts in Saudi Arabia.

1.   In fact it is the largest continuous body of sand in the world.

_____

2.   Extending over 250,000 square miles the Rub al-Khali comprises more than one-third of Saudi Arabia.

_____

3.   As a point of comparison Texas is just slightly larger.

_____

4.   Because it is almost completely devoid of rain the Rub al-Khali is one of the driest places on the planet.

_____

5.   Despite the existence of a few scattered shrubs the desert is largely a sand sea.

_____

6.   However its eastern side develops massive dunes with salt basins.

_____

7.   Except for the hardy Bedouins the Rub al-Khali is uninhabited.

_____

8.   Indeed it is considered one of the most forbidding places on earth.

_____

9.   Until Bertram Thomas crossed it in 1931 it was unexplored by outsiders.

_____

10. Even after oil was discovered in Arabia exploration in the Empty Quarter was limited.

_____

11. Losing heavy equipment in the deep sand made such exploration expensive.

_____

12. To facilitate exploration huge sand tires were developed in the 1950s.

_____

13. Shortly thereafter drilling rigs began operating in the Rub al-Khali.

_____

14. We now know that the Empty Quarter sits on huge reserves of oil.

_____

15. As it turns out the Empty Quarter is not so empty after all.

_____

B: Applying the rules governing commas and introductory elements, insert commas as needed in this paragraph.

[1]As might be expected the Rub al-Khali is hot all year round. [2]In contrast the Gobi Desert is hot in the summer but extremely cold in the winter. [3]Located in China and Mongolia the Gobi is twice the size of Texas. [4]Unlike the Rub al-Khali the Gobi has some permanent settlers. [5]Nevertheless most of its inhabitants are nomadic. [6]To avoid the subzero winters the nomads move their herds at the end of summer. [7]When the harsh winters subside they return to the sparse desert vegetation.

Using Commas in Series and with Coordinate Adjectives

A: In each sentence, first underline all items in series and all coordinate adjectives. Then rewrite each sentence, adding any necessary commas. If no commas are needed, explain why.

EXAMPLE   Vicunas guanacos llamas and alpacas are all South American members of the camel family.
Vicunas, guanacos, llamas, and alpacas are all South American members of the camel family.

1. The vicuna, the smallest member of the camel family, lives in the mountains of Ecuador Bolivia and Peru.

_____

2. The guanaco is the wild humpless ancestor of the llama and the alpaca.

_____

3. The llama stands four feet tall is about four feet long and is the largest of the South American camels.

_____

4. A llama's coat may be white brown black or shades in between.

_____

5. Indians of the Andes use llamas to carry loads to bear wool and to produce meat.

_____

6. Llamas are foraging animals that live on lichens shrubs and other available plants.

_____

7. Because they can go without water for weeks, llamas are economical practical pack animals.

_____

8. The alpaca has a longer lower body than the llama.

_____

9. It has wool of greater length of higher quality and of superior softness.

_____

10. Alpaca wool is straighter finer and warmer than sheep's wool.

_____

B: Write complete sentences as described below. Take special care to follow the rules governing the use of commas in lists and between coordinate adjectives.

EXAMPLE   Mention three favorite holidays.
My favorite holidays are Christmas, New Year's Day, and Easter.

1. Give at least three reasons to spend those holidays with relatives.

     _____

     _____

2. List your three favorite fast foods.

     _____

     _____

3. Mention your four preferred vacation activities.

     _____

     _____

4. Using two or three coordinate adjectives, describe a pet.

     _____

     _____

5. Use a series of adjectives to describe a favorite movie.

     _____

     _____

6. Use a series of prepositional phrases to tell where the groom found rice after the wedding.

     _____

     _____

7. Using a series of verbs or verb phrases, tell what John does at his fitness center.

     _____

     _____

8. Use coordinate adjectives to describe John's improved appearance as a result of working out.

     _____

     _____

Using Commas with Nonrestrictive, Parenthetical, and Transitional Elements

Rewrite these sentences to punctuate nonrestrictive clauses, phrases, appositives, and transitional expressions. If a sentence needs no commas, write *correct* on the line.

EXAMPLE   Ballet a sophisticated form of dance is a theatrical art.
           Ballet, a sophisticated form of dance, is a theatrical art.

1.   A ballet contains a sequence of dances that are performed to music.

     _____

     _____

2.   The dances both solos and ensembles express emotion or tell a story.

     _____

     _____

3.   The person who composes the actual dance steps is the choreographer.

     _____

     _____

4.   A ballet's steps called its choreography become standardized over many years of performance.

     _____

     _____

5.   The choreographer Marius Petipa created the blend of steps still used in most productions of *Swan Lake*.

     _____

     _____

6.   The steps all with French names combine solos and groups.

     _____

     _____

7.   The *corps de ballet* the ballet company excluding its star soloists may dance together or in small ensembles.

     _____

     _____

8. One soloist may join another for a *pas de deux* a dance for two.

    _____

    _____

9. Ensemble members not just soloists must be proficient at pliés and arabesques.

    _____

    _____

10. Children wanting to become professionals must practice for years.

    _____

    _____

11. It is important therefore to start lessons early.

    _____

    _____

12. In Russia which has some of the most stringent ballet training students begin at age three.

    _____

    _____

Expanding Sentences with Restrictive and Nonrestrictive Elements

Expand each sentence twice: first with a restrictive word, phrase, or clause, and then with a nonrestrictive word, phrase, or clause. Place commas as needed.

EXAMPLE   I love my neighbor.
　　　　　　1. (restrictive) *I love my new neighborhood.*
　　　　　　2. (nonrestrictive) *I love my neighborhood which is in the oldest part of the city.*

1.   My neighbors are kind.

_____

_____

2.   They help one another.

_____

_____

3.   They are friendly to strangers.

_____

_____

4.   The houses and yards are well kept.

_____

_____

5.   Trees line the streets.

_____

_____

6.   Many of the neighborhood families have pets.

_____

_____

7.   The pets are friendly.

_____

_____

8.   The park is one street away.

_____

_____

9. The park has a playground.

    _____

    _____

10. The neighborhood children play at the park.

    _____

    _____

Using Commas with Quotations   EXERCISE **22-6**

Using the rules governing commas to attach quotations to their speaker tags, place commas in these sentences.

EXAMPLE   According to Aristotle "The actuality of thought is life."
            According to Aristotle, "The actuality of thought is life."

1. George Sand was most accurate when she said "Life in common among these people who love each other is the ideal of happiness."

2. "I find that I have painted my life—things happening in my life—without knowing" said the wise Georgia O'Keeffe.

3. "I slept and dreamed that life was beauty" said Ellen Sturgis Hooper. "I woke—and found that life was duty."

4. In passing, a professor said to a student "Life, dear friend, is short but sweet."

5. "Life's a tough proposition" declared Wilson Mizner "and the first hundred years are the hardest."

6. "Life" said Forrest Gump "is like a box of chocolates: You never know what you're going to get."

7. "That it will never come again is what makes life so sweet" observed Emily Dickinson.

8. "May you live all the days of your life" advised Jonathan Swift.

9. William Cooper was right when he said "Variety's the spice of life."

10. "Live all you can; it's a mistake not to" said Henry James.

Using Commas in Dates, Names, Addresses, and Numbers

Rewrite the following sentences, inserting commas to punctuate dates, names, addresses, and numbers. If a sentence is correct as written, write correct on the line.

EXAMPLE   January 1 1975 was the beginning of a momentous year.
January 1, 1975, was the beginning of a momentous year.

1. In the northwest part of China, 6000 pottery figures were found.

    _____

2. Construction workers uncovered a terra cotta army in July 1975.

    _____

3. The life-sized warriors and horses had been buried for 2200 years.

    _____

4. The figures were in a huge tomb near the city of Xían China.

    _____

5. Archaeologists also unearthed almost 10000 artifacts from the excavation site.

    _____

6. It did not take John Doe Ph. D. to realize that this was an extraordinary find.

    _____

7. Some of the figures were displayed in Memphis Tennessee twenty years later.

    _____

8. Running from 18 April 1995 to 18 September 1995, the exhibit featured 250 objects from the imperial tombs of China.

    _____

9. The exhibit was open from 9 A.M. to 10 P.M. daily.

    _____

10. To get tickets, one could write to the Memphis Cook Convention Center 255 North Main Memphis TN 38103.

    _____

Adding Commas

A: Rewrite the following sentences, inserting commas as needed. If a sentence is correct as written, write *correct* on the line.

EXAMPLE   Ancient writers both Greek and Roman wrote about the seven wonders of the world.
Ancient writers, both Greek and Roman, wrote about the seven wonders of the world.

1.   One was the statue of Olympian Zeus which was covered with precious stones.

   _____

2.   Unfortunately it was taken to Constantinople in 576 A. D. and there destroyed by fire.

   _____

3.   The Hanging Gardens of Babylon built for Nebuchadnezzar were considered a wonder.

   _____

4.   They were probably irrigated terraces connected by marble stairways.

   _____

5.   To lift water from the Euphrates slaves had to work in shifts.

   _____

6.   The Colossus of Rhodes was a huge impressive statue built to honor the sun god Helios.

   _____

7.   Constructed near the harbor it was intended to astonish all who saw it.

   _____

8.   Another wonder was the Lighthouse at Alexandria Egypt.

   _____

9.   Because it stood on the island of Pharos the word pharos has come to mean lighthouse.

   _____

10. After the death of Mausolus king of Caria his widow erected a richly adorned monument to honor him.

   _____

11. With sculptures by famous artists the Mausoleum at Halicarnassus amazed the ancient world.

   _____

12. The Temple of Artemis at Ephesus an important Ionian city was also considered a wonder.

   _____

13. It was burned rebuilt and burned again.

   _____

14. Some wonders such as the Colossus and the Mausoleum were destroyed by earthquakes.

   _____

15. Of the seven works that astounded the ancients only the pyramids of Egypt survive.

   _____

B: Add commas as needed. You will not need to add any words or other marks of punctuation.

[1]St. Andrews Scotland is an old city. [2]Named for a Christian saint the city was once an object of devout pilgrimage. [3]Its cathedral the largest in Scotland is now a ruin. [4]It was destroyed in 1559 by followers of the reformer John Knox. [5]All the revered carefully preserved relics of St. Andrew disappeared. [6]Although the castle of St. Andrews also lies in ruins it preserves two fascinating remnants of medieval history. [7]One is a bottle-shaped dungeon and the other is a countermine. [8]When attackers tried to mine under castle walls defenders tried to intercept the tunnel with a countermine. [9]Interestingly one can actually enter both mine and countermine. [10]The University of St. Andrews which is the oldest university in Scotland was established in 1412. [11]From all parts of the globe students come to study there. [12]Nevertheless most people who think of St. Andrews associate it with golf. [13]Even golf at St. Andrews is old the first reference dating to January 25 1552. [14]The famous Old Course is only one of four courses from which the avid golfer may choose. [15]St. Andrews is still an object of pilgrimage but today's pilgrims come with drivers wedges and putters.

Eliminating Unnecessary Commas   EXERCISE 22-9

Revise this paragraph, eliminating any unnecessary commas. You will not need to add any words or marks of punctuation.

[1]Many scholars consider Ralph Waldo Emerson, who was born in Boston, Massachusetts, on May 25, 1803, to be, the most powerful writer of American literature. [2]At age 14, Emerson entered, Harvard College, graduating four years later. [3]After finishing college, he earned money while teaching school, for three years. [4]With his money, Emerson entered, the divinity school at Harvard.[5]Not long thereafter, he began preaching, and in 1829, Emerson was appointed minister, of a large Unitarian church in Boston. [6]Within the same year, he married, Ellen Louisa Tucker. [7]After her death, only two years later, and after the death of Emerson's two brothers, Emerson, began to question the church's doctrine, leading him to resign his pastorate, in 1832. [8]Soon after, Emerson sailed for Europe, where he met the great, men of, his time, including John Stuart Mill. [9]Emerson remarried in 1835 and spent the next, several decades of his life with his family, at his home in Concord, which burned down in 1872. [10]However, people nationwide donated money, to have it rebuilt. [11]Emerson died several years later, at the age of 79 after a brief illness, and he was buried, in Sleepy Hollow Cemetery.

Adding and Deleting Commas

Rewrite this paragraph, adding or deleting commas as needed. You will not have to change any words or other marks of punctuation. Number each change you make, and on the lines below, indicate the reason for each addition or omission.

Money, although valuable is really a matter, of trust and confidence in the
government. By definition money is anything that society, accepts as having value.
With such a broad definition it is not surprising, that money has, throughout history
5   taken on some forms that were both creative and unique. Precious stones, fish
hooks, nails livestock, throwing knives, and ax-heads, are just a few examples of
money that is equivalent to ours today. In a successful, society, money must serve
three, basic functions: It must serve as a store of wealth a medium of exchange and
a unit against which items are valued. Forms of money, must be portable, easy to
10 store durable, and relatively hard to acquire. Successful forms of money, like gold
and silver have all these qualities. However, trust is also, necessary in a society
such as ours that uses paper money. Although the paper itself is of little value we
trust that a bill is, worth the number printed on the front of it.

COMMAS ADDED	COMMAS DELETED
_____	_____
_____	_____
_____	_____
_____	_____
_____	_____
_____	_____
_____	_____
_____	_____
_____	_____
_____	_____
_____	_____
_____	_____

MODULE 23: SEMICOLONS

23a What are the uses of a semicolon?

While a period signals the complete separation of **independent clauses**, a semicolon indicates only a partial ("semi") separation. Use a semicolon in only two situations. A semicolon can replace a period between sentences that are closely related in meaning. Also, a semicolon belongs between sentence structures that already contain one or more commas and with certain lists.

23b When can I use a semicolon, instead of a period, between independent clauses?

When independent clauses are related in meaning, you can separate them with a semicolon instead of a period. ✤ COMMA CAUTION: Do not use only a comma between independent clauses, or you will create a comma splice. ✤

> Independent clause; independent clause.

All changes are not growth; all movement is not forward.
—ELLEN GLASGOW

23c When else can I use a semicolon between independent clauses?

Use a semicolon between two independent clauses when the second clause begins with a conjunctive adverb or other transitional word. ✤ COMMA CAUTION: Do not use only a comma between independent clauses connected by a conjunctive adverb or other words of transition, or you will create a comma splice. ✤

> Independent clause; conjunctive adverb or other transition, independent clause.

A coelacanth, a supposedly extinct fish, was caught by an African fisherman in 1938; **as a result**, some scientists believe other "extinct" animals may still live in remote parts of the world.

✤ COMMA ALERT: When you place a conjunctive adverb or a transition after the first word in an independent clause, set it off with commas: *This theory may be true; some people, however, even suggest the Loch Ness Monster may be a dinosaur.* ✤

23d How do semicolons work with coordinating conjunctions?

You will usually use a comma to separate independent clauses linked by a coordinating conjunction. When the independent clauses already contain commas, however, use a semicolon instead to separate the clauses.

> Independent clause, one that contains commas; coordinating conjunction independent clause.
>
> Independent clause; coordinating conjunction independent clause, one that contains commas.

Aim at the sun, and you may not reach it; but your arrow will fly far higher than if aimed at an object on a level with yourself.　　　　　　　　　　　　　　　　　　—JOEL HAWES

23e When should I use semicolons between items in a series?

When a sentence contains a series of words, phrases, or clauses, commas usually separate one item from the next. When the items are long and contain commas for other purposes, you can make your message clearer by separating the items with semicolons instead of commas.

> Independent clause that includes a series of items, each or all of which contain commas; another item in the series; another item in the series.

Many are always praising the by-gone time, for it is natural that the old should extol the days of their youth; the weak, the time of their strength; the sick, the season of their vigor; and the disappointed, the spring-tide of their hopes.　　　　　　— CALEB BINGHAM

23f How do I avoid misusing the semicolon?

Don't use a semicolon between a dependent clause and an independent clause; use a comma: *Because the price of new cars continues to rise, people are keeping their old cars.*

Don't use a semicolon to introduce a list; use a colon: *Keeping these old cars running can be expensive too: rebuilt engines, new transmissions, and replacement tires.*

Name _____ Date _____

Using the Semicolon

A: Insert semicolons where needed. They may be placed where there is now no punctuation or they may replace commas. Some sentences may require more than one semicolon. If an item is *correct*, write *correct* in the left margin.

EXAMPLE   Vision is our most important sense; we get most of our information about the world by seeing.

1. The sclera is the outer cover of the eye, it helps the eye keep its shape because the sclera is fairly hard.

2. The choroid is just inside the sclera it keeps out unneeded light.

3. The pupil is the opening in the eye this is where the light enters.

4. The cornea is the clear cover of the pupil, therefore, light can enter the eye.

5. The pupil is opened or closed by muscles in the iris, in fact, in bright light the iris closes to decrease the amount of light entering, in low light, it opens to increase the light.

6. After passing through the pupil, light shines on the retina, which sends messages to the brain.

7. The retina contains cells, cones and rods, which are outgrowths of the brain when light strikes them, nerve impulses travel to the brain.

8. The optic nerve connects the eye to the brain, thus any damage to the nerve can cause blindness.

9. Cone cells give us color vision, they are most effective in the day.

10. Rods are sensitive to low light they are involved in night vision.

B: This paragraph is missing seven semicolons. Insert them where needed.

    Hearing is based on sound waves these are pressure changes spreading out from a vibrating source. If we could see sound waves, they might remind us of ripples on water like ripples, sound waves vary in number, size, and speed. When these waves reach us, our ears and brain translate them into pitch, loudness, and timbre.

5   Pitch is the number of wave vibrations per second it determines whether a tone is high or low, whether a singer is a soprano or an alto. Loudness is a measure of the intensity of the waves this is called their amplitude. When we turn up the volume on the stereo, we are raising the amplitude. Sound intensity is measured in decibels. Any sound registering over 130 decibels is painful however, people still listen to loud

10 music or live near railroad tracks. Timbre is hard to describe in everyday language in physics terms, however, timbre is the main wavelength plus any other wavelengths that may come from a particular source. Timbre explains why a note played on a violin sounds different from the same note played on an electric guitar or why two people singing the same note sound different. Physics defines noise as too many unrelat-

15 ed frequencies vibrating together nevertheless, people still disagree over whether some sounds are noise or exciting music.

Using the Semicolon and the Comma

Add commas or semicolons as needed to fill in the blanks appropriately.

EXAMPLE   One out of every twenty-five people is colorblind _____ unable to tell certain colors apart.

1.   Colorblindness is inherited _____ it appears more often in men than in women.

2.   The most common colorblindness is the inability to tell red from green _____ but more than green and red are involved.

3.   Different colors, the result of differences in light wavelengths, create a spectrum _____ the spectrum of colors is red, orange, yellow, green, blue, indigo, and violet.

4.   People who are severely red-green colorblind cannot "see" any colors at that end of the spectrum _____ that is _____ they cannot tell the difference between blue-greens, reds, or yellow-greens.

5.   Colorblindness varies from person to person _____ people who can distinguish red from green a little are called color-weak.

6.   Some people have no cone cells (the cells that send signals about color to the brain) _____ so they are completely colorblind.

7.   They have achromatism _____ a rare condition.

8.   Such people can see only black, white, and grays _____ what a boring view of the world.

9.   However, their problem is much more serious than this _____ they also have trouble focusing on objects.

10. The part of the eye that usually receives images is the fovea, which contains the cone cells _____ achromatics' foveas are blank and cannot receive images.

11. To compensate, they look at objects off center _____ to pick up images with their rod (black and white) cells.

12. It is possible to be colorblind and not know it _____ how can people miss what they have never known?

13. There are several tests for colorblindness _____ most involve seeing (or not seeing) a number or word written on a background of a complementary color for example, a red *48* on a green background.

MODULE 24: COLONS

24a What are the uses of a colon?

In sentence punctuation, the colon introduces what comes after it: a quotation, a summary or restatement, or a list. The colon also has a few separating functions.

24b When can a colon introduce a list, an appositive, or a quotation?

Use a colon to introduce a list or series of items announced by an independent clause.

In selecting a major, consider these factors: your talent for the subject, the number of years needed to qualify professionally, and the availability of jobs.

When you use phrases such as *the following* or *as follows*, a colon is usually required. A colon is not called for with the words *such as* or *including*.

Woods commonly used in fine furniture include the following: black walnut, mahogany, oak, and pecan.

You can use a colon to lead into a final appositive—a word or group of words that renames a noun or pronoun.

A hot plate can enable any student to become a dormitory chef, preparing simple and satisfying meals: omelets, stir-fried vegetables, even stews.

Use a colon at the end of a grammatically complete statement that introduces a formal quotation.

Francis Bacon was referring to men and women when he wrote of the destructiveness of seeking vengeance: "A man that studieth revenge keeps his own wounds green."

24c When can I use a colon between two independent clauses?

You can use a colon at the end of an independent clause to introduce statements that summarize, restate, or explain what is said in that clause.

The makers of some movies aimed at teenagers think that their audience is interested in little more than car chases, violence, and nudity: they sadly underestimate young people.

> Independent clause containing words that introduce a quotation: "Quoted words."
>
> Independent clause: summarizing or restating words.
>
> Independent clause: listed items.

24d What standard formats require a colon?

TITLE AND SUBTITLE

Broca's Brain; Reflections on the Romance of Science

HOURS, MINUTES, AND SECONDS

The lecture began at 9:15 A.M.

CHAPTERS AND VERSES OF THE BIBLE

Ecclesiastes 3:1

LETTER SALUTATION

Dear Ms. Winters:

MEMO FORM

TO: Dean Elliot Gordon

FROM: Professor Steven Wang

RE: Honors and Awards Ceremony

24e When is a colon wrong?

A colon must follow a complete independent clause except when it separates standard material. Lead-in words must make a grammatically complete statement. When they do not, do not use a colon. Also do not use a colon after the words *such as* and *including* or forms of the verb *be*.

No	The shop sold: T-shirts, bumper stickers, posters, and greeting cards.
Yes	The shop sold T-shirts, bumper stickers, posters, and greeting cards.
No	Students work in many of the town's businesses, such as: the diner, the grocery, the laundromat, and the gas station.
Yes	Students work in many of the town's businesses, such as the diner, the grocery, the laundromat, and the gas station.
Yes	Students work in many of the town's businesses: the diner, the grocery, the laundromat, and the gas station.

Do not use a colon to separate a dependent clause from an independent clause.

No	When summer comes: the town is almost deserted.
Yes	When summer comes, the town is almost deserted.

Using the Colon

Rewrite the following sentences, adding colons as needed. If no colon is needed, write *correct* in the left margin.

EXAMPLE   On many college campuses, there's a place that students find indispensable the writing center.

On many college campuses, there's a place that students find indispensable: **the writing center**.

1. Many college writing centers are open from 800 a.m. to 800 p.m.

2. The staff of writing centers has a common goal teach students to write better.

3. Instructors and peer tutors may help students in a variety of ways from understanding an assignment to answering questions about a final draft.

4. Other ways of helping students learn to write better include the following reading a student's paper out loud, asking questions to help the writer provide more details, and explaining a difficult point of grammar.

5. Many college administrators have a problem with writing centers they're expensive to operate.

6. But usually, college administrators understand the value of learning to write well priceless.

7. Many students say the same thing to writing center staff "Thank you for your help."

8. Here is some excellent advice for students seeking help at their college writing center be prepared.

9. Being prepared means students should have the following items ready for an instructor or tutor the class assignment and their draft.

10. There is much more to know about writing centers according to the book Writing Center Research Extending the Conversation.

Writing Sentences
with the Colon

Write complete sentences in answer to these questions. Use a colon in each sentence.

EXAMPLE   What time do you wake up?
            I wake up at 5:45.

1. What is the full title and subtitle of one of your textbooks?

   _____

2. What are your favorite classes? (Use the expression *as follows*.)

   _____

3. What is your advice to someone going to a job interview?

   _____

4. Who are the star players on your favorite team?

   _____

5. What streets or geographical features mark the borders of your campus?

   _____

   _____

MODULE 25: APOSTROPHES

25a What is the role of the apostrophe?

The apostrophe plays three major roles: it helps to form the possessive of nouns and a few pronouns, it stands for omitted letters, and it helps to form the plurals of letters and numerals.

25b How do I use an apostrophe to show a possessive noun?

The possessive case shows ownership (the scientist's invention) or close relationship (*the governor's policy, the movie's ending*). It indicates the same meaning as phrases beginning *of the* (*the invention of the scientist*).

When nouns and indefinite pronouns do not end in *-s*, add *'s* to show possession.

The **doctor's** diplomas are on her office wall. [singular noun not ending in *-s*]
The class studied the **women's** rights movement. [plural noun not ending in -sl
Good health is **everyone's** wish. [indefinite pronoun not ending in *-s*]

When singular nouns end in *-s*, add *'s* to show possession.

The **waitress's** tip was less than she expected.
Les's phone bill was enormous.

When a plural noun ends in *-s*, use only an apostrophe to show possession.

The **workers'** tools were all over the room.
Their **supervisors'** reports were critical of their sloppiness.

In compound words, add *'s* to the last word.

The police **chief's** retirement party was held in the hotel ballroom.
They held their wedding in her **sister-in-law's** backyard.

In individual possession, add *'s* to each noun.

Pat's and Lee's songs are hits. [Pat and Lee each wrote some of the songs; they did not write the songs together.]
Dali's and Turner's paintings were sold for record prices. [Dali and Turner painted different canvasses.]

In joint or group possession, add *'s* to only the last noun.

Pat and Lee's songs are hits. [Pat and Lee wrote the songs together.]

Dali and Turner's show at the art museum was a hit. [Dali and Turner are featured in the same show.]

25c How do I use an apostrophe with possessive pronouns?

Some pronouns have their own possessive forms. Do not use an apostrophe with these forms: *his, her, hers, its, our, ours, your, yours, their, theirs, whose*. Be especially careful in using *its/it's* and *whose/who's*, which are often confused. *It's* stands for *it is*, its is a personal pronoun showing possession. *Who's* stands for *who is*, *whose* is a personal pronoun showing possession.

No	The state will elect **it's** governor next week.
Yes	The state will elect **its** governor next week.
No	The candidate **who's** ads appear on television daily expects to win.
Yes	The candidate **whose** ads appear on television daily expects to win.

25d How do I use an apostrophe with contractions?

In informal English, some words may be combined by omitting one or more letters and inserting apostrophes to signal the omission: *I'm (I am), aren't (are not), he'll (he will)*, and others. These words are called contractions.

Apostrophes also indicate the omission of the first two numerals in years: *The professor spoke of the sit-ins of '68*. However, no apostrophe is used when you indicate a span of years: *1948-52*.

25e How do I use an apostrophe with possessive indefinite pronouns?

An apostrophe works with a pronoun to form the **possessive case**, which shows ownership or a close relationship.

Ownership	everyone's pen
Close Relationship	something's plot

Possession in **idenfinite pronouns** can be communicated in two ways: by a **phrase** starting with *of* (comments **of** everyone) or by an apostrophe and *s* (everyone's comments).

25f How do I form the plural of miscellaneous elements?

The child practiced writing her **Q's**.

The computer went berserk and printed out pages of **4's**.

In writing the plural form of years, two styles are acceptable: with an apostrophe (1990's) or without (1990s). Whichever form you prefer, use it consistently.

25g When is an apostrophe wrong?

If you're a writer who makes the same apostrophe errors repeatedly, memorize the rules you need.

LEADING CAUSES OF APOSTROPHE ERRORS

1. Never use an apostrophe with the **present-tense verb**.
   Cholesterol **plays** (not **play's**) a crucial role in how long we live.

2. Always use an apostrophe after the *s* in a **possessive** plural.
   Patients's (or **Patients'**—but not **Patients**) questions seek detailed answers.

3. Never add an apostrophe at the end of a nonpossessive **noun** ending in *s*.
   Medical **studies** (not **studies'** or **study's**) show this to be true.

4. Never use an apostrophe to form a nonpossessive plural.
   Teams (not **Team's**) of doctors have studied the effects of smoking.

Using the Apostrophe in Possessive Nouns

Write the possessive forms, singular and plural, for each of the following words. If you are unsure how to form the plural of any word, see your dictionary.

		SINGULAR POSSESSIVE	PLURAL POSSESSIVE
EXAMPLE	cow	*cow's*	*cows'*
1	sheep		
2.	pony		
3.	turkey		
4.	lion		
5	mouse		
6.	she		
7.	gorilla		
8.	goose		
9.	gnu		
10.	ox		
11.	you		
12.	buffalo		
13.	zebra		
14.	ibex		
15.	fly		
16.	I		
17.	giraffe		
18.	dodo		
19.	zoo		
20.	zoo keeper		
21.	he		
22.	farm		
23.	farmer		
24.	ranch		
25.	it		

Using the Apostrophe in Possessive Expressions

EXERCISE 25-2

Rewrite each of these noun phrases as a possessive noun followed by another noun.

EXAMPLE   The eye of the mind
          The mind's eye

1. the work of a day

    _____

2. the worth of a dollar

    _____

3. the hooves of a horse

    _____

4. the hooves of several horses

    _____

5. the business of nobody

    _____

6. the share of the lion

    _____

7. the meow of the cat

    _____

8. the weights of the bodybuilder

    _____

9. the mail of the neighbor

    _____

10. the mail of the neighbors

    _____

Using the Apostrophe in Contractions

Write contractions of the following expressions.

EXAMPLE   he + is =   *he's* _____

1.   are + not = _____

2.   will + not= _____

3.   let + us = _____

4.   he + had = _____

5.   was + not = _____

6.   you + would = _____

7.   did + not= _____

8.   I + will = _____

9.   what + is = _____

10. I + am = _____

11. is + not = _____

12. would + not= _____

13. can + not = _____

14. does + not = _____

15. I + have = _____

16. you + are = _____

17. there + is = _____

18. we + would = _____

19. were + not = _____

20. they + are = _____

21. it + is = _____

22. we + have = _____

23. she + will = _____

24. we + are = _____

25. do + not = _____

Using Apostrophes

Insert apostrophes as needed. If no apostrophes are called for in a sentence, write *correct* in the left margin.

EXAMPLE   The detective storys roots go back to at least 1841.
          The detective story's roots go back to at least 1841.

1.   The modern detective story began with Edgar Allan Poes "The Murders in the Rue Morgue."

2.   Its detective reappeared in "The Mystery of Marie Rogêt" in 1842-43.

3.   The authors last pure detective story was "The Purloined Letter."

4.   The three stories featured amateur detective C. August Dupins ability to solve crimes by using logic.

5.   Poe didnt use the word *detective* in the stories.

6.   The publics response was not enthusiastic, perhaps because the heros personality was unpleasant.

7.   This may explain why there werent any more detective stories by Poe.

8.   Twenty years later, in 66, a Frenchman revived the detective story, and this time it was a great success.

9.   Soon after, Englishman Wilkie Collins published *The Moonstone*.

10. Collins book was the first full-length detective novel in English.

11. The books hero was a professional detective who grew roses when he wasnt working.

12. *The Moonstones* hero had a better personality than Dupin, so the publics acceptance of him is understandable.

13. Charles Dickens, Collins friend, was writing a mystery novel when he died.

14. The fragment of *The Mystery of Edwin Drood* has been studied for years, but no ones been able to figure out how Dickens planned to explain the mystery.

15. Its been one of my favorite literary puzzles for years.

16. Arthur Conan Doyles Sherlock Holmes made his debut in "A Study in Scarlet" in 1887.

17. Holmes popularity really dates from July 1891, when "A Scandal in Bohemia" was published.

18. Peoples attention was finally captured, and they demanded more and more stories featuring Holmes.

19. Conan Doyle became so tired of the character that he wrote about Holmes death, killing him in a fall over a waterfall.

20. The readers outcry was so great that Holmes was brought back for more stories in 1902.

21. Then in 1905, Holmes earlier absence was explained.

22. The explanation was weak, but the fans couldnt have been happier.

MODULE 26: QUOTATION MARKS

26a What is the role of quotation marks?

Quotation marks most frequently enclose direct quotations—spoken or written words from an outside source. Quotation marks also set off some titles, and they can call attention to words used in special senses. Always use quotation marks in pairs. Be especially careful not to forget the second (closing) quotation mark.

26b How do I use quotation marks with short direct quotations?

Direct quotations present exact words copied from an original source. Use double quotation marks to enclose short quotations (no more than four lines).

SHORT QUOTATION

According to Marvin Harris in *Cows, Pigs, Wars, and Witches*, "We seem to be more interested in working in order to get people to admire us for our wealth than in the actual wealth itself."

26c Are quotation marks used with long quotations?

Longer quotations are not enclosed in quotation marks. They are displayed, starting on a new line, and all lines of the quotation are indented ten spaces.

26d How do I use quotation marks for quotations within quotations?

When the words of a short quotation already contain quotation marks, use double quotation marks at the start and end of the directly quoted words. Then substitute single quotation marks (' ') wherever there are double quotation marks in your original source.

Carl Sagan begins his essay called "In Defense of Robots" by telling us, "The word 'Robot,' first introduced by the Czech writer Karl Capek, is derived from the Slavic root for 'worker.' "

When the words of a longer quotation already contain quotation marks, display the quotation without enclosing it in quotation marks. Then use quotation marks exactly as they were used in your original source.

26e How do I use quotation marks for quotations of poetry and dialogue?

Use double quotation marks to enclose a short quotation of poetry (no more than three lines of the poem). If you quote more than one line of poetry, use slashes to show the line divisions.

Not everyone would agree with Emily Dickinson's statement: "Success is counted sweetest / By those who ne'er succeed."

Quotation marks are also used to enclose speakers words in **direct discourse** Whether you are reporting the exact words of a real speaker or making up dialogue in, for example, a short story, quotation marks let your readers know which words belong to the speaker and which words do not. Use double quotation marks at the beginning and end of a speaker's words, and start a new paragraph each time the speaker changes.

"The marks were some twenty yards from the body and no one gave them a thought. I don't suppose I should have done so had I not known the legend."

"There are many sheep dogs on the moor?"
"No doubt, but this was no sheep dog."
"You say it was large?"
"Enormous."

—Sir Arthur Conan Doyle, *The Hound of the Baskervilles*

In contrast to direct discourse, **indirect discourse** reports only the spirit of what a speaker said. Do not enclose indirect discourse in quotation marks.

DIRECT DISCOURSE   The professor said, "Your midterm is a week from Tuesday."

INDIRECT DISCOURSE   The professor said that our midterm would be a week from Tuesday.

26f How do I use quotation marks with titles of short works?

Use quotation marks around the titles of short published works, such as pamphlets and brochures. Also use them around song titles, episodes of television series, and titles of works that are parts of longer works or parts of collected works: poems, short stories, essays, and articles from periodicals.

Stephen Jay Gould examines what we know about dinosaur intelligence in the essay "Were Dinosaurs Dumb?"
Modern readers still enjoy Edgar Allan Poe's short story "The Tell-Tale Heart."

26g How do I use quotation marks for words used as words?

Writers sometimes use quotation marks to indicate words or phrases that are not meant to be taken at face value.

The "free" records came with a bill for ten dollars—for postage and handling.

Writers sometimes put technical terms in quotation marks and define them the first time they are used. No quotation marks are used after such terms have been introduced and defined.

"Plagiarism"—the unacknowledged use of another person's words or ideas—can result in expulsion. Plagiarism is a serious offense.

Words being referred to as words can be either enclosed in quotation marks or underlined.

YES   Do not confuse "then" and "than."

YES   Do not confuse <u>then</u> and <u>than</u>.

26h How do I use quotation marks with other punctuation?

Place commas and periods inside closing quotation marks.

Besides writing such stories as "The Premature Burial," Edgar Allan Poe was also a respected literary critic and poet.

The bill read, "Registration fees must be paid in full one week before the start of classes."

Place colons and semicolons outside closing quotation marks.

The label on the ketchup said "low salt": it was also low taste.

Some people have trouble singing "The Star-Spangled Banner"; they think the United States should choose a different national anthem.

Place question marks, exclamation points, and dashes inside or outside closing quotation marks, according to the situation. If a question mark, exclamation point, or dash belongs with the words enclosed in quotation marks, put that punctuation mark *inside* the closing quotation mark.

"Where is Andorra?" asked the quiz show host.

Before her signal faded, we heard the CB'er say, "There is a radar trap on Route—"

If a question mark, exclamation point, or dash belongs with words that are *not* included in quotation marks, put the punctuation mark *outside* the closing quotation mark.

Do you know Adrienne Rich's poem "Aunt Jennifer's Tigers"?

Grieving for a dead friend, Tennyson spent seventeen years writing "In Memoriam A. H. H."!

26i When are quotation marks wrong?

Writers sometimes place quotation marks around words they are uncomfortable about using. Instead of resorting to this practice, find appropriate words.

No   Einstein's theory of relativity is very "heavy stuff."

Yes   Einstein's theory of relativity is very sophisticated.

Do not enclose a word in quotation marks merely to call attention to it.

No   The report is due on Friday, "or else."

Yes   The report is due on Friday, or else.

Do not put quotation marks around the title of your own papers (on a title page or at the top of the first page). The only exception is if your paper's title includes words that require quotation marks for one of the reasons discussed.

Using Quotation Marks   EXERCISE 26-1

Insert additional quotation marks as needed. Use double quotation marks unless single quotation marks are specifically needed. Remember to place quotation marks carefully in relation to other marks of punctuation. If a sentence needs no additional quotation marks, write *correct* in the left margin.

EXAMPLE   Speaking of an old friend, Winston Churchill said, In those days he was wiser than he is now; he used frequently to take my advice.
Speaking of an old friend, Winston Churchill said, "In those days he was wiser than he is now; he used frequently to take my advice."

1. According to Chesterfield, Advice is seldom welcome.

2. "If you are looking for trouble, offer some good advice, says Herbert V. Prochnow.

3. Marie Dressler was right: No vice is so bad as advice.

4. Someone once remarked, How we do admire the wisdom of those who come to us for advice!

5. "Free advice, it has been noted, is the kind that costs you nothing unless you act upon it."

6. "The only thing to do with good advice is to pass it on; it is never of any use to one-self," believed Oscar Wilde.

7. I sometimes give myself admirable advice, said Lady Mary Wortley Montagu, but I am incapable of taking it.

8. Says Tom Masson, " 'Be yourself! is the worst advice you can give to some people.

9. The Beatles' song With a Little Help from My Friends contains some good advice.

10. Do you seriously advise me to marry that man?

11. My uncle advised me, The next time you are depressed, read Lewis Carroll's poem *Jabberwocky*.

12. Do you recall the Beach Boys' words: Be true to your school?

13. Many marriage counselors advise us never to go to sleep angry with our mate.

14. However, comedienne Phyllis Diller suggests, Never go to bed mad. Stay up and fight.

15. Rachel Carson advised, The discipline of the writer is to learn to be still and listen to what his subject has to tell him.

16. If I had to give students advice in choosing a career, I would tell them to select a field that interests them passionately.

Writing Direct Quotations

Rewrite these indirect quotations as direct quotations. You will need to add commas, colons, capitals, and quotation marks. If necessary, change pronouns and verbs to suitable forms.

EXAMPLE   The boss said that there would be an important meeting at noon.
The boss said, "There will be an important meeting at noon."

1. She said that all employees must attend the meeting.

    _____

2. She further explained that any employee who wasn't at the meeting would be terminated.

    _____

3. I told my supervisor that I was leaving at noon and flying to Montreal to meet an important client. [Make this a split quotation.]

    _____

4. My supervisor asked whose idea it was for me to fly to Montreal.

5. I said that it was the boss's idea.

    _____

6. My supervisor told me not to worry because when I returned, he would help me find another job.

    _____

Writing Properly Punctuated Dialogue

Write an original dialogue using proper punctuation and appropriate pronouns and verb tenses. Select one of the following situations, letting each person speak at least three times. Remember to start a new paragraph each time the speaker changes. Use your own paper.

1. You are asking your boss for a raise.

2. You are asking one of your parents for advice.

3. You are trying to talk a traffic officer out of giving you a ticket.

4. You and your boyfriend/girlfriend are trying to decide what movie to see.

5. You are trying to convince your younger brother/sister not to drop out of high school.

MODULE 27: OTHER PUNCTUATION MARKS

DASH

27a When can I use a dash in my writing?

The dash, or a pair of dashes, lets you interrupt a sentence to add information. Dashes are like parentheses in that they set off extra material at the beginning, in the middle, or at the end of a sentence. Unlike parentheses, dashes emphasize the interruptions. Use dashes sparingly—so that their dramatic impact is not blunted.

Use a dash or dashes to emphasize explanations, including appositives, examples, and definitions.

EXAMPLES

In general, only mute things are eaten alive—plants and invertebrates. If oysters shrieked as they were pried open, or squealed when jabbed with a fork, I doubt whether they would be eaten alive.

—MARSTON BATES

DEFINITIONS

Personal space—"elbow room"—is a vital commodity for the human animal, and one that cannot be ignored without risking serious trouble.

—DESMOND MORRIS, "Territorial Behavior"

APPOSITIVES

Many's the long night I've dreamed of cheese—toasted, mostly.

—ROBERT LOUIS STEVENSON

Use a dash or dashes to emphasize a contrast.

I know a lot of people didn't expect our relationship to last—but we've just celebrated our two months' anniversary.

—BRITT EKLAND

Use a dash or dashes to emphasize an "aside." Asides are writers' comments within the structure of a sentence or paragraph.

These five passages have not been picked out because they are especially bad—I could have quoted far worse if I had chosen—but because they illustrate various of the mental vices from which we now suffer.

—GEORGE ORWELL, "Politics and the English Language"

Commas, semicolons, colons, and periods are not used next to dashes, but if the words you put between a pair of dashes would take a question mark or an exclamation point written as a separate sentence, use that punctuation before the second dash.

The tour guide—do you remember her name?—recommended an excellent restaurant.

Use a dash to show hesitating or broken-off speech.

"Yes," he said. "That is why I am here, you see. They thought we might be interested in that footprint."
"That footprint?" cried Dorothy. 'You mean—?"
"No, no; not your footprint, Miss Brant. Another one."

—Carter Dickson, "The Foot Print in the Sky"

PARENTHESES

27b When can I use parentheses in my writing?

Parentheses let you interrupt a sentence's structure to add information of many kinds. Parentheses are like dashes in that they set off extra or interrupting words. However, unlike dashes, which make interruptions stand out, parentheses de-emphasize what they enclose.

Use parentheses to enclose interrupting words, including explanations, examples, and asides.

EXPLANATIONS

On the second night of his visit, our distinguished guest (Sir Charles Dilke) met Laura in the passage on her way to bed; he said to her: "If you will kiss me, I will give you a signed photograph of myself." To which she answered: "It's awfully good of you, Sir Charles, but I would rather not, for what on earth should I do with the photograph?"

—Margot Asquith

EXAMPLES

Many books we read as children (*Alice in Wonderland*, for example) may be even more enjoyable when we reread them as adults.

ASIDES

I have heard of novelists who say that, while they are creating a novel, the people in it are ever with them, accompanying them on walks, for all I know on drives (though this must be distracting in traffic), to the bath, to bed itself.

—Rose Macaulay

Use parentheses for certain numbers and letters of listed items. When you number listed items within a sentence, enclose the numbers (or letters) in parentheses.

I plan to do four things during summer vacation: (1) sleep, (2) work to save money for next semester's tuition, (3) catch up on my reading, and (4) have fun.

In business and legal writing, use parentheses to enclose a numeral repeating a spelled-out number.

The monthly fee to lease a color television is forty dollars (S40).

Never put a comma before an opening parenthesis even if what comes before the parenthetical material requires a comma. Put the parenthetical material in, and then use the comma immediately after the closing parenthesis.

Even though I grew up in a big city (New York), I prefer small-town life.

You can use a question mark or an exclamation point with parenthetical words that occur within the structure of a sentence.

We entered the old attic (what a mess!) and began the dirty job of organizing the junk of three generations.

Use a period, however, only when you enclose a complete statement in parentheses outside the structure of another sentence. In this case, use a capital letter as well.

We entered the old attic and began the dirty job of organizing the junk of three generations. (The place was a mess.)

BRACKETS

27c When do I need to use brackets in my writing?

When you work quoted words into your own sentences, you may have to change a word or two to make the quoted words fit into your structure. You may also want to add explanations to quoted material. Enclose your own words within brackets.

According to John Ackerman, "He [Dylan Thomas] was aware of the extent to which his temperament and his imagination were the products of his Welsh environment."

When you find a mistake in something you want to quote—for example, a wrong date or a misspelled word—you cannot change another writer's words. So that readers do not think you made the error, insert the Latin word *sic* (meaning "so" or "thus") in brackets next to the error. Doing this indicates that this is exactly what you found in the original.

The student wrote that, "The Vikings came to North America long before Columbus's arrival in 1942 [*sic*]."

You can also use brackets to enclose very brief parenthetical material inside parentheses.

From that point on, Thomas Parker simply disappears. (His death [c. 1441] is unrecorded officially, but a gravestone marker is mentioned in a 1640 parish report.)

ELLIPSIS POINTS

27d How do I use ellipsis points in my writing?

An ellipsis is a series of three spaced dots. In quotations, it is used to show that you have left out some of the writer's original words. Ellipses can also show hesitant or broken-off speech.

Ellipses can show that you have omitted words from material you are quoting.

ORIGINAL

My aunt has survived the deaths of her husband and my parents in typical, if I may say so, West Indian fashion. Now in her 70s, and no longer principal of a New York City public school, she rises at 5 A.M. every day to prepare for another day of complicated duties as the volunteer principal of a small black private academy.

—JUNE JORDAN, "Thank You, America"

SOME MATERIAL USED IN A QUOTATION

My aunt has survived the deaths of her husband and my parents. . . . Now in her 70s, and no longer principal of a New York City public school, she rises at 5 A.M. every day to prepare for another day . . . as the volunteer principal of a small black private academy.

If an omission occurs at the beginning of your quoted words, you do not need to use an ellipsis. Also, you do not need to use an ellipsis at the end as long as you end with a complete sentence. If an ellipsis occurs after a complete sentence, use a fourth dot to represent the period of that sentence (for an example of this, see the first ellipsis in the above quotation).

Also, you can use ellipses to show broken-off speech.

"And, anyway, what do you know of him?"
"Nothing. That is why I ask you . . ."
"I would prefer never to speak of him."

—UMBERTO ECO, *The Name of the Rose*

SLASH

27e When can I use a slash in my writing?

If you quote more than three lines of a poem in writing, set the poetry off with space and indentations as you would a prose quotation of more than four lines. For three lines or less, quote poetry—enclosed in quotation marks—in sentence format, with a slash to divide one line from the next. Leave a space on each side of the slash.

Robert Frost makes an important point when he writes, "Before I built a wall I'd want to know / What I was walling in or walling out, / And to whom I was like to give offense."

Capitalize and punctuate each line as it is in the original, with this exception: end your sentence with a period, even if the quoted line of poetry does not have one.

If you have to type numerical fractions, use a slash between the numerator and denominator and a hyphen to attach a whole number to its fraction: 1/16, 1-2/3, 2/5, 3-7/8.

You will not use word combinations such as *and/or* often, but where use is acceptable, separate the words with a slash. Leave no space before or after the slash. *He/she* is one option available to you in avoiding sexist language.

HYPHEN

27f When do I need a hyphen in my writing?

A **hyphen** serves to divide words at the end of a line, to combine words into compounds, to communicate numbers, and generally help writers deliver their messages with spelling that's as clear as possible.

27g When do I use a hyphen at the end of a line?

Try not to divide words at the end of a line, but when you must do so, follow these guidelines.

GUIDELINES FOR DIVIDING WORDS AT END OF LINE

1. Never divide short words, and never divide single-syllable words at the end of a line, no matter how long the word: *cleanse*, not *cle-anse*.

2. Always divide words between syllables. The dictionary listing of a word shows its syllables clearly: *helicopter*, for example, appears in the dictionary as *he-li-cop-ter*.

3. Never leave or carry over only one or two letters on a line: *alive*, not *a-live*.

4. Follow rules for double consonants. Suffixes usually create added syllables. If a base word ends in a double consonant, divide the word *after* the double consonant: *success-ful*, not *succes-sful*. If a single consonant is doubled when the suffix is added, then divide the word between the double consonants: *omit-ting*, not *omitting*.

5. Never violate pronunciation when dividing words. Not all word endings create syllables. The *-ed* ending, for example, often simply adds the sound of the consonant *d* to a word. If you divide such a word before the *-ed* ending, you create a new syllable: *com-pelled,* not *compell-ed*.

27h How do I use a hyphen with prefixes and suffixes?

GUIDELINES FOR HYPHENS WITH PREFIXES AND SUFFIXES

- Use hyphens after the prefixes *all-*, *ex-*, *quasi-*, and *self-*.
  - **YES** all-inclusive   self-reliant

- Never use a hyphen when *self* is a root word, not a prefix.
  - **No** self-ishness   **YES** selfishness

- Use a hyphen to avoid a distracting string of letters.
  - **No** antiintellectual   **YES** anti-intellectual

- Use a hyphen to add a prefix or suffix to a numeral or a word that starts with a capital letter.
  - **No** post1950s, proAmerican   **YES** post-1950, pro-American

- Use a hyphen before the suffix *-elect*.
  - **No** presidentelect   **YES** president-elect

- Use a hyphen to prevent confusion in meaning or pronunciation.
  - **YES** re-dress (means *dress again*)   redress (means *set right*)

- Use a hyphen when two or more prefixes apply to one root word.
  - **YES** **pre-** and **post-war** eras   **two-** or **four-year** program

27i How do I use hyphens with compound words?

A **compound word** consists of two or more words used together to form one word. When a compound acts as a modifier *before* a noun, it is usually hyphenated: *fast-paced lecture, long-term commitment.* When the same modifier comes after the noun, however, there is no hyphen: *The lecture was fast paced.* Some terms have become clear enough that they do not require hyphens: *genetic engineering laboratory, health insurance policy, junior high school, state sales tax.*

The hyphen is omitted in several other situations: when the first word in the compound ends with *-ly,* when the first word is a comparative or superlative, or when the compound is a foreign phrase: *happily married couple, lowest common denominator, ad hoc committee.*

A hyphen is placed between the two parts of a combined unit of measurement: *kilowatt-hours, light-years.*

Most compound titles are not hyphenated (*state senator, vice principal*), but many are. Hyphenated titles usually are national names, actual double titles, or three-word titles: *Italian-American, father-in-law, director-producer.*

Using Dashes, Parentheses, Brackets, Ellipses, and Slashes

Add dashes, parentheses, brackets, ellipses, or slashes as needed. If more than one kind of punctuation is possible, choose the one you think best. Be prepared to explain your decision.

EXAMPLE   I'll pay by Do you accept checks?"
              I'll pay by—Do you accept checks?"

1. Chicago is not the windiest city in the United States Great Falls, Montana, is.

2. The next windiest cities are 2 Oklahoma City, Oklahoma, 3 Boston, Massachusetts, and 4 Cheyenne, Wyoming.

3. Chicago is relatively calm average wind speed equals 10.4 mph.

4. Greenland the largest island in the world was given its name by Eric the Red in 985.

5. The name was a masterstroke of publicity convincing settlers to come to what was actually an ice-covered wasteland.

6. Let's go to New Orleans for Mardi Oops! I have exams that week.

7. The most expensive part of a trip the airfare can be reduced by careful planning.

8. Contest rules say "The winner must appear to claim his her prize in person."

9. "Broadway my favorite street is a main artery of New York—the hardened artery," claimed Walter Winchell. [Note: *my favorite street* is not part of the quotation.]

10. Punctuate the shortened version of the following quotation: "Too often travel, instead of broadening the mind, merely lengthens the conversation," said Elizabeth Drew. "Too often travel merely lengthens the conversation," said Elizabeth Drew.

11. New Jersy sic has some spectacular parks for camping.

12. Once a camper has been there, he she will always want to return.

13. I can say only one thing about camping I hate it.

14. We leave as soon as Have you seen the bug spray? we finish packing.

15. "Let's take Interstate 80 across" "Are you crazy?"

16. Finding an inexpensive hotel motel isn't always easy.

17. Motels named from a combination of *motorist* and *hotel* are usually cheaper than regular hotels.

18. When traveling, always remember to a leave a schedule with friends, b carry as little cash as possible, and c use the hotel safe for valuables.

A: Add missing punctuation or change mistaken punctuation as needed. There may be more than one choice possible. If so, use the punctuation mark you think best. Be prepared to explain your answers.

The cheetah, is the fastest animal on earth, it can accelerate from one mile an hour to forty miles an hour in under two seconds. Briefly reaching speeds of up to seventy miles an hour. Its stride, may during these bursts of speed, be as much as (23 feet). To help it run at these speeds: the cheetah is built unlike any of the other large cats—powerful heart, oversized liver, long, thin leg bones, relatively small teeth, and a muscular tail (used for balance. Unlike other cats; it cannot pull in its claws. They are blunted by constant contact (with the earth), and so are of little use, in the hunt. The cheetah—instead, makes use of a strong dewclaw on the inside of its front, legs to grab and hold down prey.

B: Add whatever punctuation is needed to this completely unpunctuated paragraph. Be sure to add capital letters as needed too. If more than one kind of punctuation is suitable, select the best one. Be prepared to explain your choices.

Have you ever wondered how instant coffee is made first the coffee beans are prepared as they would be for regular coffee they are roasted blended and ground at the factory workers brew great batches of coffee 1800 to 2000 pounds at a time the coffee is then passed through tubes under great pressure at a high temperature this causes much of the water to boil away creating coffee liquor with a high percentage of solids at this point a decision must be made about what the final product will be powdered instant coffee or freeze dried coffee powdered instant coffee is made by heating the coffee liquor to 500° F in a large drier this boils away the remaining water and the powdered coffee is simply gathered from the bottom of the drier and packed if freeze dried coffee is being made the coffee liquor is frozen into pieces which are then broken into small granules the granules are placed in a vacuum box a box containing no air which turns the frozen water into steam which is removed all that is left are coffee solids some people say they prefer freeze dried coffee because the high temperature used to make regular instant coffee destroys some of the flavor either way the coffee is more convenient than home-brewed coffee

Name _____   Date _____

Dividing Words
at the Ends of Lines

EXERCISE 27-3

Using your dictionary, rewrite each word on the line to its right. Use a slash to indicate the best place to divide the word at the end of a line. Some words may be broken in more than one place. Pick the best place, and use dots to indicate all other syllable breaks. If the word cannot be divided, write it out as one unit.

EXAMPLES signaled   *sig/naled*
          brake   *brake*
          sledgehammer   *sledge/ham•mer*

1. sleepless _____
2. slenderize _____
3. referee _____
4. phlegm _____
5. palate _____
6. muscle-bound _____
7. indecent _____
8. Hollywood _____
9. expiration _____
10. echo _____
11. cuckoo _____
12. cough _____
13. butte _____
14. avocado _____
15. avoirdupois _____
16. loose _____
17. cattail _____
18. enroll _____
19. grouch _____
20. progressing _____

21. sleeve _____
22. sapsucker _____
23. Polynesia _____
24. palace _____
25. nonresident _____
26. increase _____
27. however _____
28. gesticulate _____
29. emerge _____
30. cubic _____
31. colorless _____
32. caretaker _____
33. buttermilk _____
34. await _____
35. antacid _____
36. mother-in-law _____
37. trousseau _____
38. midget _____
39. controlling _____
40. farther _____

MODULE 28: CAPITALS, ITALICS, ABBREVIATIONS, AND NUMBERS

CAPITALS

28a When do I capitalize a "first" word?

Always capitalize the first letter of the first word in a sentence, a question, or a command.

Pain is useful because it warns us of danger.

Does pain serve any purpose?

Never ignore severe pain.

Whether to capitalize the first letter of a complete sentence enclosed in parentheses depends upon whether that sentence stands alone or falls within the structure of another sentence. Those that stand alone start with a capital letter; those that fall within the structure of another sentence do not start with a capital letter.

I didn't know till years later that they called it the Cuban Missile Crisis. But I remember Castro. (We called him Castor Oil and were awed by his beard—beards were rare in those days.) We might not have worried so much (what would the Communists want with our small New Hampshire town?) except that we lived 10 miles from an air base.

—JOYCE MAYNARD, "An 18-Year-Old Looks Back on Life"

28b When do I use capitals with listed items?

A **run-in list** works its items into the structure of a sentence. When the items in a run-in list are complete sentences, capitalize the first letter of each item.

Three groups attended the town meeting on rent control: (1) Landlords brought proof of their expenses. (2) Tenants came to complain about poor maintenance. (3) Real estate agents came to see how the new rules would affect them.

When the items in a run-in list are not complete sentences, do not begin them with capital letters.

Three groups attended the town meeting on rent control: (1) landlords, (2) tenants, and (3) real estate agents.

28c When do I use capitals with sentences in parentheses?

When you write a complete sentence within parentheses that falls within another sentence, don't start with a capital or end with a period—but do use a question mark or exclamation point if needed. When you write a sentence within parentheses that doesn't fall within another sentence, capitalize the first word and end with a period (or question mark or explanation point).

I did not know till years later that they called it the Cuban Missile Crisis. But I remember Castro (We called him Castor Oil and were awed by his beard.) We might not have worried so much (what would the communists want with our small New Hampshire town?) except we lived 10 miles from a U.S. air base.

—Joyce Maynard, "An 18-Year-Old Looks Back on Life"

28d When do I use capitals with quotations?

When you quote another person's words, do not capitalize the first quoted word if you have made the quoted words part of the structure of your own sentence.

Thomas Henry Huxley called science "trained and organized common sense."

However, if your own words in your sentence serve only to introduce quoted words or if you are directly quoting speech, capitalize the first letter of the quoted words.

According to Thomas Henry Huxley, "Science is nothing but trained and organized common sense."

Do not capitalize a partial quotation or a quotation you resume within a sentence.

"We," said Queen Victoria, "are not amused."

28e When do I capitalize nouns and adjectives?

Capitalize proper nouns and adjectives made from them.

PROPER NOUNS	PROPER ADJECTIVES
Korea	the Korean language
Hollywood	a Hollywood studio

Notice that the articles (*the, a, an*) are not capitalized.

Do not capitalize common nouns (nouns that name general classes of people, places, or things) unless they start a sentence: *a country, the movies, friends, planes*. Many common nouns are capitalized when names or titles are added to them. For example, *lake* is not ordinarily capitalized, but when a specific name is added, it is: *Lake Erie*. Without the specific name, however, even if the specific name is implied, the common noun is not capitalized.

I would like to visit the **Erie Canal** because the **canal** played a big part in opening up the Northeast to trade.

On the next page is a list to help you with capitalization questions. Although it cannot cover all possibilities, you can apply what you find in the list to similar items.

CAPITALIZATION GUIDE

	Capitals	Lower-Case Letters
NAMES	Bob Ojeda	
	Mother (name)	my mother (relationship)
TITLES	the President (usually reserved for the U.S. president in office)	a president
	Professor Edgar Day	the professor
GROUPS OF HUMANKIND	Caucasian (race)	white (or White)
	African American (race)	black (or Black)
	Latino (race)	ethnic group
ORGANIZATIONS	Congress	congressional
	the Rotary Club	the club
PLACES	Los Angeles	
	India	
	the South (a region)	turn south (a direction)
	Main Street	the street
BUILDINGS	Carr High School	the high school
	the China Lights	the restaurant
SCIENTIFIC TERMS	Mars, Martian	the moon, the sun
	the Milky Way galaxy	the galaxy
LANGUAGES	Portuguese	a language
SCHOOL COURSES	Chemistry 342	the chemistry course
NAMES OF THINGS	the *Times-Union*	the newspaper
	Purdue University	the university
	the Dodge Omni	the car
TIME NAMES	Friday	spring, summer, fall,
	August	autumn, winter
HISTORICAL PERIODS	World War II	the war
	the Great Depression	the depression (any other depression)
Religious TERMS	God	a god, a goddess
	Buddhism	
	the Torah	
LETTER PARTS	Dear Ms. Tauber:	
	Sincerely yours,	
TITLES OF WORKS	"The Lottery"	
	Catcher in the Rye	
ACRONYMS	IRS	
	NATO	
	AFL-CIO	

ITALICS

28f What are italics?

In printed material, **roman type** is the standard. Type that slants to the right is called **italic**. Words in italics contrast with standard roman type, so italics create an emphasis readers can see. In typewritten and handwritten manuscripts, underline to indicate italics.

28g How do I choose between using italics and quotation marks?

Some titles require underlining: long written works, names of ships, trains, and some aircraft, film titles, titles of television series. Underlining also calls readers' attention to words in languages other than English and to letters, numbers, and words used in ways other than for their meaning. The list below shows these uses.

It also shows (and explains) some titles that call for quotation marks and some names and titles neither underlined nor in quotation marks.

28h Can I use italics for special emphasis?

Instead of counting on underlining to deliver impact, try to make word choices and sentence structures convey emphasis. Reserve underlining for special situations.

ABBREVIATIONS

28i What are standard practices for using abbreviations?

Some abbreviations are standard in all writing circumstances (*Mr.* not *Mister* (in a name); *St.* Louis, the city, not *Saint* Louis).

No   Our field hockey team left after Casey's **psych** class on **Tues.**, Oct. 10, but the flight had to make an unexpected stop (in **Chi.**) before reaching **L.A.**

Yes   Our field hockey team left after Casey's psychology class on Tuesday, October 10, but the flight had to make an unexpected stop (in **Chicago**) before reaching **Los Angeles**.

✤ PUNCTUATION ALERTS: (1) Most abbreviations call for periods: Mrs., R.N., A.M. (2) Acronyms (pronounceable words formed from the initials of a name) generally have no periods: NASA (National Aeronautics and Space Administration) and AIDS (Acquired Immune Deficiency Syndrome). (3) Postal abbreviations for states have no periods. (4) When the period of an abbreviation falls at the end of a sentence, that period serves also to end the sentence. ✤

28j How do I use abbreviations with months, time, eras, and symbols?

What you are writing and who will read that writing should help you to determine whether to use an abbreviation or a spelled-out word. A few abbreviations are standard in any writing circumstance.

A.M. AND P.M. WITH SPECIFIC TIMES

8:20 A.M. or 8:20 a.m.   9:35 P.M. or 9:35 p.m.

A.D. AND B.C. WITH SPECIFIC YEARS

A.D. 576 [A.D. precedes the year.]   33 B.C. [B.C. follows the year.]

Symbols are seldom used in the body of papers written for courses in the humanities. You can use a percent symbol (%) or a cent sign (¢), for example, in a table, graph, or other illustration, but in the body of the paper spell out *percent* and *cent*. You can, however, use a dollar sign with specific dollar amounts: *$1.29, $10 million*.

Let common sense and your readers' needs guide you. If you mention temperatures once or twice in a paper, spell them out: *ninety degrees, minus twenty-six degrees*. If you mention temperatures throughout a paper, use figures and symbols: *90° –26°*.

28k How do I use abbreviations for other elements?

TITLES OF ADDRESS BEFORE NAMES

Dr. P. C. Smith   Mr. Scott Kamiel

Ms. Rachel Wang   Mrs. Ann Wenter

ACADEMIC DEGREES AFTER NAMES

Jean Loft, Ph.D.   Peter Kim, J.D.

Asha Rohra, M.D.   Verna Johnson, D.D.

❖ ABBREVIATION CAUTION: Do not use a title of address before a name *and* an academic degree after a name. Use one or the other. ❖

If you use a long name or term often in a paper, you can abbreviate it. The first time you use it, give the full term, with the abbreviation in parentheses right after the spelled-out form. After that you can use the abbreviation alone.

Volunteers in Service to America (VISTA) began at about the same time as the Peace Corps, but VISTA participants do not go to exotic foreign countries.

You can abbreviate *U.S.* as a modifier (*the U.S. economy*), but spell out *United States* when you use it as a noun.

If you include a full address—street, city, and state—in the body of a paper, you can use the postal abbreviation for the state name, but spell out any other combination of a city and a state.

No   **Miami, FL**, has a thriving Cuban community.

Yes   **Miami, Florida**, has a thriving Cuban community.

28l When can I use *etc.*?

Etc. is the abbreviation for the Latin *et cetera*, meaning *and the rest*. Do not use it in academic writing; acceptable substitutes are *and the like, and so on*, or *and so forth*.

The Greenlawn Resort offers water sports such as snorkeling, scuba diving, windsurfing, **and the like** [not *etc.*].

NUMBERS

28m When do I use spelled-out numbers?

Depending on how often numbers appear in a paper and what they refer to, you will sometimes express numbers in words and sometimes in figures. The guidelines here are those used in the humanities. For the guidelines that other disciplines follow, ask your instructor or consult style manuals written for specific fields.

If numerical exactness is not a prime purpose in your paper and you mention numbers only a few times, spell out numbers that can be expressed in one or two words.

Most people need to take the road test for their driver's license **two or three** times.

Eating **one** extra slice of bread a day can lead to a weight gain of about **seven** pounds per year.

❖ HYPHENATION ALERT: Use a hyphen between spelled-out two-word numbers from *twenty-one* through *ninety-nine*. ❖

If you use numbers frequently in a paper, spell out numbers from *one* to *nine* and use figures for numbers *10* and above.

two shirts	12 blocks
third base	21st year

Never start a sentence with a figure. If a sentence starts with a number, spell it out or revise so that the number does not come first.

Thirteen is known as a baker's dozen because bakers used to give an extra roll or pastry to customers who placed large orders.

Nineteen fifty saw the start of the Korean War.
The Korean War started in 1950.

28n What are standard practices for writing numbers?

Give specific numbers—dates, addresses, measurements, identification numbers—in figures.

GUIDE FOR USING SPECIFIC NUMBERS	
Dates	August 6, 1941 1732-1845 34 B.C to A.D. 230
Addresses	10 Downing Street 237 North 8th Street (*or* 237 North Eighth Street) Export Falls, MN 92025
Times	8:09 A.M.; 3:30 (*but* half past three, quarter of seven, six o'clock)
Decimal and Fractions	5.55; 98.6; 3.1415; 7/8; 121/4 (*but* one quarter, one half, two thirds)
Chapter and Pages	Chapter 27; page 245
Scores and Statistics	a 6-0 score; a 5 to 3 ratio; 29 percent
Identification Number	94.4 on the FM dial; call 1-212-555-0000
Measurements	2 feet; 67.8 miles per hour; 1.5 gallons; 2 level teaspoons; 3 liters; $8\frac{1}{2}$ " x 11" paper or $8\frac{1}{2}$ -x-11-inch paper
Act, Scene, and Line Number	act II, scene 2, lines 75–79
Temperatures	43°F; -4° Celsius
Money	$1.2 billion; $3.41; 25 cents

28o How do I use hyphens with spelled-out numbers?

Fractions: Hyphens are used between the numerator and the denominator of fractions, unless a hyphen already appears in either or both: *three-hundredths (3/100)*, but *two three-hundredths (2/300)*.

Double-digit numbers: Hyphens are used between the two parts of all double-digit numbers, whether those numbers are written alone or as part of larger numbers: *sixty-two, five hundred sixty-two.*

Combined numbers and words: When numbers and words are combined to form one idea or modifier, a hyphen is placed between the number and the word: *50-minute class.* If the word in the modifier is possessive, omit the hyphen: *one week's work.*

Using Capital Letters

A: Select the passage in each pair that needs capital letters. Then rewrite the passage correctly on the line provided.

EXAMPLE   (a) going to the city next summer
            (b) going to milwaukee in june
            (b) going to Milwaukee in June

1. (a) president truman
    (b) the thirty-third president

    _____

2. (a) the ancient gods
    (b) god's love

    _____

3. (a) the federal communications
    commission
    (b) a government agency

    _____

4. (a) a meeting in the afternoon
    (b) a meeting on friday

    _____

5. (a) my favorite aunt
    (b) my aunt clara

    _____

6. (a) when i graduate
    (b) when we graduate

    _____

7. (a) the rising sun
    (b) the sun is rising.

    _____

8. (a) mother teresa
    (b) my mother

    _____

9. (a) dinner at a fine restaurant
    (b) dinner at the steak
    palace

    _____

10. (a) english 202
    (b) a literature course

    _____

11. (a) across the main street
    (b) across main street

    _____

12. (a) the los angeles lakers
    (b) a basketball team

    _____

13. (a) the election officials
    (b) election day

    _____

14. (a) northeast of town
    (b) a town in the northeast

    _____

15. (a) a college in florida
    (b) a college on the coast

    _____

16. (a) "the gift of the magi"
    (b) a story about sacrifice

    _____

17. (a) learning a second language
    (b) learning french

    _____

18. (a) nassau county medical center
    (b) the local hospital

    _____

19. (a) stars shining in the sky
    (b) the moon and venus shining in the sky

    _____

20. (a) the hudson river
    (b) the polluted river

    _____

B: Rewrite these sentences on the lines provided, adding or deleting capital letters as needed. If no capitals are needed, write *correct* on the line.

EXAMPLE London, the capital of great britain is huge and historical.
         London, the capital of Great Britain is huge and historical..

1. It began as a trading post on the banks of the thames river.

    _____

2. Now it's the largest, most populous metropolis in europe.

    _____

3. Just like new york city, london is divided into boroughs.

    _____

4. Part of the king james bible was written in westminster.

    _____

5. Many people have heard of big ben, the famous bell in the clock tower of Westminster.

    _____

6. Most tourists enjoy visiting st. paul's cathedral, a magnificent landmark designed by christopher wren.

    _____

7. The dome of st. paul's cathedral is second in size only to st. peter's cathedral in rome.

    _____

8. Another famous landmark, the tower of london, was started in 1078.

    _____

9. Several historical figures, queens, princes, and advisors to various monarchs, entered the tower of london and never came out again.

    _____

10. Just as wall street in new york city represents the stock market to many people, a number of streets in london represent entire industries and institutions.

    _____

11. For example, fleet street represents the press, and downing street represents the government of great britain.

    _____

12. Now it's possible to go to paris and back to london in one day.

_____

13. People used to have to travel by air or sea to reach paris from london.

_____

14. Now people can travel to paris by train through a tunnel beneath the english channel.

_____

15. Combining the words of the name "channel tunnel," the english came up with a shorter name, "chunnel."

_____

Using Italics   EXERCISE **28-2**

A: Select the passage in each of these pairs that needs italics added. Then rewrite the passage correctly on the line provided, using underlining to indicate italics.

EXAMPLE   (a) My favorite movie is a mystery.
           (b) My favorite movie is Citizen Kane.
           My favorite movie is Citizen Kane. _____

1. (a) a book about war and peace
    (b) War and Peace

_____

2. (a) the humor of Bill Cosby
    (b) The Bill Cosby Show

_____

3. (a) The Washington Post
    (b) a Washington newspaper

_____

4. (a) a cruise ship
    (b) The Queen Elizabeth II

_____

5. (a) a space ship
    (b) the U.S.S. Enterprise

_____

6. (a) We are Homo sapiens.
    (b) We are human beings.

_____

7. (a) pay particular attention
    (b) nota bene

_____

8. (a) Many words have the common root, cycle.
   (b) Many words come from the same source.

   _____

9. (a) Don't tease your pets.
   (b) Never tease a hungry crocodile.

   _____

10. (a) The Orient Express was the setting of a famous mystery novel.
    (b) Amtrak goes all over the United States.

    _____

B: Rewrite these sentences on the lines provided, adding italics (underlining) as needed. If no italics are needed, write *correct* on the line.

EXAMPLE   How do you pronounce chamois?
          How do you pronounce <u>chamois</u>? [sham´e]

1. The word cool has many meanings.

   _____

2. The new hospital is shaped like the letter H.

   _____

3. Scientifically the chimpanzee is called Pan troglodytes and the gorilla is Gorilla
   gorilla.

   _____

4. I'm feeling muy bien after seeing the play Man of La Mancha.

   _____

5. The H.M.S. Bounty was a real ship.

   _____

6. The troubles of its crew are told in the book Mutiny on the Bounty.

   _____

7. I subscribe to a Memphis newspaper.

   _____

8. William Randolph Hearst began his career in journalism in 1887 running his father's
   paper, the San Francisco Examiner.

   _____

   _____

9. By the end of his career, he had a nationwide chain of papers, and his policies had
   given rise to the term "yellow journalism."

   _____

   _____

10. The movie Citizen Kane (1941) was an unflattering portrait of a thinly disguised
    Hearst.

    _____

Using Abbreviations

A. Rewrite each of these sentences, replacing inappropriate abbreviations with their full forms. If a sentence is correct as given, write *correct* on the line.

EXAMPLE   It takes years to become a dr.
           It takes years to become a doctor.

1.   The Chang bros. are opening a fishing charter co.

_____

2.   It will be off pier no. 17, not far from L.A., Calif.

_____

3.   They plan to go after game fish, e.g., shark, some of which are as much as 45 ft. long.

_____

4.   Election Day is always the 2nd Tues. in Nov.

_____

5.   What did you get for Xmas?

_____

6.   Everyone ought to know the story of Wm. Henry Harrison, 9th pres. of the U.S.

_____

7.   He is mentioned in my textbook on the hist. of poli. sci. and philo.

_____

8.   The prof. says the midterm will cover chaps. 1-5.

_____

9.   The midterm & final each count 40%.

_____

10. The body contains about 10 pts. of blood.

_____

11. Some people sell their blood for a few $'s.

_____

12. A kilo. equals 2.2 lbs.

_____

13. The counselor had an MSW degree from NYU.

_____

14. She had put herself through school working as an assist. mgr. in a fast-food rest.

_____

15. Mr. and Mrs. McDonald live on Maple Ave. in Duluth, Minn.

_____

B: Rewrite each of these sentences, replacing inappropriate full forms with standard abbreviations. It may be necessary to slightly rearrange some sentences.

EXAMPLE   Americans celebrate independence on the fourth day of July.
            Americans celebrate independence on July 4th.

1.   The bank's loan officer awoke at 2:00 *ante meridiem*.

     _____

2.   He was thinking about the family that had applied for a loan of thirty thousand dollars.

     _____

3.   Doctor Jones had given them a letter of reference.

     _____

4.   Bill Smith, a Certified Public Accountant, had also sent a letter.

     _____

5.   For collateral, they offered a Spanish doubloon dated 1642 *Anno Domini*.

     _____

6.   The doubloon had been in the family since nineteen nineteen.

     _____

7.   Mister and Missus Grossman wanted to use the money to set up a company to make precision measuring devices.

     _____

8.   They already had a contract with the National Aeronautics and Space Administration.

     _____

9.   The banker wanted to give his okay, but loans this big had to be co-authorized by the bank president.

     _____

10. However, the president had taken her Self-Contained-Underwater-Breathing-Apparatus and gone on a vacation.

     _____

Using Figures   EXERCISE 28-4

Rewrite each of these sentences, replacing inappropriate figures with words or inappropriate words with figures. If a sentence is correct as given, write *correct* on the line.

EXAMPLE   He is six feet four and a half inches.
           He is 6'4½ " _____

1. There are a hundred and seven women in the freshman class at the law school this year.

    _____

2. Ten years ago there were only 47.

    _____

3. 1/3 the faculty is female now compared with1/10 then.

    _____

4. Many students share apartments in a building that charges six hundred dollars for two rooms, $700 for three rooms, and $775 for 4 rooms.

    _____

5. The semester begins on September fourteenth.

    _____

6. The entering class will graduate on June first, nineteen ninety-six.

    _____

7. Entrance requirements are on pages thirty to thirty-five.

    _____

8. The average law student is expected to drink 1½ gallons of coffee a day over the next 3 years.

    _____

9. The drop-out rate is about twenty-nine percent.

    _____

10. The law school is located at Fifteen Clark Street.

    _____

Using Hyphens in Numbers

Formal usage in the humanities requires that numbers, including common fractions, be written in words. Write out each of these numbers, using hyphens as needed.

EXAMPLE   2102   ___*twenty-one hundred and two*___

1. 35 _____

2. $\frac{1}{2}$ _____

3. $\frac{4}{5}$ _____

4. 101 _____

5. 1st _____

6. 3457 _____

7. 495 _____

PART 3: | *Writing Research*

MODULE 29: USING SOURCES AND AVOIDING PLAGIARISM

29a How do I use sources well?

Now's the time to turn from researching to writing your research paper. When you use sources well, your chances of writing a successful research paper increase greatly. In your work so far, you've built a solid foundation by choosing a research-suitable topic, one that's neither too general nor too narrow; formulating a research question; establishing a search strategy for finding sources to answer that question; locating sources that apply to your particular treatment of the topic; writing a working bibliography of what you've found; evaluating each source carefully to make sure it's reliable and trustworthy; and taking content notes on the sources that have passed your careful evaluation.

Now you're ready to use critical thinking to pull together a synthesis of your sources combined with your own thinking about the topic. To synthesize well, you think through the information gathered from your sources by:

- Mastering the information from each source
- Finding relationships among the sources' information
- Adding your own thinking to the mix

Your written synthesis is your research paper. To write effectively, you organize your paper around a logical sequence based on the main points in your synthesis. Further, you want to support each main point and important subpoint with specific ideas or words drawn from your sources to show that your claims originate with authorities on your topic.

As you marshal your support, keep the RENNS formula, discussed in 4f, in mind: Be specific by using **R**easons, **E**xamples, **N**ames, **N**umbers, and the five **S**enses. Also, if your purpose is persuasive rather than informative, remember to present opposing viewpoints even-handedly and then refute them reasonably.

A successful research paper relies on your drawing from your sources. You integrate suitable material into your paper by using quotations, paraphrases, and summaries, while always being sure to avoid plagiarism. Your source-based writing needs to be:

- Accurate
- Effective
- Honest (the only way to avoid plagiarism)

The final step in using sources well is to use correct **documentation**. Documentation means making two types of entries in your research paper each time you draw upon a source for support.

1. Writing a parenthetical citation for each quotation, paraphrase, and summary you take from sources.

2. Composing a Works Cited list, MLA's name for a bibliography for the end of your paper. This list needs to include full bibliographic information on each source from which you have quoted, paraphrased, and summarized in your paper.

Today's bibliographies differ from those of the past. The root word biblio- means "book," so traditionally, the bibliographic information referred to a book's title, author, publisher, and place and year of publication. Now that the age of the Internet, CD-ROMs, and other technologies is here, researchers include in their bibliographies all the sources they've used not only in print but also from the various technologies.

A **documentation style** refers to a specific system for providing information on sources used in a research paper. Documentation styles vary among the disciplines.

29b What is plagiarism?

To **plagiarize** is to present another person's words or ideas as if they were your own. Plagiarism, like stealing, is a form of academic dishonesty or cheating. Because it's a serious offense, plagiarism can be grounds for a failing grade or expulsion from college.

29c How do I avoid plagiarism?

Here's how to avoid plagiarism. First, understand that researchers use sources carefully by honestly and suitably **quoting, paraphrasing,** and **summarizing** their ideas and words—a popular memory device for this is **Use QPS.** Second, become comfortable with the concept of **documentation,** which you need to use each time you quote, paraphrase, and summarize your sources. The box below describes the main strategies you can use to avoid plagiarism.

STRATEGIES FOR AVOIDING PLAGIARISM

- Use DOCUMENTATION to acknowledge your use of the ideas or phrasings of others, taken from the sources you've compiled on your topic.

- Become thoroughly familiar with the documentation style that your instructor tells you to use for your research paper. To work efficiently, make a master list of the information required to document all sources that you quote, paraphrase, or summarize according to your required documentation style.

- Write down absolutely all the documentation facts that you'll need for your paper, keeping careful records as you search for sources. Otherwise, you'll waste much time trying to retrace your steps to get a documentation detail you missed.

- Use a consistent system for taking CONTENT NOTES. Perhaps use different colors of ink or another coding system to keep these three uses of sources separate:

  1. Quotations from a source (require documentation)

  2. Material paraphrased or summarized from a source (requires documentation)

  3. Thoughts of your own triggered by what you've read or experienced in life (no documentation required), making sure to maintain the distinction between your own thinking and the ideas that come directly from a source

- Write clear, perhaps oversized, quotation marks when you're directly quoting a passage. Make them so distinct that you can't miss seeing them later.

- Consult with your instructor if you're unsure about any phase of the documentation process.

Never assume that your instructor can't detect plagiarism. Instructors have keen eyes for writing styles different from the ones students generally produce and from your own style in particular. In addition, instructors can access Web sites that electronically check your submitted work against all material available online. Further Internet sites such as <http://www.turnitin.com> allow instructors to check your writing against hundreds of thousands of paper for free or for sale on the World Wide Web and the Internet. (Also, that site adds your paper to its huge database of student papers so that no one can plagiarize your work.) Moreover, when instructors receive papers that they suspect contain plagiarized passages, they can check with other professors to see whether a student paper looks familiar.

Another important way to avoid plagiarism is to dive willingly into any interim tasks your instructors build into their research assignments. These tasks can help you enormously as you conduct your research and write your paper. For example, many instructors today set interim deadlines such as a date for handing in a working bibliography, a list of all documentation details for sources you've located in your search but haven't yet evaluated for their value and reliablity. Another possible assignment is to prepare an **annotated bibliography**, which includes all documentation information and a brief summary or commentary on each source that you've evaluated as trustworthy and useful for your research paper. Further, some instructors want to read and coach you about how to improve one or more of your research paper drafts. In some cases, they might want to look over your research log, content notes, and/or photocopies of your sources.

29d How do I work with Internet Sources to avoid plagiarism?

The Internet can both greatly help researchers and create potential new problems. One problem is that the Internet allows anyone to say anything, so many Internet sources lack reliability and aren't legitimate for research purposes. The second problem is that students might plagiarize more readily from Internet sources.

For example, you might be tempted to download a completed research paper from the Internet. *Don't.* That's intellectual dishonesty—which can get you into real trouble not only with your instructor but also with the college. Or you might be tempted to borrow wording from what you wrongly consider an "obscure" Internet source. *Don't.* Not only is this intellectual dishonesty, but instructors will easily detect it. The box below provides guidelines for avoiding plagiarism of Internet sources.

GUIDELINES FOR AVOIDING PLAGIARIZING FROM THE INTERNET

- Never cut and paste directly into your paper from online sources. You can too easily lose track of what language is your own and what material came from a source. You'll need to document each item.

- Keep downloaded or printed Internet sources in computer files that are separate from your draft, whether you intend to draw upon the sources as quotations, summaries, or paraphrases. Be extremely careful about how you manage those copies. Whenever you know the exact place where you think an item would fit in your paper, record that location very clearly (use another color or a much larger font), but never paste it in.

- Make sure that you write every detail of information that identifies the source and is called for in the documentation style you need to use.

(continued next page)

**GUIDELINES FOR AVOIDING PLAGIARIZING FROM
THE INTERNET** *(continued)*

- If you're taking CONTENT NOTES in a computer file, copy or paste material onto a blank page if you intend to use it as a direct quotation from a printed or downloaded source. Make certain to place quotation marks around the quoted material and to include proper documentation. Do this at the moment you copy or paste the quotation. If you put off documenting until later, you may forget to do it or get it wrong. Also, in a different font or color, type your reason for thinking the quotation might be useful.

- SUMMARIZE or PARAPHRASE materials *before* you include them in your paper. If for the sake of convenience you've printed or downloaded Internet sources into separate files, never copy directly from those files into your paper. On the spot, summarize or paraphrase the sources.

- QUOTE carefully if you decide you must quote a passage directly from a source. Make sure to use quotation marks; perhaps signal with a different font or color that you have quoted.

- Keep all documentation information together as you work with each source. Then, at the very moment you put a quote, paraphrase, or summary in your paper, enter all documentation information in a parenthetical citation and in your bibliography. Never put this off until later, because the details might slip your mind, you might forget to do the documentation entirely, or you might get it wrong as you try to reconstruct your thinking.

- If you think that you may have plagiarized by mistake, check your work against papers and files on the Internet. Try typing one or two sentences—always putting them in quotation marks—into the search window at google.com. You might also submit your work to one of the for-profit plagiarism-detection services. These for-profit services charge you money for their work, and they also keep a copy of your paper in their databases.

29e What don't I have to document?

You don't have to document common knowledge or your own thinking. **Common knowledge** is information that most educated people know, although they may need to remind themselves of certain facts by looking up information in a reference book. For example, here are a few facts of common knowledge that you don't need to document.

- Bill Clinton was the U.S. president before George W. Bush.
- Mercury is the planet closest to the sun.
- Normal human body temperature is 98.6°F.
- All the oceans on our planet contain salt water.

A very important component of a research paper that doesn't need documentation is **your own thinking**, which is based on what you've learned as you've built on what you already knew about your topic. It consists of your analysis, synthesis, and interpretation of new material as you read or observe it. You don't have to document your own thinking. Your own thinking helps you formulate a thesis statement and organize your research paper by composing topic sentences that carry along your presentation of information. For example, suppose that you're drawing on an article about the connections between emotions and logic in people. While reading the article, you come to a personal conclusion that computers can't have emotions. This idea is not stated anywhere in the article you are reading or in any other source you use. Obviously, you need to cite the ideas from the article that led to your conclusion, but you don't need to cite your own thinking. On the other hand, if you find a source that states this very idea, you must cite it.

29f What must I document?

You must document everything that you learn from a source. This includes ideas as well as specific language. Expressing the ideas of others in your own words doesn't release you from the obligation to tell exactly where you got those ideas—you need to use complete, correct documentation.

29g How can I effectively integrate sources into my writing?

Integrating sources means blending information and ideas from others with your own writing. Before trying to integrate sources into your writing, you need to have analyzed and then synthesized the material. Analysis requires you to break ideas down into their component parts so that you can think them through separately. The best time to do this is while you're reading your sources and taking content notes. Synthesis requires you to make connections among different ideas, seeking relationships and connections that tie them together.

29h How can I use quotations effectively?

A **quotation** is the exact words of a source enclosed in quotation marks. You face conflicting demands when you use quotations in your writing. Although quotations provide support, you can lose coherence in your paper if you use too many quotations. If more than a quarter of your paper consists of quotations, you've probably written what some people call "cut and paste special"—merely stringing together a bunch of quotations. Doing so gives your readers—including instructors—the impression that you've not bothered to develop your own thinking, and you're letting other people do your talking.

In addition to avoiding too many quotations, you also want to avoid using quotations that are too long. Readers tend to skip over long quotations and lose the drift of the paper. Also, your instructor might assume that you just didn't take the time required to paraphrase or summarize the material. Generally, summaries and paraphrases are more effective for reconstructing someone else's argument. If you do need to quote a long passage, make absolutely sure every word in the quotation counts. Edit out irrelevant parts,using ellipsis points to indicate deleted material. The box on the next page provides guidelines for using quotations.

When you use quotations, the greatest risk you take is that you'll end up with incoherent, choppy sentences. You can avoid this problem within each sentence, when the words you quote fit smoothly with three aspects of the rest of your sentence: grammar, style, and logic.

After writing sentences that contain quotations, read the material aloud and listen to whether the language flows smoothly and gracefully. Perhaps you need to add a word or two placed in brackets within the quotation so that its wording works grammatically and effortlessly with the rest of

---

GUIDELINES FOR USING QUOTATIONS

1. Use quotations from authorities on your subject to support or refute what you write in your paper.

2. Never use a quotation to present your thesis statement or topic sentences.

3. Select quotations that fit your message. Choose a quotation only in these cases:

   • Its language is particularly appropriate or distinctive.

   • Its idea is particularly hard to paraphrase accurately.

   • The authority of the source is especially important to support your thesis or main point.

   • The source's words are open to interpretation.

4. Never use quotations in more than a quarter of your paper. Instead, rely on paraphrase and summary.

5. Quote accurately. Always check each quotation against the original source—and then recheck it.

6. Integrate quotations smoothly into your writing.

7. Avoid PLAGIARISM.

8. Enter all DOCUMENTATION precisely and carefully.

---

your sentence. Of course, make sure your bracketed additions don't distort the meaning of the quotation.

Perhaps the biggest complaint instructors have about student research papers is that sometimes quotations are simply stuck in, for no apparent reason. Whenever you place words between quotation marks, they take on special significance for your message as well as your language. Without context-setting information in the paper, the reader can't know exactly what logic leads the writer to use a particular quotation.

Furthermore, always make sure your readers know who said each group of quoted words. Otherwise, you've used a *disembodied quotation* (some instructors call them "ghost quotations"). Although quotation marks set off someone else's words, they need explanation and context, or they'll tell the reader nothing about who is being quoted and why. This reflects poorly on the clarity of your writing.

Rarely can a quotation begin a paragraph effectively. Start your paragraph by relying on your topic sentence, based on your own thinking. Then, you can fit in a relevant quotation somewhere in the paragraph, if it supports or extends what you have said.

Another stategy for working quotations smoothly into your paper is to integrate the name(s) of the author(s), the source title, or other information into your paper. You can prepare your reader for a quotation using one of these methods:

• Mention in your sentence directly before or after the quotation the name(s) of the author(s) you're quoting.

• Mention in your sentence the title of the work you're quoting from.

- Give additional authority to your material. If the author of a source is a noteworthy figure, you can gain credibility when you refer to his or her credentials.

- Mention the name(s) of the author(s) with or without the name of the source and any author credentials, along with your personal introductory lead to the material.

You can also integrate a quotation into your own writing by interrupting the quotation with your own words. If you insert your own words within the quotation, you are required to put those words between brackets, as with the word "eight" in the following example:

"While we all possess all of the [eight] intelligences," Howard Gardner explains, "perhaps no two persons—not even identical twins—exhibit them in the same combination of stengths" (72). [This citation is arranged in MLA documentation style.]

After using an author's full name in the first reference, you can decide to use only the author's last name in subsequent references. This holds true unless another source has that same last name.

29i How can I write good paraphrases?

A **paraphrase** precisely restates in your own words and your own writing style the written or spoken words of someone else. Select for paraphrase only the passages that carry ideas that you need to reproduce in detail. Because paraphrasing calls for a very close approximation of a source, avoid trying to paraphrase a whole chapter—or even a whole page; use summary instead. Expect to write a number of drafts of your paraphrases, each time getting closer to effectively rewording and revising the writing style so that you can avoid plagiarism. The box below provides guidelines for writing paraphrases.

GUIDELINES FOR WRITING PARAPHRASES

1. Decide to paraphrase authorities on your subject to support or counter what you write in your paper.

2. Never use a paraphrase to present your thesis statement or topic sentences.

3. Say what the source says, but no more.

4. Reproduce the source's sequence of ideas and emphases.

5. Use your own words and writing style to restate the material. If some technical words in the original have awkward or no synonyms, you may quote the original's words—but do so very sparingly.

6. Never distort the source's meaning as you reword and change the writing style.

7. Expect your material to be as long as, and often longer than, the original.

8. Integrate your paraphrases smoothly into your writing.

9. Avoid plagiarism.

10. Enter all DOCUMENTATION precisely and carefully.

29j How can I write good summaries?

A **summary** differs from a paraphrase in one important way: A paraphrase restates the original material completely, but a summary provides only the main point of the original source. A summary is much shorter than a paraphrase. Summarizing is the technique you will probably use most frequently in writing your research paper, both for taking notes and for integrating what you have learned from sources into your own writing.

As you summarize, you trace a line of thought. This involves deleting less central ideas and sometimes transposing certain points into an order more suited to summary. In summarizing a longer original—say, ten pages or more—you may find it helpful first to divide the original into subsections and summarize each. Then, group your subsection summaries and use them as the basis for further condensing the material into a final summary. You will likely have to revise a summary more than once. Always make sure that a summary accurately reflects the source and its emphases.

When you're summarizing a source in your content notes, take care not to be tempted to include your personal interpretation along with something the author says. Similarly, never include in your summary your own judgment about the point made in the source. Your own opinions and ideas, although they have value, don't belong in a summary. Instead, jot them down immediately when they come to mind, but separate them clearly from your summary.

GUIDELINES FOR WRITING SUMMARIES

1. Use summaries from authorities on your subject to support or refute what you write in your paper.

2. Identify the main points you want to summarize and condense them using your own words without losing the essence of the original source.

3. Never use a summary to present your thesis statement or topic sentences.

4. Keep your summary short.

5. Integrate your summaries smoothly into your writing.

6. Avoid plagiarism.

7. Enter all documentation precisely and carefully.

Write your notes so that when you go back to them you can be sure to distinguish your opinions or ideas from your summary. Highlight your personal writing with a screen of yellow or some other color or use an entirely different font for it. The box on the next page provides guidelines for writing good summaries.

29k Which verbs can help me weave source material into my sentences?

The verbs listed in the box on the next page can help you work quotations, paraphrases, and summaries smoothly into your writing. Some of these verbs imply your position toward the source material (for example, *argue, complain, concede, deny, grant, insist,* and *reveal*). Other verbs imply a more neutral stance (for example, *comment, describe, explain, note, say,* and *write*).

VERBS USEFUL FOR INTEGRATING QUOTATIONS, PARAPHRASES, AND SUMMARIES

acknowledges	discusses	points out
agrees	distinguishes between/among	prepares
analyzes	emphasizes	promises
argues	endeavors to	proves
asks	establishes	questions
asserts	estimates	recognizes
balances	explains	recommends
begins	expresses	refutes
believes	finds	rejects
claims	focuses on	remarks
comments	grants	reports
compares	illuminates	reveals
complains	illustrates	says
concedes	implies	sees
concludes	indicates	shows
confirms	informs	signals
connects	insists	specifies
considers	introduces	speculates
contends	maintains	states
contradicts	means	suggests
contrasts	negates	supports
declares	notes	supposes
demonstrates	notices	thinks
denies	observes	wishes
describes	offers	writes
develops	organizes	

Name _____   Date _____

Quoting

A. Select the portions of this passage that could be usefully quoted in an essay on marketing. Carefully and accurately incorporate those portions of the passage into your writing.

Then came the brand equity mania of the eighties, the defining moment of which arrived in 1988 when Philip Morris purchased Kraft for $12.6 billion - six times what the company was worth on paper. The price difference, apparently, was the cost of the word "Kraft." Of course Wall Street was aware that decades of marketing and brand bolstering added value to a company over and above its assets and total annual sales. But with the Kraft purchase, a huge dollar value had been assigned to something that had previously been abstract and unquantifiable - a brand name. This was spectacular news for the ad world, which was now able to make the claim that advertising spending was more than just a sales strategy: it was an investment in cold hard equity. The more you spend, the more your company is worth. Not surprisingly, this led to a considerable increase in spending on advertising. More important, it sparked a renewed interest in puffing up brand identities, a project that involved far more than a few billboards and TV spots. It was about pushing the envelope in sponsorship deals, dreaming up new areas in which to "extend" the brand, as well as perpetually probing the zeitgeist to ensure that the "essence" selected for one's brand would resonate karmically with its target market. For reasons that will be explored in the rest of this chapter, this radical shift in corporate philosophy has sent manufacturers on a cultural feeding frenzy as they seize upon every corner of unmarketed landscape in search of the oxygen needed to inflate their brands. In the process, virtually nothing has been left un-branded. That's quite an impressive feat, considering that as recently as 1993 Wall Street had pronounced the brand dead, or as good as dead.

—NAOMI KLEIN, *No Logo*

B. Select any sample paragraph from your handbook and write a paraphrase that includes the most important passages as quotations.

C. Select a paragraph from one of your textbooks or any other nonfiction work, and take notes that combine paraphrase with careful, selective quotation.

Paraphrasing

A. Paraphrase the following paragraph.

Though the words are often used interchangeably, branding and advertising are not the same process. Advertising any given product is only one part of branding's grand plan, as are sponsorship and logo licensing. Think of the brand as the core meaning of the modern corporation, and of the advertisement as one vehicle used to convey that meaning to the world. The first mass-marketing campaigns, starting in the second half of the nineteenth century, had more to do with advertising than with branding as we understand it today. Faced with a range of recently invented products — the radio, phonograph, car, light bulb and so on — advertisers had more pressing tasks than creating a brand identity for any given corporation; first, they had to change the way people lived their lives. Ads had to inform consumers about the existence of some new invention, then convince them that their lives would be better if they used, for example, cars instead of wagons, telephones instead of mail and electric light instead of oil lamps. Many of these new products bore brand names — some of which are still around today — but these were almost incidental.

—Naomi Klein, *No Logo*

B. Select any sample paragraph in your handbook and paraphrase it.

C. Select a paragraph from one of your textbooks or any other nonfiction work and paraphrase it.

Summarizing

A. Summarize the following passage.

The astronomical growth in the wealth and cultural influence of multi-national corporations over the last fifteen years can arguably be traced back to a single, seemingly innocuous idea developed by management theorists in the mid-1980s: that successful corporations must primarily produce brands, as opposed to products.

Until that time, although it was understood in the corporate world that bolstering one's brand name was important, the primary concern of every solid manufacturer was the production of goods. This idea was the very gospel of the machine age. An editorial that appeared in *Fortune* magazine in 1938, for instance, argued that the reason the American economy had yet to recover from the Depression was that America had lost sight of the importance of making things.

This is the proposition that the basic and irreversible function of an industrial economy is the making of things; that the more things it makes the bigger will be the income, whether dollar or real; and hence that the key to those lost recuperative powers lies ... in the factory where the lathes and the drills and the fires and the hammers are. It is in the factory and on the land and under the land that purchasing power originates. And for the longest time, the making of things remained, at least in principle, the heart of all industrialized economies. But by the eighties, pushed along by that decade's recession, some of the most powerful manufacturers in the world had begun to falter. A consensus emerged that corporations were bloated, oversized; they owned too much, employed too many people, and were weighed down with too many things. The very process of producing – running one's own factories, being responsible for tens of thousands of full-time, permanent employees – began to look less like the route to success and more like a clunky liability.

At around this same time a new kind of corporation began to rival the traditional all-American manufacturers for market share; these were the Nikes and Microsofts, and later, the Tommy Hilfigers and Intels. These pioneers made the bold claim that producing goods was only an incidental part of their operations, and that thanks to recent victories in trade liberalization and labor-law reform, they were able to have their products made for them by contractors, many of them overseas. What these companies produced primarily were not things, they said, but images of their brands. Their real work lay not in manufacturing but in marketing. This formula, needless to say, has proved enormously profitable, and its success has companies competing in a race toward weightlessness: whoever owns the least, has the fewest employees on the payroll and produces the most powerful images, as opposed to products, wins the race.

—Naomi Klein, *No Logo*

B. Select any sample paragraph in your handbook and summarize it.

C. Select a paragraph from one of your textbooks or any other nonfiction work and summarize it.

PART 4: | *Writing Across the Curriculum and Beyond*

MODULE 30: COMPARING THE DISCIPLINES

30a What is writing Across the Curriculum?

Writing Across the Curriculum refers to the writing you do in college courses beyond first-year composition. Good writing in various subject areas has many common features, but there are also important differences.

Academic disciplines are commonly grouped into three broad categories: the humanities, the social sciences, and the natural sciences. Each of these disciplines has its own knowledge, vocabulary, and perspectives on the world; its own specialized assignments and purposes; its own common types of SOURCES; and its own expected documentation styles. Despite these differences, writing processes and strategies interconnect and overlap across the curriculum. Types of writing such as SUMMARIES, ANALYSES, and SYNTHESIS are common in various disciplines.

30b What are primary research and secondary research in the disciplines?

Research methods differ among the disciplines where sources are concerned. This is true of both primary sources (those that offer firsthand exposure to information) and secondary sources (articles and books that draw on primary sources).

In the humanities, existing documents are the primary sources, and it is the task of the researcher to analyze and interpret them directly. Secondary sources represent other writers' efforts to do this.

In the social and natural sciences, primary research means designing and carrying out experiments involving direct observation. Researchers must either conduct the experiments themselves or read firsthand reports by those who have conducted them. Secondary sources in these disciplines summarize and synthesize findings and draw parallels that offer new insights.

30c What can help me write assignments in various disciplines?

A useful strategy for writing assignments in different disciplines is to analyze successful writings that match the requirements of your assignment. The expectations for an assignment can vary greatly across the disciplines. Your instructor may provide model papers for you to evaluate.

30d

30d How do I use documentation in the disciplines?

Styles of documentation — the way in which writers give credit to the sources they have used — also differ among the disciplines.

In the humanities, most fields of study use the documentation style of the Modern Language Association (MLA). CM (Chicago Manual) style is sometimes used as an alternative.

In the social sciences, most fields use APA (American Psychological Association) style. In the natural sciences, documentation styles vary widely.

Sources and Documentation

A. Look at the Works Cited list for one of the secondary sources you are using. Underline those you feel might help you understand the secondary source — and hence the primary source — better. Locate and read at least one additional secondary source.

B. Find out the correct method of documentation for the types of secondary sources used most often in your discipline.

MODULE 31: WRITING ABOUT THE HUMANITIES AND LITERATURE

HUMANITIES

31a What are the humanities?

The humanities consist of a set of disciplines that seek to represent and understand human experience through art, thought, and values. These disciplines include literature, languages, philosophy, and history, although at some colleges history is grouped with the social sciences. Also, many colleges consider the fine arts (music, art, dance, theater, and creative writing) part of the humanities, while other colleges group them separately.

31b What types of papers do I write in the humanities?

In the humanities, existing documents or artifacts are PRIMARY SOURCES, and the writer's task generally is to analyze and interpret them. Typical primary source material for humanities research could be a poem by Billy Collins, the floor plans of Egyptian pyramids, or the early drafts of musical scores. A humanities class assignment might invite you to create primary sources yourself. For example, in a studio art class, you paint, draw, or sculpt. In a music composition class, you create pieces of music. Some humanities papers will require SECONDARY SOURCES. These are articles and books that someone has written to explain or interpret a primary source. For example, suppose you're writing about a movie you saw. The movie is a primary source. If you consult a review of that movie, the review would be a secondary source.

31c What types of papers do I write in the humanities?

Inquiry calls for thinking beyond the obvious by intelligently questioning, investigating, and examining a subject. Because the humanities cover an impressively broad range of knowledge, writing in the various disciplines involves several forms of intellectual inquiry. These include responses, narratives, interpretations, critiques, and analysis of works or objects or ideas. In practice, many writing assignments in the humanities require you to combine these activities, but I present each of them individually here for ease of reference.

Synthesis in the humanities

Synthesis plays a major role in the habits of mind involved in inquiry. Synthesis relates several texts, ideas, or pieces of information to one another. For example, you might read several accounts of the events leading up to the Civil War and then write a synthesis that explains what caused that war. Or you might read several philosophers' definitions of morality and then write a synthesis of the components of a moral life. Unsynthesized ideas and information are like separate spools of thread, neatly lined up, possibly coordinated but not integrated. Synthesized ideas and information are threads woven into a tapestry—a new whole that shows relationships.

Responses in the humanities

In a response, you give your personal reaction to a work, supported by explanations of your reasoning. For example, do you like Hamlet? What is your reaction to America's dealings with Hitler in the 1930s? Do you agree with Peter Singer's philosophical arguments against using animals in scientific experiments? Some instructors want you to justify your response with references to a text, while other instructors do not. Clarify what your instructor wants before you begin.

Narrative in the humanities

When you write a NARRATIVE, you construct a coherent story out of separate facts or events. Historians, for example, assemble public records, diaries and journals, news events, laws, incidents, and related materials to create a chronological version of what happened. Similarly, biographers take isolated events in people's pasts, interviews with the people themselves if possible, interviews of those who know or knew the people, letters written to or from the people, and related SOURCES to form a coherent story of their subjects' lives.

Interpretation in the humanities

An interpretation explains the meaning or significance of a particular text, event, or work of art. For example, what does Plato's *Republic* suggest about the nature of a good society? What message does Picasso's painting *Guernica* convey about the nature of war? What was the significance of President Richard Nixon's visit to China in the early 1970s? What does it suggest when language authorities in some countries try to ban new words that originated in other languages (such as the French trying to exclude English terms like *skateboard*)? Your reply isn't right or wrong; rather, you present your point of view and explain your reasoning.

Critique in the humanities

In a critique (also called a CRITICAL RESPONSE or a review), you present judgments about a particular work, supported by your underlying reasoning. For example, movie, book, music, and art reviews present a writer's carefully reasoned, well-supported opinion of a work. Critical responses and reviews may focus on the literary form, or genre, of a work (for example, "How does this poem satisfy the conventions of a sonnet?" or "Is this painting an example of Expressionism or Impressionism?"). Responses or reviews may focus on a work's accuracy, logic, or conclusions ("Is this history of the development of rap music complete and accurate?"). Finally, responses or reviews may analyze a work's relations to other works ("Is the Broadway version of *The Producers* better or worse than the earlier film version?") or a work's similarities to and diffrences from the "real" world ("To what extent does *Everybody Loves Raymond* accurately portray middle-class family life?").

Analysis in the humanities

When you engage in analysis, you examine material by breaking it into its component parts and discovering how the parts interrelate. You examine and explain texts, events, objects, or documents by identifying and discussing important elements in them. These elements can include formal matters (how the work is put together) or the ideas, assumptions, and evidence they include. The humanities use a number of analytic frameworks, or systematic ways of investigating a work. The box below summarizes some common analytic frameworks used most notably in literary analysis. Nearly all writing in the humanities depends on analysis to some extent.

SELECTED ANALYTIC FRAMEWORKS USED IN THE HUMANITIES

Cultural/New Historical

Explores how social, economic, and other cultural forces influence the development of ideas, texts, art, laws, customs, and so on. Also explores how individual texts or events provide broader understandings of the times in which they were written or occurred or in today's world.

Deconstructionist

Assumes that the meaning of any given text is not stable or "in" the work. Rather, that meaning always depends on contexts and the interests of those in power. The goal of deconstruction is to produce multiple possible meanings of a work, usually in order to undermine traditional interpretations.

Feminist

Focuses on how women are presented and treated, concentrating especially on power relations between men and women.

Formalist

Centers on matters of structure, form, and traditional literary devices (plot, rhythm, images, symbolism, diction).

Marxist

Proceeds from the assumption that the most important forces in human experience are economic and material ones. Focuses on power differences between economic classes of people and the effects of those differences.

Reader-Response

Emphasizes how the individual reader determines meaning. The reader's personal history, values, experiences, relationships, and prior reading life all contribute to how he or she interprets a particular work or event.

31d Which documentation style do I use to write about the humanities?

Most fields in the humanities use the documentation style of the Modern Language Association (MLA), as explained and illustrated in Chapter 34. Some disciplines in the humanities use Chicago Manual (CM) style, as explained in Chapter 36.

LITERATURE

31e What is literature?

Literature includes fiction (novels and short stories), drama (plays, scripts, and some films); poetry (poems and lyrics); as well as nonfiction with artistic qualities (memoirs, personal essays, and the like). Since ancient times, literature has represented human experiences, entertained, and enlarged readers' perspectives about themselves, others, diverse cultures, and different ways of living.

By writing about literature, you shape and refine the insights that result from your reading. Writing about reading, more than reading without writing, helps you move to a deeper understanding of other people and of ideas, times, and places. Writing about literature facilitates your investigations of how authors use language to stir the imaginations, emotions, and intellects of their readers. And, of course, writing allows you to share your own reading experiences and insights with other readers.

31f Why write about literature?

Writing about literature generates insights about your reading. It helps you understand other people, ideas, times, and places. It shows you how authors use language to stir the imaginations, emotions, and intellects of their readers. Finally, writing is a way to share your own reading experiences and insights with other readers.

31g What general strategies can help me write about literature?

In academic work, although you may initially read a work for sheer enjoyment, doing further readings you need to attend more closely to various elements in the text. Interestingly, many readers are surprised to discover that CRITICAL READING actually enhances their enjoyment of the text.

Critical reading means reading systematically, closely, and actively. Above all, it means asking questions: What does the work mean? Why has the author made particular choices in plot, characterizations, and word choice? What other works influenced the author's choices? How do readers react to the work?

Sometimes instructors ask students to answer questions that deal with material on a literal level: that is, to tell exactly what is said on the page. If a question asks what happens in the plot or what a passage is saying, you need to answer with a SUMMARY or PARAPHRASE of the work. If a question asks about the historical context of a work, or asks for biographical or situational information about the author, you likely need to do some research and then report exactly what you find.

More often, assignments call for making INFERENCES, which I discuss in detail in section 5c. Making inferences means reading "between" the lines to figure out what is implied but not stated. This reading skill is especially crucial for reading literature because it tends to "show" rather than to "tell." It depicts events, characters, conversations, and settings, but the author doesn't say precisely what the work means. For example, your instructor might ask you to discuss why a character does something for which the author provides no explicit reason; to explain the effect of images in a poem; to investigate how a work depicts the roles of women, men, and/or children; or to explore the author's stance on a social issue. In such papers you're not only analyzing the literary text but also examining your own experiences and beliefs.

To read a literary work closely, and then to write about it, you look for details or passages that relate to each other. In doing so, you can form a TOPIC or THESIS STATEMENT for writing about the text. As you read, mark up the text by selectively underlining or highlighting passages, by writing notes, comments, or questions in the margin, or by taking notes separately on paper or on a computer. If you use the third method, be sure to note exactly what part of the text you're referring to so that you don't lose track of what applies to what.

31h How do I write different types of papers about literature?

Several different types of inquiry are used for writing about literature. They include all types discussed, with the following adaptations.

Personal response to literature

In a personal response you explain your reaction to a work of literature or some aspect of it. As with all effective papers about literature, you explain your response through discussions of specific passages or elements from the text. You might write about whether you enjoyed reading the work –and why. You might discuss whether situations in the work are similar to your personal experience, and why such observations are worth the reader's consideration. You might explain whether you agree with the author's point of view—and why. You might answer a question or explore a problem that the work raised for you—for example, how you reacted when a likeable character broke the law.

Interpretation of literature

Most works of literature are open to more than one interpretation. Your task, then, is not to discover the single right answer. Instead, you determine a possible interpretation and provide an argument that supports it. The questions in the following box can help you write an effective interpretation paper.

QUESTIONS FOR A LITERARY INTERPRETATION PAPER

1. What is the central theme of the work?

2. How do particular parts of the work relate to the central theme of the work?

3. What do patterns, if they exist in various elements of the work, mean?

4. What meaning does the author create through the major elements of formal analysis?

5. Why does the work end as it does?

Formal analysis of literature

A formal analysis explains how elements of a literary work function to create meaning or effect. The term "formal analysis" refers to analysis of formal elements that make up a work of literature, such as the plot structure of a novel or the rhythm of a poem. The box describes many of these formal elements. Your instructor may ask you to concentrate on just one formal element (for example, "How does the point of view in the story affect its meaning?") or to discuss how a writer develops a theme through several elements (for example, "How do setting, imagery, and symbolism reveal the author's vieiwpoint?").

MAJOR ELEMENTS OF FORMAL ANALYSIS IN LITERARY WORKS

PLOT	The events and their sequence
THEME	Central idea or message
STRUCTURE	Organization and relationship of parts to each other and to the whole
CHARACTERIZATION	Traits, thoughts, and actions of the people in the plot
SETTING	Time and place of the action
POINT OF VIEW	Perspective or position from which the material is presented—by a narrator, a main character, or another person either in the plot or observing the plot
STYLE	Words and sentence structures chosen to present the material
IMAGERY	Pictures created by the words according to other aspects (simile, figurative language, etc.) discussed in this box
TONE	Author's attitude toward the subject of the work—and sometimes toward the reader—expressed through choice of words, imagery, and point of view
FIGURE OF SPEECH	Unusual use or combination of words, as in metaphor and simile, for enhanced vividness or effect
SYMBOLISM	Meaning beneath the surface of the words and images
RHYTHM	Beat, meter
RHYME	Repetition of similar sounds for their auditory effect

To prepare to write your formal analysis, read the work thoroughly, looking for patterns and repetitions. Write notes as you read to help you form insights about those patterns and repetitions. For example, if you need to analyze a character, you want to pay attention to everything that character says or does, everything that other characters say about him or her, and any descriptions of the character.

Cultural analysis of literature

A cultural analysis relates the literary work to broader historical, social, cultural, and political situations. Instructors might ask you to explain how events or prevailing attitudes influence the writing of a work or the way readers understand it. For example, "How did Maxine Hong Kingston's experience as a Chinese American affect the way she tells her story in *The Woman Warrior*?" or "How do differences between the institution of marriage in the early nineteenth century and today affect readers' interpretations of *Pride and Prejudice*?" The box lists some common focuses for cultural analysis.

MAJOR TOPICS FOR CULTURAL ANALYSIS

GENDER	How does a work portray women or men and define—or challenge—their respective roles in society?
CLASS	How does a work portray relationships among the upper, middle, and lower economic classes? How do characters' actions or perspectives result from their wealth and power—or the lack thereof?
RACE AND ETHNICITY	How does a work portray the influences of race and ethnicity on the characters' actions, status, and values?
HISTORY	How does a work reflect—or challenge—past events and values in a society?
AUTOBIOGRAPHY	How might the writer's experiences have influenced this particular work? Similarly, how might the times in which the writer lives or lived have affected his or her work?
GENRE	How is the work similar to, or different from, other works of its type, often—but not always—those written at the same general time? Literature's genres include fiction and memoirs, plays, and poems.

31i What special rules apply to writing about literature?

When you write about literature, certain special elements come into play.

Many instructors require students to use the FIRST PERSON (*I*, *we*, *our*) only when writing about their personal point of view in evaluations; they want students to use the THIRD PERSON (*he*, *she*, *it*, *they*) for all other content. These rules are becoming less rigid, but be sure to ask about your instructor's requirements.

Always use the PRESENT TENSE when you describe or discuss a literary work or any of its elements: *George Henderson* [a character] *takes control of the action and tells the other characters when they may speak.* The present tense is also correct for discussing what the author has done in a specific work: *Because Susan Glaspell* [the author] *excludes Minnie and John Wright from the stage as speaking characters, she forces her audience to learn about them through the words of others.*

Use a PAST-TENSE VERB to discuss historical events or biographical information: *Susan Glaspell was a social activist who was strongly influenced by the chaotic events of the early twentieth century.*

Some assignments call for only your own ideas about the literary work that is the subject of your essay. In such cases, you are dealing only with a PRIMARY SOURCE. in writing about literature, a primary source is the original creative work (a poem, play, story, novel, memoir, diary). Other assignments require you additionally to use SECONDARY SOURCES, which consist of interpretations of literary works. As with all source-based writing, you need to DOCUMENT primary sources and secondary sources because you want to ensure that readers never mistake someone else's ideas as yours. Otherwise, you're PLAGIARIZING, which is a serious academic offense.

Most literature instructors require students to use the DOCUMENTATION STYLE of the Modern Language Association (MLA). However, some instructors prefer APA style or CM or CSE style, so check with your instructor before you begin to conduct your research.

Secondary sources include books, articles, and Web sites in which experts discuss some aspect of the literary text or other material related to your topic. You might use secondary sources to support your own ideas, perhaps by drawing upon the ideas of a scholar who agrees with you or debating the ideas of a scholar who disagrees with you. Or, if you think that you have a new or different interpretation, you might summarize, analyze, or critique what others have written, in order to provide a framework for your own analysis. You can locate secondary sources by using the research process. A particularly important resource for research about literature is the *MLA International Bibliography*, which is the most comprehensive index to literary scholarship.

Verb Tenses and Analysis

A. Look at a draft paper you are writing. Check that present and past tenses have been used correctly and consistently.

B. Consider a literary work you have been asked to analyze. What aspects of the work seem most accessible to you as you try to interpret it?

MODULE 32: WRITING IN THE SOCIAL SCIENCES AND NATURAL SCIENCES

SOCIAL SCIENCES

32a What are the social sciences?

The social sciences focus on the behavior of people as individuals and in groups. They include disciplines such as economics, education, geography, political science, psychology, and sociology. History is sometimes considered a social science; otherwise, it is treated as part of the humanities.

32b What kinds of sources do I use in the social sciences?

Surveys and questionnaires

Surveys and questionnaires systematically gather information from a representative number of individuals. For example, you might survey people to see how and why they will vote in an upcoming election, or you might interview students to explain the effects of peer pressure on behavior in high schools.

Observations

Some writing in the social sciences requires direct observations of people's behaviors. Use whatever tools you need to take complete notes: a laptop or notebook, sketching materials, tape recorders, or cameras. In reporting your observations, tell what tools you used, because they might have influenced what you saw. For example, it would be important to state whether a photo was posed or candid because human subjects behave differently when they know they are being photographed.

Interviews

You might interview people to gather opinions and impressions. Remember that interviews aren't always reliable because people's memories are imprecise, and their first impulse is to present themselves in the best light. Try to interview as many people as possible so that you can cross-check information.

Experiments

The social sciences sometimes use data from experiments as a source. For example, if you want to learn how people react in a particular situation, you can set up that situation artificially and bring individuals (known as "subjects") into it to observe their behavior. With all methods of inquiry in the social sciences, you need to be ethical. You're required to treat subjects fairly and honestly, not in ways that could cause them harm in body, mind, or reputation. Professional social scientists must seek explicit written permission from their subjects, and colleges have official panels to review research proposals to make sure the studies are ethical. Check with your instructor to see whether you need to have your study approved.

32c What are writing purposes and practices in the social sciences?

Summary and *synthesis* are fundamental strategies for analytical writing in the social sciences. *Analysis* is useful for breaking problems down into their constituent parts. Social scientists may also use *analogy* for clarity's sake. *Definition of terms* is particularly important. Social scientists must be very clear about the boundaries of what they mean by a particular word.

In social science college courses, it is acceptable to use the first person when writing about your own reactions and experiences. However, your goal is usually to be a neutral observer, so most of the time writers use the third person.

32d What are different types of papers in the social sciences?

A case study is an intensive study of one group or individual. You should describe situations as a neutral observer, refraining from interpreting them unless your assignment states that you can add an interpretation at the end. Be careful not to present something as fact when it is really your interpretation or opinion of something you have seen.

Most case studies about an individual or a group will present the following:

1. Basic identifying information.
2. History.
3. Observations of behavior.
4. Conclusions (and perhaps recommendations).

Research Reports

Research reports in the social sciences can be based on primary field research or on secondary sources (articles and books that present the findings of other people's research).

Research Papers (Or Reviews of the Literature)

More often for students, social science research requires you to summarize, analyze, and synthesize SECONDARY SOURCES. These sources are usually articles and books that report or discuss the findings of other people's primary research. To prepare a review of literature, comprehensively gather and analyze the sources that have been published on a specific topic. "Literature" in this sense simply means "the body of work on a subject" and not creative work. Sometimes a review of the literature is a part of a longer paper, usually the "background" section of a research report. Other times the entire paper might be an extensive review of the literature.

32e What documentation style should I use in the social sciences?

The most commonly used documentation style for writing in the social sciences is that of the American Psychological Association (APA). APA style uses parenthetical references in the body of a paper and a reference list at the end. Chicago Manual style (CM) is also sometimes used.

NATURAL SCIENCES

32f What are the natural sciences?

The natural sciences include disciplines such as astronomy, biology, chemistry, geology, and physics. Scientists form and test hypotheses in order to explain cause and effect as systematically and objectively as possible.

The *scientific method* is a procedure for gathering information related to a specific hypothesis.

32g What are writing purposes and practices in the natural sciences?

Because scientists usually write to inform their AUDIENCE about factual information, SUMMARY and SYNTHESIS are important fundamental writing techniques.

Exactness is extremely important in scientific writing. Readers expect precise descriptions of procedures and findings, free of personal bias. Scientists expect to be able to replicate—repeat step by step—the experiment or process the researcher carried out and obtain the same outcome.

Completeness is as important as exactness in scientific writing. Without complete information, a reader can misunderstand the writer's message and reach a wrong conclusion. For example, a researcher investigating how plants grow in different types of soil needs to report these facts: an analysis of each soil type, the amount of daylight exposure for each plant, the soil's moisture content, the type and amount of fertilizer used, and all other related facts. By including all of this information, the researcher tells the reader how the conclusion in the written report was founded in the experiment or analysis.

Because science writing depends largely on objective observation rather than subjective comments, scientists generally avoid using the FIRST PERSON (I, we, our) in their writing. Another reason to avoid the first person is that the sciences generally focus on the experiment rather than on the person doing the experimenting. When writing for the sciences, you're often expected to follow fixed formats, which are designed to summarize a project and present its results efficiently. In your report, organize the information to achieve clarity and precision. Writers in the sciences sometimes use charts, graphs, tables, diagrams, and other illustrations to present material. In fact, illustrations, in many cases, can explain complex material more clearly than words can.

32h What documentation style should I use in the natural sciences?

If you use secondary sources in writing about the sciences, consult your instructor about which documentation style to use. The Council of Science Editors (CSE) has compiled style and documentation guidelines for the life sciences, the physical sciences, and mathematics.

32i How do I write different types of papers in the natural sciences?

Science reports tell about observations and experiments. They feature eight elements.

Parts of a science report:

1. Title	A precise description of what your report is about.	
2. Abstract	A short overview of your report.	
3. Introduction	A statement of your purpose and hypothesis. Background information and a review of any relevant literature.	
4. Methods and Materials	A description of your equipment, material, and procedures.	
5. Results	The information obtained from your efforts. Charts, graphs, and photographs to help present the data.	
6. Discussion	Your interpretation and evaluation of the results.	
7. Conclusion	Your conclusions about the hypothesis and the outcomes of your efforts. Theoretical implications that can be drawn from your work. Specific suggestions for further research.	
8. References Cited	A properly formatted list of references cited in any review of the literature.	

Writing Science Reviews

A *science review* is a paper discussing published information on a scientific topic or issue. Its usual purpose is to summarize for readers all the current knowledge about the topic or issue.

Some science reviews will synthesize information, i.e. put forward a new interpretation of existing material in the light of more recent evidence.

If you are required to write a science review, use the following guidelines:

1. Choose a very limited issue that is currently being researched.

2. Use the most current sources you can.

3. Accurately summarize and paraphrase source material.

4. Document your sources.

Interviewing and Citation   EXERCISE 32-1

A. Consider any research you have carried out involving interviews. Did you learn anything new about the interviewing process? What is it most important for you to remember next time?

B. Identify a *type* of secondary source which you have not used before in writing a science report. Locate an example of this type of source and cite it, using the documentation style your teacher requires.

MODULE 33: BUSINESS AND PUBLIC WRITING

BUSINESS WRITING

33a Who writes in the workplace?

Writing infuses most job situations, from corporate offices, not-for-profit agencies, schools, and health care facilities to farms and factories. People write to co-workers inside organizations; they write to customers or service providers outside them.

Even people who work independently (consultants, therapists, artists, craftspeople, and so on) keep records, apply for grants, correspond with customers, and advertise their services. Work-related correspondence needs to be professional in TONE, concise, and well informed. It can't contain slang, abbreviations, or informal words or expressions. Recipients expect it to use standard EDITED AMERICAN ENGLISH grammar, spelling, and punctuation. To be effective, always address the recipient by name, preferably last name until a relationship is established, and say straight out in the first paragraph what the communication is about. All workplace writing benefits from moving its way through the WRITING PROCESS as it seeks to INFORM or to PERSUADE. Indeed, never before in your writing have the acts of revising, editing, and proofreading carried as much weight as they do in business writing. The slightest error reflects negatively on the writer personally.

33d What are special considerations concerning business email?

E-mail is the primary form of written business communication today. Therefore, use it with special care, even though you might use it quite informally in your personal life. Here are some overriding guidelines for business use.

- Find out whether personal e-mail is tolerated. (You can usually find email policies in an employee manual.) Even if personal e-mail is permitted, realize that monitoring systems in most workplaces can quickly identify such e-mails. Therefore, you might want to avoid sending or receiving personal e-mails on your workplace computer.

- Avoid risking infecting your organization's entire computer system by scanning for viruses. If you aren't sure how to do this skillfully, ask before trying to scan your first attachment.

- Ask your supervisor whether there are restrictions regarding the size of attachments that you can send or receive. (Large attachments can overload the computer system at work.) If there are restrictions, use ETIQUETTE and alert your recipients about the size of any large attachments before you send them. In turn, ask senders to alert you before sending large ones to you.

- Protect the ID numbers and passwords you're assigned or have created to access your organization's electronic systems. As an employee, you're accountable for all activity conducted on password-protected accounts.

Some businesses automatically insert or require employees to insert a DISCLAIMER—a statement appended to the top or bottom of e-mails designed to protect the company from legal liability. The value of disclaimers is limited. Only a court of law can determine the effectiveness of such statements, but they might prove effective in limiting a company's liability in some cases.

33e How do I format and write memos?

Memos are usually exchanged internally (within an organization or business). Today e-mail takes the place of most memos, unless the correspondence requires a paper record or signature. The guidelines for writing e-mail also pertain to memos. The appropriate form of communication— paper memos or e-mail—depends on what's customary in your work environment.

The standard format of a memo includes two major parts: the headings and the body.

To: [Name your audience—a specific person or group.]

From: [Give your name and your title, if any.]

Date: [Give the date on which you write the memo.]

Re: [State your subject as specifically as possible in the "Subject" or "Re" line.]

The content calls for a beginning, middle, and end, with all parts holding closely to your topic. Don't ramble. If you need more than one or, at most, two pages, change your format into that of a brief report. Here are some guidelines for preparing a memo.

33f How do I write business letters?

Business letters are more formal and official than business e-mails or business memos. Choose to write a business letter, rather than a business e-mail, to add appropriate weight and respect to your message, for ceremonial occasions, and to ensure that your message is placed on the record and thereby becomes part of a "paper trail." Business letters generally fall into two official categories based on their purposes.

Regular business letters are business-to-business communications. These letters make up the majority of business correspondence. Always use company letterhead stationery, and follow any special guidelines for style or format that your company uses.

Social business letters are letters to business colleagues on matters that serve a business-related social function, such as congratulations on an achievement, condolences in a time of loss, thank you letters, invitations to social events, and the like. Given that these letters are written in a business context, social business letters may be written on company letterhead stationery.

There are some general guidelines for addressing recipients in business letters. The old-fashioned "To Whom It May Concern" rarely reaches the right person in an organization. Use the full name of your recipient whenever possible. If you can't locate a name, either through a phone call to a central switchboard or on the Internet, use a specific category—for example, "Dear Billing Department," placing the key word "Billing" first (not "Department of Billing"). Always use gender-neutral language.

33g How do I write a resume?

A resume details your accomplishments and employment history. Its PURPOSE is to help a potential employer (the AUDIENCE) determine whether you'll be a suitable candidate for employment. To make favorable impression, follow the guidelines for writing a resume in your handbook.

33h How do I write a job application letter?

A job application letter always needs to accompany your resume. Avoid repeating what's already on the resume. Instead, connect the company's expectations to your experience by emphasizing how your background has prepared you for the position. Your job application letter, more than your resume, reflects your energy and personality. Here are guidelines for writing a job application letter.

- Use one page only.
- Overall, think of your letter as a polite sales pitch about yourself and what benefits you can bring to the company. Don't be shy, but don't exaggerate.
- Use the same name, content, and format guidelines as for a business letter.
- Address the letter to a specific person. If you can't discover a name, use a gender-neutral title such as Dear Personnel Director.
- Open your letter by identifying the position for which you're applying.
- Mention your qualifications, and explain how your background will meet the job requirements.
- Make clear that you're familiar with the company or organization; your research will impress the employer.
- End by being specific about what you can do for the company. If the job will be your first, give your key attributes—but make sure they're relevant. For instance, you might state that you're punctual, self-disciplined, eager to learn, and hard-working.
- State when you're available for an interview and how the potential employer can reach you.
- Edit and proofread the letter carefully. If you have to hand-correct even one error, print out the letter again.

PUBLIC WRITING

33l What is public writing?

Public writing is writing addressed to members of your community, the community as a whole, or public officials. It might take the form of a letter to a newspaper, a magazine, or even your congressional representative. You might write a newspaper article or a local government proposal. On the Internet, you might post a book review or a message for a newsgroup. In all cases, you are writing for an audience you do not know personally and which does not know you. You should therefore take special care to analyze your audience and establish your credibility. Think about things you might have in common with your audience. Mention experiences you have had or research you have done which qualifies you to speak.

33m How do I write reports for the public?

Reports for the public vary in length, format, and content. An action brief from a political organization might consist of a few pages detailing recent developments on an issue of concern, such as a proposed law. Often these are published on Web sites or distributed through e-mail messages. A product update might contain news of technological advances, along with critical reviews and, perhaps, information on where to purchase an item. An impact study might explain the effect that a proposed construction project or new policy will have on the local environment, economy, or groups of people.

33n How do I write letters to my community or its representatives?

Letters to your community include letters to newspapers and magazines, statements of position for local or national newsletters, and similar self-published material. Such letters allow you to participate in discussion with a community of peers. When responding to a letter in the same publication, always state precisely what you are responding to. When writing to propose a solution to a community problem, keep the following guidelines in mind:

- Briefly explain the problem.
- State how your solution will solve all elements of the problem.
- Briefly address possible objections or alternatives.
- State why your solution is the best one.

Letters to civic and political leaders can be very effective. You might write in reaction to a proposed law, to object to an existing one, or to thank someone for action taken. State your purpose, be concise, and end by clearly stating what response, if any, you require.

33o What other types of pubic writing exist?

Many people write simply to express themselves or to entertain others. The most obvious examples are fiction, poetry, plays, film scripts, journals, and scrapbooks. In addition, many people produce newsletters, brochures, or similar documents, using not only words, but also graphic designs and images.

Writing for the Internet is perhaps the broadest form of public writing, in the sense that anything you post there is available to any reader with online access. On the Internet, you might post book reviews on a bookseller's Web site or a message about an upcoming concert to a newsgroup. You might create a Web site about your talents, interests, or accomplishments, or a Web site for an organization, a social cause, or a special interest group.

Business Writing

A. Compare the e-mails you write to friends with those you write to strangers. Which conventions do you ignore when you are writing to friends? Which conventions are you particularly careful to observe when writing to strangers?

B. Find examples of business letters you have received (e.g., unsolicited mail, letters from the government, replies from companies or colleges). Have the senders followed all the guidelines in your handbook? If not, has this affected the impact of the letters?

C. Locate advertisements for two different jobs which interest you. Adapt your résumé to each one and draft suitable job application letters.

A. Identify a problem in your home or school community to which you believe you have a solution. Draft a letter addressing community leaders in which you explain the problem and put forward your solution.

B. Choose any local organization that serves the public (for example, a political group or charity) and prepare a report detailing the organization's goals for the upcoming year and the strategy they plan to use to achieve those goals.

MODULE 34: MAKING ORAL PRESENTATIONS AND USING MULTI-MEDIA

34a What are oral presentations?

Oral presentations, which are speeches often supported with multimedia tools, are common not only in academic disciplines across the curriculum, but also in work and public settings. Preparing a presentation and drafting a paper involve similar processes. The rest of this module will provide additional information for preparing presentations and using multimedia tools.

34b How does my purpose focus my presentation?

Just as writing purposes change from one situation to the next, so do speaking purposes. The three main purposes for presentations are to entertain, to INFORM and to PERSUADE. In academic and work situations, the last two are most important.

For an oral presentation, determine your purpose, and keep it in mind as you draft and revise your speech. Common INFINITIVE PHRASES for an informative presentation include: *to explain why, to clarify, to show how, to report, to define, to describe*, and *to classify*. Common phrases for a persuasive presentation include: *to convince, to argue, to agree with, to disagree with, to win over, to defend*, and *to influence*.

34c How do I adapt my message to my listening audience?

Adapting your presentation to your listening audience means grabbing and holding their interest and being responsive to their viewpoints. Especially consider your listeners' prior knowledge of your topic, their desire to learn more, and whether they agree with your point of view. You'll find that your audience falls into one of three categories: *uninformed, informed*, or *mixed*.

34d How do I organize my presentation?

As with essays, an oral presentation has three parts: INTRODUCTION, BODY, and CONCLUSION. Within the body, you present your major points, with two to three supports for each point. Drafting a SENTENCE OUTLINE gets you close to your final form and forces you to sharpen your thinking.

All audience members want to know three things about a speaker: **Who are you? What are you going to talk about? Why should I listen?** To respond effectively to these unasked questions, try these suggestions.

- Grab your audience's attention with an interesting question, quotation, or statistic; a bit of background information; a compliment; or an anecdote. If necessary to establish your credibility—even if someone introduced you—briefly and humbly mention your qualifications speaker about your topic.

- Give your audience a road map of your talk: Tell where you're starting, where you're going, and how you intend to get there. Your listeners need to know that you won't waste their time.

Listening to a presentation is very different from reading an essay. When you're reading an article and lose sight of the main point, you can reread a few paragraphs. But when you're listing to a speech, you can't go back. As a result, audiences generally need help following the speaker's line of reasoning. To help your listeners keep sight of your main points, follow these guidelines:

- Signal clearly where you are on your road map by using cue word transitions such as *first, second*, and *third*; or *subsequently, therefore*, and *furthermore*; or *before, then*, and *next*.

- Define unfamiliar terms and concepts, and follow up with strong, memorable examples.

- Occasionally tell the audience what you consider significant, memorable, or especially relevant, and why. Do so sparingly, at key points.

- Provide occasional summaries at points of transition. At each interval, recap what you've covered and say how it relates to what's coming next.

When wrapping up your presentations, demonstrate that you haven't let key points simply float away. Try ending with these suggestions.

- Never let your voice volume fall or your clarity of pronunciation falter because the end is in sight.

- Don't introduce new ideas at the last minute.

- Signal that you're wrapping up your presentation using verbal cues, such as "In conclusion" and "Finally." When you say "finally," mean it!

- Make a dramatic, decisive statement; cite a memorable quotation; or issue a challenge. Allow a few seconds of silence, and then say "thank you." Use body language, such as stepping slightly back from the podium, and then sit down.

34e How do I research and write a presentation?

Doing research for an oral presentation requires the same kind of planning as doing research for written documents. To keep yourself calm and focused, divide the preparation into manageable tasks according to a realistic time line. Set small goals and stick to them to give yourself enough time to research, organize, and practice your presentation. An oral presentation won't have a

WORKS CITED or REFERENCES list to be read out, but your instructor might ask you to turn it in before or after you give your presentation.

Most of the preparation involved in an oral presentation is written work. Writing helps you take four important steps in your preparation:

(1) to organize your thoughts;

(2) to distance yourself from the ideas and remain objective;

(3) to pay attention to words and language;

(4) to polish for clarity and impact.

An oral presentation calls for the same careful language selection that you employ in your writing. Here are some tips on using language in oral presentations.

- Recognize the power of words. For example, read this statement by Winston Churchill, made after World War II: "Never in the field of human conflict was so much owed by so many to so few." Now try substituting the word *history* for "the field of human conflict." Note that while the single word *history* is more direct, using it destroys the powerful impact of the original words.

- Never alienate your audience by using words, phrases, or examples that could offend your listeners or people connected with them.

- Use GENDER-NEUTRAL LANGUAGE by avoiding sexist terms and inappropriate words and expressions.

- Present yourself with dignity in body language, tone of voice, and dress.

34f How do I incorporate multimedia into my oral presentation?

Multimedia elements such as visual aids, sound, and video can reinforce key ideas in your speech by providing illustrations or concrete images for the audience. If done well, they can make long explanations unnecessary and add to your credibility. Still, they can never take the place of a well prepared presentation.

34h What presentation styles can I use?

Presentation style is the way you deliver what you have to say. You may memorize it, read it, map it, or speak without notes. In general, avoid the last style until you have considerable experience giving speeches, unless otherwise instructed by your professor or someone in your workplace.

Memorizing Your Presentation

Memorized talks often sound unnatural. Unless you've mastered material well enough to recite it in a relaxed way, choose another presentation style. After all, no safety net exists if you forget a word or sentence. Fortunately, instructors rarely require you to memorize long presentations.

Reading Your Presentation

You can bore your audience when you read your entire presentation aloud. Burying your nose in sheets of paper creates an uncomfortable barrier between you and your audience because you appear painfully shy, unprepared, or insincere. If you have no choice but to read, avoid a monotone voice. Vary your pitch and style so that people can listen more easily.

Mapping Your Presentation

Mapping means creating a brief outline of the presentation's main points and examples and then using that outline to cue yourself as you talk.

34i How do I use my voice effectively?

Your voice is the vehicle for the presentation, so be aware of it. If you are unsure of your volume, ask the audience if they can hear you. If using a microphone, remember that you do not need to raise your voice. Speak fairly slowly and deliberately — but not slowly that there is no pace to the speech. Change the tone of your voice for emphasis. Insert planned pauses. In general, try to sound like yourself, but an intensified version.

34j How do I use nonverbal communication?

Body language will either add to or detract from your presentation. Make eye contact with your audience immediately; it will communicate confidence. If walking up to a podium, do not begin speaking before you have gotten there, squared off, and looked directly at the audience.

Use appropriate facial expressions to mirror the emotion contained in your message. Gestures, if natural and not overdone, can also help add emphasis. If you are unsure of where to place your hands, rest them on the podium. Body movements should be kept to a minimum and used in pace with the speech. Step forward or backward to indicate transitions, but do not sway from side to side. Dress appropriately for your audience and venue.

34k What can I do to practice for my oral presentation?

- Practice conveying ideas rather than particular words.
- Time yourself, cutting or adding material as necessary.
- Practice in front of a mirror or videotape yourself. Are your gestures natural? Do you make nervous movements that could be distracting?
- Practice in front of a friend. Ask if your main point was evident, if your points flowed, if the information seemed to fit in, if you looked and sounded natural, and if your visuals helped.

34l How do I make a collaborative presentation?

A common practice in many academic settings—and in business and public situations—is to present an oral report as part of a group. When you find yourself in this situation, use the following guidelines to create a successful collaborative presentation.

* Make sure, when choosing a topic or a position about an issue, that most members of the group are familiar with the subject.

* Lay out clearly each member's responsibilities for preparing the presentation. Try to define roles that complement one another; otherwise, you may end up with overlap in one area and no coverage in another.

* Agree on firm time limits for each person, if all members of the group are expected to speak for an equal amount of time. If there is no such requirement, people who enjoy public speaking can take more responsibility for delivery, while others can do more of the preparatory work or contribute in other ways.

* Allow enough time for practice. Good delivery requires practice. Plan at least four complete run-throughs of your you use them. Although each member can practice on his or her own part alone, schedule practice sessions for the entire presentation as a group. This will help you (a) work on transitions, (b) make sure the order of presenters, is effective, (c) clock the length of the presentation, and (d) cut or expand material accordingly.

* As you practice your presentation, have different group members watch in order to make suggestions, or videotape the practices. Notice your gestures. Do you look natural? Do you speak clearly and at an effective pace?

Oral Presentation

A. Imagine that you have been asked to speak to a group of high schoolers on an issue you know well. The talk should last 20 minutes. Formulate a working thesis and prepare an organizational outline. Consider what presentation aids would help you to get your message across.

B. Write a ten-minute speech on a topic of your choice to deliver in class. Highlight the key elements that you used to both capture and hold your audience's attention.

PART 5: | *Writing When English Is A Second Language*

MODULE 35: SINGULARS AND PLURALS

35a What are count and noncount nouns?

Count nouns name items that can be counted: *hand, ball, ring, interpretation.* Count nouns can be singular or plural (*hands, balls*).

Noncount nouns name things that are thought of as a whole and not separated into individual parts: *flour, heritage.* (Noncount nouns are used in the singular form only.) The following chart lists eleven categories of uncountable items, and it gives examples of noncount nouns in each category

If you want to check whether a noun is count or noncount, look it up in a dictionary such as the *Longman Dictionary of Contemporary English* or the *Oxford Advanced Learner's Dictionary.* These two dictionaries use the terms *countable* and *uncountable.* Noncount nouns are indicated by the letter *U.* Nouns without a *U* are always count.

Some nouns, including some listed in the previous Chart, can be countable or uncountable. Most such nouns name things that can be meant individually or as "wholes" made up of individual parts depending on the meaning you want to deliver in each sentence.

COUNT	Our instructor expects ten **papers** this semester. [In this sentence, *papers* is meant as individual, countable items.]
NONCOUNT	I ran out of **paper** before I finished. [In this sentence, *paper* is meant as a whole.]
COUNT	The **chickens** escaped from the coop. [In this sentence, *chickens* is meant as individual, countable items.]
NONCOUNT	Fried **chicken** is John's favorite food. [In this sentence, *chicken* is meant as a whole.]

When you are editing your writing, be sure that you have not added a plural -s to any noncount nouns, for they are always singular in form. ✤ VERB ALERT: Be sure to use a singular verb with any noncount noun that functions as a subject in your sentences. ✤

UNCOUNTABLE ITEMS

Groups of similar items making up "wholes":

baggage, fruit, garbage, hardware, makeup, and *others*

Abstractions

education, evidence, patience, luck, and *others*

Liquids

tea, milk, oil, ginger ale, wine, and *others*

Gases

air, hydrogen, nitrogen, oxygen, pollution, and *others*

Materials

gold, iron, paper, silver, wood, and *others*

Food

cheese, chicken, lamb, pasta, venison, and *others*

Particles or grains

com, grass, pepper, rye, sand, and *others*

Sports, games, activities

baseball, bridge, checkers, football, tennis, and *others*

Languages

French, German, Japanese, Latin, Thai, and *others*

Fields of study

architecture, chemistry, engineering, geology, nursing, and *others*

Events in nature

darkness, dew, fog, snow, lightning, and *others*

35b How do I use determiners with singular and plural nouns?

Determiners, also called *expressions of quantity*, are a group of words that traditionally are called adjectives but that are used to tell "how much" or "how many" about nouns. Additional names for determiners include *limiting adjectives, noun markers*, and *articles*.

Choosing the correct determiner with a noun depends first on whether the noun is count or noncount. For count nouns, you must also decide whether the noun is singular or plural. The following Chart lists many determiners and singular count nouns, noncount nouns, plural (count) nouns that they can accompany.

❖ USAGE ALERT: The phrases *a few* and *a little* convey the meaning "some": *I have a few worries* means "I have some worries." *The Joneses spend a little time with their children* means "The Joneses spend some time with their children."

Without the word *a few* and *a little* convey the meaning "almost none" or "not enough": *I have a few [or very few] worries* means "I have almost no worries." *The Joneses spend little time with their children* means "The Joneses spend almost no time with their children." ♣

DETERMINERS TO USE WITH COUNT AND NONCOUNT NOUNS

With every **singular count noun**, always use one of the determiners listed in Group 1.

    No   We live in **apartment** in large, white **house**.

    Yes   We live in **an apartment** in **that** large white **house**.

GROUP 1: DETERMINERS FOR SINGULAR COUNT NOUNS

a, an, the

    a chair   **an apple**   **the room**

one, any, some, every, each, either, neither, another, the other

    any chair   **each apple**   **another room**

my, our, your, his, her, its, their, nouns with 's or s'

    your chair   **its apple**   **Connie's room**

this, that

    this chair   **that apple**   **this car**

one, no, the first, the second, and so on

    one chair   **no apple**   **the fifth room**

With every **plural count noun**, use one of the determiners listed in Group 2. Count nouns are sometimes used without determiners.

    Yes   Be sure that the tomatoes you select are ripe.

    Yes   Tomatoes are tasty in salad.

GROUP 2: DETERMINERS FOR PLURAL COUNT NOUNS

the

    the signs   **the rugs**   **the headaches**

some, any, both, many, more, most, few, fewer, the fewest, a number of, other, several, all, all the, a lot of

    some signs   **many rugs**   **all headaches**

my, our, your, his, her, its, their, nouns with 's or s'

    our signs   **her rugs**   **students' headaches**

these, those

    these signs   **those rugs**   **these headaches**

no, two, three, four, and so on, the first, the second, the third, and so on

    no signs   **four rugs**   **the first headaches**   *(continued next page)*

DETERMINERS TO USE WITH COUNT AND NONCOUNT NOUNS *(continued)*

With every **noncount noun** (always singular), use one of the determiners listed in Group 3. Noncount nouns can also be used without determiners.

> **YES**   I bought the fish we ate for supper.

> **YES**   I bought fish for supper.

GROUP 3: DETERMINERS FOR NONCOUNT NOUNS

the

> **the cream**   **the light**   **the progress**

some, any, much, more, most, other, the other, little, less, the least, enough, all, all the, a lot of

> **enough cream**   **a lot of light**   **more progress**

my, our, your, his, her, its, their, nouns with 's or s'

> **their cream**   **its light**   **your progress**

this, that

> **this cream**   **that light**   **this progress**

no, the first, the second, the third, and so on

> **no cream**   **the first light**   **no progress**

35c How do I use *one of*, nouns as adjectives, and *states* in names or titles?

One of constructions include *one of the* and *one of* followed by a pronoun in the possessive case (*one of my, one of your, one of the, one of her, one of its, one of their*). Always use a plural noun as the object when you begin a phrase with *one of*.

> **No**   One of our **goal** is progress.
> **YES**   One of our **goals** is progress.

> **No**   One of his **pet** has died.
> **YES**   One of his **pets** has died.

The verb in *one of* constructions is always singular. The verb agrees with *one*, not with a plural noun: *One of the most important inventions of the twentieth century* **is** [not *are*] *television.*

Nouns Used as Adjectives

Some words that function as nouns can also function as adjectives.

> The bird's wingspan in ten **inches**. [*Inches* functions here as a noun.]

> The bird has a ten-**inch** wingspan. [*Inch* functions here as an adjective.]

Adjectives in English do not have plural forms. When you use a noun as an adjective, therefore, do not add -*s* or -*es* to the adjective even when the noun or pronoun it modifies is plural.

No	Many **Americans** students are basketball fans.
Yes	Many *American* students are basketball fans.

Names and Titles that Include the Word States

The word *states* is always plural. However, names such as the *United States* or the *Organization of American States* refer to singular things—a country and an organization—so they are singular nouns and therefore require singular verbs.

No	The United **State** has a large entertainment industry.
No	The **United States** have a large entertainment industry.
Yes	The United **States has** a large entertainment industry.

35d How do I use nouns with irregular plurals?

Some English nouns have irregular spellings. Here are some categories of nouns that often cause difficulties.

Plurals of Foreign Nouns and Other Irregular Nouns

Whenever you are unsure whether a noun is plural, look it up in a dictionary. If no plural is given for a singular noun, add an -*s*.

Many nouns from other languages that are used unchanged in English have only one plural. If two plurals are listed in the dictionary, look carefully for differences in meaning. Some words for example, keep the plural form from the original language for scientific usage and have another English-form plural that is used in non-science contexts. Examples include *antenna, antennae, antennas; formula, formulae, formulas; appendix, appendices, appendixes; index, indices, indexes; medium, media, mediums; cactus, cacti, cactuses;* and *fungus, fungi, funguses*.

Words of Latin origin that end in -*is* in their singular form become plural by substituting -*es*: *parenthesis, parentheses; thesis, theses; oasis, oases*, for example.

Other Words

Medical terms for diseases involving an inflammation end in -*itis*: *tonsillitis, appendicitis*. They are always singular.

The word *news*, although it ends in -*s*, is always singular: *The news is encouraging*. The words *people, police*, and *clergy* are always plural even though they do not end in -*s*: *The police are prepared*.

Identifying Nouns

Divide the following list of words into count and noncount nouns. Give the plural forms of the count nouns. List in all columns any words that can be both count and noncount.

advice	fern	jewelry	paragraph
book	flour	library	physics
calculator	gold	lightning	pollution
chocolate	hair	man	rain
desk	happiness	news	report
earring	homework	novel	storm
essay	honesty	occupation	time
experiment	information	paper	weather

	Noncount	**Count**	**Plural**
1.	_____	_____	_____
2.	_____	_____	_____
3.	_____	_____	_____
4.	_____	_____	_____
5.	_____	_____	_____
6.	_____	_____	_____
7.	_____	_____	_____
8.	_____	_____	_____
9.	_____	_____	_____
10.	_____	_____	_____
11.	_____	_____	_____
12.	_____	_____	_____
13.	_____	_____	_____
14.	_____	_____	_____
15.	_____	_____	_____
16.	_____	_____	_____
17.	_____	_____	_____
18.	_____	_____	_____
19.	_____	_____	_____

Noncount	Count	Plural
20. _____	_____	_____
21. _____	_____	_____
22. _____	_____	_____
23. _____	_____	_____
24. _____	_____	_____
25. _____	_____	_____
26. _____	_____	_____
27. _____	_____	_____
28. _____	_____	_____
29. _____	_____	_____
30. _____	_____	_____
31. _____	_____	_____
32. _____	_____	_____

Correct Forms   EXERCISE **35-2**

Choose the correct forms of the nouns in parentheses and write them on the lines at the right.

Example   Some _____ (hiker) return to   _____*hikers*_____
            _____ (nature) by walking the   _____*nature*_____
            Appalachian Trail.

1. Hikers with little _____ (money) but much _____   _____
    (fortitude) can begin the hike in Georgia   _____
    and continue to Maine.

2. The 2,015- _____ (mile) trail extends through   _____
    fourteen _____ (state).   _____

3. The trail passes cultivated _____ (farm) and   _____
    untamed _____ (wilderness).   _____

4. Since 1968 it has been one of two federally   _____
    protected _____ (trail) in the United   _____
    _____ (state).

5. Few _____ (hiker) have anything but praise for   _____
    their _____ (experience) on the trail.   _____

6. Many _____ (youngster) would gladly give   _____
    up _____ (piano) lessons or _____   _____
    (homework) to be climbing wooded _____   _____
    (path).

7. The Appalachian Trail is one of the nation's   _____
    _____ (treasure).

MODULE 36: ARTICLES

36a How do I use *a*, *an*, or *the* with singular count nouns?

The words *a* and *an* are called **indefinite articles**. The word *the* is called a **definite article**. Articles are one type of determiner. Articles signal that a noun will follow and that any modifiers between the article and the noun refer to that noun.

> **a** sandwich
> **a** fresh tuna sandwich
> **the** guest
> **the** welcome guest

Every time you use a singular count noun, the noun requires some kind of determiner. To choose between *a* or *an* and *the*, you need to determine whether the noun is **specific** or **nonspecific**. A noun is considered specific when anyone who reads your writing can understand from the context of your message exactly and specifically to what the noun is referring.

For nonspecific singular count nouns, use *a* (or *an*). When a singular noun is specific, use *the* or some other determiner. Use the following Chart to help you determine when a noun is specific and therefore requires the article *the*.

One common exception affects Rule 4 in the following Chart. Even when a noun has been used in an earlier sentence, it may require *a* (or *an*) if one or more descriptive adjectives come between the article and the noun: *I bought a computer today. It was a* [not *the*] *used computer.* Other information may make the noun specific so that *the* is correct. For example, *it was the used computer that I saw advertised on the bulletin board* uses *the* because the *that* clause lets a reader know which specific used computer is meant.

♣ USAGE ALERT: Use *an* before words that begin with a vowel sound. Use *a* before words that begin with a consonant sound. Words that begin with *h* or *u* can have either a vowel or a consonant sound. Make the choice based on the sound of the first word after the article even if that word is not the noun.

a cat	**an** axiom	**a** fine day
a unicorn	**an** underpass	**a** united front
a heretic	**an** herb	**a** happy smile ♣

> ## FOUR RULES: WHEN A SINGULAR COUNT NOUN IS SPECIFIC AND REQUIRES *THE*
>
> **Rule 1: A noun is specific and requires *the* when it names something unique or generally known.**
>
> > **The stars** lit his way. [Because *stars* is a generally known noun, it is a specific noun in the context of this sentence.]
>
> **Rule 2: A noun is specific and requires *the* when it names something used in a representative or abstract sense.**
>
> > **The termite** is actually a fascinating insect. [Because *termite* is a representative reference rather than a reference to a particular termite, it is a specific noun in the context of this sentence.]
>
> **Rule 3: A noun is specific and requires *the* when it names something defined elsewhere in the same sentence or in an earlier sentence.**
>
> > **The disease bilharzia** is a serious threat in some parts of the world. [The word *bilharzia* means a specific disease.]
> >
> > **The face in the painting** startled me. [*In the painting* defines exactly which *face* is meant, so *face* is a specific noun in this context.]
> >
> > I know **a good place** to eat. **The** *place* is near my home. [*Place* is not specific in the first sentence, so it uses *a*. In the second sentence *place* has been made specific by the first sentence, so it uses *the*.]
>
> **Rule 4: A noun is specific and requires *the* when it names something that can be inferred from the context.**
>
> > **The chef** is excellent. [If this sentence follows the two sentences about a place in Rule 3 above, *chef* is specific in this context.]

One common exception affects Rule 3 in the Four Rules Chart. A noun may still require *a* (or *an*) after the first use if one or more descriptive adjectives comes between the article and the noun: *I bought **a sweater** today. It was a* [not *the*] **red sweater.**

Other information may make the noun specific so that *the* is correct. For example, **It was the red sweater that I saw in the store yesterday** uses *the* because the *that* clause makes specific which red sweater is meant.

36b How do I use articles with plural nouns and with noncount nouns?

With plural nouns and noncount nouns, you must decide about articles whether to use *the* or to use no article at all.

What you learned about nonspecific and specific nouns can help you make the choice between using *the* or using no article. The Four Rules Chart explains when a singular count noun's meaning is specific and calls for *the*. Plural nouns and noncount nouns with specific meanings usually use *the* in the same circumstances. However, a plural noun or a noncount noun with a general or nonspecific meaning usually does not use *the*.

I need **nuts** and **chocolate chips** for this recipe. I also need **flour**.

Plural Nouns

A plural noun's meaning may be specific because it is widely known.

The crops may not survive the drought. [Because the meaning of *crops* is widely understood, *the* is correct to use. This example is related to Rule 1 in the Four Rules Chart.]

A plural noun's meaning may also be made specific by a word, phrase, or clause in the same sentence.

I don't know **the students** in my apartment building. [Because the phrase *in my apartment building* makes *students* specific, *the* is correct to use. This example is related to Rule 3 in the Four Rules Chart.]

A plural noun's meaning usually becomes specific by being used in an earlier sentence.

We have begun doing **exercises**. We hope **the exercises** will develop our stamina. [*Exercises* is used in a general sense in the first sentence, without *the*. Because the first sentence makes *exercises* specific, *the exercises* is correct in the second. This example is related to Rule 4 in the Four Rules Chart.]

A plural noun's meaning may be made specific by the context.

The aerobics should be particularly beneficial. [In the context of the sentences about exercises, *aerobics* is specific and calls for *the*. This example is related to Rule 4 in the Four Rules Chart.]

Noncount Nouns

Noncount nouns are always singular in form. Like plural nouns, noncount nouns use either *the* or no article. When a noncount noun's meaning is specific, use *the* before it. If its meaning is general or nonspecific, do not use *the*.

Li served us **tea**. He had brought the tea from China. [*Tea* is a noncount noun. This example is related to Rule 4 in the Four Rules Chart. By the second sentence, tea has become specific, so *the* is used.]

Li served us **the tea that he had brought from China**. [*Tea* is a noncount noun. This example is related to Rule 3 in the Four Rules Chart: *Tea* is made specific by the clause *that he had brought from China*, so *the* is used.]

Generalizations with Plural or Noncount Nouns

Rule 2 in the Four Rules Chart tells you to use *the* with singular count nouns used in a general sense. With generalizations using plural or noncount nouns, omit *the*.

No   The elephants live longer than the zebras.

YES   Elephants live longer than zebras.

36c How do I use *the* with proper nouns and with gerunds?

Proper Nouns

Proper nouns name specific people, places, or things. Most proper nouns do not require articles: *I spent my holidays with Asda at Cape Cod.* As shown in the following Chart, however, certain types of proper nouns do require *the*.

PROPER NOUNS THAT USE *THE*

Nouns with the pattern *the . . . of . . .*

    the United States **of** America
    the Isle **of** Wight
    the Fourth **of** July
    the University **of** Illinois

Plural proper nouns

    the Randalls   **the** Atlanta Braves
    the Trossachs
    the Smoky Mountains   [but Mount Everest]
    the Virgin Islands   [but Staten Island]
    the Great Lakes   [but Lake Titicaca]

Collective proper nouns (nouns that name a group)

    the Lions Club
    the League of Women Voters

Some (but not all) geographical features

    the Amazon River   **the** Gobi Desert
    the Indian Ocean

Two countries and one city

    the Congo   **the** Sudan
    the Hague [capital of the Netherlands]

Gerunds

Gerunds are present participles (the *-ing* form of verbs) used as nouns: *Skating* is *challenging*. Gerunds usually are not preceded by *the*.

    No   The **constructing** new bridges is necessary to improve traffic flow.

    Yes   **Constructing** new bridges is necessary to improve traffic flow.

Use *the* before a gerund when two conditions are met: (1) the gerund is used in a specific sense and (2) the gerund does not have a direct object.

    No   The **designing** fabric is a fine art. [*Fabric* is a direct object of *designing*, so *the* should not be used.]

    Yes   **Designing** fabric is a fine art. [*Designing* is a gerund, so *the* is not used.]

    Yes   The **designing** of fabric is a fine art. [*The* is used because *fabric* is the object of the preposition *of* and *designing* is meant in a specific sense.]

Articles

In the following blanks write *a, an,* or *the* as needed. If no article is necessary, put a *0* in the blank.

In 1872 _____ Congress passed _____ Yellowstone Act, establishing Yellowstone as _____ first national park in _____ United States and indeed in _____ world. For centuries _____ wealthy set aside _____ private preserves for their own recreational use, but except for _____ few public parks in _____ major cities, setting aside _____ vast area for _____ national enjoyment was _____ novel idea. It became _____ popular one. Since _____ founding of _____ Yellowstone, forty-nine other national parks have been established in _____ United States and its territories.

_____ Yellowstone is _____ largest of this country's national parks. It occupies 3,472 square miles at _____ juncture of _____ states of _____ Wyoming, Montana, and _____ Idaho. Although _____ Native American habitation goes back 800 years, _____ park's remoteness from _____ centers of _____ population left it undiscovered by _____ white settlers until _____ nineteenth century.

_____ John Colter is thought to be _____ first explorer to venture into _____ area. Colter was _____ member of _____ Lewis and Clark Expedition. When _____ expedition returned to _____ St. Louis, he remained in _____ region of _____ upper Missouri River to become _____ mountain man. In 1807 he explored _____ Yellowstone Basin. When he later wrote about _____ thermal wonders of _____ area, many people did not believe such natural phenomena existed. They continue to amaze _____ tourists today.

Yellowstone is truly _____ natural fantasy land. Its features include _____ geysers, hot springs, and _____ mud volcanoes along with _____ forests, _____ lakes, mountains, and _____ waterfalls. _____ most famous of _____ park's attractions is _____ "Old Faithful," _____ geyser which erupts on _____ average of every 65 minutes. It shoots _____ steaming water from 120 to 170 feet into _____ air. Each eruption lasts approximately four minutes and spews out 10,000 _____ gallons of _____ water.

Other active geysers in _____ six geyser basins may be less predictable but are no less spectacular. Some of _____ more than 200 just emit _____ steam and _____ spooky underground noises. _____ silica in _____ geyser water builds up around _____ walls of _____ geyser craters, making _____ craters very colorful and beautiful to view even when _____ geysers are not spouting.

_____ hot springs are another Yellowstone attraction. There are more than 3,000 of them ranged throughout _____ park. Some, such as _____ Emerald Spring, are remarkable because of their color. _____ Morning Glory Spring looks like its flower namesake.

_____ Yellowstone Lake, _____ Golden Gate Canyon, and _____ Tower Falls are just some of _____ features that combine with _____ geysers and _____ hot springs to make _____ Yellowstone National Park _____ extraordinary place to visit.

MODULE 37: WORD ORDER

37a How do I understand standard and inverted word order in sentences?

In **standard word order**, the most common pattern for declarative sentences in English, the subject comes before the verb.

With **inverted word order**, the main verb or an auxiliary verb comes before the subject. The most common use of inverted word order in English is forming direct questions. Questions that can be answered with "yes" or "no" begin with a form of *be* used as a main verb, or with an auxiliary verb (*be*, *do*, or *have*), or with a modal auxiliary.

QUESTIONS THAT CAN BE ANSWERED WITH YES OR NO

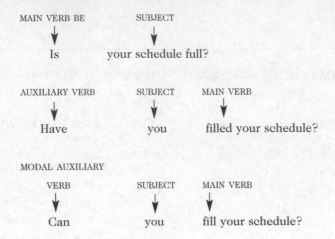

MAIN VERB BE → Is   SUBJECT → your schedule full?

AUXILIARY VERB → Have   SUBJECT → you   MAIN VERB → filled your schedule?

MODAL AUXILIARY VERB → Can   SUBJECT → you   MAIN VERB → fill your schedule?

To form a **yes/no question** with a verb other than *be* as the main verb and when there is no auxiliary or modal as part of a verb phrase, use the appropriate form of the auxiliary verb *do*.

AUXILIARY VERB → Does   SUBJECT → Mako   MAIN VERB → wear only black?

You may sometimes see a question formed with the main verb at the beginning.

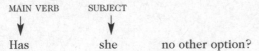

MAIN VERB → Has   SUBJECT → she   no other option?

It is equally correct and more common to see the question formed with *do* as an auxiliary and *have* as a main verb, following the pattern of auxiliary verb- subject-main verb: *Does she have no other option?*

A question that begins with a question-forming word like *why*, *when*, *where*, or *how* cannot be answered with "yes" or "no": *Why did the doorbell ring?* Such a question communicates that information must be provided to answer it; the answer cannot be "*yes*" or "*no*." Information is needed: for example, *Suki rang it*.

Most information questions follow the same rules of inverted word order as yes/no questions.

INFORMATION QUESTIONS: INVERTED ORDER

QUESTION WORD → Why   MAIN VERB BE → is   SUBJECT → Suki early?

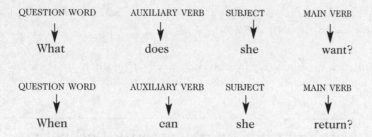

When **who** or **what** functions as the subject in a question, however, use standard word order.

INFORMATION QUESTIONS: STANDARD ORDER

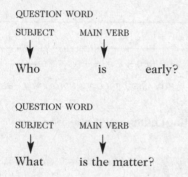

♣ ALERT: When a question has more than one auxiliary verb, put the subject after the first auxiliary verb:

The same rules apply to emphatic exclamations: *Was that soup delicious! Did it hit the spot!*

Also, when you use negatives such as *never, hardly ever, seldom, rarely, not only,* or *nor* to start a clause, use **inverted order**. These sentence pairs show the differences:

I have never been so embarrassed.
  (**standard order**)
Never have I been so embarrassed!
  (**inverted order**)
Jo is not only a chemist but also a writer.
Not only is Jo a chemist, but she is also a writer.

Paul did not study, and his brother didn't either.
Paul did not study, and neither did his brother.

✣ USAGE ALERT: With indirect questions, use standard word order: *She asked when Suki could return* (not *She asked when could Suki return.*) ✣

✣ STYLE ALERT: Word order deliberately inverted can be effective, when used sparingly, to create emphasis in a sentence that is neither a question nor an exclamation.✣

37b How can I understand the placement of adjectives?

Adjectives modify—that is, they describe or limit—nouns, pronouns, and word groups that function as nouns. In English, an adjective comes directly before the noun it describes. However, when more than one adjective describes the same noun, several sequences may be possible. The following Chart shows the most common order for positioning several adjectives.

WORD ORDER FOR MORE THAN ONE ADJECTIVE

1. **Determiners, if any**: *a, an, the, my, your, Jan's, this, that, these, those,* and so on

2. **Expressions of order, including ordinal numbers, if any**: *first, second, third, next, last, final,* and so on

3. **Expressions of quantity, including cardinal (counting) numbers, if any**: *one, two, three, few, each, every, some,* and so on

4. **Adjectives of judgment or opinion, if any**: *pretty, happy, ugly, sad, interesting, boring,* and so on

5. **Adjectives of size and/or shape, if any**: *big, small, short, round, square,* and so on

6. **Adjectives of age and/or condition, if any**: *new, young, broken, dirty, shiny,* and so on

7. **Adjectives of color, if any**: *red, green, blue,* and so on

8. **Adjectives that can all be used as nouns, if any**: *French, Protestant, metal, cotton,* and so on

9. **The noun**

1	2	3	4	5	6	7	8	9
A		few		tiny		red		ants
The	last	six					Thai	carvings
My			fine		old		oak	table

37c How can I understand the placement of adverbs?

Adverbs modify—that is, describe or limit—verbs, adjectives, other adverbs, or entire sentences. Adverbs are usually positioned first, in the middle, or last in a clause. The following chart summarizes adverb types, what they tell about the words they modify, and where each type can be placed.

TYPES OF ADVERBS AND WHERE TO POSITION THEM

ADVERBS OF MANNER

- describe how something is done
- usually are in middle or last position

> Boris **thoroughly** cleaned his car.
> Boris cleaned his car **thoroughly**.

ADVERBS OF TIME

- describe when or how long about an event
- usually are in the first or last position

> **First**, he scrubbed the wheels.
> He scrubbed the wheels **first**.

- include *just*, *still*, and *already*, and similar adverbs, which usually are in the middle position

> He had **already** vacuumed the interior.

ADVERBS OF PLACE

- describe *where* an event takes place
- usually are in the last position

> He cleaned the car **outdoors**.

ADVERBS OF FREQUENCY

- describe *how often* an event takes place
- usually are in the middle position

> Boris **rarely** takes the car to a car wash.

- are in the first position when they modify an entire sentence (see Sentence Adverbs below)

> **Occasionally**, he waxes the car.

ADVERBS OF DEGREE OR EMPHASIS

- describe how much or to what extent about other modifiers
- are directly before the word they modify

> Boris is **extremely** proud of his car. [*Extremely* modifies *proud*.]

- include *only*, which is easy to misplace

SENTENCE ADVERBS

- modify the entire sentence rather than just one word or a few words
- include transitional words and expressions as well as *maybe*, *probably*, *possibly*, *fortunately*, *unfortunately*, *incredibly*, and others
- are in first position

Surprisingly, he doesn't mind loaning it.

❖ PUNCTUATION ALERT: Unless they are very short (fewer than five letters), adverbs in the first position are usually followed by a a comma. ❖

❖ USAGE ALERT: Do not let an adverb in a middle position separate a verb from its direct object or indirect objective. ❖

Question Form

Convert the following sentences into questions.

EXAMPLE   We should have called first.
Should we have called first?

1. That pizza is enough for all of us.

   _____

2. Henri understood the lesson.

   _____

3. You have my lab manual. (two ways)

   _____

4. Juanita will have finished by the time we return.

   _____

5. Everyone in the room can see the screen.

   _____

Rewrite the following sentences using correct word order.

EXAMPLE   Our English class took a field final trip to an auction large house.
           Our English class took a final field trip to a large auction house.

1. Katrina purchased two Limoges lovely boxes.

     _____

2. A black leather comfortable chair appealed to Nils.

     _____

3. He waited to bid on it patiently.

     _____

4. We left unfortunately before it was auctioned.

     _____

5. Marios wanted a wooden old table but bought a silver worn spoon.

     _____

6. Suchen outbid someone for a green round interesting hatbox.

     _____

7. She was delighted extremely to get it.

     _____

8. She has wanted often one.

     _____

9. The English entire class bought something except Ingrid.

     _____

10. Because she brought an empty small purse, she bought nothing at all.

     _____

MODULE 38: PREPOSITIONS

Prepositions function with other words in prepositional phrases. Prepositional phrases usually indicate **where** (direction or location), **how** (by what means or in what way), or **when** (at what time or how long), about the words they modify.

This chapter can help you with several uses of prepositions, which function in combination with other words in ways that are often idiomatic. An idiom's meaning differs from the literal meaning of each individual word. For example, *Yao-Ming broke into a smile* means that a smile appeared on Yao-Ming's face. However, the dictionary definitions of *break* and *into* imply that *broke into a smile* means "shattered the form of" a smile. Knowing which preposition to use in a specific context takes much experience reading, listening to, and speaking the language. A dictionary like the *Longman Dictionary of Contemporary English* or the *Oxford Advanced Learner's Dictionary* can be especially helpful when you need to find the correct preposition to use in cases not covered by this chapter.

38a How can I recognize prepositions?

The following Chart shows many common prepositions.

COMMON PREPOSITIONS		
about	despite	out
above	down	out of
according to	during	outside
across	except	over
after	except for	past
against	excepting	regarding
along	for	round
along with	from	since
among	in	through
apart from	in addition to	throughout
around	in back of	till
as	in case of	to
as for	in front of	toward
at	in place of	under
because of	inside	underneath
before	in spite of	unlike
behind	instead of	until
below	into	up
beneath	like	upon
beside	near	up to
between	next	with
beyond	of	within
but	off	without
by	on	
by means of	onto	
concerning	on top of	

38b How do I use prepositions with expressions of time and place?

The following Chart shows how to use the prepositions *in, at*, and *on* to deliver some common kinds of information about time and place. The Chart, however, does not convey every preposition that indicates time or place, nor does it cover all uses of *in, at*, and *to*. For example, it does not explain the subtle different in meaning delivered by the prepositions *at* and *in* in these two correct sentences: I have a checking account **at** that bank and I have a safe-deposit box **in** that bank. Also, the Chart does not include expressions that operate outside the general rules. (Both these sentences are correct: You ride **in** the car and You ride **on** the bus.)

USING *IN*, *AT*, AND *ON* TO SHOW TIME AND PLACE

TIME

in **a year or a month** (*during* is also correct but less common)
    in 1995   **in** May

in **a period of time**
    in a few months (seconds, days, years)

in **a period of the day**
    in the morning (afternoon, evening)
    in the daytime (morning, evening), but **at** night

on **a specific day**
    on Friday   **on** my birthday

at **a specific time or period of time**
    at noon   **at** 2:00
    at dawn   **at** nightfall
    at takeoff (the time a plane leaves)
    at breakfast (the time a specific meal takes place)

PLACE

in **a location surrounded by something else**
    in the province of Alberta
    in Utah   **in** downtown Bombay
    in the kitchen   **in** my apartment
    in the bathtub

at **a specific location**
    at your house   **at** the bank
    at the corner of Third Avenue and Main Street

on the top or the surface of something
    on page 20   **on** the mezzanine
    on Washington   **on** street level
    on the second floor, but **in** the attic or **in** the basement

38c How do I use prepositions in phrasal verbs?

Phrasal verbs, also called *two-word verbs* and *three-word verbs*, are verbs that combine with prepositions to deliver their meaning.

In some phrasal verbs, the verb and the preposition should not be separated by other words: *Look at the moon* [not ***Look** the moon **at**.*]

In **separable phrasal verbs**, other words in the sentence can separate the verb and the preposition without interfering with meaning: *I **threw away** my homework* is as correct as *I **threw** my homework **away***.

Here is a list of some common phrasal verbs. The ones that cannot be separated are marked with an asterisk (*).

LIST OF SELECTED PHRASAL VERBS

ask out	get along with*	look into
break down	get back	look out for*
bring about	get off*	look over
call back	go over*	make up
drop off	hand in	run across*
figure out	keep up with*	speak to*
fill out	leave out	speak with*
fill up	look after*	throw away
find out	look around	throw out

Position a pronoun object between the words of a separable phrasal verb: *I threw **it** away*. Also, you can position an object phrase of several words between the parts of a separable phrasal verb: *I threw **my research paper** away*. However, when the object is a clause, do not let it separate the parts of the phrasal verb: *I threw away **all the papers that I wrote last year***.

Many phrasal verbs are informal and are used more in speaking than in writing. For academic writing, a more formal verb may be more appropriate than a phrasal verb. In a research paper, for example, *propose* or *suggest* might be better choices than *come up with*. For academic writing acceptable phrasal verbs include *believe in, benefit from, concentrate on, consist of, depend on, dream of* (or *dream about*), *insist on, participate in, prepare for*, and *stare at*. None of these phrasal verbs can be separated.

38d How do I use prepositions with past participles?

Past participles are verb forms that function as ADJECTIVES. Past participles end in either –*ed* or –*d*, or in an equivalent irregular form.When past participles follow the LINKING VERB *be*, itg is easy to confuse them with PASSIVE verbs, which have the same endings. Passive verbs describe actions. Past participles, because they act as adjectives, modify NOUNS and PRONOUNS and often describe situations and conditions. Passive verbs follow the pattern *be* + past participle + *by: The child **was frightened by** a snake*. An expression containing a past participle, however, can use either *be* or another linking verb, and it can be followed by either *by* or a different preposition.

The child **seemed frightened by** snakes.

The child **is frightened** of all snakes.

Here is a list of expressions containing participles and the prepositions that often follow them. Look in a dictionary for others.

SELECTED PAST PARTICIPLE PHRASES + PREPOSITIONS

be accustomed to	be interested in
be acquainted with	be known for
be composed of	be located in
be concerned/worried about	be made of (*or* from)
be disappointed with (*or* in someone)	be married to
be discriminated against	be pleased/satisfied with
be divorced from	be prepared for
be excited about	be tired of (*or* from)
be finished/done with	

38e How do I use prepositions in expressions?

In many common expressions, different prepositions convey great differences in meaning. For example, four prepositions can be used with the verb *agree* to create five different meanings:

agree to = to give consent (*I cannot **agree to** buy you a new car.*)

agree about = to arrive at a satisfactory understanding (*We **agree about** your needing a car.*)

agree on = to arrive at a satisfactory understanding (*You and the seller must **agree on** a price for the car.*)

agree with = to have the same opinion (*I **agree with** you that you need a car.*)

agree with = be suitable or healthful (*The idea of having such a major expense does not **agree with** me.*)

You can find entire books filled with English expressions that include prepositions. This list shows a few that you are likely to use often.

LIST OF SELECTED EXPRESSIONS WITH PREPOSITIONS

ability in	different from	involved with [*someone*]
access to	faith in	knowledge of
accustomed to	familiar with	made of
afraid of	famous for	married to
angry with *or* at	frightened by	opposed to
authority on	happy with	patience with
aware of	in charge of	proud of
based on	independent of	reason for
capable of	in favor of	related to
certain of	influence on *or* over	suspicious of
confidence in	interested in	time for
dependent on	involved in [*something*]	tired of

In, At, On

In the following blanks, use *in*, *at*, or *on* to show time or place.

EXAMPLE   The University of Virginia, located _____ Charlottesville, was founded
by Thomas Jefferson.

The University of Virginia, located _____*in*_____ Charlottesville, was founded
by Thomas Jefferson.

1.   Others wanted to put the new university _____ Staunton or Lexington.

2.   _____ August 1818, Jefferson convinced legislators to place it _____
Albermarle County.

3.   Jefferson designed the university so that students and faculty lived together
_____ an "academical village."

4.   A rotunda building for classes sits _____ one end of a lawn.

5.   _____ both sides of the lawn are sets of student rooms.

6.   Faculty members lived _____ pavilions between the sets of student rooms.

7.   The university opened _____ 1825.

8.   _____ his last visit to the university, Jefferson stood _____ a window
_____ the rotunda and surveyed the campus.

9.   _____ his deathbed, Jefferson included founding the university as one of the
three accomplishments for which he hoped to be remembered.

10. Today students at the University of Virginia consider it an honor to live
_____ the rooms Jefferson designed.

Phrasal Verbs

A: Fill in each blank with a phrasal verb from page 452. Use each phrasal verb only once. More than one phrasal verb may be appropriate for some blanks.

EXAMPLE   Walid cannot _____ why it takes so long to register.

Walid cannot _*figure out*_ why it takes so long to register.

1. Ravi will _____ Walid and explain.

2. First he must _____ all the forms.

3. He must _____ all his records to make sure he does not _____ anything.

4. He must then _____ the forms at the registrar's office.

5. Should he _____ the forms without some vital information, the registrar will _____ him _____ to get it.

6. Walid will have to _____ the forms and _____ what is missing.

7. He must not _____ any records until he has finished the procedure.

B: Now rewrite the sentences above using as many formal verbs as possible.

1. _____

2. _____

3. _____

4. _____

5. _____

6. _____

7. _____

MODULE 39: GERUNDS, INFINITIVES, AND PARTICIPLES

39a How can I use gerunds and infinitives as subjects?

Gerunds are used more commonly than infinitives as subjects. Sometimes, however, either is acceptable.

Choosing the best instructor is difficult.
To choose the best instructor is difficult.

❖ VERB ALERT: When a gerund or an infinitive is used alone as a subject, it is singular and requires a singular verb. When two or more gerunds or infinitives create a compound subject, they require a plural verb. ❖

39b When do I use a gerund, not an infinitive, as an object?

Some verbs must be followed by gerunds used as direct objects. Other verbs must be followed by infinitives. Still other verbs can be followed by either a gerund or an infinitive. (A few verbs can change meaning depending on whether they are followed by a gerund or an infinitive.) The following Chart lists common verbs that must be followed by gerunds, not infinitives.

Sasha **considered** *dropping* [not to *drop*] her accounting class.
She **was having** trouble *understanding* [not to *understand*] the teacher.
Her advisor **recommended** *hiring* [not to *hire*] a tutor.

VERBS AND EXPRESSIONS THAT USE GERUNDS AFTER THEM		
acknowledge	detest	mind
admit	discuss	object to
advise	dislike	postpone
anticipate	dream about	practice
appreciate	enjoy	put off
avoid	escape	quit
cannot bear	evade	recall
cannot help	favor	recommend
cannot resist	finish	regret
complain about	give up	resent
consider	have trouble	resist
consist of	imagine	risk
contemplate	include	suggest
defer from	insist on	talk about
delay	keep (on)	tolerate
deny	mention	understand

Gerund After go

Go is usually followed by an infinitive: *We can **go to hear** [not go hearing] a band after the show.* Sometimes, however, *go* is followed by a gerund in phrases such as *go swimming, go fishing, go shopping,* and *go driving: I will **go swimming** [not go to swim] after class.*

Gerund After be + *Complement* + *Preposition*

Many common expressions use a form of the verb *be* plus a complement plus a preposition. In such expressions, use a gerund, not an infinitive, after the preposition. Here is a list of some of the most frequently used expressions in this pattern.

LIST OF SELECTED *BE* + COMPLEMENT + PREPOSITION EXPRESSIONS

be (get) accustomed to	be interested in
be angry about	be prepared for
be bored with	be responsible for
be capable of	be tired of
be committed to	be (get) used to
be excited about	be worried about

Hari **is tired** *of waiting* [not to *wait*] for his grades.
Katrina **is bored with** *learning* [not to *learn*] to ski.

❖ USAGE ALERT: Always use a gerund, not an infinitive, as the object of a preposition. Be especially careful when the word *to* is functioning as a preposition in a phrasal verb: *We are **committed to changing** [not to change] the rules.* ❖

39c When do I use an infinitive, not a gerund, as an object?

The following Chart lists selected common verbs and expressions that must be followed by infinitives, not gerunds, as objects.

Niki **hoped** *to go* [not hoped *going*] home for the holidays.
Astrid **decided** *to remain* [not *remaining*] in the dormitory.

VERBS AND EXPRESSIONS THAT USE INFINITIVES AFTER THEM			
afford	claim	hope	promise
agree	consent	intend	refuse
aim	decide	know how	seem
appear	decline	learn	struggle
arrange	demand	like	tend
ask	deserve	manage	threaten
attempt	do not care	mean	volunteer
be left	expect	offer	vote
beg	fail	plan	wait
cannot afford	give permission	prepare	want
care	hesitate	pretend	would like

Infinitives After be + Complement

Gerunds are common in constructions that use forms of the verb *be*, a complement, and a preposition. However, use an infinitive, not a gerund, when *be* plus a complement is not followed by a preposition.

We **are glad** *to see* [not *seeing*] you so happy.
Maria **is ready** *to learn* [not *learning*] to cook.

Infinitives to Indicate Purpose

Use an infinitive in expressions that indicate purpose: *I wore an old shirt **to gather** berries.* This sentence means "I wore an old shirt for the purpose of gathering berries." *To gather* delivers the idea of purpose more concisely than expressions such as "so that I can" or "in order to."

Infinitives with the first, the last, the one

Use an infinitive after the expressions *the first, the last,* and *the one*: *Colin is the first **to start** [not starting] and the last **to quit** [not quitting] on this project.*

Unmarked Infinitives

Infinitives used without the word *to* are called **unmarked infinitives** or **bare infinitives**. An unmarked infinitive may be hard to recognize because it is not preceded by *to*. Some common verbs followed by unmarked infinitives are *feel, have, hear, let, listen to, look at, make,* (meaning "compel") *notice, see,* and *watch*.

> Please make your son **behave.** [not to *behave*]
> [unmarked infinitive]

> I asked your son **to behave.**
> [marked infinitive]

The verb *help* can be followed by either a marked or an unmarked infinitive. Either is correct: *Help me* **count** [or **to count**] *the receipts.*

❖ USAGE ALERT: Be careful to use parallel structure correctly when you use two or more gerunds or infinitives after verbs. If two or more verbal objects follow one verb, put the verbals into the same form.

No	We like **skating** and **to ski**.
YES	We like **skating** and **skiing**.
YES	We like **to skate** and **to ski**.

Conversely, if you are using verbal objects with compound predicates be sure to use the kind of verbal that each verb requires.

| **No** | We enjoyed **scuba diving** but do not plan **sailing** again. [*Enjoyed* requires a gerund object and *plan* requires an infinitive object.] |
| **YES** | We enjoyed **scuba diving** but do not plan **to sail** again. ❖ |

39d How does meaning change when certain verbs are followed by a gerund or an infinitive?

With Stop

The verb *stop* followed by a gerund means "finish, quit." *Stop* followed by an infinitive means "stop or interrupt one activity to begin another."

> We **stopped eating.** [We finished our meal.]
> We **stopped to eat.** [We stopped another activity, such as driving, in order to eat.]

With remember and forget

The verb *remember* followed by an infinitive means "not to forget to do something": *I **must remember to talk** with Isa. Remember* followed by a gerund means "recall a memory": *I **remember talking** in my sleep last night.*

The verb *forget* followed by an infinitive means "to not do something": *If you **forget to put** a stamp on that letter, it will be returned. Forget* followed by a gerund means "to do something and

GERUNDS, INFINITIVES, AND PARTICIPLES

not recall it": *I forget having put the stamps in the refrigerator*.

With try

The verb *try* followed by an infinitive means "made an effort": *I tried to find your jacket.* Followed by a gerund, *try* means "experimented with": *I tried jogging but found it too difficult.*

39e Why is the meaning unchanged whether a gerund or an infinitive follows sense verbs?

Sense verbs include words such as *see, notice, hear, observe, watch, feel, listen to,* and *look at.* The meaning of these verbs is usually not affected whether it is followed by a gerund or an infinitive as an object. I **saw** the water **rise** and I **saw** the water **rising** both have the same meaning in American English.

39f How do I choose between *-ing* and *-ed* forms for adjectives?

Deciding whether to use the *-ing* form (present participle) or the *-ed* (past participle of a regular verb) as an adjective in a specific sentence can be difficult. For example, I am **amused** and I am **amusing** are both correct in English, but their meanings are very different. To make the right choice, decide whether the modified noun or pronoun is causing or experiencing what the participle describes.

Use a present participle (*-ing*) to modify a noun or pronoun that is the agent or the cause of the action.

Mica described your **interesting** plan. [The noun *plan* causes what its modifier describes—*interest*, so *interesting* is correct.]

I find your plan **exciting**. [The noun *plan* causes what its modifier describes— *excitement*, so *exciting* is correct.]

Use a past participle (*-ed* in regular verbs) to modify a noun or pronoun that experiences or receives whatever the modifier describes.

An **interested** committee wants to hear your plan. [The noun *committee* experiences what its modifier describes—*interest*, so interested is correct.]

Excited by your plan, I called a board meeting. [The pronoun *I* experiences what its modifier describes—*excitement*, so *excited* is correct.]

Here is a list of some frequently used participles that require your close attention when you use them as adjectives. To choose the right form, decide whether the noun or pronoun experiences or causes what the participle describes.

amused, amusing

frightened, frightening

annoyed, annoying

insulted, insulting

appalled, appalling

offended, offending

bored, boring

overwhelmed, overwhelming

confused, confusing

pleased, pleasing

depressed, depressing

reassured, reassuring

disgusted, disgusting

satisfied, satisfying

fascinated, fascinating

shocked, shocking

Use of Verbals

Complete each sentence with the appropriate gerund, infinitive, or participle form of the verb in parentheses.

EXAMPLE   Most students at a university hope _____ (prepare)
themselves for a career.

       Most students at a university hope _to prepare_ themselves for a career.

1. They are worried about _____ (get) jobs after graduation.

2. They may want _____ (study) for the pure enjoyment of learning.

3. They may even dream about _____ (be) philosophers or writers.

4. However, many parents refuse _____ (support) students who lack a
   definite career goal.

5. They are happy _____ (help) their children reach their goals.

6. They resist _____ (aid) children who lack direction.

7. Yet _____ (read) widely in the liberal arts is one way for students
   _____ (know) themselves.

8. Students of the humanities are the first _____ (see) the value of
   a liberal education.

9. When they hear their parents _____ (complain) about wasting
   money, students try _____ (explain) their positions.

10. They recommend _____ (learn) about life before _____
    _____ (train) for a specific job.

MODULE 40: MODAL AUXILIARY VERBS

    Auxiliary verbs are known as *helping verbs* because adding an auxiliary verb to a main verb helps the main verb convey additional information. For example, the auxiliary verb *do* is important in turning sentences into questions. *You have to sleep* becomes a question when *do* is added: *Do you have to sleep?* The most common auxiliary verbs are forms of *be*, *have*, and *do*.

    The charts in section 8e list the forms of these three verbs.

    Modal auxiliary verbs are one type of auxiliary verb. They include *can, could, may, might, should, had better, must, will, would,* and others discussed in this chapter. They have only two forms: the present-future and the past. Modals differ from *be, have,* and *do* used as auxiliary verbs in the ways discussed in the following Chart.

SUMMARY OF MODALS AND THEIR DIFFERENCES FROM OTHER AUXILIARY VERBS

Modals in the present or future are always followed by the simple form of a main verb

> *I might **go** tomorrow.*

One-word modals have no -s ending in the third person singular

> *She **could** go with me, you **could** go with me, they **could** go with me.* (The two-word modal *have to* changes form to agree with its subject: *I **have to** leave, she **has to** leave.*)

Auxiliary verbs other than modals usually change form for third-person singular

> *I **have** talked with her, he **has** talked with her.*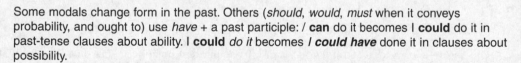

Some modals change form in the past. Others (*should, would, must* when it conveys probability, and *ought to*) use *have* + a past participle: / **can** do it becomes I **could** do it in past-tense clauses about ability. I **could** *do it* becomes *I **could have*** done it in clauses about possibility.

    Modals convey meaning about ability, advisability, necessity, possibility, and other conditions: for example, I *can go* means / am able to go. Modals do not indicate actual occurrences.

40a How do I convey ability, necessity, advisability, possibility, and probability with modals?

Conveying Ability

The modal *can* conveys ability now (in the present) and *could* conveys ability before (in the past). These words deliver the meaning of "able to." For the future, use *will be able to*.

> Luis **can** beat Pepe at tennis. [*Can* conveys present ability.]
> He **could** beat him last month too. [*Could* conveys past ability.]
> If he practices, he **will be able to** beat him next month. [*Will* be able to conveys future ability.]

Adding *not* between a modal and the main verb makes the clause negative: *Mondana* **can not** (or **cannot**) *attend the study session; she* **could not** *attend last night; she* **will not be able** *to attend next Monday*.

❖ USAGE ALERT: You will often see negative forms of modals turned into contractions: *can't, couldn't, won't, wouldn't*, and others. Because contractions are considered informal usage by some instructors, you will never be wrong if you avoid them in academic writing except for reproducing spoken words. ❖

Conveying Necessity

The modals *must* and *have to* convey the message of a need to do something. Both *must* and *have to* are followed by the simple form of the main verb. In the present tense, *have to* changes form to agree with its subject.

> You **must** turn your paper in on time.
> You **have** to meet the minimum requirements.

In the past tense, *must* is never used to express necessity. Instead, use *had to*.

PRESENT TENSE	We **must** submit our papers today. We **have to** abide by the rules.
PAST TENSE	We **had to** [not *We must*] write our first paper yesterday.

The negative forms of *must* and *have to* also have different meanings. *Must not* conveys that something is forbidden; *do not have to* conveys that something is not necessary.

> You **must not** miss the lecture. [Missing the lecture is forbidden.]

> You **do not have to** miss the lecture. [Missing the lecture is not necessary. You can watch it on television.]

Conveying Advisability or the Notion of a Good Idea

The modals *should* and *ought to* express the idea that doing the action of the main verb is advisable or is a good idea.

> You **should** write in your journal daily.

In the past tense, *should* and *ought to* convey regret or knowing something through hindsight. They mean that good advice was not taken.

You **should have** written in it yesterday.

I **ought to have** written in mine too.

The modal *had better* delivers the meaning of good advice or warning or threat. It does not change form for tense.

You **had better** start writing before you get behind.

Need to is often used to express strong advice, too. Its past-tense form is *needed to*.

You **need to** be a more conscientious student.

Conveying Possibility

The modals *may*, *might*, and *could* can be used to convey an idea of possibility or likelihood.

We **may** travel during our fall break.

We **could** leave Friday after classes end.

The past-tense forms for *may*, *might*, and *could* use these words followed by *have* and the past participle of the main verb.

We **could have** traveled during the summer, but we both attended summer school.

Conveying Probability

The modal *must* can convey probability or likelihood in addition to its conveying necessity (see Conveying Necessity). It means that a well-informed guess is being made.

Shakir **must** be a gregarious person. Everyone on campus seems to know him.

When *must* conveys probability, the past tense is *must have* plus the past participle of the main verb.

We hoped Marisa would come to the party; she **must have** had to study.

40b How do I convey preferences, plans, and past habits with modals?

Conveying Preferences

The modals *would rather* and *would rather have* express a preference. *Would rather* (present tense) is used with the simple form of the main verb and *would rather have* (past tense) is used with the past participle of the main verb.

Carlos **would rather** work on the computer than sleep.

He **would rather have** had an earlier class.

Conveying Plan or Obligation

A form of *be* followed by *supposed to* and the simple form of a main verb delivers a meaning of something planned or of an obligation.

Lucia **was supposed to** be here an hour ago.

Conveying Past Habit

The modals *used* to and *would* express the idea that something happened repeatedly in the past.

> Inger **used to** dream of studying in the States.

> She **would** imagine what it would be like.

♣ USAGE ALERT: Both *used to* and *would* can be used to express repeated actions in the past, but *would* cannot be used for a situation that has lasted for a duration of time in the past.

No	I **would** be a physics major.
Yes	I **used to** be a physic major. ♣

40c How can I recognize modals in the passive voice?

Modals use the active voice, as shown. In the active voice, the subject does the action expressed in the main verb.

Modals can also use the passive voice. In the passive voice, the doer of the main verb's action is either unexpressed or is expressed as an object in a prepositional phrase starting with the word *by*.

Passive	The rooftop **can be reached** from a door in the east tower.
Active	I **can reach** the rooftop from a door in the east tower.
Passive	The assignment **must be completed** by Friday.
Active	Everyone **must complete** the assignment by Friday.

Modal Auxiliaries

Fill in the blanks with the correct modal auxiliary forms.

EXAMPLE   _____ (present ability) you imagine a more interesting place to
                 visit than New Orleans?

                 ___*Can*___ you imagine a more interesting place to visit than
                 New Orleans?

1. I _____ (present advisability, negative) brag, but I went there for spring
    vacation.

2. You _____ (present possibility, negative) know it, but New Orleans was
    founded in 1718 by two brothers from Montreal.

3. They _____ (past probability) been looking for a warmer climate.

4. They _____ (past advisability) looked for higher ground.

5. Much of New Orleans is below sea level and _____ (present passive
    necessity) kept dry by using dikes and pumps.

6. Early settlers _____ (past necessity) build with cypress timbers.

7. Because cypress wood came from the surrounding swamps, it
    _____ (past ability) withstand the moisture of the climate.

8. Owners of plantations near the Mississippi River _____ (past habit)
    expect to be flooded occasionally.

9. They _____ (past possibility) moved, but they preferred to keep their
    rich soil and their beautiful view.

10. I _____ (preference) visit New Orleans than any other city in the South.

Workbook for Writers, 1/e

Exercise Answer Key

Module 1: Thinking Like a Writer

Exercise 1–1: Answers will vary.

1. This letter should seek to inform your audience about the disaster and also persuade them to help. The tone should be medium level and the vocabulary simple.

2. This letter should explain the writer's attitude toward earthquakes and also assure the grandmother that the writer is safe and knows what to do in case of an emergency. The tone should be informal.

3. This article should detail the earthquake while emphasizing that no one was fatally injured. The tone should be formal.

4. This letter should relate the earthquake damage to the use of cheap material. The letter should emphasize the company's negligence. The tone should be between medium and formal.

Module 2: Planning, Shaping, Drafting, and Revising

Exercise 2–1: Answers will vary.

1. talent: how to nurture talent in young musicians
2. someone I can count on: the ways in which my sister has helped me
3. traveling alone: safety tips for the young solo traveler
4. happiness: how the author's definition of happiness has changed with age
5. graduation: thoughts on moving out into the "real" world
6. breakfast: the nutritional value of the breakfasts sold in fast food restaurants
7. the beach: the effect of pollution on the local beaches
8. my grandparents: the obstacles faced by the author's grandparents in raising their families
9. a personal loss: reaction to the death of a loved one
10. choosing a car: how to conduct a safety check of a used car

Exercise 2–2: Answers will vary.

Exercise 2–3A: Answers will vary.

1. Unacceptable. Planned budget cuts will affect university services, housing, and scholarships.

2. Unacceptable. A regular study schedule can improve student grades.

3. Unacceptable. Recent theories suggest three principal causes of contemporary violence.

4. Unacceptable. The Indianapolis 500 is now a much safer race than it was twenty years ago.

5. Unacceptable. My first adolescent crush was a painful experience.

6. Unacceptable. Giving brief but complete answers on a job application will make the best impression.

7. Acceptable.

8. Acceptable.

9. Unacceptable. My May visit to Turkey provided an opportunity to learn about history and archaeology.

10. Unacceptable. The Norman Conquest brought dramatic changes to Britain.

Exercise 2–3B: Answers will vary.

1. success: Definitions of success vary from person to person, but I will consider myself successful if I have a well-paying job that I enjoy doing and a happy, healthy family.

2. being a good friend: The hardest thing a good friend has to do is tell the truth even when it might hurt.

3. summer in the city: The heat of summer brings people together because it is too hot to stay inside.

4. laughter: Recent scientific studies indicate that laughter, as well as the positive mental attitude it represents, speeds up recovery from illness.

5. marriage: A good marriage is one that is based on love, trust, and mutual responsibility.

6. restaurants: Restaurant prices are not as unreasonable as they may seem; they are set by using standard formulas that take all the restaurant's expenses into account.

7. concerts: I stopped going to rock concerts when the prices and the violence increased.

8. children: Child abuse can be stopped if parents develop trusting relationships with their youngsters.

9. sacrifice: My grandparents gave up everything they had to come to the United States.

10. shopping: Buying by mail is an easy way to beat the Christmas crowds at the malls.

Exercise 2–4:

Thesis Statement: Leaving a roommate for a single apartment can have definite drawbacks.

I. Unsatisfactory furnishings
    A. Appliances
        1. Major
            a. Stove
            b. Refrigerator
            c. Washer
            d. Dryer
        2. Minor
            a. Microwave
            b. Blender
            c. Toaster
            d. Mixer
    B. Furniture
        1. Bedroom
            a. Futon
            b. Dresser
        2. Living room
            a. Sofa
            b. Chairs
            c. Tables
        3. Kitchen
            a. Table
            b. Chairs
    C. Equipment
        1. For entertainment
        2. For exercise
II. Insufficient finances
    A. Rent
    B. Utilities
        1. Gas
        2. Electricity
        3. Phone
    C. Food
    D. Entertainment

    III. Inadequate companionship

        A. Frequent loneliness

        B. Occasional fear

Exercise 2–5: Answers will vary.

Exercise 2–6: Answers will vary.

A: A Brief History of Utensils

Forks, knives, and spoons seem so natural to most of us that it is hard to imagine eating dinner without them. Yet, many people, such as the Chinese, use chopsticks instead, and others use their hands to eat.

Knives are the oldest Western utensils. The first ones were made of stone 1.5 million years ago. They were originally used to cut up animals after a hunt. The same knife was used to butcher game, slice cooked food, and kill enemies. Even later in history, nobles were the only ones who could afford separate knives for different uses. People used all-purpose knives, pointed like today's steak knives. The round-tipped dinner knife is a modern invention. It became popular in seventeenth-century France because hostesses wanted to stop guests from picking their teeth with the points of their dinner knives.

The spoon is also an ancient tool. Wooden spoons twenty thousand years old have been found in Asia; spoons of stone, wood, ivory, and even gold have been found in Egyptian tombs. Spoons were originally used to scoop up foods that were too thick to sip from a bowl.

The fork is a newcomer. Forks did not become widely accepted until the eighteenth century, when the French nobility adopted the fork as a status symbol and eating with one's hands became unfashionable. At about the same time, individual settings became the rule too. Previously, even rich people had shared plates and glasses at meals, but now the rich demanded individual plates, glasses, forks, spoons, and knives. Today in America, a full set of utensils is considered a necessity. We forget that as recently as the American Revolution, some people considered anyone who used a fork to be a fussy showoff.

B: Why I Live in the Suburbs

I was insulted this morning at registration. I had carefully filled out all my forms and was checking out when the clerk reviewing my program said, "Why do you live all the way out there?" She said it as if I were a fool to live in the suburbs. There was a long line behind me, so I did not answer her. This, however, is what I wanted to say: I like living in the suburbs.

City dwellers often have pity on me: "You're so far away from everything," they say. This remark only shows how little they know. I am not as isolated as they imagine. To get to school, I drive for about forty minutes on a smooth, uncrowded highway. My city-friends take overcrowded buses for forty minutes—or longer, if there is a traffic jam. When I graduate and begin to work full time, I probably will not have even the forty-minute drive because local businesses are expanding. There are factories, shopping malls, and large insurance, law, and advertising firms all within twenty miles of my home.

I think that if my classmates knew how pleasant suburban life can be, they would join me in a minute. People here are friendlier than in the city. When I first moved onto my block, people I didn't recognize waved to me as I walked my dog. I thought they had me confused with someone else. I later found out that they were just being friendly. When I lived in the city, the only people who noticed me when I walked my dog were the ones who sternly reminded me to keep the dog off their lawns. Neighbors here keep an eye on one another. Once when I did not move my car for three days, a neighbor knocked on my door to see if I was feeling all right. When I lived in the city, my neighbors did not care what I did or how I was, as long as I kept the volume down on the stereo.

Maybe I do not live in the most sophisticated area in the world, but I am not deprived. My stores carry the same fashions as stores in the city, my television receives the same programs, and my radio carries the same stations. Given the advantages of suburban life and these things being equal, I feel that the city may be a nice place to visit, but I would not want to leave the suburbs.

Module 3: Writing Paragraphs

Exercise 3–1: Topic Sentence; Irrelevant Sentence

1. 2; 3
2. 1; 4
3. 1; 3; 7
4. 1; 7
5. 1; 7; 9

Exercise 3–2:

1. but; and; in contrast
2. however; in the United States; but; in fact
3. despite its name; nor; when; finally; since the 1920s; from 1928 to 1943; since 1943
4. finally; because; or; certainly; unfortunately; actually; so
5. although; in most places; during the French Revolution; within a year

Exercise 3–3:

1. so; before; it; while; of course; instead; so; for other reasons as well; and; in fact
2. painted/painting; lines; straight; machine/machines; marks; road; truck; one-person/four-person; hot plastic; paint; crew
3. sentence 6: same structure on either side of semicolon highlights contrast; sentence 9: two items in list in same form
4. road or street: it; truck: it; crewmembers: they

Exercise 3–4:

1. b, d, a, e, c
2. c, a, e, b, d
3. d, c, e, b, f, a
4. c, d, e, a, b, f

Exercise 3–5: Answers will vary. Here are some likely details:

1. many high school students become parents while still in school; because of smaller families, students do not see how to take care of babies; grandparents may not be available to help; parenting classes teach responsibility
2. credit doesn't feel like real money; easy to forget how much one has already spent; high interest rates; adverse credit ratings
3. music, food, vocabulary; art
4. the thrill of the crowd; long-standing rivalries; close scores; skillful playing
5. based on an old, outdated view; too harsh; discriminatory; don't affect behavior
6. size; academic ranking; sports; location

Exercise 3–6: Answers will vary.

1. preparing for vacation

   Topic Sentence: A few simple steps can reduce the tension sometimes connected with a major vacation.

   Details:
   1. Begin planning early.
   2. Arrange for time off from work.
   3. Use a travel agent to get the best details.
   4. Get maps and/or booklets about local attractions.
   5. Make a packing list early enough to purchase needed items in advance.
   6. Take enough cash or travelers' checks.

2. the floor plan of the local video rental store

   Topic Sentence: The floor plan at Jim's Video makes finding the tapes I want easy.

   Details:
   1. movie classics on the left wall
   2. comedies on the right wall
   3. science fiction and horror in the front center
   4. kids' movies in the rear center
   5. the counter across the back wall

3. the disadvantages of working while attending school full time

   Topic Sentence: The difficulty with working while attending school full time is that I never have any time for myself.

Details: 1. heavy classload
            2. homework and studying for tests
            3. hours at work
            4. required overtime at holidays
            5. family responsibilities

4. why I've chosen my career

Topic Sentence: I think I would enjoy being a college professor.

Details: 1. summers off
            2. opportunity to work with young people
            3. high status
            4. chance to study what interests me

Exercise 3–7: Answers will vary.

1. Topic Sentence: Walking alone at night on campus can be risky.

    Examples: a. It's easy to trip on cracked pavement in the dark.
                b. Drunks bother women in front of the Rathskeller.
                c. Two purses were snatched last week.
                d. Someone was robbed at the bus stop a few days ago.

2. Topic Sentence: Peer pressure can be hard to resist.

    Example: My first semester grades were low because I could not say no to all the invitations to go out and party after classes.

Exercise 3–8: Answers will vary.

1. a success story

    Topic Sentence: Sometimes the hardest part about succeeding is just deciding to try.

    Events: 1. invited to a gathering in Baltimore
                2. fearful of driving that far alone
                3. trying to get someone else to go—and drive
                4. studying the map
                5. the ease of the trip itself

2. an odd person in my neighborhood

    Topic Sentence: You wouldn't expect to find someone like Stan living in an upscale neighborhood.

    Details: 1. Drives a beat-up truck which leaks oil.
                2. Has a couple of wrecked cars in his yard.
                3. Has long hair and a grizzly beard.
                4. Never mows his lawn.
                5. Threatens anyone who comes near his house.

3. how to study for a test

   Topic Sentence: Studying for a test does not begin the night before the examination.

   Steps:
   1. Read assignments as they are given.
   2. Highlight or take notes.
   3. Answer review questions or work sample problems.
   4. Ask questions in class.
   5. Review in short study sessions.

4. my ideal job

   Topic Sentence: My ideal job would enable me to help other people at the same time that it would allow me to be creative and earn a living wage.

   Qualities:
   1. importance of contributing to my community
   2. helping others take care of themselves
   3. not routine
   4. challenging
   5. money

5. bosses

   Topic Sentence: In my experience, bad bosses fall into a few distinct categories.

   Subgroups:
   1. bullies
   2. socializers
   3. the disorganized
   4. control freaks

6. my sister and I

   Topic sentence: No one believes my sister and I are related.

   Points:
   1. looks
   2. choice of friends
   3. career choices
   4. political choices
   5. treatment of others

7. a lie and a forest fire

   Topic Sentence: Sometimes even a small lie can be like a match tossed carelessly into a forest.

   Similarities:
   1. a thoughtless act
   2. may land where it can't be controlled
   3. destructive
   4. can hurt the person who began it all

8. why you chose the college you are now attending

Topic Sentence: Picking a college was not easy, but I finally chose X for several reasons.

Causes or Effects: a. far away enough to live on campus, close enough to visit home on weekends

 b. good Art Department

 c. reasonable tuition

 d. friends going too

 e. near sports arena and theaters

Exercise 3–9: Revised paragraphs will vary. Students should, however, note the following weaknesses.

1. Introduction: apologies

 Conclusion: announces what has been done; gives a key definition too late to be of use

2. Introduction: lacks thesis or main idea sentence; all specifics, no generalization; has no apparent connection to topic

 Conclusion: too abrupt

3. Introduction: refers to the title instead of stating thesis; doesn't show connection between capital punishment and getting criminals off streets (a logical fallacy)

 Conclusion: contains several absolute claims

4. Introduction: an unadorned thesis statement, not a complete introduction

 Conclusion: has no conclusion; this is a body paragraph

5. Introduction: announces what will be done

 Conclusion: introduces new material

Exercise 3–10: Answers will vary.

Module 4: Thinking, Reading, and Writing Critically

Exercise 4–1A:

1. fact
2. fact
3. opinion
4. fact
5. fact
6. opinion
7. fact
8. fact
9. opinion
10. opinion
11. fact
12. opinion
13. fact
14. opinion
15. opinion

Exercise 4–1B:

1. fact
2. fact
3. fact
4. opinion
5. fact
6. fact
7. fact
8. opinion
9. fact
10. fact
11. opinion
12. fact
13. opinion
14. fact

Module 5: Writing Arguments

NO EXERCISES

Module 6: Parts of Speech

Exercise 6–1: Identifying Nouns

1. Many <u>people</u> have now seen, or at least heard about, "<u>e-books</u>."
2. They may replace traditional, manuscript-based <u>books</u>.
3. It is essential, however, to distinguish between a digital <u>book</u> and a book-reading <u>appliance</u>.
4. At its simplest, a digital <u>book</u> is a literal <u>translation</u> of a printed <u>work</u>.
5. It is created by scanning or generating a PDF <u>file</u>.
6. Book-reading <u>appliances</u> are <u>devices</u> resembling small <u>laptops</u>.
7. They enable you to read digital <u>books</u>.
8. Costing a few hundred <u>dollars</u>, the <u>appliances</u> feature high-quality <u>screens</u> but no <u>keyboards</u>.
9. They run for a long <u>time</u> on <u>batteries</u> and can store several <u>books</u>.
10. Some book-reading <u>appliances</u> are designed to work with your own <u>library</u> of downloaded digital <u>books</u>.
11. Without the <u>appliance</u>, you would be unable to read the <u>books</u>, which are encrypted and stored on your <u>computer</u>.
12. Other book-reading <u>appliances</u> use <u>modems</u> to download <u>works</u> directly from library <u>services</u> over phone <u>lines</u>.
13. Some <u>companies</u> are working on <u>software</u>, which will enable digital <u>books</u> to be displayed on general-purpose <u>computers</u>.
14. Even so, digital <u>books</u> may never be as popular as their traditional <u>counterparts</u>.
15. <u>Screens</u> do not offer a pleasant <u>environment</u> for reading very long <u>texts</u>.
16. In addition, highlighting or making <u>notes</u> in a digital <u>book</u> is awkward.
17. Some <u>books</u> are already very popular in electronic <u>form</u>.

18. They include <u>dictionaries</u>, <u>encyclopedias</u>, <u>directories</u>, product <u>catalogs</u>, and maintenance <u>manuals</u>.

19. <u>Readers</u> of such <u>books</u> are generally in search of a small <u>amount</u> of specific <u>information</u>.

20. When doing lengthy <u>reading</u>, however, <u>people</u> seem to prefer to print on-screen <u>text</u>.

21. They are using <u>paper</u> – a simple but effective viewing <u>technology</u> – as their pre-ferred user <u>interface</u>.

Exercise 6–2: Identifying Pronouns

1. their
2. they, her, she
3. they, her, she
4. she
5. that
6. this, their
7. their, themselves
8. none
9. she, her
10. she, anyone, who
11. what, they
12. whose, them
13. us
14. everyone, this
15. some, one another
16. what, you
17. you, your

Exercise 6–3: Identifying Verbs

1. These tips <u>can lead</u> to such a life.
2. Always <u>recognize</u> your good qualities.
3. Everyone <u>has</u> positive traits, such as sympathy or generosity.
4. You <u>should think</u> of these qualities often.
5. Sometimes, another person <u>may cause</u> us problems.
6. <u>Discuss</u> that problem with a friend or a loved one.
7. You <u>might ask</u> yourself several questions.
8. Who <u>is</u> at fault, and why <u>is</u> that person at fault?
9. Always <u>take</u> responsibility for your part of the problem.
10. A solution to the problem <u>may require</u> a joint effort.
11. What else <u>might lead</u> to a happy life?
12. <u>Tolerate</u> other people's behaviors.
13. <u>Accept</u> their differences.
14. Also, <u>do</u> not <u>dwell</u> upon the past mistakes of your own life.
15. Mistakes <u>are</u> part of a continuous learning process.
16. Without mistakes, you <u>might</u> not <u>learn</u> the right way.
17. <u>Look</u> back at all your successes, not your failures.
18. <u>Be</u> available to assist others.

19. They <u>would do</u> the same for you in most cases.

20. Above all, always <u>find</u> time for relaxation, and <u>enjoy</u> everything around you.

Exercise 6–4: Identifying Forms of Verbs

1. Verb
2. Gerund
3. Infinitive
4. Verb
5. Verb
6. Past Participle
7. Verb
8. Past Participle
9. Verb
10. Verb
11. Infinitive
12. Verb
13. Present Participle
14. Present Participle
15. Verb
16. Infinitive
17. Verb
18. Gerund
19. Verb
20. Infinitive

Exercise 6–5: Identifying Adjectives

1. <u>arithmetic</u>
2. <u>familiar</u>; <u>Chinese</u>; <u>***suan p'an***</u>
3. <u>small</u>; <u>parallel</u>
4. <u>rectangular</u>
5. <u>first</u>; <u>straight</u>; <u>shallow</u>
6. <u>Later</u>; <u>firm</u>; <u>entire</u>
7. <u>portable</u>; <u>parallel</u>
8. <u>each</u>; <u>exact</u>; <u>unique</u>
9. <u>fundamental</u>; <u>place-value</u>
10. <u>ingenious</u>; <u>few</u>; <u>large</u>
11. <u>numerical</u>; <u>one</u>
12. <u>each</u>; <u>previous</u>
13. <u>first</u>; <u>new</u>
14. <u>other</u>
15. <u>memory</u>; <u>mental</u>
16. <u>Asian</u>
17. <u>Japanese</u>; <u>***soroban***</u>
18. <u>Russian</u>; <u>***tschoty***</u>
19. <u>one</u>; <u>their complex</u>
20. <u>These</u>; <u>physical</u>; <u>mental</u>

Exercise 6–6: Identifying Adverbs

1. <u>only</u> (adverb)
2. <u>most</u> (adverb)
3. <u>most easily</u> (adverbs)
4. <u>Typically</u> (adverb); however (conj. adverb); <u>mostly</u> (adverb)
5. <u>more</u> (adverb)
6. <u>extremely</u> (adverb); indeed (conj. adverb); <u>often</u> (adverb)
7. However (conj. adverb); <u>usually</u> (adverb)
8. <u>not just</u> (adverbs)
9. also (adverb); <u>quite</u> (adverb)
10. <u>Generally</u> (adverb); still (conj. adverb); <u>sometimes</u>, <u>much</u> (adverbs)
11. (***none***)

Exercise 6–7: Identifying Prepositions

prepositions	objects
1. <u>In</u>	<u>China</u>
<u>over</u>	<u>300 million bicycles</u>
<u>on</u>	<u>the railroad</u>
2. <u>after</u>	<u>a French model</u>
3. <u>to</u>	<u>"wooden horse"</u>
<u>unlike</u>	<u>those</u>
4. <u>of</u>	<u>a German baron</u>
<u>of</u>	<u>the stationary front wheel</u>
5. <u>for</u>	<u>this bicycle</u>
6. <u>in</u>	<u>a Scottish workshop</u>
<u>with</u>	<u>pedals</u>
7. <u>to</u>	<u>the real wheels</u>
<u>by means of</u>	<u>cranks</u>
8. <u>During</u>	<u>the 1860s</u>
<u>to</u>	<u>the front wheels</u>
9. <u>In</u>	<u>England</u>
<u>in</u>	<u>1879</u>
<u>with</u>	<u>a chain and sprocket</u>
10. <u>for</u>	<u>today's bicycle</u>
11. <u>Instead of</u>	<u>a larger front wheel</u>
<u>in</u>	<u>size</u>

12. <u>During</u>   <u>the 1880s</u>
  <u>with</u>   <u>compressed air</u>
13. <u>along with</u> <u>the derailleur gear</u>
  <u>in</u>   <u>the 1890s</u>
14. <u>of</u>   <u>the bicycle</u>
  <u>to</u>   <u>attempts</u>

Exercise 6–8: Identifying Conjunctions

1. When: (SC)
2. No conjunctions
3. and: (CC)
4. Whereas: (SC)
5. No conjunctions
6. Although: (SC)
7. No conjunctions
8. but: (CC)
9. so that: (SC)
10. yet: (CC)
11. so: (CC)
12. before: (SC)
13. and: (CC)
14. Although: (SC) for: (CC)
15. and: (CC)

Exercise 6–9: Identitying the Parts of Speech: Review

1. adjective
2. verb
3. preposition
4. noun
5. noun
6. conjunction
7. adverb
8. preposition
9. verb
10. pronoun
11. verb
12. conjunctions
13. adjective
14. preposition
15. verb
16. verb
17. preposition
18. verb
19. verb
20. preposition
21. noun
22. adverb
23. adjective
24. adverb
25. adjective

Exercise 6–10A: Identifying Subjects and Predicates

1. Warm air/cannot . . .
2. The temperature beneath the ice/is . . .
3. This/keeps . . .
4. The ice at a figure-skating rink/is . . .
5. Ice hockey rinks/have . . .
6. The ice/is . . .
7. The concrete/contains . . .
8. An Olympic-sized rink/has . . .
9. A very cold liquid, like the antifreeze in cars/circulates . . .
10. The liquid/absorbs . . .

11. Machinery/keeps . . .
12. More and more people/are . . .

Exercise 6–10B:

<u>subject</u> <u>verb</u>

	subject	verb
1.	toothbrushes	were
2.	people	rubbed
3.	toothbrushes	originated
4.	bristles	came
5.	hogs	grew
6.	Europeans	brushed
7.	toothbrushes	were used
	sponges	
8.	men	picked
	women	
9.	stems	were employed
	toothpicks	
10.	toothpicks	were
11.	germs	developed
12.	solution	was
13.	discovery	led
		made
14.	nylon	was
		resisted
15.	brushes	were sold
16.	they	were
17.	tissue	scratched
		bled
18.	version	was developed
19.	It	cost
20.	care	improved
21.	dentists	have made
	surgeons	
22.	toothbrushes	should be used
		should be replaced
23.	bristles	are
		can cut

Exercise 6–11: Identifying Objects

direct object	indirect object
1. popcorn	children
2. necklaces	Columbus
3. strings	—
4. machines	friends
5. popcorn	themselves
6. dollar	customers
7. poppers	—
8. popcorn	customers
9. origin	—
10. hot dogs	people
11. hot dogs	New Yorkers
12. buns	customers
13. gloves	customers
14. fortune	vendors

Exercise 6–12: Identifying Complements

1. Strawberries are not true *berries*. (SC, noun)
2. They are an *offshoot* of the rose plant family. (SC, noun)
3. Strawberries taste *sweet*. (SC, adj)
4. Harpo Marx was not a *mute*. (SC, noun)
5. Many considered his silence *charming*. (OC, adj)
6. In fact, friends have called him *talkative*. (OC, adj)
7. Many people consider elephants *fearless*. (OC, adj)
8. However, mice can make them *frantic* with fright. (OC, adj)
9. Carrots are not a *remedy* for poor eyesight. (SC, noun) .
10. This belief is a *myth*. (SC, noun)
11. Only for improving night vision are they *helpful*. (SC, adj)
12. Indian ink is not *Indian*. (SC, adj)
13. It is *Chinese*. (SC, adj)
14. Lions are *cats*, or felids. (SC, noun)
15. Many people mistakenly call them the *largest cats in the cat family*. (OC, noun phrase as object complement)
16. Yet the largest cat is the *tiger*. (SC, noun)
17. The Siberian tiger is the *king* of all felids. (SC, noun)
18. A rabbit is a *lagomorph*. (SC, noun)

19. It is not a *rodent*. (SC, noun)

20. Its distinguishing feature is its *digestive system*. (SC, noun phrase)

21. People mistakenly consider *pigs dirty*. (OC, adj)

22. Yet pigs are very *clean*. (SC, adj)

23. Often, their owners leave pig sties *unclean*. (OC, adj)

Exercise 6–13A: Identifying and Using Adjectives and Adverbs

1. *Each*[d] player's chances of winning depend *entirely*[e] on the numbers that are drawn. (d: adjective; e: adverb)

2. Because it is so easily[f] mastered, the game attracts many[g] players. (f: adverb; g: adjective)

3. Bingo cards are *universally*[h] *designed; they have five*[i] rows of five squares each. (h: adverb; i: adjective)

4. The letters B-I-N-G-O are *clearly*[j] printed on the top of each card; each letter heads a *vertical*[k] row. (j: adverb; k: adjective)

5. *Any*[l] number from one to seventy-five is placed in a box on the card, except for the center square, which is *always*[m] a free square. (l: adjective; m: adverb)

6. There are seventy-five *corresponding*[n] balls, each with a letter and a number that is drawn *randomly*[o] from a bowl or box by the caller. (n: adjective; o: adverb)

7. The *bingo*[p] caller chooses a ball and *quickly*[q] announces its letter and number. (p: adjective; q: adverb)

8. *Those*[r] players who have a square with a number matching the one that was called must *carefully*[s] place a marker over the square. (r: adjectives; s: adverb)

9. The *first*[t] player to cover five boxes *vertically*[u] or horizontally yells, "Bingo!" and wins the game. (t: adjective; u: adverb)

10. *Usually,*[v] the winner receives a prize: *typically,*[w] a *grand*[x] prize is given to the player who can cover the entire card. (v: adverb; w: adverb; x: adjective)

Exercise 6–13B: Answers will vary.

1. early: adverb

2. empty: adjective

3. brightly: adverb

4. new: adjective

5. much: adverb

6. even: adverb; great: adjective

7. Luckily: adverb; cozy: adjective

8. really: adverb; fine: adjective

9. crystal: adjective; fortunately: adverb

10. finally: adverb; completely: adverb

Exercise 6–14: Identifying Appositives

1. futurist and author
2. ARPA
3. Leonard Kleinrock
4. Packet switching
5. the long periods of "silence"
6. ARPAnet
7. Ray Tomlinson
8. "killer application"
9. NSF
10. a similar, parallel network of its own
11. scientist
12. hyperlinks
13. Mosaic
14. One of the developers of Mosaic ... Netscape Navigator

Exercise 6–15A: Identifying Phrases

1. NP	6. VP	11. PP
2. PP	7. PP	12. PP
3. VP	8. VP	13. VP
4. AP	9. VP	
5. NP	10. AP	

Exercise 6–15B:

1. part	6. part	11. ger
2. part	7. part	12. ger
3. part	8. part	13. inf
4. part	9. inf	14. ger
5. inf	10. ger	15. ger

Exercise 6–16: Identifying Dependent Clauses

1. The London Eye Ferris Wheel, which was designed as part of London's Millennium celebrations, is the largest attraction of its kind in the world.
2. The structure, which stands 443 feet high, was built by British Airways at a cost of 35 million pounds.
3. There was disappointment, however, on New Year's Eve 1999, when technical problems delayed the opening of the wheel.
4. A fault was discovered in the clutch mechanism of one of its 32 glass pods, which meant the wheel had to be shut down.

5. Rather than close just one pod, BA decided on a complete overhaul.

6. The 250 people <u>who had been invited to ride the wheel that night</u> were given a rain check.

7. <u>Although each pod can carry 25 people</u>, fewer people are admitted in hot weather.

8. The wheel does not cause motion sickness, <u>as it travels extremely slowly</u>.

9. However, <u>when one passenger suffered vertigo</u>, the wheel had to be reversed to let her off.

10. One thing that most people enjoy about the wheel is <u>that it is noiseless</u>.

11. The wheel sold its millionth ticket in April 2000, <u>which was well ahead of schedule</u>.

12. Because of the success of the wheel, other cities—including Boston and Toronto—have asked <u>if they can copy it</u>.

Exercise 6–17: Using Subordination Answers will vary.

1. <u>Since</u> potatoes grown from seed may not inherit the parent plant's characteristics, potatoes are usually grown from the eye of a planted piece of potato.

2. <u>Because</u> potato blossoms look like those of the poisonous nightshade plant, centuries ago Europeans were afraid to eat potatoes.

3. <u>Although</u> tomatoes, tobacco, and eggplant are all relatives of the potato, they do not look alike.

4. The sweet potato is not related to the potato <u>even though</u> its Indian name, <u>batata</u>, was mistakenly taken to mean "potato" by its European "discoverers."

5. Most people throw away the potato skin, <u>which</u> is a good source of dietary fiber.

6. <u>While</u> thirty-two percent of the U.S. potato crop is eaten fresh, twenty-seven percent is made into frozen products, such as commercial french fries. (The use of "while" for "although" is informal.)

7. Would you believe <u>that</u> twelve percent of the U.S. crop is made into potato chips?

8. There are misinformed people <u>who</u> believe that the potato is only a poor person's food.

9. They overlook <u>that</u> potatoes have nourished the masses of Europe since the eighteenth century.

10. Nutritious potatoes allowed the population to expand, <u>until</u> 1845, when Europe—especially Ireland—was devastated by a potato blight that destroyed the crop.

11. Potato chips were created in New England <u>because</u> a hotel chef became angry with a fussy customer.

12. <u>Although</u> no one else had ever complained, the customer sent back his French fries twice, saying they were not crisp enough.

13. The chef, <u>who</u> apparently had a bad temper, decided to teach the man a lesson.

14. He cut the potatoes paper-thin and fried them <u>until</u> they were too crisp to pick up with a fork.

15. <u>Once</u> the customer tasted these potatoes, he was delighted.

16. These "chips" became very popular, <u>so that</u> that chef never got his revenge, but he did get his own restaurant.

Exercise 6–18: Identifying Different Types of Sentences

1. <u>Forgetting</u> <u>is</u> not always permanent. Simple

2. <u>Interference</u> sometimes <u>keeps</u> us from remembering. Simple

3. When $^{(SC)}$ <u>this</u> <u>happens</u>, <u>we</u> <u>may</u> not <u>be able</u> to stop thinking about something else even though $^{(SC)}$ <u>we</u> <u>know</u> it <u>is</u> wrong. Complex

4. For example, <u>we</u> <u>may</u> not <u>recall</u> a friend's name, and $^{(CC)}$ <u>we</u> <u>may</u> even <u>want</u> to call her by someone else's name. Compound

5. Other times, <u>we</u> <u>try</u> hard to remember, but $^{(CC)}$ our <u>memories</u> <u>may</u> not <u>work</u> at all. Compound

6. The <u>information</u> <u>seems</u> lost until $^{(SC)}$ <u>we</u> <u>receive</u> a clue <u>that</u> $^{(RP)}$ <u>helps</u> us remember. Complex

7. Some <u>scientists</u> <u>believe</u> that $^{(RP)}$ <u>memories</u> <u>may</u> completely <u>fade</u> away, and $^{(CC)}$ then <u>we</u> <u>can</u> never <u>retrieve</u> them. Compound-complex

8. Recent <u>studies</u> <u>show</u> that $^{(RP)}$ <u>storing</u> memory <u>changes</u> the brain tissue. Complex

9. However, $^{(CA)}$ <u>no one</u> <u>has shown</u> that $^{(RP)}$ these <u>changes</u> <u>can be erased</u>, so $^{(CC)}$ the "fading-away" <u>theory</u> of forgetting <u>remains</u> unproven. Compound-Complex

10. <u>Scientists</u> <u>who</u> $^{(RP)}$ <u>believe</u> in the interference theory of forgetting <u>identify</u> different kinds of interference. Complex

11. Sometimes <u>learning</u> new material <u>is</u> <u>made</u> difficult by conflicting old material. Simple

12. <u>Confusion</u> between the old material and the new <u>makes</u> it hard to remember either one. Simple

13. <u>Coming</u> upon similar material soon after learning something <u>can</u> also <u>interfere</u>. Simple

14. <u>Scientists</u> <u>have</u> <u>shown</u> this in experiments, but $^{(CC)}$ everyday <u>experience</u> <u>can convince</u> us too. Compound

15. <u>Anyone</u> trying to learn two similar languages, such as French and Spanish, at the same time <u>knows</u> the feeling of confusion. Simple

Exercise 6–19A: Writing Different Types of Sentences Answers will vary.

1. Psychoanalysis helps people deal with these forgotten memories, for it works at exploring them consciously.

2. Repression, which is the burying in the unconscious of fearful experiences, can make life difficult.

3. People repress frightening thoughts and experiences, and then they try to go on living normally.

4. When people repress experiences, they avoid having to relive them, so they feel better for a time.

5. Experiments show that people forget bad experiences more quickly (than they forget) good experiences.

6. Repression occurs in the mentally ill, but it also occurs in healthy people.

7. A learning atmosphere where people can relax leads to better memory.

8. Any student knows this, and so does any teacher.

9. Because people are often distracted in stressful situations, they simply do not see everything; therefore, they cannot remember everything.

10. This may explain why accident victims often do not recall details of their experiences.

11. Many people do not remember much from their childhoods, but this does not mean that they are repressing bad memories.

12. They may have been too interested in some events to notice others that were happening at the same time, or maybe their childhoods were simply too boring to remember.

Exercise 6–19B: Answers will vary.

1. Compound: Fast food is not cheap, and it is not especially healthful.

   Complex: Although it is less expensive than other options, fast food is not cheap.

   Compound-Complex: Although it is very popular, fast food is not cheap, nor is it appetizing.

2. Compound: The movie theater was crowded, so the manager turned up the air conditioner.

   Complex: Because too many tickets were sold, the movie theater was crowded.

   Compound-Complex: After the announcement that the star would make a personal appearance, the movie theater was crowded, and the line stretched around the block.

3. Compound: Read contracts before you sign them, or you could end up in financial trouble.

   Complex: Whenever you purchase goods or services, read contracts before you sign them.

   Compound-Complex: When you rent an apartment, always ask for a written lease, but read contracts before you sign them.

4. Compound: Ice cream is a popular dessert, and sales increase every year.

   Complex: Although it is fattening, ice cream is a popular dessert.

   Compound-Complex: Since the opening of the new diner, more people are eating out, and ice cream is a popular dessert.

5. Compound: Grocery stores should be open twenty-four hours a day, and so should banks.

Complex: If staff can be hired, grocery stores should be open twenty-four hours a day.

Compound-Complex: Because more and more people are working off schedules, grocery stores should be open twenty-four hours a day, and bus service should be frequent.

Exercise 6–19C: Answers will vary.

1. Because she had a pet snake, she has learned a lot about cold-blooded animals.
2. Whoever has the flu should stay home until the symptoms are gone.
3. Let both sides speak before the union votes on the contract.
4. Even though they paid the electric bill, service was suspended until the check cleared.
5. Do you know where the keys are?
6. The pen that cost a dollar isn't as good as the cheaper one.
7. I know who has the prize-winning ticket.
8. Since she learned to drive, she's traveled all over the state.
9. I forget whether the bus stops on that corner.
10. If the milk is sour, pour it down the drain.

Module 7: Verbs

Exercise 7–1:

1. rushes	14. warns
2. ties	15. posts
3. weighs	16. stops
4. needs	17. requires
5. attempts	18. knows
6. fails	19. hears
7. starts	20. allows
8. opens	21. remains
9. waits	22. brakes
10. occurs	23. causes
11. reports	24. faces
12. affects	25. practices
13. recommends	

Exercise 7–2:

1. started
2. recorded
3. developed
4. used
5. inserted
6. issued, startled
7. perceived
8. jerked, headed
9. employed
10. pulled
11. experimented
12. imagined

Exercise 7–3:

1. The woman <u>woke</u> early and looked at the clock. It was five a.m.
2. Sensing something was wrong, she <u>got</u> up and opened the door to the utility room, where her dog normally <u>slept</u>.
3. She <u>froze</u> at what she saw: the room was empty and the door <u>stood</u> open.
4. The woman <u>shook</u> her husband awake and <u>told</u> him that the dog was missing.
5. Then she <u>threw</u> on some clothes and jumped in the car.
6. She <u>drove</u> up and down nearby streets looking for her pet.
7. She even <u>swung</u> by her friend's house two miles away to see if he was there.
8. However, she <u>drew</u> a blank. Finally she admitted defeat and came home.
9. When she <u>saw</u> her husband, she <u>burst</u> into tears.
10. They both <u>thought</u> they would never see their dog again.
11. The woman <u>went</u> to work and <u>spent</u> the entire day wondering if her dog was safe.
12. When she <u>got</u> home, she <u>spoke</u> to her neighbor and asked if he had seen the animal.
13. Then she <u>heard</u> a rustling behind her.
14. She <u>spun</u> around, and <u>saw</u> the dog cowering in the bushes.
15. At the sound of his name, however, he <u>sprang</u> out.
16. He <u>shook</u> his coat, which was muddy and matted.
17. She immediately <u>swept</u> him up in her arms and <u>took</u> him inside.
18. He <u>clung</u> to her as if traumatized.
19. However, she <u>felt</u> no broken bones, and he <u>ate</u> and <u>drank</u> normally.
20. When her husband <u>rang</u> to say he was on his way home, she <u>told</u> him the good news.

Exercise 7–4:

person	present tense	past tense
first	am	was
second	are	were
third	is	was
first	are	were
second	are	were
third	are	were
present	participle: being	past participle: been

Exercise 7–5:

For some people a garden <u>is</u> a hobby. For others it is a necessity. In either case, <u>being</u> a gardener is hard work.

The first thing you must do each spring <u>is</u> prepare the garden plot with spade, plow, or rototiller. Your muscles <u>are</u> sure to ache after a day of turning the soil. Planting and mulching <u>are</u> next. I <u>am</u> always excited to see new plants coming up. You will <u>be</u> too. However, weeds <u>are</u> apt to grow faster than the seeds you planted.

Unless your idea of an aerobic workout <u>is</u> thirty minutes with a hoe, you should <u>be</u> enthusiastic about mulch. Mulch can <u>be</u> straw mounded around plants or plastic sheets covering the ground between rows. If you <u>are</u> using plastic, <u>be</u> sure you have the kind that can breathe. Otherwise, there will <u>be</u> inadequate moisture for your plants.

A garden <u>is</u> guaranteed to cultivate your patience while you are cultivating it. It cannot <u>be</u> rushed. If you hope <u>to be</u> a successful gardener, you must <u>be</u> willing to work at it.

Exercise 7–6: Some sentences have several possible answers, but each helping verb except "are" must be used at least once.

1. seem
2. was
3. may
4. can
5. does
6. were
7. should
8. will
9. would
10. is
11. can
12. may
13. could
14. do
15. may
16. be
17. has
18. have

Exercise 7–7:

1. transitive
2. linking
3. intransitive
4. transitive
5. transitive
6. transitive
7. linking
8. intransitive
9. transitive
10. intransitive
11. transitive
12. linking
13. transitive
14. intransitive
15. transitive
16. linking

Exercise 7–8: Answers will vary.

1. He answered confidently.
   She answered the phone after the third ring.
2. She walked very quietly to the kitchen cabinet.
   Celia walked the dog on the beach early this afternoon.
3. The dinner was prepared at the last minute.
   She prepared her homework for tomorrow's classes.
4. The car drives very well in the snow.
   Sheryl drives her father's car to work every morning.
5. Jeremy painted over the stain on the wall.
   John painted the living room with the paint you gave him.

Exercise 7–9:

1. lying
2. rises; raise
3. sit; set
4. lay
5. set
6. lay
7. laid; set
8. raise
9. lay; lying
10. set; setting

Exercise 7–10:

1. have discovered
2. have been kissing
3. are beginning
4. has been studying
5. has found
6. had been involved
7. are earning
8. had said
9. has been linked; are living
10. have been having
11. have suggested
12. are starting
13. have known
14. have understood
15. have been studying

Exercise 7–11:

1. The Louvre in Paris <u>was</u> not <u>built</u> as an art museum. passive
2. The original Louvre <u>was constructed</u> in the twelfth century as a fortress. passive
3. Francis I <u>erected</u> the present building as a residence. active
4. A gallery connecting it with the Tuileries Palace <u>was started</u> by Henry IV and <u>completed</u> by Louis XIV. passive
5. A second gallery, begun by Napoleon, <u>would have enclosed</u> a great square. active
6. However, it <u>was</u> not <u>justified</u> until after his abdication. passive
7. Revolutionaries <u>overthrew</u> the Bastille on July 14, 1789. active
8. Just four years later the art collection of the Louvre <u>was opened</u> to the public. passive
9. The collection <u>can be traced</u> back to Francis I. passive
10. Francis, an ardent collector, <u>invited</u> Leonardo da Vinci to France in 1515. active
11. Leonardo <u>brought</u> the *Mona Lisa* with him from Italy. active
12. Nevertheless, the royal art collection <u>may have been expanded</u> more by ministers than by kings. passive
13. Cardinals Richelieu and Mazarin <u>can take credit</u> for many important acquisitions. active
14. Today the Louvre <u>has</u> a new entrance. active
15. A glass pyramid in the courtyard <u>was designed</u> by I. M. Pei. passive
16. Pei's name <u>can be added</u> to a distinguished list of Louvre architects. passive

Exercise 7–12A: Answers will vary.

1. The French did not build the Louvre in Paris as an art museum.
2. The French constructed the original Louvre as a twelfth century fortress.
4. Henry IV started a gallery connecting it with the Tuileries Palace, and Louis XIV completed the gallery.
6. However, workers did not finish it until after his abdication.
8. Just four years later authorities opened the art collection of the Louvre to the public.
9. We can trace the collection back to Francis I.
12. Nevertheless, ministers may have expanded the royal art collection more than kings.

15. I. M. Pei designed the glass pyramid entrance in the courtyard.
16. We can add Pei's name to a distinguished list of Louvre architects.

Exercise 7–12B:

1. passive   People outside Africa did not know the ruins until 1868.
2. active
3. passive   Acceptable: The building is more important than who built it.
4. passive   Acceptable: The unknown builders are less important than the way it was built.
5. passive   A thirty-foot wall encircles a lower, elliptical building.
6. active
7. passive   Acceptable: Emphasis on the sculptures; not the discoverers.
8. active
9. active
10. passive   Acceptable: Tools are stressed, not the scavengers who found them.
11. active

Module 8: Pronoun Case and Reference

Exercise 8–1:

	person	subject	object	possessive
singular	first	I	me	my/mine
	second	you	you	you/yours
	third	he	him	his
		she	her	her/hers
		it	it	its
plural	first	we	us	our/ours
	second	you	you	your/yours
	third	they	them	their/theirs

Exercise 8–2:

pronoun	case
1. me	objective
2. they	subjective
you	objective
3. his	possessive
4. he	subjective
5. him	objective
6. their	possessive
they	subjective
7. they	subjective
8. them	objective
9. it	subjective
10. they	subjective
11. its	possessive
12. she	subjective
their	possessive
13. they	subjective
their	possessive
14. them	objective
15. its	possessive
16. us	objective
they	subjective
17. our	possessive
them	objective
18. we	subjective
our	possessive
them	objective

Exercise 8–3:

1. we, we
2. It
3. us
4. he
5. He, I
6. our
7. I, he, themselves

11. us
12. my
13. himself
14. me, us
15. her
16. her
17. you, you

8. him, himself
9. them, itself
10. their

18. them
19. themselves
20. yours

Exercise 8–4A:

1. <u>he</u> and <u>she</u>: appositives of <u>the comediens</u>
2. <u>he</u>: complement of <u>a comic legend</u>
3. <u>ours</u>: appositive of <u>the best comedy act</u>
4. <u>they</u>: complement of <u>the first ones</u>
5. <u>me</u>: appositive of <u>the comedien</u>

Exercise 8–4B:

1. she
2. me
3. he
4. him
5. I

Exercise 8–5:

1. who
2. who
3. whoever
4. whom
5. whoever
6. who
7. who
8. who

9. whom
10. who
11. whom
12. whomever
13. who
14. who
15. whom
16. whom

Exercise 8–6:

1. himself
2. him
3. its
4. theirs
5. him

6. his
7. themselves
8. them
9. His
10. his

11. itself
12. him
13. his
14. he
15. us

Exercise 8–7:

1. they, them

   House of Representatives and Senate members work with young people called pages. <u>The pages</u> run errands for <u>the members of Congress</u>.

2. he

   The longest filibuster in the U. S. Senate was delivered by Senator Wayne Morse of Oregon. However, Texas State Senator Mike McKool spoke far longer. <u>Senator McKool</u> spoke for 42 hours and 33 minutes.

3. he

   For religious reasons, Zachary Taylor refused to take the presidential oath of office on a Sunday, so David Rice Atchison (president of the Senate) was president for a day. <u>Atchison</u> spent the day appointing his temporary cabinet.

4. his

   Correct

5. he

   An American Indian, Charles Curtis, became vice-president when Herbert Hoover was elected president in 1928. <u>Curtis</u> was one-half Kaw.

6. he

   William De Vance King, vice-president under Franklin Pierce, was in Cuba during the election and had to be sworn in by an act of Congress, never bothering to return to Washington. A month later, never having carried out any official duties, <u>King</u> died.

7. their, their

   Correct

8. she

   The first woman presidential candidate was Victoria Woodhull. Years before Geraldine Ferraro ran for vice president, <u>Woodhull</u> was on the Equal Rights Party ticket— in 1872.

9. it, he, it, himself

   Correct

10. He, he

    As a child, president-to-be Andrew Johnson was sold as an indentured servant to a tailor. <u>Johnson</u> was supposed to work for seven years, but <u>he</u> ran away.

11. he, it, it

    President William McKinley had a pet parrot. Whenever <u>McKinley</u> whistled the beginning of "Yankee Doodle," the bird would complete the song.

Exercise 8–8: Answers will vary.

1. A California company called the Space Island Group is planning to recycle one of the shortest-lived components of the space shuttle. <u>The idea</u> is ingenious.

2. Engineers at SIG plan to construct dozens of wheel-shaped space stations using empty shuttle fuel tanks. <u>The fuel tanks</u> are eminently suited to the task.

3. A shuttle's fuel tanks are huge. Each one is 28 feet in diameter and nearly 160 feet long – approximately the size of a jumbo jet. <u>The shuttle</u> jettisons them just before it reaches orbit, leaving them to burn up and crash into the ocean.

4. Over 100 of these tanks, known as ETs, have been used and destroyed since the first shuttle launch in 1981. So <u>one</u> can see how much hardware has gone to waste.

5. Using ETs to form manned space stations – and developing passenger shuttles to take people to them – was originally NASA's idea. At first, <u>NASA scientists</u> were enthusiastic about this possibility.

6. However, it would have taken too long for NASA to develop and test passenger shuttles, so <u>the idea</u> was dropped.

7. SIG's plan is to build the passenger shuttles and lease them to commercial air-lines. <u>The company</u> believes that this is the fastest way to get ordinary people into space.

8. The space stations will also be leased – at a rate of $10-$20 per cubic foot per day – to anyone wishing to run a business in space. <u>A person</u> will simply take the shuttle, transfer to the space station, and set up his or her office.

9. While the space stations have a projected life of 30 years, <u>SIG</u> claims that tenants would fully pay for them within 2–3 years. This means that the passenger shuttle program could actually operate at a profit.

Exercise 8–9: Answers may vary.

People have to be careful when buying on credit. Otherwise, **they** may wind up so heavily in debt that it may take years to straighten out **their lives**. Credit cards are easy for **people** to get if **they are** working, and many finance companies are eager to give **customers** installment loans at high interest rates. Once **people** are hooked, **they** may find **themselves** taking out loans to pay **their** loans. When this happens, **they are** doomed to being forever in debt.

There are, of course, times when using credit makes sense. If **people** have the money (or will have it when the bill comes), a credit card can enable **them** to shop without carrying cash. **Consumers** may also want to keep a few gasoline credit cards with **them** in case **their** car breaks down on the road. Using credit will allow **people** to deal with other emergencies (tuition, a broken water heater) when **they** lack the cash. **They** can also use credit to take advantage of sales. However, **they** need to recognize the difference between a sale item **they** need and one **they** wants. If **they** can't do this, **they** may find **themselves** dealing with collection agents, car repossessors, or even bankruptcy lawyers.

Module 9: Agreement

Exercise 9–1A:

1. occupy
2. associates
3. wear
4. refers
5. work
6. consists
7. use
8. bastes
9. cuts
10. reveal

Exercise 9–1B:

1. needs
2. makes
3. are
4. deserve
5. seems
6. are
7. means
8. is
9. becomes
10. are

Exercise 9–1C:

	subject	verb	correction
1.	place	are	is
2.	region	are	is
3.	names	is	are
4.	name	reveal	reveals
5.	kinds	is	are
6.	It	is	correct
7.	alligators	are	correct
8.	species	is	are
9.	region	are	is
10.	Majorie Stoneman Douglas	deserve	deserves

Exercise 9–1D:

1. is
2. are
3. is
4. have
5. are
6. share
7. is
8. is
9. prefers
10. are

Exercise 9–1E:

1. mystery/continues
2. anyone/sees
3. book/is
4. no one/studies
5. paintings/are
6. decoration/appears
7. pictures/stem
8. birds/wear
9. humor/pervades
10. text/is

Exercise 9–1F:

1. seems
2. show
3. argues
4. look
5. belong
6. makes
7. publish
8. deals
9. gets
10. ask

Exercise 9–1G:

1. knows, dream
2. occur
3. stands
4. gets
5. are, means
6. suggest
7. represent
8. believe
9. spend
10. receive
11. devote
12. form
13. think
14. lacks
15. have
16. claim
17. protect
18. exists, proposes
19. learn
20. combines, are

Exercise 9–2:

1. their
2. their
3. they
4. his or her
5. its
6. themselves
7. its
8. his or her
9. its
10. their
11. its
12. her
13. their
14. their
15. their
16. her
17. her
18. its
19. their
20. their

Exercise 9–3:

1. Many people assume that a person who makes a lot of money has <u>his or her</u> happiness guaranteed.

2. However, a person who owns a lot of things is not necessarily as happy as <u>he or she</u> would like to be.

3. An individual who isn't able to buy much beyond life's necessities may not be happy with <u>his or her</u> life either.

4. How do most people define happiness and how can <u>they</u> achieve it?

5. The answer is that everyone has <u>his or her</u> own idea of what makes <u>him or her</u> happy.

6. Therefore, each individual should take time to reflect on what makes <u>him or her</u> happy.

7. One of the oldest and wisest sayings is "Know yourself." That's the only way to know what makes <u>you</u> happy.

8. It's also important to understand that no matter how much somebody may care for you, <u>he or she</u> is not responsible for your happiness. You are responsible for your own happiness.

9. To be happy, it seems that most people need more than just life's necessities, but <u>they</u> probably don't need nearly as much as <u>they</u> may think.

Module 10: Adjectives and Adverbs

Exercise 10–1:

1. adjective	8. adjective	15. adverb
2. adverb	9. adverb	16. adverb
3. adverb	10. adjective	17. adjective
4. adjective	11. adjective	18. adverb
5. adverb	12. adjective	19. adjective
6. adjective	13. adjective	20. adverb
7. adjective	14. adverb	

Exercise 10–2:

1. annually	8. dangerous	15. quickly
2. available	9. slowly	16. popular
3. well	10. high	17. lately
4. serious	11. lengthy	18. regularly
5. commonly	12. ancient	19. quick
6. bad	13. chemically	20. carefully
7. delicate	14. recently	

Exercise 10–3A:

comparative	superlative
1. worse	worst
2. worse	worst
3. more forgiving	most forgiving
4. freer	freest
5. better	best
6. more gracefully	most gracefully
7. handsomer	handsomest
8. hotter	hottest
9. littler	littlest
10. more loudly	most loudly
11. more	most
12. more	most
13. more powerfully	most powerfully
14. prettier	prettiest
15. more quickly	most quickly
16. more	most
17. more sweetly	most sweetly
18. more sympathetically	most sympathetically
19. more talented	most talented
20. better	best

Exercise 10–3B: Answers will vary.

Exercise 10–4: Answers will vary.

Module 11: Sentence Fragments

Exercise 11–1A:

1. This is a dependent adverb clause.
   When March 21st arrives, so does spring.
2. This is a dependent noun clause.
   Whichever participants arrive first, Serena will be there to greet them.
3. There is no subject.
   At the village dances, the elderly always join the younger dancers.
4. This is a prepositional phrase.
   In the spring, the air feels soft and smells sweet.

5. This lacks a helping verb.

   <u>Happily, the dancers are participating</u>.

6. This is part of a participial phrase.

   <u>June 21st is known to be the longest day of the year in the northern hemisphere</u>.

7. This is a dependent adjective clause.

   <u>Everyone knows that most people like to celebrate</u>.

8. This is a noun phrase.

   <u>The garden tour is many people's favorite event</u>.

9. This is either a gerund phrase or a participial phrase.

   Gerund: <u>Visiting with my family, friends, and neighbors is something I take the time to do</u>.

   Participial phrase: <u>Visiting with my family, friends, and neighbors, I was able to hear about everyone I know</u>.

10. This is part of a compound predicate.

    <u>While I'm away, I'll call and write love letters</u>.

Exercise 11–1B: Answers will vary.

1. Someone who gets to class on time will not miss any of the lecture. (adjective)

   Autumn always gets to class on time. (part of the predicate)

2. There lay the manuscript that we thought had been entered in the literary contest. (adjective)

   The manuscript that we entered in the literary contest will not be returned. (adjective)

3. I need to buy a textbook for my creative writing class. (infinitive phrase as direct object)

   To buy a textbook is a requirement. (infinitive phrase as subject)

4. When I took the exam, my professor allowed me to stay later. (adverb)

   When I took the exam is irrelevant! (noun)

5. I never see my friend working to pay for college. (part of the predicate)

   Working to pay for college shouldn't take away too much study time. (gerund phrase as subject)

6. In many of the city's coffee houses, we saw students studying for exams during spring break. (adjective)

   A small group of students were studying for exams during spring break. (part of the predicate)

7. Administrators, faculty, staff, and students will all get an extra week of summer vacation. (compound subject)

   Everyone at the college, administrators, faculty, staff, and students, will be glad when fall semester begins. (appositive)

8. The power going off suddenly, we hoped and prayed our work on the computers would be saved. (absolute phrase)

   The power going off is something that has happened too many times when I've been working on my computer. (subject)

9. The retired electrical contractor who attends night classes thought Literature 101 was a superb class. (adjective)

   Who attends night classes? (question)

10. Working in the writing center is one of the best jobs on campus. (prepositional phrase as part of the subject)

    Students tutored in the writing center often learn more than they expect to learn. (prepositional phrase as adjective)

Exercise 11–2:

1. When he first met with Mary Burch, a Tallahassee-based therapist, Jason sat listlessly and expressionless in her office. After that first meeting, Burch decided to bring a visitor to the next meeting.

2. The surprise visitor was Burch's Border collie. During their fifth session, Jason began speaking to the dog and eventually began to open up to Burch.

3. Burch is heavily involved in a pet therapy program, which is designed to help children who were born addicted to cocaine. It is the only program of its kind in the United States.

4. Why animals have such blatant effects on human health is still largely unknown. Yet in recent years scientists have found proof of such connections, allowing them to confirm what people have suspected to be true for centuries.

5. In fact, at a Quaker retreat in York, England, in 1790, patients were encouraged to spend time with the animals. Leaders suspected that this would help improve their patients' states of mind.

6. Recent evidence suggests that the human bond with animals is uniquely helpful to human health. Many organizations across the country have begun donating time and funds for further research as a result of this evidence.

7. Many jails, hospitals, and nursing homes have also begun to support the human-animal connection by allowing pet visitation and therapy programs.

8. Scientists suspect that the relationship between humans and animals is so helpful because it is so uncomplicated. Animals offer comfort, love, and affection without criticism or judgment.

9. Family and friends who visit loved ones at nursing homes get more of a response when they arrive with a pet than do those who come alone.

10. According to research conducted by Suzanne Robb, elderly people in nursing homes smile more when they are exposed to the company of animals. They are even more alert around animals than when not.

11. For children who are mentally challenged, the effects of animals are even more positive than they are with the elderly. College students at the Julia Dyckman Andrus home in Yonkers, New York, can attest to that.

12. For eight weeks, these students made weekly trips to visit emotionally disturbed children, each accompanied by a cat or a dog. The students discovered that the children misbehaved less after spending time with the animals.

13. The leader of this experiment was Stephen Daniel, who is a psychologist at Mercy College. Even he was surprised by the results.

14. Daniel suggests that animals increase a child's self-control by acting in a predictable manner. The child, it seems, mimics the calm actions of the animals.

15. Although just the presence of an animal is enough to heal children, nurturing it helps children even more. Nursing an animal back to health nurses a sick child back to health as well.

16. Most children delight in seeing an animal recover, because the children themselves can identify with the injured animal. When children see that an animal can survive with a physical disability, they believe that they can survive as well.

17. Animals affect humans on a physical level as well. There are confirmed reports that say the heart rate is lowered when people sit in the presence of an animal.

18. Elderly people living at home also benefit from animals. Those elderly who live with pets visit the doctor less frequently than do those without pets.

19. Doctors aren't sure why animals have these effects on humans. Yet scientists do suggest that with an animal present people feel less lonely and enjoy having an understanding and loving companion.

20. Whether scientifically proven or not, animals are a sure way to help relieve physical and emotional problems while making a friend at the same time.

Exercise 11–3: Answers will vary. The following passages are fragments.

A: 2, 4, 6, 7, 9, 10, 12, 13, 15, 16, 18, 19, 22, 24, 25, 27, 29, 31

B: 2, 3, 5, 7, 8, 10, 11, 14, 16, 17, 20, 22, 23, 27

Module 12: Comma Splices and Run-On Sentences

Exercise 12–1A: Answers will vary. Possible answers are shown below.

1. . . . ounces of salt; without it . . .
2. . . . became difficult, so they . . .
3. . . . like money; it was a . . .
4. . . . are very salty. There's enough salt . . .
5. . . . used as seasoning; most of the rest
6. Although people get some salt...
7. . . . to crave salt. Now so much salt . . .

Exercise 12–1B:

1. Salt is a major ingredient in pesticides and herbicides which are used to kill insects and plants.

2. The Romans destroyed the city of Carthage. They plowed the ground with salt and made the area uninhabitable.

3. Constructive or destructive, salt has many uses; moreover, it is used far more than any other mineral.

4. The Romans knew the value of salt as a commodity; they named their major highway the Via Salaria (Salt Road).

5. The word *salary* comes from the word *salarium*, which meant money used to pay soldiers so they could buy salt.

6. Salt has long been used to preserve food, and the expression "salted away" means to keep for a future time.

7. Salt may become even more important to us than it already is; we may be able to use it to bury radio-active waste.

Exercise 12–1C:

1. . . . tree. It satisfies . . .

   . . . tree; it satisfies . . .

   . . . tree, for it satisfies . . .

   . . . tree, which satisfies . . .

2. . . .ungainly. They . . .

   . . .ungainly; they . . . . . .

   . . . ungainly, but they . . . . . .

   Although to most people giraffes appear ungainly, . . .

3. . . .giraffes. They . . .

   . . . giraffes; they . . .

   . . . giraffes, so they . . .

   Because people have greatly reduced . . .

4. . . . fingerprints. Giraffes . . .

   . . . fingerprints; giraffes . . .

   . . . fingerprints, and giraffes . . .

   ...fingerprints while giraffes . . .

5. ...leopard. Its . . .

   ...leopard; its . . .

   ...leopard, so . . .

   ...leopard so that...

Exercise 12–2: Answers will vary. Possible answers are shown below.

1. The king Jayavarman II introduced into the empire an Indian royal cult. The cult held that the king was related spiritually to one of the Hindu gods; consequently, the king was thought to fill on earth the role the gods had in the universe.

2. Each king was expected to build a stone temple. The temple, or *wat*, was dedicated to a god, usually Shiva or Vishnu. When the king died, the temple became a monument to him as well.

3. Over the centuries the kings erected more than seventy temples within seventy-five square miles. They added towers and gates, and they created canals and reservoirs for an irrigation system.

4. The irrigation system made it possible for farmers to produce several rice crops a year. Although such abundant harvests supported a highly evolved culture, the irrigation system and the rice production were what we would call labor-intensive.

5. The greatest of the temples is Angkor Wat, which was built by Suryavarman II in the 12th century. Like the other temples, it represents Mount Meru, the home of the Hindu gods. The towers represent Mount Meru's peaks while the walls represent the mountains beyond.

6. The gallery walls are covered with bas-reliefs that depict historical events. They show the king at his court, and they show him engaging in activities that brought glory to his empire.

7. The walls also portray divine images. There are sculptures of *apsarases*, who are attractive women thought to inhabit heaven. There are mythical scenes on the walls as well.

8. One scene shows the Hindu myth of the churning of the Sea of Milk. On one side of the god Vishnu are demons who tug on the end of a long serpent; on the other are heavenly beings who tug on the other end. All the tugging churns the water.

9. Vishnu is the god to whom Angkor Wat is dedicated. In Hindu myth he oversees the churning of the waters. That churning is ultimately a source of immortality.

10. Another temple is the Bayon, which was built by Jayavarman VII around 1200 A. D. Jayavarman VII was the last of the great kings of Angkor. He built the Bayon in the exact center of the city.

11. The Bayon resembles a step pyramid. It has steep stairs which lead to terraces near the top. Around its base are many galleries. Its towers are carved with faces which look out in all directions.

12. Because Jayavarman VII was a Buddhist, the representations on Bayon are different from those on earlier temples. Some scholars think they depict a Buddhist deity with whom the king felt closely aligned.

13. To build each temple required thousands of laborers who worked for years. After cutting the stone in far-off quarries, they had to transport it by canal or cart. Some stone may have been brought in on elephants.

14. Once cut, the stones had to be carved and fitted together into lasting edifices. Thus, in addition to requiring laborers, each project needed artisans, architects, and engineers. Each temple was a massive project.

15. After Angkor was conquered by the Thais in the 1400's, it was almost completely abandoned. The local inhabitants did continue to use the temples for worship, however, and a few late Khmer kings tried to restore the city.

16. The Western world did not learn about Angkor until the nineteenth century, when a French explorer published an account of the site. French archaeologists and conservators later worked in the area and restored some of the temples. More recent archaeologists have come from India.

17. Today the Angkor Conservancy has removed many of the temple statues. Some of the statues need repair; all of them need protection from thieves. Unfortunately, traffic in Angkor art has become big business among people with no scruples. There is even a booming business in Angkor fakes.

18. Theft is just one of the problems Angkor faces today. Political upheaval has taken its toll. Although Angkor mostly escaped Cambodia's civil war, some war damage has occurred.

19. More damage has been done by nature, however. Trees choke some of the archways, vines strangle the statues, and monsoons undermine the basic structures.

20. Today many Cambodians do what they can to maintain the temples of Angkor. They clean stones or sweep courtyards or pull weeds. No one pays them; they do it for themselves and their heritage.

Module 13: Misplaced and Dangling Modifiers

Exercise 13–1A: Answers will vary.

[1]Sailors developed scrimshaw, the art of carving or engraving marine articles, while sailing on long voyages. [2]Because scrimshaw was practiced primarily by whalermen, sperm whale teeth were the most popular articles. [3]Baleen, which was also called whalebone, was another popular choice. [4]With whaling voyages taking several years, a sailor needed something to occupy his time. [5]Only imagination or available material limited scrimshaw. [6]All kinds of objects—canes, corset busts, cribbage boards—were produced by the scrimshander. [7]The sailor used everything from whaling scenes to mermaids to decorate his work. [8]Often a sailor doing scrimshaw drew his own ship. [9]The most frequently depicted ship, the *Charles W. Morgan*, is presently a museum ship at Mystic Seaport. [10]It is easily possible to see it on a visit to Connecticut.

Exercise 13–2A:

1. To paint one's house, one must <u>frequently</u> do it oneself.

2. <u>Almost</u> all homeowners try to paint at one time or another.

3. They <u>usually</u> try to begin on a bedroom.

4. <u>By doing so</u>, they think no one will see it if they botch the job.

5. <u>In no time</u>, most people can learn to paint.

6. <u>Only</u> the uncoordinated should not try it.

7. People <u>who have strong arm muscles</u> have a direct advantage.

8. <u>Lacking strength</u>, prospective painters can always exercise.

9. Novices need to purchase all supplies such as brushes, rollers, and dropcloths <u>carefully</u>.

10. They must bring home paint chips to match <u>exactly</u> the shade desired.

11. It takes <u>nearly</u> as much time to prepare to paint as it does to do the actual job.

12. Painters <u>who think they are done with the last paint stroke</u> are in for a surprise.

13. Painters need to clean their own brushes <u>immediately</u> and put away all equipment.

14. <u>In the long run</u>, they can be proud of their accomplishment.

15. <u>Only</u> then can they enjoy the results of their labor.

16. <u>When all is said and done</u>, painting one's own home can be extremely satisfying.

Exercise 13–2B:

1. Playing the role of a caring and wise father, <u>Richardson told the girls</u> how to handle various situations.

2. To help the girls, <u>Richardson sometimes wrote</u> letters to their suitors.

3. After writing a number of successful letters, <u>Richardson had the idea</u> to write a book of model letters.

4. To prepare the books, <u>Richardson wrote letters</u> as if from adults to sons, daughters, nieces, and nephews.

5. When ready to send advice, <u>a parent copied out a letter and just</u> changed the names.

6. Bought by many, <u>Richardson's book was a success</u>.

7. While working on one letter (. . .), Richardson thought of enough <u>ideas for a whole book</u>.

8. By writing a series of letters between a girl and her faraway parents, <u>Richardson hoped to entertain and instruct young readers</u>.

9. Upon finishing *Pamela*, or *Virtue Rewarded* in 1740, <u>Richardson knew he had invented a new form of literature</u>.

10. After years of development, <u>this form became the novel</u>.

11. Being a nasty person, <u>Horace Walpole wrote an only novel</u> that wasn't very attractive.

12. Correct.

13. Although badly written, <u>it contained</u> the themes, atmosphere, mood, and plots that have filled gothic novels ever since.

14. Featuring gloomy castles filled with dark secrets, <u>gothic movies also entertain people</u>.

Module 14: Shifting and Mixed Sentences

Exercise 14–1A: Answers will vary.

If you ever visit Miami, be sure to see Vizcaya. The estate was one of the homes of James Deering. He hired three young geniuses to build it: Hoffman, the architect; Chalfin, the artistic director; and Suarez, the landscape architect. Together they built Deering's winter home on the shore of Biscayne Bay. As the estate was built, it took almost ten percent of Miami's 1913 population to work on it. Deering was able to spend his first winter at Vizcaya in 1916. Other extremely wealthy people have also built great estates, but they didn't have the exquisite taste of Deering and his geniuses. Today, Vizcaya is a museum of the European decorative arts, a place you won't want to miss.

Exercise 14–1B: Answers will vary.

No one knows why sailors wear bell-bottom pants. However, three theories are popular. First, bell-bottom pants fit over boots and keep sea spray and rain from getting in. Second, bell-bottoms can be rolled up over the knees, so they stay dry when a sailor must wade ashore and stay clean when he scrubs the ship's deck. Third, because bell-bottoms are loose, they are easy to take off in the water if a sailor falls overboard. In boot camp, sailors are taught another advantage to bell-bottoms. By taking them off and tying the legs at the ends, a sailor who has fallen into the ocean can change his bell-bottom pants into a life preserver.

Exercise 14–1C: Answers will vary.

1. 2. The Aran Isles are situated off the coast of Ireland. <u>They are not far from Galway</u>.

2. 1. <u>Islanders have difficult lives</u>. They must make their living by fishing in a treacherous sea.

3. 2. They use a simple boat called a *curragh* for fishing. <u>They also use it</u> to ferry their market animals to barges.

4. 3. Island houses <u>stand</u> out against the empty landscape. Their walls provide scant protection from a hostile environment.

5. 2. In 1898 John Millington Synge first visited the Aran Isles. <u>He used them</u> as the setting for *Riders to the Sea* and other of his works.

6. 1. Whether people see the Synge play or Ralph Vaughan Williams' operatic version of *Riders to the Sea*, <u>they</u> will feel the harshness of Aran life.

7. 3. The mother Maurya has lost her husband and several sons. They <u>have</u> all drowned at sea.

8. 2. When the body of another son is washed onto the shore, <u>it is identified</u> from the pattern knitted into his sweater.

9. 3.   Each Aran knitter develops her own combination of patterns. The patterns not only produce a beautiful sweater, but <u>they have</u> a very practical purpose.

10. 3.   The oiled wool <u>protects</u> the fisherman from the sea spray while the intricate patterns offer symbolic protection as well as identification when necessary.

11. 4.   When you knit your first Aran Isle sweater, you should learn what the stitches mean. <u>You should not</u> choose a pattern just because it is easy.

12. 2.   A cable stitch represents a fisherman's rope; <u>a zigzag stitch depicts winding cliff paths</u>.

13. 3.   Bobbles symbolize men in a curragh while the basket stitch <u>represents</u> a fisherman's creel and the hope that it will come home full.

14. 3.   The tree of life signifies strong sons and family unity. It <u>is</u> also a fertility symbol.

15. 5.   When someone asks you <u>whether</u> you knitted your <u>Aran</u> Isle yourself, you can proudly say that you did and you also chose the patterns.

Exercise 14–2A: Answers will vary.

1. Carl Fabergé created Easter eggs for the tsars.
2. Because Fabergé was a talented goldsmith, he was able to make exquisite objects.
3. Working for the court of Imperial Russia enabled him to combine craftsmanship and ingenuity.
4. Fabergé pleased his clients by creating unique works of art.
5. He included gems in his creations, but they did not overshadow his workmanship.
6. In adapting enameling techniques, he achieved a level seldom matched by other artisans.
7. Buyers in Europe expanded his clientele beyond the Russian royal family.
8. Because he had no money worries, he had few restrictions on imagination.
9. Although Fabergé created other examples of the jeweler's art, it is the Imperial Easter eggs for which he is most remembered.
10. The most famous eggs contained surprises inside—a hen, a ship, a coach.
11. One egg opened to reveal a model of a palace.
12. The most ambitious creation represented an egg surrounded by parts of a cathedral.
13. An artist is one who practices an imaginative art.
14. One reason Fabergé is so admired is that he was a true artist.

Exercise 14–2B: Answers will vary. These are possible answers only.

1. The use of cuneiform began <u>in</u> and spread throughout ancient Sumer.
2. This picture language of the Sumerians is thought to be older than <u>that of</u> the Egyptians.

3. Like hieroglyphics, early cuneiform used easily recognizable pictures <u>to</u> represent objects.

4. When scribes began using a wedge-shaped stylus, <u>great</u> changes occurred.

5. The new marks were different <u>from the early pictographs</u>.

6. They had become so stylized <u>that the origin was often unrecognizable</u>.

7. Early Sumerian tablets recorded practical things such <u>as</u> lists of grain in storage.

8. Some tablets were put <u>into</u> clay envelopes that were themselves inscribed.

9. Gradually ordinary people used cuneiform as much as official scribes <u>did</u>.

10. *The Epic of Gilgamesh*, written in Akkadian cuneiform, is older than any <u>other</u> epic.

11. The Code of Hammurabi recorded in cuneiform a more comprehensive set of laws <u>than any previously set down</u>.

12. Correct.

13. Because it was written in three languages, it served the same purpose <u>as the Rosetta Stone</u>.

14. Today we understand cuneiform as much <u>as,</u> if not more than, we understand hieroglyphics.

Exercise 14–2C: Answers will vary.

[1]Wild rice may be the caviar of grains, but it is not really rice. [2]It is, however, truly wild. [3]One reason is that it needs marshy places in order to thrive. [4]Planting it in man-made paddies can produce abundant crops. [5]Nevertheless, most wild rice grows naturally along rivers and lake shores in the northern states and Canada. [6]In certain areas only Native Americans are allowed to harvest the rice. [7]Connoisseurs think wild rice tastes better than any other grain. [8]It is surely the most expensive of all grains. [9]Some hostesses serve it with Cornish hens exclusively, but the creative cook serves it with many dishes. [10]Try it in quiche or pancakes; your guests will be so pleased that they will ask for more.

Module 15: Conciseness

Exercise 15–1:

1. Art Deco took its name from a 1925 Paris exposition.

2. Art Deco used bold and streamlined shapes and experimented with new materials.

3. In the 1920s public fascination with futuristic technology influenced Art Deco.

4. In addition to dominating architecture, the style pervaded glassware, appliances, furniture, and even advertising art.

5. The Empire State Building and the Chrysler Building exemplified Art Deco's dynamic style.

6. After the 1929 stock market crash, Art Deco expressed modern ideas and themes less extravagantly.
7. The Art Deco of the Great Depression had restraint and austerity.
8. Architects used rounded corners, glass blocks, and porthole windows.
9. They liked flat roofs.
10. Buildings with plain exteriors often had lavish interiors and furniture to match.

Exercise 15–2:

1. The Romans gave sacrifices to the goddess Maia on the first day of the month named for her.
2. The Celts also celebrated May Day as the midpoint of their year.
3. One of the most important of the May Day celebrations is the Maypole.
4. The Maypole represented rebirth.
5. In Germany a Maypole tree was often stripped of all but the top branches to represent new life.
6. In Sweden floral wreaths were suspended from a crossbar on the pole.
7. The English had a different tradition.
8. Holding streamers attached to the top of the Maypole, villagers danced around it enthusiastically.
9. Because May Day had pagan beginnings, the Puritans disapproved of it.
10. Thus it never became popular in the United States.

Exercise 15–3:

1. Many new collectors express amazement at the number of stamps to be collected.
2. They get excited about each new stamp they acquire.
3. They hope to make their collection complete.
4. Soon it becomes clear that a complete collection is impossible.
5. Then they may take the pragmatic approach.
6. They confine their collections to one country, continent, or decade.
7. At that point, their collections will again provide great satisfaction.
8. It is a consensus that collecting stamps can be educational.
9. It can teach about history or geography.
10. Nevertheless, a new collector should not become discouraged by trying to collect too much.

Exercise 15–4A: Answers will vary.

The Puerto Rican city of San Juan is interesting not only because it is an expanding metropolis but also because of its historical roots. Founded in 1521 and the oldest city on United States soil, San Juan was originally enclosed in a seven-square-block walled area known as Old San Juan. The city experienced a large population explosion in the nineteenth century. By 1898, at the time of the Spanish-American war, parts of the wall had been knocked down to allow for the expansion. San Juan today, home to 1.5 million people, is considered to be influential in the Puerto Rican community because it is both the island's political capital as well as its cultural, financial, and social capital.

Exercise 15–4B: Answers will vary.

Auguste Escoffier was the most famous chef between 1880 and World War I. He was the leader of the culinary world of his day. Until then the best chefs were found in private homes. With Escoffier came an era of fine dining at restaurants to which the nobility and wealthy flocked. After Escoffier joined César Ritz, the luxury hotel owner, they worked together to attract such patrons as the Prince of Wales. Ritz made each guest feel personally welcome. Escoffier added the crowning touch by preparing dishes especially for guests. He created dishes for the prince and for celebrities in the entertainment world. He concocted *consommé favori de Sarah Bernhardt* for the actress. For an opera singer he created *poularde Adelina Patti*. Another singer was fortunate to have more than one dish named for her. When the Australian Nellie Melba sang in *Lohengrin*, Escoffier served *pêches melba*, a combination of poached peaches and vanilla ice cream. To commemorate the swans of *Lohengrin*, he served the dessert in an ice swan. Melba toast was created by Escoffier during one of Melba's periodic diets. Today although many people have not heard of Nellie Melba, they are familiar with melba toast. As a young army chef, Escoffier had to prepare horse meat and even rat meat to feed the troops. Obviously he left those days far behind him when he became the most renowned chef of his day.

Module 16: Coordination and Subordination

Exercise 16–1: Answers will vary.

1. In 1952 publisher Walter H. Annenberg heard that someone was considering starting a national television magazine, and he became interested in the idea himself.

2. He wanted to learn about his competition, so he had one of his assistants find out if such magazines already existed.

3. The assistant found local television magazines being published in . . . and Los Angeles; Annenberg bought them all.

4. Articles to appear in the first issue were written quickly, for there was no supply of already completed work to rely on.

5. One of the first people hired was sportswriter Red Smith, but this was before he won a Pulitzer Prize for sports reporting.

6. Starting the magazine was hard work, but one decision was not hard at all.

7. *I Love Lucy* was the most popular show on the air in 1953, and the star, Lucille Ball, had just given birth to a baby boy.

8. The whole country had followed Lucy's pregnancy, so the editors decided to take advantage of this interest and to feature the baby, Desi Arnaz, Jr.

9. They could not ignore the baby's popularity, nor could they ignore Lucy's popularity.

10. The cover had a big picture of Desi, Jr., and it had a smaller picture of Lucy in the upper right-hand corner.

11. From the beginning *TV Guide* has been a national magazine, but it has different editions, giving local listings.

12. Sales fell soon after the first successful issue, for summer had come, and people preferred to sit outside in the cool night air rather than watch television in their hot living rooms.

13. The editors had to have a sudden great idea, or the magazine would fail.

14. They needed to increase interest in their subject, so they decided to devote one issue to the new shows scheduled for the 1953–54 season.

15. That first Fall Preview issue sold out, and it started a tradition that is repeated at the start of every new television season.

Exercise 16–2:

1. A company in Toronto, Canada, was one of the first ones to install a fragrancing unit in its office ventilation system in order to control employee behavior.

2. The company was careful about what fragrances it introduced into the workplace, because some fragrancies rev people up, and some calm them down.

3. The scents were designed by Toronto-based Aromasphere, Inc., which created a time-release mechanism to send the scents directly into the work area.

4. Once Bodywise Ltd. in Great Britain received a patent for a fragrance, it began to market its scent, which contains adrostenone, an ingredient of male sweat.

5. The scent was adopted by a U.S. debt-collection agency after another agency in Australia reported that chronic debtors who received scented letters were 17 percent more likely to pay than were those who received unscented letters.

6. Researchers have recently discovered how much odor can influence behavior even though smell is still the least understood of the five senses.

7. Aromasphere's employees have been asked to keep logs of their moods whenever they are in the workplace.

8. Researchers have raised many concerns about trying to change human behavior, because they feel that this kind of tampering may lead to too much control over employees.

9. Smells can have an effect on people, who may be completely unaware of what is happening.

10. If employees are forewarned, however, that they will be exposed to mood-altering fragrances, they may protest against the introduction of such scents in the workplace.

11. Even psychiatric wards emit a scent, which makes the patients calm.

12. As the world's largest manufacturer of artificial flavors and aromas, International Flavors and Fragrances of New York has developed many of the scents commonly used today.

13. It has even created a bagel scent, because bagels lose their aroma when they are contained in plexiglass.

14. There wasn't a true commercial interest in these products until researchers began to understand somewhat the anatomy of smell.

15. It turns out that olfactory signals travel to the limbic region of the brain, where hormones of the automatic nervous system are regulated.

Exercise 16–3: Answers will vary.

1. There are severe winter storms, and they last for days.

   There are severe winter storms, which last for days.

2. The electricity often goes out, and sometimes people are without electricity for days.

   Because the storms are so intense, the electricity often goes out.

3. Flooding occurs, and people are forced to stay home.

   After it rains for two or three days, flooding occurs.

4. Roads may be blocked by landslides, and residents must find alternate routes to their homes.

   Roads may be blocked by landslides, when one winter storm follows another.

5. Wind and surf advisories are frequent, and people take them seriously.

   As the storms approach, wind and surf advisories are frequent.

6. Summers on the north coast of California are cool and foggy, but the redwoods thrive in those conditions.

   While summers in most of the country are hot, summers on the north coast of California are cool and foggy.

7. The average ocean temperature is about 55 degrees, so resident swim in the rivers instead of the ocean.

   The average ocean temperature is about 55 degrees which is fine for wading but not for swimming.

8. Large rogue waves thunder onto the beaches and jetties, and these waves can knock people down.

   After they travel hundreds of miles across the Pacific Ocean, large rogue waves thunder onto the beaches and jetties.

9. Shaking from earthquakes can be unnerving, but the residents are used to it.

   When people are trying to relax, shaking from earthquakes can be unnerving.

10. The area's natural beauty is worth the many challenges of living there, but visitors are often surprised at the dangerous natural phenomena.

    Although some people don't agree, the area's natural beauty is worth the many challenges of living there.

Exercise 16–4: Answers will vary.

Senet is a game that was played by ancient Egyptians. Because it was very popular, Egyptians began putting senet boards into tombs as early as 3100 B.C. Tomb objects were intended for use in the afterlife, yet they give us a good idea of daily life.

Many senet boards and playing pieces have been found in tombs, where the hot, dry air preserved them well. Tomb paintings frequently show people playing the game while hieroglyphic texts describe it. Because numerous descriptions of the game survive, Egyptologists think it was a national pastime.

Senet was a game for two people who played it on a board marked with thirty squares. Each player had several playing pieces. They probably each had seven, but the number did not matter as long as it was the same for both. Opponents moved by throwing flat sticks that were an early form of dice although sometimes they threw pairs of lamb knuckles instead. Players sat across from each other, and they moved their pieces in a backward S line. The squares represented houses through which they moved.

By the New Kingdom the game began to take on religious overtones. The thirty squares were given individual names, and they were seen as stages on the journey of the soul through the netherworld. When New Kingdom tomb paintings showed the deceased playing senet with an unseen opponent, the object was to win eternal life. The living still played the game, but they played it in anticipation of the supernatural match to come.

Module 17: Parallelism

Exercise 17–1:

1. exploration, travel
2. proud, evil
3. he had made plans for a helicopter, he made plans for an underwater ship
4. designed by a British mathematician, built by a Dutch inventor
5. designed in 1578, built in 1620, tested from 1620–24
6. on the surface, below the surface
7. boarded the submarine, took a short ride
8. the talk of the town, the focus of scientific investigation
9. When the vessel was to submerge, the bags would fill with water and pull the ship downward; when the vessel was to rise, a twisting rod would force water from the bags and the lightened ship would surface
10. designed, built
11. sneak up on British warships, attach explosives to their hulls
12. launching, steering
13. small four-person ships called "Davids," a full-sized submarine called the "Hunley"

14. providing dependable power, seeing to navigate
15. the development of the gasoline engines, the invention of the periscope

Exercise 17–2: Answers will vary.

1. Sometimes after a demanding day at work, it's relaxing to turn on the TV, lie down on the couch, and be entertained.
2. TV shows can be entertaining and informational.
3. Because there are more channels than ever before, channel surfing can be fun or frustrating.
4. Relaxing and interesting are ways some people describe TV viewing.
5. Others describe TV viewing as boring and stupid.
6. Those people claim that finding a good TV show is much more difficult than finding a bad one.
7. But the wonderful range of programs now available means that people of all ages and tastes can find something they want to watch on TV.
8. Like anything else, watching too much TV may cause physical and emotional problems.
9. Just be sure to balance TV viewing with physical activities such as walking or jogging.
10. Also be sure to balance TV viewing with mental activities such as reading or doing a puzzle.
11. It can be upsetting when your favorite TV show is scheduled while you are away from home either working or running errands.
12. However, many people are adept at recording the TV shows they want to watch or can't bear to miss.
13. TV is especially important for people who live in rural areas where live entertainment and sports events are rare.
14. These people can enjoy an evening at the New York Metropolitan Opera or at Yankee Stadium in the quiet and comfort of their own homes.
15. In spite of what naysayers may think of TV, I would rather have one than not have one.

Module 18: Variety and Emphasis

Exercise 18–1: Answers will vary.

1. The first task is choosing a house plan.
2. To choose just the right plan among all the architectural styles and floor plans is difficult.

3. By talking to loan officers at different banks, people can get their finances in order.

4. Most people want to borrow from the bank that gives the lowest interest rate.

5. Every homeowner's dream come true is a contractor who is trustworthy and competent.

6. Once all the permits have been signed by city and county officials, it's time to begin building the house.

7. The homeowners get a little break as the contractor clears the lot and lays the foundation.

8. Choosing all the materials and colors to use in a new home is exciting and demanding for the homeowners.

9. Before the contractor calls and asks if they have their flooring, counters, cabinets, and paint colors picked out, people who are building a new home should do lots of shopping.

10. Stories people enjoy telling their friends are what went right, what changes they made, and what they would do differently if they could go back in time and build their house again.

Exercise 18–2A: Answers will vary. These are suggestions only.

1. The <u>little</u> children walk to school. (adjective)

    <u>Because they live so close</u>, the children walk to school. (adverb clause)

    <u>Laughing and shouting</u>, the children walk to school. (participial phrase)

2. The shopkeepers open their stores <u>early</u>. (adverb)

    The shopkeepers, <u>who seem eager to do business</u>, open their stores. (adjective clause)

    <u>Daylight occurring earlier</u>, the shopkeepers open their stores. (absolute phrase)

3. People go shopping <u>in the morning</u>. (prepositional phrase)

    People go <u>grocery</u> shopping. (adjective)

    <u>Happily</u>, people go shopping. (adverb)

4. Delivery trucks are seen <u>holding up traffic</u>. (participial phrase)

    Delivery trucks are seen <u>frequently</u>. (adverb)

    Delivery trucks, <u>which are quite noisy</u>, are seen. (adjective clause)

5. <u>Every customer demanding service</u>, the coffee shops are crowded. (absolute phrase)

    <u>Before ten a.m.</u>, the coffee shops are crowded. (prepositional phrase)

    The <u>best</u> coffee shops are crowded. (adjective)

Exercise 18–2B: Answers will vary.

1. The <u>centennial</u> celebration included a <u>large</u> parade <u>down Main Street</u>.
2. <u>Taking advantage of the sunny day</u>, the crowd was dressed in shorts and <u>short-sleeved</u> shirts.
3. The mayor, <u>who was recently elected</u>, stopped traffic <u>because several children had run out into the street</u>.
4. The <u>aging</u> astronaut rode <u>proudly</u> in an <u>open</u> car.
5. Youngsters, <u>who admired the astronaut</u>, tried to get autographs <u>even if it meant waiting for over an hour</u>.
6. <u>Recounting the town's last 100 years</u>, the mayor gave a <u>long</u>, but <u>interesting</u> speech.
7. <u>Even though it lasted for an hour</u>, everyone cheered <u>after he had finished</u>.
8. The celebration ended <u>outside of Town Hall</u>.
9. <u>Exhausted by the long day</u>, everyone headed home.
10. <u>Rather</u> than wait <u>until morning to clean</u>, the street cleaners came out after the celebration.

Exercise 18–3: Answers will vary.

1. Managers hope that the new emphasis on trust and teamwork in the work place will increase business quality in the United States.
2. Companies are trying to make a difference by experimenting with group talks among employees that discuss issues dealing with workers as individuals and team members.
3. The talks, which are very helpful for managers, involve workers who have survived massive cutbacks and need a boost in morale.
4. These experimental groups also break down departmental barriers that tend to separate and take away any feelings of teamwork and cooperation in the workplace.
5. These groups strive to remove obstacles that prevent communication and respect among workers. Teamwork, a necessary step in the right direction, is critical for companies that want to regain competitiveness.

Module 19: The Impact of Words

Exercise 19–1:

1. informal
2. between medium and formal
3. formal
4. medium
5. between medium and formal

Exercise 19–2A:

1. commanded
2. intact
3. overthrown
4. accuracy
5. foul
6. divided
7. dispersed
8. withheld
9. tall
10. restored
11. immoderate
12. suspend
13. capacity
14. donated
15. guffawed
16. praised
17. rewards
18. impolite
19. secretly
20. skin

Exercise 19–2B: Answers will vary.

1. There was <u>danger</u> wherever the private investigator went.

    The skiers were in <u>peril</u> of being buried by the avalanche.

    College students who plagiarize <u>hazard</u> expulsion.

    The game-show contestant decided to <u>risk</u> everything for a chance to win a car.

2. His <u>rich</u> uncle left him $10,000.

    <u>Wealthy</u> people often travel to Europe to shop.

    The <u>affluent</u> sometimes own several homes around the world.

    The <u>opulent</u> mansion contained a private movie theater and a large indoor pool.

3. The president agreed to <u>speak</u> at our meeting.

    Let's <u>talk</u> about where to go on vacation.

    The priest and the rabbi frequently <u>converse</u> about how to get better attendance at services.

    Academic <u>discourse</u> is sometimes confusing to college students.

4. The philosophy course required students to <u>think</u> about their most deeply held convictions.

    Sherlock Holmes gave no <u>reason</u> for his sudden departure.

    Take some time every day to <u>reflect</u> on your actions.

    Scientists <u>speculate</u> on the origins of life.

    The various departments <u>deliberate</u> today about the areas designated for smokers.

5. Having a cold made him <u>irritable</u>.

    Don't disagree with her; she's <u>choleric</u>.

    He's very <u>touchy</u> about his height.

    She always gets <u>cranky</u> if people don't do as she says.

    Ask the boss for an increase later; she's <u>cross</u> about the shipping delay.

Exercise 19–3A:

1. food
   sandwich
   cheese sandwich
   Swiss cheese on rye
2. business
   store
   supermarket
   A&P
3. mail
   letter
   bill
   record club charges
4. clothing
   pants
   jeans
   stone-washed jeans
5. land
   islands
   tropical paradise
   Hawaii

6. book
   how-to-book
   cookbook
   The Joy of Cooking
7. animal
   hunter
   cat
   lion
8. entertainment
   television show
   family comedy
   The Bill Cosby Show
9. art
   painting
   portrait
   Blue Boy
10. sports
    track
    running
    100-yard dash

Exercise 19–3B: Answers will vary.

1. Trans-Am
2. azaleas
3. sour
4. strode
5. Mobile, Alabama
6. your boyfriend
7. the unification of Italy
8. pigeon
9. accurate
10. drug-runners
11. sprained

12. a gold chain
13. grinding
14. difficult
15. considerate of
16. Eddie Murphy's latest movie
17. scratched
18. in need of new plumbing
    and wiring
19. steady, well-paying
20. all her patients who smoke

Exercise 19–4:

1. man
2. edible
3. please
4. address
5. regardless
6. slacks
7. students
8. cars
9. motorcycle
10. dormitories, checked in

Exercise 19–5: Answers will vary.

1. Before I tried skydiving, I thought skydivers were insane.
2. It seemed so extreme.
3. But now that I've done it, I think skydiving is wonderful.
4. The day of the jump, I was so excited.
5. My friends were worried about me, though.
6. But then, they are anxious types.
7. I felt nauseated just before I jumped out of the plane.
8. But it was great – exhilarating.
9. It's far better than bungee-jumping, which is over too quickly.
10. Yes, skydiving is definitely a great experience.

Exercise 19–6: Answers will vary.

Exercise 19–7: Answers will vary.

1. Once I began acting, I felt as though I were living in a fantastic dream.
2. Acting was as easy for me as playing is for a child.
3. I was always able to remember my lines.
4. Sometimes the famous lines I spoke filled me with awe.
5. On stage, I danced with the grace of a gazelle.
6. I sang as so sweetly and clearly that I made the audience cry.
7. I succeeded in getting every part I auditioned for.
8. The teachers, the students, and the students' parents all thought I was a phenomenal actor.
9. Being in a television commercial let to instant fame.
10. I made the product for the commercial seem like the most valuable object in the universe.
11. After that, my agent was so busy she needed a vacation every three months.
12. My schedule became a staccato of public appearances.
13. During these public appearances, I signed autographs until my hand became as limp as a deflated balloon.

14. I soon learned that being rich and famous doesn't bring inner peace.

15. But my passion for acting continues to expand without bounds like the universe itself.

Exercise 19–8: Answers will vary.

1. The horse seemed to float past us, like a silken banner in a gentle wind.

2. The shack stood off alone in the woods, looking like a moldy gingerbread house.

3. XYZ sound like a dozen monkeys trapped in a garbage can.

4. Grease oozed off the fries onto the paper plate, creating an oil slick that no EPA regulation could control.

5. At 5 A.M. I was awoken by my alarm clock, sounding like the finale at the demolition derby.

6. Professor ABC must think he is an Egyptian pharaoh; he treats his students like slaves.

7. The salesman had a grin like the Cheshire cat's—and like the cat itself, the grin faded away when I said, "I'm not interested."

8. It was so hot that the pigeons were fanning themselves with tattered sheets from last week's newspapers.

9. The library books were so overdue that the records showing they had been charged out were written on parchment.

10. Her voice is so shrill it could shatter plexiglass.

Exercise 19–9A: Answers will vary.

1. Every year, college students throughout the country look forward to spring break.

2. Many travel to warm, sunny beaches to rest and relax.

3. Many others return home to visit their families and friends.

4. However, many students use spring break to catch up on their course work.

5. No matter how students spend spring break, it's difficult to imagine college life without it.

Exercise 19–9B: Answers will vary.

Module 20: Spelling and Hyphenation

Exercise 20–1:

1. bitten
2. framed
3. management
4. foreign
5. dining
6. incredible
7. jumping
8. leisure
9. reluctantly
10. dissatisfied
11. courageous
12. laid
13. trapped
14. used
15. illegible
16. magically
17. permanent
18. proceeds
19. reliable
20. paid
21. believed
22. interaction
23. inventories
24. leaves
25. profitable

Exercise 20–2:

1. oranges
2. kisses
3. strays
4. lives
5. radios
6. pairs
7. speeches
8. flies
9. monkeys
10. pianos
11. mothers-in-law
12. data
13. ice skates
14. themselves
15. echoes
16. halves
17. children
18. women
19. phenomena
20. mice

Exercise 20–3A:

1. motivation
2. guidance
3. noticeable
4. graceful
5. truly
6. accurately
7. mileage
8. argument
9. driving
10. outrageous

Drop the final *e* before a suffix beginning with a vowel, but keep it if the suffix begins with a consonant.

Exercise 20–3B:

1. dutiful
2. playing
3. drier
4. supplied
5. noisiest
6. strayed
7. sloppier
8. gravies
9. happiness
10. buying

If the final *y* is preceded by a consonant, change the *y* to *i* before adding a suffix, unless the suffix begins with *i*. If the final *y* is preceded by a vowel, retain the *y*.

Exercise 20–3C:

1. gripping
2. mendable
3. steamed
4. beginner
5. planting
6. stopper
7. poured
8. splitting
9. occurrence
10. reference

If a one-syllable word ends in a consonant preceded by a single vowel, double the final consonant before adding a suffix. With two-syllable words, double the final consonant only if the last syllable of the stem is accented.

Exercise 20–4:

1. believe
2. receive
3. neither
4. ceiling
5. foreign
6. field
7. counterfeit
8. weird
9. freight
10. niece

Exercise 20–5: Answers will vary.

Exercise 20–6:

1. you're / to
2. Weather / rain / affect
3. clothes / wear / where
4. Buy / weigh / too / which
5. waste
6. stationery / write / diary
7. country / all ready
8. course / board / plane
9. personnel / assistance
10. aisle / breathe / ascent / descent
11. effect / your
12. whole
13. capitol or capital / desert / dominate
14. It's / meet / where
15. human / hear / through / seen / sights
16. presence / there / already
17. counsel / may be
18. ensure
19. alter / fares
20. break / buy / presents
21. piece / advice
22. stationary / quite / bored
23. patience
24. sense / scene
25. passed / conscious / principle

Exercise 20–7:

1. open-heart surgery
2. free-for-all
3. high school
4. pear-shaped
5. birdhouse
6. accident-prone
7. pothole
8. bathing suit
9. breadwinner
10. handmade
11. headache
12. head cold
13. headphone
14. head-to-head
15. headstone
16. free agent
17. freehand
18. free-form
19. free-spoken
20. freestyl

Module 21: Periods, Question Marks, and Exclamation Points

Exercise 21–1A:

1. operating?
2. purity.
3. correct
4. 1914.
5. disgusting.
6. blood.
7. green.
8. correct
9. blue-gray.
10. again?
11. does?
12. not!
13. students.

Exercise 21–1B:

Do you know who Theodor Seuss Geisel is? Sure you do. He's Dr. Seuss, the famous author of children's books. After ten years as a successful advertising illustrator and cartoonist, Seuss managed to get his first children's book published. <u>And to Think That I Saw It on Mulberry Street</u> was published in 1937 by Vanguard Press. It had been rejected by 27 other publishers. I wonder why. They certainly were foolish! What is your favorite Dr. Seuss book? Mine is <u>The Cat in the Hat</u>, published in 1957. Everyone has a favorite. And I do mean everyone! His books have been translated into 17 languages, and by 1984 over a hundred million copies had been sold worldwide. In fact, in 1984 Seuss received a Pulitzer Prize for his years of educating and entertaining children. How fitting! Sadly Dr. Seuss died in 1991. We will all miss him.

Exercise 21–2: Answers will vary.

1. The doctor asked me what was wrong.
2. Please close the door.
3. How much does the piano weigh?
4. Dr. Jones specialized in delivering twins.
5. Oscar Wilde said, "To love oneself is the beginning of a lifelong romance."
6. Wow!
7. Eggs are a good source of protein.
8. Sit down!
9. He asked, "What time does the train reach New York?"
10. The shoemaker said that my boots would be ready tomorrow.
11. When I saw my birthday present, all I could say was "Great!"

Module 22: Commas

Exercise 22–1A:

1. . . . along, and . . .
2. . . . however, and . . .
3. . . . plasmodium, for . . .
4. correct
5. . . . direction, and . . .
6. . . . colors, but . . .
7. correct
8. correct
9. . . . wood, yet . . .
10. . . . water, so . . .
11. . . . sporangia, and . . .
12. correct
13. . . . sporangia, and . . .
14. . . . ground, or . . .

Exercise 22–1B:

1. Some, however, leave the forest, <u>and</u> they live on cultivated plants.

2. They can cause clubroot <u>or</u> cabbage, or they can create powdery scab of potato.

3. Slime molds sound disagreeable, <u>yet</u> some are quite attractive.

4. One form produces unappealing stalks, <u>but</u> the stalks are topped with tiny balls.

5. The balls appear to be woven, <u>so</u> they look rather like baskets.

6. The woven balls are really sporangia, <u>and</u> they contain spores for distribution.

7. Another form looks like tiny ghosts, <u>for</u> its white molds could be small sheeted figures.

8. Serpent slime mold is yellow, <u>and</u> it can look like a miniature snake on top of a decaying log.

9. One would have to work hard to find it in New England, <u>for</u> it is most common in the tropics.

10. After one learns about slime molds, they no longer seem disgusting, <u>nor</u> do they even seem disagreeable.

Exercise 22–2A:

1. In fact, it is the largest continuous body of sand in the world.

2. Extending over 250,000 square miles, the Rub al-Khali . . .

3. As a point of comparison, Texas is just slightly larger.

4. Because it is almost completely devoid of rain, the Rub al-Khali . . .

5. Despite the existence of a few scattered shrubs, the desert is largely a sand sea.

6. However, its eastern side develops massive dunes with salt basins.

7. Except for the hardy Bedouins, the Rub al-Khali is uninhabited.

8. Indeed, it is considered one of the most forbidding places on earth.

9. Until Bertram Thomas crossed it in 1931, it was unexplored by outsiders.

10. Even after oil was discovered in Arabia, exploration . . .

11. correct

12. To facilitate exploration, huge sand tires were developed in the 1950s.

13. Shortly thereafter, drilling rigs began operating in the Rub al-Khali.

14. correct

15. As it turns out, the Empty Quarter is not so empty after all.

Exercise 22–2B:

[1]As might be expected, the Rub al-Khali is hot all year round. [2]In contrast, the Gobi Desert is hot in the summer but extremely cold in the winter. [3]Located in China and Mongolia, the Gobi Desert is twice the size of Texas. [4]Unlike the Rub al-Khali, the Gobi has some permanent settlers. [5]Nevertheless, most of its inhabitants are nomadic. [6]To avoid the subzero winters, the nomads move their herds at the end of summer. [7]When the harsh winters subside, they return to the sparse desert vegetation.

Exercise 22–3A:

1. The vicuna, the smallest member of the camel family, lives in the mountains of <u>Ecuador</u>, <u>Bolivia</u>, and <u>Peru</u>.
2. The guanaco is the <u>wild</u>, <u>humpless</u> ancestor of the llama and the alpaca.
3. The llama <u>stands four feet tall</u>, <u>is about four feet long</u>, and <u>is the</u> <u>largest of the South American camels</u>.
4. A llama's coat may be <u>white</u>, <u>brown</u>, <u>black</u>, or <u>shades</u> in between.
5. Indians of the Andes use llamas <u>to carry loads</u>, <u>to bear wool</u>, and <u>to produce meat</u>.
6. Llamas are foraging animals that live on <u>lichens</u>, <u>shrubs</u>, and <u>other</u> <u>available plants</u>.
7. Because they can go without water for weeks, llamas are <u>economical</u>, <u>practical</u> pack animals.
8. The alpaca has a <u>longer</u>, <u>lower</u> body than the llama.
9. It has wool <u>of greater length</u>, <u>of higher quality</u>, and <u>of superior softness</u>.
10. Alpaca wool is <u>straighter</u>, <u>finer</u>, and <u>warmer</u> than sheep's wool.

Exercise 22–3B: Answers will vary.

1. I like to spend those holidays with relatives because I like my relatives, I rarely get other chances to see them, and I enjoy their company.
2. My favorite fast foods are hot dogs, hamburgers, and pizza.
3. Swimming, hiking, reading, and sleeping are my preferred vacation activities.
4. My new puppy is a soft, silky cocker spaniel.
5. I found *Ghandi* long, disturbing, but compelling.
6. The groom found rice in his hair, in his ears, and in his shoes.
7. John lifts weights, does pushups, and uses a treadmill.
8. John is developing a sleek, streamlined physique as a result of working out.

Exercise 22–4:

1. correct
2. The dances, both solos and ensembles, express emotion or tell a story.
3. correct
4. A ballet's steps, called its choreography, become standardized over many years of performance.
5. correct
6. The steps, all with French names, combine solos and groups.
7. The *corps de ballet*, the ballet company excluding its star soloists, may dance together or in small ensembles.
8. One soloist may join another for a *pas de deux*, a dance for two.
9. Ensemble members, not just soloists, must be proficient at pliés and arabesques.

10. correct

11. It is important, therefore, to start lessons early.

12. In Russia, which has some of the most stringent ballet training, students begin at age three.

Exercise 22–5: Answers will vary.

1. My neighbors are kind to me.

   My neighbors, who have known each other a long time, are kind.

2. They often help one another.

   They help one another, which surprises some people.

3. They are usually friendly to strangers.

   They are friendly to strangers, waving or calling hello.

4. Along my street, the houses and yards are well kept.

   The houses and yards are well kept, which makes the neighborhood pleasant.

5. Trees that are well maintained line the streets.

   Trees, which were planted over fifty years ago, line the streets.

6. Many of the neighborhood families with children have pets.

   Many of the neighborhood families, who seem to love animals, have pets.

7. The pets that I like best are friendly.

   The pets, mostly cats and small dogs, are friendly.

8. The park that the neighborhood residents help to maintain is one street away.

   The park, which is the size of ten city blocks, is one street away.

9. The park has a playground that meets all safety requirements.

   The park has a playground, which has swings and slides.

10. When they aren't doing homework, the neighborhood children play at the park.

    The neighborhood children play at the park, which closes at sundown.

Exercise 22–6:

1. George Sand was most accurate when she said, "Life in common among these people who love each other is the ideal of happiness."

2. "I find that I have painted my life—things happening in my life—without knowing," said the wise Georgia O'Keeffe.

3. "I slept and dreamed that life was beauty," said Ellen Sturgis Hooper. "I woke—and found that life was duty."

4. In passing, a professor said to a student, "Life, dear friend, is short, but sweet."

5. "Life's a tough proposition," declared Wilson Mizner, "and the first hundred years are the hardest."

6. "Life" said Forrest Gump, "is like a box of chocolates: You never know what you're going to get."

7. "That it will never come again is what makes life so sweet," observed Emily Dickinson.

8. "May you live all the days of your life," advised Jonathan Swift.

9. William Cooper was right when he said, "Variety's the spice of life."

10. "Live all you can; it's a mistake not to," said Henry James.

Exercise 22–7:

1. In the northwest part of China, 6,000 pottery figures were found.

2. correct

3. The life-sized warriors and horses had been buried for 2,200 years.

4. The figures were in a huge tomb near the city of Xian, China.

5. Archaeologists also unearthed almost 10,000 artifacts from the excavation site.

6. It did not take John Doe, Ph.D., to realize that this was an extraordinary find.

7. Some of the figures were displayed in Memphis, Tennessee, twenty years later.

8. correct

9. correct

10. To get tickets, one could write to the Memphis Cook Convention Center, 255 North Main, Memphis, TN 38103.

Exercise 22–8A:

1. One was the statue of Olympian Zeus, which was covered with precious stones.

2. Unfortunately, it was taken to Constantinople in 475 A.D. and there destroyed by fire.

3. The hanging gardens of Babylon, built for Nebuchadnezzar, were considered a wonder.

4. correct

5. To lift water from the Euphrates, slaves had to work in shifts.

6. The Colossus of Rhodes was a huge, impressive statue built to honor the sun god Helios.

7. Constructed near the harbor, it was intended to astonish all who saw it.

8. Another wonder was the Lighthouse at Alexandria, Egypt.

9. Because it stood on the island of Pharos, the word pharos has come to mean lighthouse.

10. After the death of Mausolus, king of Caria, his widow erected a richly adorned monument to honor him.

11. With sculptures by famous artists, the Mausoleum at Halicarnassus amazed the ancient world.

12. The Temple of Artemis at Ephesus, an important Ionian city, was also considered a wonder.

13. It was burned, rebuilt, and burned again.

14. Some wonders, such as the Colossus and the Mausoleum, were destroyed by earthquakes.

15. Of the seven works that astounded the ancients, only the pyramids of Egypt survive.

Exercise 22–8B:

[1]St. Andrews, Scotland, is an old city. [2]Named for a Christian saint, the city was once an object of devout pilgrimage. [3]Its cathedral, the largest in Scotland, is now a ruin. [4]It was destroyed in 1559 by followers of the reformer John Knox. [5]All the revered, carefully preserved relics of St. Andrew disappeared. [6]Although the castle of St. Andrews also lies in ruins, it preserves two fascinating remnants of medieval history. [7]One is a bottle-shaped dungeon, and the other is a countermine. [8]When attackers tried to mine under castle walls, defenders tried to intercept the tunnel with a countermine. [9]Interestingly, one can actually enter both mine and countermine. [10]The University of St. Andrews, which is the oldest university in Scotland, was established in 1412. [11]From all parts of the globe, students come to study there. [12]Nevertheless, most people who think of St. Andrews associate it with golf. [13]Even golf at St. Andrews is old, the first reference dating to January 25, 1552. [14]The famous Old Course is only one of four courses from which the avid golfer may choose. [15]St. Andrews is still an object of pilgrimage, but today's pilgrims come with drivers, wedges, and putters.

Exercise 22–9:

[1]Many scholars consider Ralph Waldo Emerson, who was born in Boston, Massachusetts, on May 25, 1808, to be the most powerful writer of American literature. [2]At age 14, Emerson entered Harvard College, graduating four years later. [3]After finishing college, he earned money while teaching school for three years. [4]With his money, Emerson entered the divinity school of Harvard. [5]Not long thereafter, he began preaching, and in 1829, Emerson was appointed minister of a large Unitarian church in Boston. [6]Within the same year, he married Ellen Louisa Tucker. [7]After her death only two years later and after the death of Emerson's two brothers, Emerson began to question the church's doctrine, leading him to resign his pastorate in 1832. [8]Soon after, Emerson sailed for Europe, where he met the great men of his time, including John Stuart Mill. [9]Emerson remarried in 1935 and spent the next several decades of his life with his family at his home in Concord, which burned down in 1872. [10]However, people nationwide donated money to have it rebuilt. [11]Emerson died several years later at the age of 79 after a brief illness, and he was buried in Sleepy Hollow Cemetery.

Exercise 22–10:

Commas Added	*Commas Deleted*
valuable, is	really a matter of trust
By definition, money is	anything that society accepts as
broad definition, it is	not surprising that money
throughout history, taken on	ax-heads are
nails, livestock	In a successful society
store of wealth, a medium of exchange,	Forms of money must be
easy to store,	trust is also necessary
gold and silver, have	that a bill is worth the number
is of little value, we trust	

Module 23: Semicolons

Exercise 23–1A:

1. The sclera is the outercover of the eye; it helps . . .
2. The choroid is just inside the sclera; it keeps . . .
3. The pupil is the opening in the eye; this is where . . .
4. The cornea is the clear cover of the pupil; therefore . . .
5. The pupil is opened or closed by muscles in the iris; in fact, in bright light the iris closes to decrease the amount of light entering; in low light . . .
6. correct
7. The retina contains cells, cones, and rods, which are outgrowths of the brain; when light . . .
8. The optic nerve connects the eye to the brain; thus . . .
9. Cone cells give us color vision; they . . .
10. Rods are sensitive to low light; they . . .

Exercise 23–1B: Semicolons appear in the following lines.

line 1	Hearing is based on sound waves; these are . . .
line 3	made by a thrown rock; like ripples . . .
line 6	Pitch is the number of wave vibrations per second; it . . .
line 7	waves; this is called . . .
line 10	130 decibels is painful; however, people . . .
line 12	Timbre is hard to describe in everyday language; in physics terms . . .
line 16	as too many unrelated frequencies vibrating together; nevertheless . . .

Exercise 23–2:

1. Color-blindness is inherited; it appears . . .

2. The most common color-blindness is the inability to tell red from green; but more . . .

3. Different colors, the result of differences in light wavelengths, create a spectrum; the spectrum . . .

4. People who are severely red-green color-blind cannot "see" any colors at that end of the spectrum; that is, they cannot . . .

5. Color-blindness varies from person to person; people . . .

6. Some people have no cone cells (the cells that send signals about color to the brain), so they . . .

7. They have achromatism, a rare condition.

8. Such people can see only black, white, and grays; what . . .

9. However, their problem is much more serious than this; they also have . . .

10. The part of the eye that usually receives images is the fovea, which contains the cone cells; achromatics' . . .

11. To compensate, they look at objects off center, to pick . . . **No comma or semicolon is necessary**.

12. It is possible to be color-blind and not know it; how . . .

13. There are several tests for color-blindness; most involve seeing (or not seeing) a number or word written on a background of a complementary color, for example . . .

Module 24: Colons

Exercise 24–1:

1. Many college writing centers are open from 8:00 a.m. to 8:00 p.m.

2. The staff of writing centers has a common goal: teach students to write better.

3. correct

4. Other ways of helping students learn to write better include the following: reading a student's paper out loud, asking questions to help the writer provide more details, and explaining a difficult point of grammar.

5. Many college administrators have a problem with writing centers: they're expensive to operate.

6. But usually, college administrators understand the value of learning to write well: priceless.

7. Many students say the same thing to writing center staff: "Thank you for your help."

8. Here is some excellent advice for students seeking help at their college writing center: Be prepared.

9. Being prepared means students should have the following items ready for an instructor or peer tutor: a copy of the writing assignment and their draft.

10. There is much more to know about writing centers according to the book *Writing Center Research: Extending the Conversation*.

Exercise 24–2: Answers will vary.

1. Parallel Lives: Five Victorian Marriages

2. My favorite classes are as follows: English, Drama, and History.

3. Here is some advice about what to do when you go on a job interview: Don't be afraid to tell what you can do, but don't brag needlessly.

4. The star plays on the X are these: a, b, c, and d.

5. Hofstra University has a large campus bordered by public streets and a nature preserve: California Avenue, Braxton Avenue, Hamilton Road, Jones Street, Broadfield Avenue, and the Mitchell Field Preserve.

Module 25: Apostrophes

Exercise 25–1:

	singular possessive	plural possessive
1.	sheep's	sheep's
2.	pony's	ponies'
3.	turkey's	turkeys'
4.	lion's	lions'
5.	mouse's	mice's
6.	her	their
7.	gorilla's	gorillas'
8.	goose's	geese's
9.	gnu's	gnus'
10.	ox's	oxen's
11.	your	your
12.	buffalo's	buffalos'
13.	zebra's	zebras'
14.	ibex's	ibexes'
15.	fly's	flies'
16.	my	our
17.	giraffe's	giraffes'

18. dodo's	dodos'
19. zoo's	zoos'
20. zoo keeper's	zoo keepers'
21. his	their
22. farm's	farms'
23. farmer's	farmers'
24. ranch's	ranches'
25. its	their

Exercise 25–2:

1. a day's work
2. a dollar's worth
3. a horse's hooves
4. the horses' hooves
5. nobody's business
6. the lion's share
7. the cat's meow
8. the bodybuilder's weights
9. the neighbor's mail
10. the neighbors' mail

Exercise 25–3:

1. aren't
2. won't
3. let's
4. he'd
5. wasn't
6. you'd
7. didn't
8. I'll
9. what's
10. I'm
11. isn't
12. wouldn't
13. can't
14. doesn't
15. I've
16. you're
17. there's
18. we'd
19. weren't
20. they're
21. it's
22. we've
23. she'll
24. we're
25. don't

Exercise 25–4:

1. Poe's
2. correct
3. author's
4. Dupin's
5. didn't
6. public's, hero's
7. weren't
8. '66
9. correct
10. Collins's
11. book's, wasn't
12. *The Moonstone's*, public's
13. Collins's
14. one's
15. It's
16. Doyle's
17. Holmes's
18. People's
19. Holmes's
20. readers'
21. Holmes's
22. couldn't

Module 26: Quotation Marks

Exercise 26–1:

1. According to the Chesterfield, "Advice is seldom welcome."
2. "If you are looking for trouble, offer some good advice," says Herbert V. Prochnow.
3. Marie Dressler was right: "No vice is so bad as advice."
4. Someone once remarked, "How we do admire the wisdom of those who come to us for advice!"
5. "Free advice," it has been noted, "is the kind that costs you nothing unless you act upon it."
6. correct
7. "I sometimes give myself admirable advice," said Lady Mary Wortley Montagu, "but I am incapable of taking it."
8. Says Tom Masson, "'Be yourself!' is the worst advice you can give to some people."
9. The Beatles' song "With a Little Help from My Friends" contains some good advice.
10. correct
11. My uncle advised me, "The next time you are depressed, read Lewis Carroll's poem 'Jabberwocky.'"
12. Do you recall the Beach Boys' words: "Be true to your school"?
13. correct
14. However, comedienne Phyllis Diller suggests, "Never go to bed mad. Stay up and fight."

15. Rachel Carson advised, "The discipline of the writer is to learn to be still and listen to what his subject has to tell him."
16. correct

Exercise 26–2: Answers may vary slightly.

1. She said, "All employees must attend the meeting."
2. "Any employee who isn't at the meeting will be terminated," she said.
3. "I'm leaving at noon," I told my supervisor, "and I'm flying to Montreal to meet an important client."
4. My supervisor asked, "Whose idea was it for you to fly to Montreal?"
5. I replied, "It was the boss's idea!"
6. My supervisor said, "Don't worry. When you return, I'll help you find a new job."

Exercise 26–3: Answers will vary.

Module 27: Other Punctuation Marks

Exercise 27–1: Answers may vary slightly.

1. Chicago is not the windiest city in the United States — Great Falls, Montana, is.
2. The next windiest cities are (2) Oklahoma City, Oklahoma, (3) Boston, Massachusetts, and (4) Cheyenne, Wyoming.
3. Chicago is relatively calm — average wind speed . . .
4. Greenland (the largest island in the world) was given . . .
5. The name was a masterstroke of publicity — convincing . . .
6. Let's go to New Orleans for Mardi — Oops! . . .
7. The most expensive part of a trip — the airfare — can be reduced . . .
8. . . . "the winner must appear to claim his/her prize in person."
9. "Broadway [my favorite street] is a . . .
10. "Too often travel . . . merely lengthens the conversation," . . .
11. New Jersey [sic] has . . .
12. . . . he/she will always want to return.
13. I can only say one thing about camping — I hate it.
14. We leave as soon as — Have you seen the bug spray? — we finish packing.
15. "Let's take Interstate 80 across —" "Are you crazy?"
16. Finding an inexpensive hotel/motel isn't always easy.
17. Motels (named for a combination of *motorist* and hotel) . . .
18. When traveling, always remember to (a) leave a schedule with friends, (b) carry as little cash as possible, and (c) use the hotel safe for valuables.

Exercise 27–2A: Answers will vary.

The cheetah is the fastest animal on earth. It can accelerate from one mile an hour to forty miles an hour in under two seconds, briefly reaching speeds of up to seventy miles an hour. Its stride may, during these bursts of speed, be as much as 23 feet. To help it run at these speeds, the cheetah is built unlike any of the other large cats: powerful heart; oversized liver; long, thin leg bones; relatively small teeth; and a muscular tail used for balance. Unlike other cats, it cannot pull in its claws. They are blunted by constant contact with the earth, and so are of little use in the hunt. The cheetah, instead, makes use of a strong dewclaw on the inside of its front legs to grab and hold down prey.

Exercise 27–2B: Answers will vary.

Have you ever wondered how instant coffee is made? First the coffee beans are prepared as they would be for regular coffee. They are roasted, blended, and ground. At the factory, workers brew great batches of coffee—1,800 to 2,000 pounds at a time. The coffee is then passed through tubes under great pressure at a high temperature. This causes much of the water to boil away, creating coffee liquor (coffee with a high percentage of solids). At this point a decision must be made about what the final product will be: powdered coffee or freeze-dried coffee. Powdered instant coffee is made by heating the coffee liquor 500°F in a large drier. This boils away the remaining water, and the powdered coffee is simply gathered from the bottom of the drier and packed. If freeze-dried coffee is being made, the coffee liquor is frozen into pieces which are then broken into small granules. The granules are placed in a vacuum drier (a box containing no air), which turns the frozen water into steam which is removed. All that is left are coffee solids. Some people say they prefer freeze-dried coffee because the high temperature used to make regular instant coffee destroys some of the flavor. Either way, the coffee is more convenient than home-brewed coffee.

Exercise 27–3

1. sleep/less
2. slen•der/ize
3. ref•er/ee
4. phlegm
5. pal/ate
6. mus•cle-/bound
7. in-de/cent (rule #3)
8. Hol•ly/wood
9. ex•pi•ra/tion
10. echo (rule #3)
11. cuck•oo (rule #3)
12. cough
13. butte
14. av•o/ca•do
15. av•oir/du•pois or av•oir-du/pois
16. loose
17. cat/tail
18. en•roll (rule #3)
19. grouch
20. pro/gress
21. sleeve
22. sap/suck•er
23. Pol•y/ne•sia
24. pal/ace
25. non/res•i•dent

26. increase (rule #3)
27. how/ev•er
28. ges•tic/u•late,
    or ges•tic•u/late
29. e•merge (rule #3)
30. cu•bic (rule #3)
31. col•or/less
32. care/tak•er

33. but•ter/milk
34. a•wait (rule #3)
35. ant/ac•id
36. moth•er-/in-•law or moth•er-•in/law
37. trous/seau
38. midg•et (rule #3)
39. con·trol·ling
40. far/ther

Module 28: Capitals, Italics, Abbreviations, and Numbers

Exercise 28–1A:

1. President Truman
2. God's love
3. the Federal Communication Commission
4. a meeting on Friday
5. my Aunt Clara
6. when I graduate
7. The sun is rising.
8. Mother Teresa.
9. dinner at the steak palace
10. English 202
11. across Main Street
12. the Los Angeles Lakers
13. Election Day
14. a town in the Northeast
15. a college in Florida
16. "The Gift of the Magi"
17. learning French
18. getting a job at Nassau County Medical Center
19. the moon and Venus shining in the sky
20. the Hudson River

Exercise 28–1B:

1. It began as a trading post on the banks of the Thames River.
2. Now it's the largest, most populous metropolis in Europe.
3. Just like New York City, London is divided into boroughs.

4. Part of the King James Bible was written in Westminster.

5. Many people have heard of Big Ben, the famous bell in the clock tower of Westminster.

6. Most tourists enjoy visiting St. Paul's Cathedral, a magnificent landmark designed by Christopher Wren.

7. The dome of St. Paul's Cathedral is second in size only to St. Peter's Cathedral in Rome.

8. Another famous landmark, the Tower of London, was started in 1078.

9. Several historical figures, queens, princes, and advisors to various monarchs, entered the Tower of London and never came out again.

10. Just as Wall Street in New York City represents the stock market to many people, a number of streets in London represent entire industries and institutions.

11. For example, Fleet Street represents the press, and Downing Street represents the government of Great Britain.

12. Now it's possible to go to Paris and back to London in one day.

13. People used to have to travel by air or sea to reach Paris from London.

14. Now people can travel to Paris by train through a tunnel beneath the English Channel.

15. Combining the words of the name "Channel Tunnel," the English came up with a shorter name, "Chunnel."

Exercise 28–2A:

1. b. <u>War and Peace</u>

2. b. <u>The Bill Cosby Show</u>

3. a. The <u>Washington Post</u>

4. b. <u>The Queen Elizabeth II</u>

5. b. The U.S.S. <u>Enterprise</u>

6. a. We are <u>homo sapiens</u>.

7. b. <u>nota bene</u>

8. a. Many words have the common root—<u>cycle</u>.

9. b. <u>Never</u> tease a hungry crocodile.

10. a. <u>The Orient Express</u> was the setting of a famous mystery novel.

Exercise 28–2B:

1. The word <u>cool</u> has many meanings.

2. The new hospital is shaped like the letter <u>H</u>.

3. Scientifically, the chimpanzee is called <u>Pan troglodytes</u> and the gorilla is <u>Gorilla gorilla</u>.

4. I'm feeling <u>muy bien</u> after seeing the play <u>Man of La Mancha</u>.

5. The H.M.S. <u>Bounty</u> was a real ship.

6. The troubles of its crew are told in the book <u>Mutiny on the Bounty</u>.

7. correct

8. William Randolph Hearst began his career in journalism in 1887 running his father's paper, the <u>San Francisco Examiner</u>.

9. correct

10. The movie <u>Citizen Kane</u> (1941) was an unflattering portrait of the thinly disguised Hearst.

Exercise 28–3A:

1. The Chang brothers are opening a fishing charter company.

2. It will be off pier number 17, not far from Los Angeles, California.

3. They plan to go after game fish, for example shark, some of which are as much as 45 feet long.

4. Election Day is always the second Tuesday in November.

5. What did you get for Christmas?

6. Everyone ought to know the story of William Henry Harrison, ninth president of the United States.

7. He is mentioned in my textbook on the history of political science and philosophy.

8. The professor says the midterm will cover chapters 1 through 5.

9. The midterm and the final each count 40 percent.

10. The body contains about 10 pints of blood.

11. Some people sell their blood for a few dollars.

12. A kilogram equals 2.2 pounds.

13. The counselor had an MSW (or Master of Social Work) degree from New York University.

14. She had put herself through school working as an assistant manager in a fast food restaurant.

15. Mr. and Mrs. McDonald live on Maple Avenue in Duluth, Minnesota.

Exercise 28–3B:

1. 2:00 A.M.
2. $30,000
3. Dr. Jones
4. Bill Smith, a CPA
5. A.D. 1642
6. 1919
7. Mr. and Mrs. Grossman
8. NASA
9. OK
10. SCUBA gear

Exercise 28–4:

1. There are 107 women . . .

2. Ten years ago there were only forty-seven. (Note: A case could be made for "47," as this is a precise discussion involving numerous figures.)

3. One-third of the faculty is female now compared with one-tenth then.

4. . . . $300 for two rooms, $400 for three rooms, and $475 for four rooms.

5. correct or . . . September 14.

6. . . . June 1, 1993.

7. correct

8. . . . to drink one-and-a-half gallons of coffee a day over the next three years.

9. correct or . . . 29 percent.

10. correct or . . . 15 Clark Street.

Exercise 28–5:

1. thirty-five

2. one-half

3. four-fifths

4. one hundred and one

5. first

6. three thousand four hundred and fifty-seven

7. four hundred and ninety-five

Module 29: Using Sources and Avoiding Plagiarism

Exercise 29–1A:

In her book *No Logo*, Naomi Klein writes of the "brand equity mania" of the 1980s, summed up in the purchase of the Kraft brand name for six times the company's worth on paper. A brand name no longer simply added value; it contained enormous value in itself. Klein describes the struggles of the corporations to promote something as intangible as a name. She has them "perpetually probing the zeitgeist" to ensure that a brand image "would resonate karmically with its target market." In the age of branding, new marketing opportunities were vital, and manufacturers went "on a cultural feeding frenzy . . . in search of the oxygen needed to inflate their brands."

Exercise 29–1B: Answers will vary.

Exercise 29–1C: Answers will vary.

Exercise 29–2A:

The words "branding" and "advertising" are often used as if they meant the same thing. However, advertising a product, like choosing sponsors for it or licensing a logo, is only one part of the masterplan which is branding. The brand is the very essence of the modern corporation – what the corporation stands for – and advertising is just one way of making that identity known. In contrast, early mass-marketing, beginning prior to 1900, concentrated on telling people about products. A host of new products had just been invented – including the radio, the phonograph, the automobile, and the light bulb – and advertisers had a more important job to do than raising brand awareness. They had to tell people about these new inventions and get them to believe that they would improve their lives. They had to persuade people to use motorized transport rather than the horse-drawn kind, to make telephone calls rather than write letters, and to use electricity rather than oil to light their homes. Brand names existed, and some of them are still with us, but they were relatively unimportant.

Exercise 29–2B: Answers will vary.

Exercise 29–2C: Answers will vary.

Exercise 29–3A:

Around 1985, management scientists came up with the idea that a successful company sells brands, not products. This concept alone probably accounts for the amazing rise of multinational corporations in recent years. Traditionally, manufacturers were more concerned with the things they made. Producing goods was the key to economic success: the more you produced, the more wealth you would generate. The factory and the land were the sources of production and hence of economic well-being.

With the 1980s, however, came recession and a re-evaluation of the idea that bigger was necessarily better. Manufacturers with giant facilities – and matching payrolls – began to look like dinosaurs. New companies like Nike and Microsoft were doing things a different way. They offloaded production, often to overseas contractors, and concentrated on what they claimed was the real job: marketing. The role of the corporation was to produce brand images, not products *per se*. In demonstrating that marketing is more profitable than production, the modern multinationals have set a new standard. It is the company with the least overhead – and the best-known brand – which will succeed.

Exercise 29–3B: Answers will vary.

Exercise 29–3C: Answers will vary.

Module 30: Comparing the Disciplines

Exercise 30–1A: Answers will vary.

Exercise 30–1B: Answers will vary.

Module 31: Writing About the Humanities and Literature

Exercise 31–1A: Answers will vary.

Exercise 31–1B: Answers will vary.

Module 32: Writing in the Social Sciences and Natural Sciences

Exercise 32–1A: Answers will vary.

Exercise 32–1B: Answers will vary.

Module 33: Business and Public Writing

Exercise 33–1A: Answers will vary.

Exercise 33–1B: Answers will vary.

Exercise 33–1C: Answers will vary.

Exercise 33–2A: Answers will vary.

Exercise 33–2B: Answers will vary.

Module 34: Making Oral Presentations and Using Multi-Media

Exercise 34–1A: Answers will vary.

Exercise 34–1B: Answers will vary.

Module 35: Singulars and Plurals

Exercise 35–1:

Noncount	Count	Plural
1. advice	——	——
2. ——	book	books
3. ——	calculator	calculators
4. chocolate	chocolate	chocolates
5. ——	desk	desks
6. ——	earring	earrings
7. ——	essay	essays
8. ——	experiment	experiments
9. ——	fern	ferns
10. flour	——	——
11. gold	——	——
12. hair	hair	hair
13. happiness	——	——
14. homework	——	——
15. honesty	——	——
16. information	——	——
17. jewelry	——	——
18. ——	library	libraries
19. lightning	——	——
20. ——	man	men
21. news	——	——
22. ——	novel	novels
23. ——	occupation	occupations
24. paper	paper	papers
25. ——	paragraph	paragraphs
26. physics	——	——
27. pollution	——	——
28. rain	rain	rains
29. ——	report	reports
30. ——	storm	storms
31. time	time	times
32. weather	——	——

Exercise 35–2:

1. Hikers with little <u>money</u> but much <u>fortitude</u> can begin the hike in Georgia and continue to Maine.
2. The 2,015-<u>mile</u> trail extends through fourteen <u>states</u>.
3. The trail passes cultivated <u>farms</u> and untamed <u>wilderness</u>.
4. Since 1968 it has been one of two federally protected <u>trails</u> in the United <u>States</u>.
5. Few <u>hikers</u> have anything but praise for their <u>experiences</u> on the trail.
6. Many <u>youngsters</u> would gladly give up <u>piano</u> lessons or <u>homework</u> to be climbing wooded <u>paths</u>.
7. The Appalachian Trail is one of the nation's <u>treasures</u>.

Module 36: Articles

Exercise 36–1:

In 1872 Ø Congress passed <u>the</u> Yellowstone Act, establishing Ø Yellowstone as the first national park in the United State and indeed in <u>the</u> world. For centuries <u>the</u> wealthy set aside Ø private preserves for their own recreational use, but except for <u>a</u> few public parks in Ø major cities, setting aside <u>a</u> vast area for Ø national enjoyment was <u>a</u> novel idea. It became <u>a</u> popular one. Since <u>the</u> founding of Ø Yellowstone, forty-nine other national parks have been established in <u>the</u> United States and its territories.

Ø Yellowstone is <u>the</u> largest of this country's national parks. It occupies 3,472 square miles at <u>the</u> juncture of <u>the</u> states of Ø Wyoming, Ø Montana, and Ø Idaho. Although Ø Native American habitation goes back 800 years, <u>the</u> park's remoteness from <u>the</u> centers of Ø population left it undiscovered by Ø white settlers until <u>the</u> nineteenth century.

Ø John Colter is thought to be <u>the</u> first explorer to venture into <u>the</u> area. Colter was <u>a</u> member of <u>the</u> Lewis and Clark Expedition. When <u>the</u> expedition returned to Ø St. Louis, he remained in <u>the</u> region of <u>the</u> upper Missouri River to become <u>a</u> mountain man. In 1807 he explored <u>the</u> Yellowstone Basin. When he later wrote about <u>the</u> thermal wonders of <u>the</u> area, many people did not believe such natural phenomena existed. They continue to amaze Ø tourists today.

Yellowstone is truly <u>a</u> natural fantasy land. Its features include Ø geysers, Ø hot springs, and Ø mud volcanoes along with Ø forests, Ø lakes, Ø mountains, and Ø waterfalls. <u>The</u> most famous of <u>the</u> park's attractions is Ø "Old Faithful," <u>a</u> geyser which erupts on <u>an</u> average of every 65 minutes. It shoots Ø steaming water from 120 to 170 feet into <u>the</u> air. Each eruption lasts approximately four minutes and spews out 10,000 Ø gallons of Ø water.

Other active geysers in <u>the</u> six geyser basins may be less predictable but are no less spectacular. Some of <u>the</u> more than 200 just emit Ø steam and Ø spooky underground noises. Ø Silica in <u>the</u> geyser water builds up around <u>the</u> walls of <u>the</u> geyser craters, making <u>the</u> craters very colorful and beautiful to view even when <u>the</u> geysers are not spouting.

∅ Hot springs are another Yellowstone attraction. There are more than 3,000 of them ranged throughout <u>the</u> park. Some, such as ∅ Emerald Spring, are remarkable because of their color. ∅ Morning Glory Spring looks like its flower namesake.

∅ Yellowstone Lake, ∅ Golden Gate Canyon, and ∅ Tower Falls are just some of <u>the</u> features that combine with <u>the</u> geysers and ∅ hot springs to make ∅ Yellowstone National Park <u>an</u> extraordinary place to visit.

Module 37: Word Order

Exercise 37–1:

1. Is that pizza enough for all of us?
2. Did Henry understand the lesson?
3. Do you have my lab manual?; Have you my lab manual?
4. Will Juanita have finished by the time we return?
5. Can everyone in the room see the screen?

Exercise 37–2:

1. Katrina purchased two lovely Limoges boxes.
2. A comfortable black leather chair appealed to Nils.
3. He patiently waited to bid on it.
4. Unfortunately, we left before it was auctioned.
5. Marios wanted an old wooden table but bought a worn silver spoon.
6. Suchen outbid someone for an interesting round green hatbox.
7. She was extremely delighted to get it.
8. She has often wanted one.
9. The entire English class bought something except Ingrid.
10. Because she brought a small empty purse, she bought nothing at all.

Module 38: Prepositions

Exercise 38–1:

1. Others wanted to put the new university <u>in</u> Staunton or Lexington.
2. In August 1818, Jefferson convinced legislators to place it <u>in</u> Albemarle County.
3. Jefferson designed the university so that students and faculty lived together <u>in</u> an "academical village."
4. A rotunda building for classes sits <u>at</u> one end of a lawn.

5. <u>On</u> both sides of the lawn are sets of student rooms.

6. Faculty members lived <u>in</u> pavilions between the sets of student rooms.

7. The university opened <u>in</u> 1825.

8. <u>On</u> his last visit to the university, Jefferson stood <u>at</u> a window <u>in</u> the rotunda and surveyed the campus.

9. <u>On</u> his deathbed, Jefferson included founding the university as one of the three accomplishments for which he hoped to be remembered.

10. Today students at the University of Virginia considered it an honor to live <u>in</u> the rooms Jefferson designed.

Exercise 38–2A: Answers will vary.

1. Ravi will <u>speak to</u> Walid and explain.

2. First he must <u>fill out</u> all the forms.

3. He must <u>go over</u> all his records to make sure he does not leave out anything.

4. He must then <u>drop off</u> the forms at the registrar's office.

5. Should he <u>hand in</u> the forms without some vital information, the registrar will call him back to get it.

6. Walid will have to <u>look over</u> the forms and find out what is missing.

7. He must not <u>throw away</u> any records until he has finished the procedure.

Exercise 38–2B: Answers will vary.

1. Ravi will <u>speak to</u> Walid and explain.

2. First he must <u>complete</u> all the forms.

3. He must <u>review</u> all his records to make sure he does not omit anything.

4. He must then <u>leave</u> the forms at the registrar's office.

5. Should he <u>submit</u> the forms without some vital information, the registrar will <u>call him back</u> to get it.

6. Walid will have to <u>examine</u> the forms and <u>discover</u> what is missing.

7. He must not <u>discard</u> any records until he has finished the procedure.

Module 39: Gerunds, Infinitives, and Participles

Exercise 39–1:

1. They are worried about <u>getting</u> jobs after graduation.

2. They may want <u>to study</u> for the pure enjoyment of learning.

3. They may even dream about <u>being</u> philosophers or writers.

4. However, many parents refuse <u>to support</u> students who lack a definite career goal.

5. They are happy <u>to help</u> their children reach their goals.

6. They resist <u>aiding</u> children who lack direction.

7. Yet <u>reading</u> widely in the liberal arts is one way for students to know themselves.

8. Students of the humanities are the first <u>to see</u> the value of a liberal education.

9. When they hear their parents <u>complain</u> about wasting money, students try to <u>explain</u> their position.

10. They recommend <u>learning</u> about life before <u>training</u> for a specific job.

Module 40: Modal Auxiliary Verbs

Exercise 40–1:

1. I <u>should not</u> (present advisability, negative) brag, but I went there for spring vacation.

2. You <u>may not</u> (present possibility, negative) know it, but New Orleans was founded in 1718 by two brothers from Montreal.

3. They <u>must have</u> (past probability) been looking for a warmer climate.

4. They <u>should have</u> (past advisability) looked for higher ground.

5. Much of New Orleans is below sea level and <u>must be</u> (present passive necessity) kept dry by using dikes and pumps.

6. Early settlers <u>had to</u> (past necessity) build with cypress timbers.

7. Because cypress wood came from the surrounding swamps, it <u>could</u> (past ability) withstand the moisture of the climate.

8. Owners of plantations near the Mississippi River <u>used to</u> (past habit) expect to be flooded occasionally.

9. They <u>might have</u> or <u>could have</u> (past possibility) moved, but they preferred to keep their rich soil and their beautiful view.

10. I <u>would rather</u> (preference) visit New Orleans than any other city in the South.